Anarchist, Artist, Sufi

Islam of the Global West

Series editors: Kambiz GhaneaBassiri and Frank Peter

Islam of the Global West is a pioneering series that examines Islamic beliefs, practices, discourses, communities, and institutions that have emerged from "the Global West." The geographical and intellectual framing of the Global West reflects both the role played by the interactions between people from diverse religions and cultures in the development of Western ideals and institutions in the modern era, and the globalization of these very ideals and institutions.

In creating an intellectual space where works of scholarship on European and North American Muslims enter into conversation with one another, the series promotes the publication of theoretically informed and empirically grounded research in these areas. By bringing the rapidly growing research on Muslims in European and North American societies, ranging from the United States and France to Portugal and Albania, into conversation with the conceptual framing of the Global West, this ambitious series aims to reimagine the modern world and develop new analytical categories and historical narratives that highlight the complex relationships and rivalries that have shaped the multicultural, poly-religious character of Europe and North America, as evidenced, by way of example, in such economically and culturally dynamic urban centres as Los Angeles, New York, Paris, Madrid, Toronto, Sarajevo, London, Berlin, and Amsterdam where there is a significant Muslim presence.

American and Muslim Worlds before 1900
Edited by John Ghazvinian & Arthur Mitchell Fraas
Amplifying Islam in the European Soundscape: Religious Pluralism and Secularism in the Netherlands
Pooyan Tamimi Arab
The British Muslim Convert Lord Headley, 1855–1935
Jamie Gilham
Islam and Nationhood in Bosnia-Herzegovina: Surviving Empires
Xavier Bougarel
Islam and the Governing of Muslims in France
Frank Peter
Islam as Critique: Sayyid Ahmad Khan and the Challenge of Modernity
Khurram Hussain
Sacred Spaces and Transnational Networks in American Sufism
Merin Shobhana Xavier

Anarchist, Artist, Sufi

The Politics, Painting, and Esotericism of Ivan Aguéli

Edited by
Mark Sedgwick

BLOOMSBURY ACADEMIC
LONDON · NEW YORK · OXFORD · NEW DELHI · SYDNEY

BLOOMSBURY ACADEMIC
Bloomsbury Publishing Plc
50 Bedford Square, London, WC1B 3DP, UK
1385 Broadway, New York, NY 10018, USA
29 Earlsfort Terrace, Dublin 2, Ireland

BLOOMSBURY, BLOOMSBURY ACADEMIC and the Diana logo are trademarks of
Bloomsbury Publishing Plc

First published in Great Britain 2021
Paperback edition published 2022

Series design by Dani Leigh
Cover image © Brian Stablyk/gettyimages.co.uk

A catalogue record for this book is available from the British Library.

Library of Congress Control Number: 2020950622

ISBN: HB: 978-1-3501-7789-5
         PB: 978-1-3502-2956-3
         ePDF: 978-1-3501-7790-1
         eBook: 978-1-3501-7791-8

Series: Islam of the Global West

Typeset by Integra Software Services Pvt. Ltd.

To find out more about our authors and books visit www.bloomsbury.com
and sign up for our newsletters

In commemoration of the 150th anniversary of the birth of Ivan Aguéli

Contents

Figures

Full-color visuals of most images may be found online at aguelimusset.se.
A pdf of images in full color is also available on the publisher's website.

Acknowledgments

I would like to thank Susanne Olsson of Stockholm University for her help in making the idea for this book become reality, especially in connection with the preliminary meeting at the Thiel Gallery in Stockholm at which contributors to this book presented and discussed drafts of its chapters. I would also like to thank Patrik Steorn, the director of the Thiel Gallery, for hosting that meeting, and the Riksbankens Jubileumsfond for paying for it.

Notes on Transliteration and Updates

The transliteration of Arabic follows the practice of the *International Journal of Middle East Studies* (IJMES). Technical terms are fully transliterated, but diacritics (macrons and dots) are not used for proper names and titles of books, though *'ayn* and *hamza* are still marked. When an accepted English spelling exists, that is always used. When quotations have been translated from another language (often French), standard modern IJMES transliteration is used instead of whatever system was used in the original. People's chosen spelling of their own names, however, has always been retained, even when it varies (as Aguéli's did).

Updates to this book and any new information relating to Aguéli will be found online at traditionalistblog.blogspot.com. This is a blog for the study of Traditionalism and the Traditionalists, and covers Aguéli among other related topics. Anyone with relevant information is invited to email the blog's moderator; contact details are on the blog.

Ivan Aguéli: Politics, Painting, and Esotericism

Mark Sedgwick

The life of Ivan Aguéli (1869–1917) takes us through some of the most important territory of the late nineteenth century. Born in Sweden, where he first encountered the Western esoteric tradition, Aguéli spent much of his adult life in the French avant-garde milieu. Settled in Paris, he painted, wrote, read, and spent time in jail for revolutionary offences. After converting to Islam in 1898, he moved to Cairo, where he was known as 'Abd al-Hadi. He became a Sufi, and his translations from Arabic into French at the start of the 1910s introduced the work of the great mystic theologian Muhyiddin ibn 'Arabi (1165–1240) to the Parisian esoteric milieu. It was also Aguéli who introduced the turn-of-the-century French philosopher René Guénon (1886–1951), founder of the Traditionalist movement, to Sufism and Islam.

Aguéli is notable as one of the earliest Western intellectuals to convert to Islam and to explore Sufism, and he is also notable as an artist, an anarchist, and an esotericist. This book treats all these different aspects of his life and activities, exploring various facets of his complex personality in their own right, and also showing how they all fitted together—how, in the end, esotericism, art, and anarchism found their fulfillment in Sufism.

Aguéli's life and conversion show that Islam occupied a more central place in modern European intellectual history than is often realized. His life reflects several major modern intellectual, political, and cultural trends, some better studied and understood than others. As is well known, the late nineteenth century saw many groundbreaking painters, much radical politics, widespread interest in esoteric alternatives to Christianity, and growing knowledge (accurate or inaccurate) of the "Orient." Aguéli, however, was one of only a very few Europeans to synthesize these trends into what was then still a very unusual destination: conversion to Islam.

This synthesis was idiosyncratic, but not unique. Echoes of parts of it, and occasionally all of it, are found in other individuals and in later periods, especially in the Traditionalist movement that derived in part from Aguéli, and that later adopted Aguéli as one of its canonical figures. Although apparently disparate, all the movements with which Aguéli engaged had something in common. Esotericism overlapped with art, as artists turned to the esoteric for help in their quest to see the

Figure 1.1 French police photograph of Ivan Aguéli, March 1894. Made by Alphonse Bertillon. Albumen silver print from glass negative, 10.5 x 7 cm. The Metropolitan Museum of Art, New York, Gilman Collection, Museum Purchase, 2005.

world a new. Progressive and revolutionary approaches to art combined comfortably with progressive and revolutionary approaches to politics, and hence with anarchism, which in turn combined with resistance to colonialism. Resistance to colonialism encouraged a sympathetic approach to Islam, as so many of those suffering from the effects of colonialism were Muslim. Western esotericism also encouraged a sympathetic approach to Islam, since the apparently pure monotheism of Islam appealed to many who had rejected the Christian churches and Christian myth and doctrine but still hoped for access to the transcendent. Western esotericism also combined comfortably with the Islamic esotericism of Ibn ʿArabi, and thus with Sufism. Many, then, combined art with esotericism, art with anarchism, or esotericism and anarchism with sympathy for Islam and Sufism. Aguéli combined all of these.

Aguéli's Life

Ivan Aguéli started life in provincial Sweden as "John Gustaf Agelii," but was known under a succession of different names that marked successive phases of his life. He replaced "John" with its Russian equivalent, "Ivan," in 1889, when he was twenty, probably under the impact of his enthusiasm for the Russian literature he was then reading; this change was associated with the transition from his problematic schooldays to his first years as an artist in Sweden. The next change, when he replaced "Agelii" with "Aguéli," marked his emigration from Sweden to France, which after 1892 became his primary domicile; not only does "Aguéli" look more normal in French than "Agelii," but it is also easier to pronounce, and follows the rules of French orthography.[1] The final change, to ʿAbd al-Hadi, marked his conversion to Islam and subsequent move from France to Egypt, in 1902; often he signed articles as "Abdul Hadi El-Maghrabi," a pun, as although "al-Maghrabi" is a fairly common surname in Egypt, its literal meaning is "the westerner,"[2] and Aguéli was, indeed, a Westerner. Egypt replaced France as his primary domicile, although he did spend 1909–13 back in France, and was expelled from Egypt by the British authorities, who suspected him of opposing their war effort, in 1916. After taking the first available ship to Europe, he was stranded penniless in Spain, where in 1917 he was run over by a train.

It was as a young man in Sweden that Aguéli (or Agelii, as he was known then) first encountered esotericism in the form of the work and followers of the Swedish Christian visionary and mystic Emmanuel Swedenborg (1688–1772). Swedenborg was a visionary in that his life was transformed by a series of visions of angels that inspired his later work, and a mystic in that he emphasized the transcendent reality (or "spiritual world") of which the "earthly world" is a reflection, the connection of the human soul ("inner self") to transcendent reality, and the central role of divine light ("heaven's light").[3] Similar understandings, which may be termed emanationist (the earthly world "emanates" from transcendent reality), are found in many other thinkers and traditions, and may be traced back to Plato, or alternatively to the later Neoplatonic philosophers, of which Plotinus (died 270) is the most important.[4] This understanding and genealogy of mysticism is not the only one possible, and has indeed recently been subjected to much criticism,[5] but it is the most useful one in this context, as it is the scholarly version of the understanding to which thinkers from William Blake (1757–1827) to Ralph Waldo Emerson (1803–82), and from Aguéli to Kathleen Raine (1908–2003), subscribed.

Swedenborg's followers never became numerous, but founded what came to be known as the New Church. After moving to Stockholm in 1888, Aguéli became friends with the family of a pastor of the New Church, Adolph Boyesen (1823–1916).[6] Swedenborg was to remain of great importance to him throughout his life, and is discussed in many chapters in this book.

In Paris, Aguéli encountered a new form of esotericism, that of the Theosophical Society, and a new political engagement, with anarchism. The Theosophical Society had been established in New York in 1875 by Helena Blavatsky (1831–91), and by the time that Aguéli joined, it had become a global organization with headquarters in Adyar, near Madras (now Chennai), in India. Blavatsky, who had become a Buddhist, claimed to be in communication with hidden spiritual masters known as Mahatmas, but in fact drew on Neoplatonism, on the Western Hermetic-Kabbalistic esoteric tradition, and on understandings of Buddhism and Hinduism in her own writings,[7] which were supplemented by the writings of many other Theosophists in a variety of books and journals. The teachings of the Theosophical Society were eclectic, and also broad: there was no central official creed that had to be adhered to. The Theosophical Society also had a political agenda, aiming at the "universal brotherhood of humanity," which in practice often meant opposing European colonialism.[8] The Theosophical Society, then, was important for its teachings and its reinterpretation of religious myth, and for the social and organizational framework it provided for the investigation of a variety of religious and spiritual ideas. It was not a major source of social identity for most of its members, as there was no need to "convert" to Theosophy away from any other denominational allegiance. It had little or no ritual.

The political agenda of Anarchism was much more radical than that of the Theosophical Society. It was part of the large family of political theory that can be described as socialist, but differed from the parliamentary or "democratic" forms of socialism that later became dominant in Western Europe, and from the Marxist-Leninist forms of socialism that later became dominant in Eastern Europe, in that rather than seeking to use the state, it saw the state as a major part of the problem. Even though "anarchy" is now generally understood as meaning "chaos," the anarchists aimed at social justice, not chaos. Some of them used what was then called "propaganda of the deed" and is now called "terrorism" to promote their cause, resulting in a popular association between anarchism and terrorism, and even between terrorism and chaos. This, however, again misrepresents anarchism. Aguéli came to subscribe to anarchist theory and anarchist ideals; he was also close to Parisian anarchists who used propaganda of the deed, which is how he came to be arrested in 1894. The police photograph taken of him after his arrest is shown as Figure 1.1.

As well as encountering Theosophy and anarchism in Paris, Aguéli also became friends with a prominent animal-rights activist (and anarchist), Marie Huot

(1846–1930, Figure 2.4). Huot was twenty-three years older than Aguéli and married; in what sense the relationship between her and Aguéli was romantic is unclear, but it was extremely close, and of lasting importance.

One of the most celebrated French painters of the period, Paul Gauguin (1848–1903), spent 1891–3 painting in Tahiti, and this was one reason that Aguéli began a series of trips outside Europe, starting immediately after his release from prison. He spent 1894–5 in Egypt and, in 1899, traveled to Colombo in Ceylon (now Sri Lanka). In 1898, under unknown circumstances, he converted to Islam; he had been studying Arabic and the Qur'an for many years. At this time, the Swedish painter Fritz Lindström (1874–1962) portrayed Aguéli in Muslim style in his 1898 painting "Ivan Aguéli", now in the National Museum, Stockholm.

Soon after his return to France from Ceylon via India, Aguéli gained fame in France after one of the earliest and most successful acts of animal-rights activism. Huot had already used the propaganda of the deed in her campaign against vivisection, interrupting a lecture by Louis Pasteur (1822–95) in 1886, and on another occasion beating the physiologist and neurologist Charles-Édouard Brown-Séquard (1817–94) with a parasol. In 1901, she and Aguéli went to a bullfight in Deuil, a little to the north of Paris, where Aguéli fired at the bullfighters as they arrived at the bull-ring. No-one was killed, but one Spanish bullfighter was wounded. Public opposition to bullfighting, and thus support for Aguéli, reached the point where Spanish-style bullfighting was banned in France. At his trial, which took place in an atmosphere more favorable to Aguéli than to the wounded bullfighter, who had returned to Spain and did not appear, Aguéli was sentenced to pay a small fine and given a suspended sentence, even though he was arguably guilty of attempted murder.

The following year, in 1902, Aguéli moved to Cairo, where he assisted an Italian friend, Enrico Insabato (1878–1963), in publishing and writing for a bilingual Arabic-Italian periodical, *Il Convito/Al-Nadi*. Insabato's objective in publishing this journal was to promote the image of Italy as a friend of the Arabs and Islam; Aguéli's objective was probably to promote Islam and to oppose colonialism. Aguéli's articles in *Il Convito/Al-Nadi* are discussed in several chapters of this book.

One of the Egyptians who wrote in *Il Convito/Al-Nadi* was ʿAbd al-Rahman ʿIllaysh (1840–1921), who helped Aguéli read classic Islamic texts, including some by Muhyiddin ibn ʿArabi, the preeminent mystical writer of the Sufi tradition, and who admitted Aguéli into a Shadhili *ṭarīqa* (Sufi order). Sufism is often described as the mystical branch of Islam, and it is true that the greatest interest in the Arabic-language mystical philosophy and theology that resembles the thought of Swedenborg and can be traced back to the Arab and Islamic reception of Plotinus and other Neoplatonists is to be found among Sufis. Not all Islamic philosophers are Sufis, however—some are just philosophers—and most Sufis are not philosophers. Sufism is a major tradition of practice across the Muslim world, generally organized into lineages and groups known as *ṭarīqa*s (a term normally translated as "order"), most members of which were, until the recent development of mass education, illiterate. Sufism itself has an important literature, but for most Sufis, ascetic practice and the example of the *shaykh* or spiritual guide has been paramount. ʿIllaysh became Aguéli's *shaykh*.

Although a major tradition of practice across the Muslim world, at the start of the twentieth century Sufism was under attack from a rising group of modernist reformers, who tended to dismiss it as superstitious and obscurantist. 'Illaysh was associated with the religious establishment based around al-Azhar, Egypt's preeminent mosque and madrasa (later modernized into a state-run university). Aguéli thus stood with the traditionalist religious establishment against modernist reform.

Aguéli's Context

Aguéli was not the only Western Sufi of this period. There was a long-standing interest in Sufism in Western Europe, going back to the beginnings of modern Orientalism. It can be dated to the publication in 1671 of the first translation of a Sufi text to be widely read in Western Europe, the *Hayy ibn Yaqzan* of Ibn Tufayl (1105–85), translated by Sir Edward Pococke (1604–91), the first ever professor of Arabic at the University of Oxford, and his son. The *Hayy ibn Yaqzan* was generally regarded as an expression of Deism, not of Sufism,[9] but Sufism and Deism were then enduringly connected in Western Europe (and later the Americas) by another great British Orientalist, Sir William Jones (1746–94), in an important lecture given in 1789.[10]

Though there were Sufi texts in Western Europe during the eighteenth century, there were no Western European Sufis;[11] post-Christian and non-Christian religious organizations (other than Jewish ones) were not established in Western Europe and America until the nineteenth century. The most important of these was the Theosophical Movement. Blavatsky and the Theosophists emphasized Buddhism, not Sufism, but one American who was active in Theosophical circles was interested in Sufism, and a Sufic Circle was established in America in 1887, though it did not develop enough to leave any mark on the historical record.[12] During the 1890s, a German resident in Turkey, Rudolf von Sebottendorf (1875–1945[?]), seems to have joined the Bektashi *tarīqa*, though details are few; Sebottendorf later wrote a book on his rather occultist understanding of Sufism, published in Germany by the press of the German branch of the Theosophical Society in 1924.[13] An American, Ada Martin (1871–1947), became a Sufi in San Francisco in 1911; her Sufi master, an Indian, Inayat Khan (1882–1927), published his first book in English on Sufism in London in 1914. Again, this was published by the local branch of the Theosophical Society.[14]

The historical circumstances that lie behind Aguéli's Sufism, then, include the growth of alternative religious thought and of Orientalism during the eighteenth century, and the growth of alternative religious organizations, notably the Theosophical Society, during the nineteenth century. Behind these developments lie the Enlightenment, the Industrial Revolution, and the decline of the hegemony of the Christian churches, without which the developments in first religious thought and then religious organization could not have happened. Globalization and imperialism were also important, as these led to the increased availability of Oriental and Sufi texts in Western Europe, and then to the facility with which people like Aguéli, Gauguin, Sebottendorf, and Inayat Khan could travel around the world. When Pococke, the English translator of the *Hayy ibn Yaqzan*, traveled to Syria in 1630, the journey was a long and dangerous one by a sail ship; when Aguéli visited Ceylon, he bought a ticket on a steamship that followed a timetable.

Traditionalism

After the closure of *Il Convito/Al-Nadi* and the departure of Insabato in 1907, Aguéli returned to France between 1909 and 1913, partly for lack of money—he spent almost the whole of his life in severe financial difficulties. Back in Paris, he met the young French philosopher René Guénon, and in 1910–11 wrote in Guénon's journal, *La Gnose*. Although Guénon and *La Gnose* probably never seemed a very important part of his life to Aguéli himself, his engagement with them later proved to be of great importance, as the esoteric philosophy that Guénon first developed in *La Gnose* with the help of Aguéli became one of the most important, if least-studied, intellectual movements of the twentieth and then the twenty-first centuries, Traditionalism. "Traditionalism" is spelled with a capital *T* to distinguish it from general uses of the term "tradition," for example, when describing the resistance to modernism of ʿIllaysh and al-Azhar, mentioned above.

The Traditionalist movement is an intellectual movement (not an organization), and combines a radical critique of modernity with a respect for tradition, understood in a very specific sense, as ancient and primordial knowledge, now mostly preserved in and transmitted through "Oriental" esoteric traditions, notably the Indian tradition, Sufism, and Taoism (also spelled Daoism). Traditionalism, then, is a "perennialist" system, based on a conception of an enduring truth that has always existed and is not the exclusive property of any one religion or philosophy. Perennialism has always been popular, partly because it helps resolve the problem of the differences between religions and philosophies. Forms of it can be found in antiquity, but its modern expressions are generally dated to Renaissance Florence.[15] One widely read twentieth-century expression was in *The Perennial Philosophy* of Aldous Huxley (1894–1963), published in 1945;[16] Huxley's perennialism, however, differs from Traditionalism in various ways, most importantly in that it lacks Traditionalism's critique of modernity.

Tradition is understood by Traditionalists primarily as metaphysical knowledge, but this knowledge has important implications for how an individual should live and also for how human societies should be organized. These two different but related sets of implications give rise to two different but related forms of Traditionalism, one spiritual and one political. Spiritual Traditionalism is today associated mostly with Islam and with the writings of Guénon and the writings and activities of Frithjof Schuon (1907–98), a Swiss Traditionalist who, as Shaykh ʿIsa Nur al-Din, established his own *ṭarīqa*, the Maryamiyya, during the 1950s and 1960s. Schuon's successor in America was Seyyed Hossein Nasr (born 1933), a prominent scholar and public intellectual of Iranian origin. Political Traditionalism is associated mostly with the radical right and with the writings of Julius Evola (1898–1974), an Italian who was active both before and after the Second World War, and Alexander Dugin (born 1962), a Russian who became prominent during the early years of Vladimir Putin's presidency. The relationship between spiritual and political Traditionalism is asymmetrical; many spiritual Traditionalists have little or no interest in politics, and might even question the identification of Evola with Traditionalism; political Traditionalists, in contrast, are generally also interested in Guénon and his work, though not normally in Schuon.[17]

The Traditionalist movement is not associated with the progressive, especially today. This presents an apparent paradox. How did a progressive figure such as Aguéli, an anarchist, become entangled in this movement? One answer is that Aguéli died before the Traditionalist movement became established, and so had nothing to do with its subsequent development. Another answer is perhaps to be found in a short article that he published in *La Gnose* in 1911, entitled "La polarisation" (Polarization). This dealt with the apparent dichotomy between past and future, in which "past implies tradition, habit, collectivity. In aesthetics, classicity and style; in politics, conservativism. The future means: emotion, initiative and individuality. In art, romanticism; in politics, liberalism, at least in principle. Individualism is always futuristic, because secret and strictly personal aspirations always tend towards the future." However, wrote Aguéli, "The ideal tradition is that which develops individuality through all the means of ancient wisdom, that is to say, through the intellectual heritage of all of humanity." In Sufism, the best shaykh "returns you to yourself, and enlarges your own self. You think you are walking in the footsteps of the shaykh, while in reality you are following your own path, that is to say the road which is personal to you according to divine destiny."[18] The greatest initiative and individualism, then, lies not in the future, but in the transcendent, and so in tradition.

Writing about Aguéli

Although this is the first book devoted to Aguéli in English, much has been written about him in Swedish, starting in 1926 with the recollections of a Finnish artist, Werner von Hausen (1870–1951), who had known Aguéli in Paris, in what was then Sweden's leading cultural journal, *Ord och Bild*.[19] Even before this, in 1919, the artist Yngve Berg (1887–1963) had published an abbreviated translation of Aguéli's most important article on art, "L'art pur" (Pure Art), in the modern art journal, *Flamman: tidskrift för modern konst*.[20] This was followed by a biographical article, focusing on Aguéli's painting, also in *Ord och Bild*, in 1934,[21] and then in 1940 by the first volume of a massive two-volume study by Axel Gauffin (1877–1964),[22] published by the Swedish Public Art Association (Sveriges allmänna konstförening) in a long-running series on Swedish artists. Gauffin's finely illustrated volumes were based on painstaking research: Aguéli's correspondence and interviews with persons who had known him. In some ways, this remains the definitive study. Gauffin, however, was interested most of all in Aguéli's painting career, although he still covered other aspects of his life—the esotericism, the anarchism, and the Sufism.

Gauffin's study was the basis of the first detailed study to appear in a language other than Swedish, in the biography of Guénon by Paul Chacornac (1884–1964), in 1958.[23] After 1958, then, Aguéli was known primarily as an artist in Sweden, and primarily as a Sufi and associate of Guénon outside Sweden. There have been several exhibitions of Aguéli's paintings in Sweden,[24] and in 1969 the 100th anniversary of his birth was commemorated by the Swedish Post Office with a special set of postage stamps. His paintings are now exhibited in several Swedish galleries. There has only been one minor exhibition outside Sweden, however, organized in Paris by the Swedish Cultural Center in 1983.[25]

A different side of Aguéli was emphasized in 1981 when the Swedish novelist Torbjörn Säfve (born 1941), a former Maoist who in 1968 had memorably directed a short film entitled "Masturbation Drama," published a novel based on Aguéli's life, *Ivan Aguéli: en roman om frihet* (Ivan Aguéli: A Novel about Freedom),[26] drawing mostly on Gauffin. Säfve was more interested in Aguéli's anarchism than his art, and was also interested in his Islam; Säfve himself became Muslim, and as Ali Touba wrote in the Swedish Muslim journal *Minaret*,[27] and even published a novel based on the life of the Prophet Muhammad and the early development of Islam, *De sanna och de falska* (The True and the False). In this novel, the tolerant and woman-friendly religion that the Prophet preached was true; the repressive and hierarchical religion that developed afterward is false.[28] After 1981, Aguéli became an ever more important symbol for Swedish Muslims, including converts, not all of whom found Islam quite as Säfve had presented it.[29] One contemporary Swedish Muslim intellectual, Mohamed Omar (born 1976), named his blog *Nya Il Convito* (The New *Il Convito*),[30] reviving the name of the bilingual Italian- and Arabic-language Cairo periodical, *Il Convito/Al-Nadi*, in which Aguéli had published his first articles.

The year 1988 saw the publication of the first postwar scholarly work on Aguéli, by the Swedish art historian Viveca Wessel,[31] the author of the next chapter in this book. Since then, numerous scholarly articles have appeared, as the select bibliography of this book shows, usually in Swedish, but sometimes in other languages. Many of their authors are among the authors of other chapters in this book.

This Book

This book is divided into two unequal parts. The first and longest part, consisting of three sections, contains chapters written for this study of the Aguéli's politics, painting, and esotericism. The second and shorter part translates five texts by Aguéli himself, only one of which ("Universality in Islam") has appeared in English before.

The first section in the book's first part focuses on Aguéli's painting and politics. It opens with a chapter in which Viveca Wessel traces Aguéli's life and work, focusing especially on his painting, and discussing the distinct periods in his life: childhood and youth; his first trip to France and his engagement with synthetism and symbolism; his early studies, in Paris, Stockholm, and Gotland; his involvement with anarchism and with Marie Huot; his two first trips to Egypt and his conversion to Islam; his engagement with Sufism and his application of Sufi theology to art; his encounter with cubism; and his final periods of painting, in France, Egypt, and Spain.

The following chapter, by Annika Öhrner, connects Aguéli's painting and career to the networks and institutions of the historical avant-garde, positioning his work in the space of European modernism. Öhrner explains how Aguéli was connected to Swedish institutions that were the equivalent of those that provided the framework of the Parisian avant-garde, and how these connections provided his point of entry in France, from which he improved his position in various ways, notably through his connection with Huot and the *Encylopédie universelle illustrée*, and with Félix Fénéon (1861–1944). She shows how his art was formed by these institutions and connections; the yearning for lands beyond Europe that ultimately led him to Egypt, for example, followed the example of Gauguin's residence in Tahiti. Öhrner also shows that Aguéli's encounter with Islam and Sufism was likewise prepared by his studies in Paris at two major institutions of the time, the École spéciale des langues orientales vivantes (special school for living Oriental languages) and the École pratique des hautes études (special school for higher studies).

In the third chapter in this section, Per Faxneld contextualizes Aguéli in a different way, focusing on his relationship with Swedenborg and Theosophy, a relationship that Aguéli shared with other artists of the period, both in Sweden and in Paris. Faxneld questions the general view of such engagements as transgressive, pointing out that Aguéli's interest in Theosophy was shared with the king of Sweden. He describes Aguéli's esoteric connections and readings, which included Papus (Gérard Encausse, 1865–1916), and figures such as Éliphas Lévi (1810–75). He also points out that the esoteric had faded from Swedish public consciousness by the 1920s, when the reception of Aguéli's work began, with the result that Aguéli's esotericism was generally ignored, and that Säfve deliberately toned down esotericism in his novel, instead bringing out anarchism and Sufism. After a very successful exhibition of the work of Hilma af Klint (1862–1944) in 2013, however, esotericism returned to Swedish public consciousness, and Aguéli is now also appreciated as an esotericist.

In the following chapter, Simon Sorgenfrei moves from the general to the specific, looking at how landscape painting, philosophy of religion—especially Swedenborg's—and art theory all informed and nourished each other in a symbiotic relationship. Swedenborg can perhaps explain both the layered skies and the choice of color in Aguéli's Swedish paintings—Sorgenfrei both explores and questions this possibility. The Egyptian paintings, however, follow a different logic, as Aguéli's views shifted toward classic Islamic understandings of light.

In the last chapter on Aguéli the artist, Thierry Zarcone moves outwards, looking not just at Aguéli but at cubism as a whole. He draws especially on Aguéli's article on "L'art pur" (Pure Art), which is translated in the final part of the book, to show how Aguéli viewed cubism in terms that are ultimately Neoplatonic, so that painting becomes an occult art of transformation akin to alchemy. He shows how Aguéli understood pure art as cerebral, relating to rhythm and number, and draws parallels with the work of Henri Matisse (1869–1954), and also, in another direction, with the work of Ibn ʿArabi.

In the final chapter in the section on Aguéli's painting and politics, Anthony T. Fiscella looks at "Ivan Aguéli's universal utopia of anarchism and Islam." He starts by showing how Aguéli's anarchism and Islam were closely interwoven with both Theosophy and concern for animals, a concern that he traces back to the Swedenborgian Pastor Boyesen, who the young Aguéli knew, and to his early engagement with anarchism. Although Aguéli's degree of enthusiasm for anarcho-syndicalism and animal welfare seemed to fluctuate throughout his life, the underlying values continued in some form and always attached to his Islam, as Fiscella demonstrates by reference to Aguéli's "L'Universalité en l'Islam" (Universality in Islam), an article which is translated in the final section of the book. Fiscella uses this to explain Aguéli's dramatic intervention at the bullfights in Deuil, and argues that, in the end, his anarchism, Islam, and defense of animals were inextricable from one another.

The book's next section moves to Cairo and looks at Aguéli's Sufism. It opens with a chapter by Paul-André Claudel, looking at the intellectual spheres around *Il Convito/Al-Nadi*. Claudel provides a comprehensive overview of this important period in Aguéli's life, of the content of the journal, and of the connections that its contributors indicate. On the Italian (and non-Sufi) side, contributors to *Il Convito* indicate connections with Orientalists, French critics of colonialism, and the Italian radical exile Romolo Garbati (1873–1942). On the Arabic side, 'Abd al-Rahman 'Illaysh connected Aguéli and *Al-Nadi* not just to Sufism but also to Egyptian Azhari and religious circles that were traditionalist in contrast to the Egyptian modernists of the time. The short-lived Turkish section, however, linked the journal to Abdullah Cevdet (1869–1932) and modernist reform. Claudel notes, but does not seek to resolve, this paradox.

In the next chapter in this section, Alessandra Marchi asks to what extent Aguéli's conversion to Islam was political, and to what extent it was religious, and how the sociopolitical and the spiritual dimensions intertwine. For several other well-known European converts to Islam of the time, conversion has been associated with radicalism. Marchi therefore looks at how Aguéli and Insabato presented Islam in the Italian section of *Il Convito/Al-Nadi*, showing how while on the one hand Aguéli defended Islam against Islamophobia, he also stressed the universal validity of Islamic ideas, especially Sufi ones.

In the following chapter, Iheb Guermazi reverses perspectives, looking not at the European approach to Sufism, but at the Sufi approach to Europe or, more specifically, that of the Emir 'Abd al-Qadir (1808–83), to whom 'Illaysh had been close. 'Abd al-Qadir thought that Sufism might make possible an esoteric rapprochement between East and West, a possibility explored in *Dhikra al-'aqil wa tanbih al-ghafil* (Reminder to the Intelligent, Warning to the Indifferent), which Guermazi discusses. He then argues that the new Sufi school that 'Abd al-Qadir established in Damascus provided the theoretical framework used by 'Illaysh and thus by Aguéli in *Il Convito/Al-Nadi*, and then by Guénon and the Traditionalists. Traditionalism, in this understanding, is ultimately a universalism based on Ibn 'Arabi.

In the next chapter, Meir Hatina takes yet another perspective, looking at Aguéli's Humanist vision, providing an in-depth analysis of the ideas expressed in *Il Convito/Al-Nadi* and also in "L'Universalité en l'Islam." While some later Western Sufis blurred the boundaries between Sufism and other cultures, or even detached Sufism from Islam, Aguéli (in Hatina's view) combined Sufism with Humanism, synthesizing Western anarchist and Islamic mystical values. Aguéli promoted a tolerant, pluralistic, and pacifist version of Islam, and advocated solidarity and morality. He presented Sufism as the purest expression of Islam, and (like 'Abd al-Qadir, though Hatina himself does not make this comparison) as a bridge between East and West. By placing mysticism at the center of Islam and reframing Sufism as a universal philosophical and moral system, Aguéli softened, though he never criticized, exoteric Islam. Hatina closes by looking at some contradictions between Aguéli's earlier anarchist ideals and his later Sufi understanding.

In the final chapter in this section, Marcia Hermansen shows that despite writing on "femminismo," Aguéli cannot be described as a feminist in contemporary terms. In fact, he was often most concerned, at least in *Il Convito*, with defending Islam against charges brought in relation to the status of women. She asks what his view of the "woman question" actually was, looking at his use of the idea of the "exceptional woman." Aguéli was in favor of female education, though with reservations, as he found Western education as a whole wanting. Hermansen ends her chapter by comparing Aguéli's views on gender with those of later Traditionalists, finding that they differ significantly. Aguéli's views, she concludes, drew both on his European sensibilities and experiences, and on Islam.

The last section in the book's first part consists of two chapters looking at Aguéli's relationship with Traditionalism, which is where his importance for the development of Western esotericism lies. In the first, Mark Sedgwick looks at his broader significance for the Traditionalist movement, through Aguéli's personal influence on Guénon, through his writings in *La Gnose*, and through his role in the "sacred history" of Traditionalism. Aguéli was responsible for Guénon's conversion to Islam in 1911, even though this conversion remained latent in its impact until after 1930, and although there is only one documented instance of discussions with Aguéli affecting Guénon's views, it can be assumed that there were also other instances. Aguéli's articles in *La Gnose* established Sufism as a major form of esotericism in Traditionalist thought, thus laying the ground for Traditionalism's later predominantly Sufi and Islamic forms. Finally, the role of Aguéli in Traditionalism's sacred history has varied. At first he and 'Illaysh provided the living connection to Islam that helped legitimize Guénon's thought, but under the assault of revisionist historians, this role was first downgraded and finally mostly dropped.

In the second chapter in this last section, Patrick Ringgenberg looks at Ivan Aguéli's art in relation to the Traditionalists' "traditional Art." He compares Aguéli's views on art, expressed most importantly in his "L'art pur," with those of three later Traditionalists, Ananda K. Coomaraswamy (1877–1947), Schuon, and Titus Burckhardt (1908–84). He starts by explaining the Traditionalist view of art in terms of symbolism, canonical aesthetics, and its ritual and initiatic character. He contrasts this with Aguéli's understandings, showing especially how his idea of the role of passion, and his eclecticism, which would be rejected by the later Traditionalists, were important to Aguéli. He also discusses the contradictions between the theories and the artistic production of Schuon, who painted, and of Nader Ardalan (born 1939), the celebrated Iranian Traditionalist architect. The "traditional art" of the Traditionalists, he concludes, is a retrospective vision of the past, very unlike the art of Aguéli.

The book's second and shorter part, consisting of only one section, contains translations of five texts by Aguéli. The first two, letters written from Paris and Colombo, show us Aguéli at a personal level. The third, translated from *Il Convito*, illustrates Aguéli's politics in his Cairo period. The last two, translated from *La Gnose*, show where Aguéli's thought ultimately led, one with regard to art, and the other with regard to Islam and Sufism.

The letter from Paris was written in Swedish in 1893 and is addressed to the painter and art theorist Richard Bergh (1858–1919), a former teacher and patron of Aguéli. Composed with youthful verve, it covers many topics—anarchism, Aguéli's life in Paris and his friends there (especially Fénéon), beautiful girls, art, his own painting, books, August Strindberg (1849–1912), and how Aguéli wants to follow Gaugin and get away to the tropics. One passing reference to the Qur'an hints at what is to come. In the letter from Colombo, written in French in 1899 to Huot, Aguéli has converted to Islam and reached the tropics. The letter tells of his arrival in Colombo, and his chance encounter with some Muslims whom he surprised by reading aloud from a copy of the Qur'an. Aguéli delights in his description of Ceylon and the Ceylonese, or at least of Ceylonese Muslims, among whom he has decided to spend his time, keeping away from the Buddhists.

The third text, on "The Enemies of Islam," was written in Italian in 1904 and published in *Il Convito* over the name of Abdul Hadi El Maghrabi. It examines European "Islamophobia," and may be the first ever use of this term. He blamed Islamophobia in part on Europeans who may hate Muslims out of Catholic or sometimes Protestant prejudice or because they believe ignorant rumors, or, if they are German, out of pro-Aryan racism. Some Europeans, however, are characterized not by Islamophobia but Islamophilia, born of admiration of Islam as a religion, and of past architectural and poetic glories. Islamophobia, however, is not only the fault of Europeans: some Muslims behave like "Levantines," a rightly despised class of persons who follow no particular religion and speak no particular language, and are interested primarily in money; they are most likely to be Armenian(!). Although good Sunni Egyptians and simple Egyptian farmers are not at all like this, it is unfortunately the Westernized Egyptian of the Levantine type whom Europeans generally encounter.

The fourth text, "L'art pur," was published in *La Gnose* in 1911, translated in *Flamman* in 1919, and is the main text discussed by Ringgenberg in his chapter. Despite occasional references to esotericism, it is really about art. It distinguishes cerebral and sentimental art. Most art is sentimental, and operates indirectly, by association with ideas in the viewer's memory. Cerebral art, in contrast, communicates directly, is pure, and is about number and dimension, not matter. It resembles music. Pure art links the concrete and the abstract, and Aguéli discusses the significance of the three axes and their relationship to color. Aguéli makes a parallel distinction between feeling and style, both of which are needed. For Purist painters, he argues, among whom he numbers Cezanne and Pablo Picasso (1881–1973), what is central and essential is tone.

The fifth and final text, "L'Universalité en l'Islam," was also published in *La Gnose* in 1911, is the text discussed by Fiscella and, especially, Hatina in their chapters, and is in many ways Aguéli's masterpiece. It is remarkable for its passion, clarity, and fidelity to Islamic mystical theology and ability to communicate its nuances to a general Western audience. It is built around a distinction between collective, temporal, apparent reality and the personal reality that is an awareness of eternity, the ultimate reality that is understood in the same way in all religions. The two realities need to operate together, as the exoteric and the esoteric, which in Christianity they do not. Only Islam merges these opposites perfectly, in the person of the Prophet, which is what makes Islam universal. The Shari'a may sometimes seem absurd to modern Europeans, but it has proved its universality by uniting in solidarity disparate races, types, periods, and classes. Its esoteric counterpart, equally part of Islam, can be understood in various ways, so long as they remain within the Shariʿa and thus the universality of Islam. Ultimately, Islam's esotericism leads to the Absolute. Altruism draws one to God, but ultimately there is no such thing as altruism, as properly speaking, the "other" does not exist. This is what is most important to understand.

Part One

Ivan Aguéli the Anarchist Artist

Ivan Aguéli's Life and Work

Viveca Wessel

John Gustaf Agelii, known by his artist name Ivan Aguéli, placed the act of painting at the center of his activities. "My art will one day explain the eccentricities of my life," he stated.[1] Yet there is still a need to clarify his Sufi identity, his contribution to the philosophy of religions and of art, and, finally, his political activities. To detach any single area of interest from the kaleidoscopic pattern that his life-course constitutes makes it more difficult to understand Aguéli. As Anton Ehrenzweig has argued, "All artistic structure is essentially 'polyphonic;' it evolves not in a single line of thought, but in several superimposed strands at once. Hence creativity requires a diffuse, scattered kind of attention that contradicts our normal logical habits of thinking."[2]

The deeper one studies Aguéli, the more one becomes convinced that the scattered fields of interest belong only to a superficial consideration, and that from a different perspective there is a profound unity and consistency to be found.

1869–89: Life and Work; Childhood and Youth

Aguéli was born in Sala, central Sweden, on May 24, 1869. He was the only child of his parents' marriage, since although his father, veterinarian Johan Gabriel Agelii (1821–96), had been married more than once, all his other children except for one son from a previous marriage had died. Aguéli's mother, Anna Kristina Nyberg (1838–1925), was the daughter of a farmer from Dalarna, central Sweden. She was warm-hearted and intelligent, though without formal education. Ivan Aguéli was a sensitive child, troubled by his father's strict upbringing practices. Anna Agelii's financial help for her adult son was given secretly and continued throughout his life. Aguéli was eager to calm his mother with selective information about his whereabouts, and as he visited Sala only a few times, he wrote letters to her during all stages of his life.

Aguéli's schooling points to a failure on the part of his teachers to discover his unusual talent for languages, philosophy, and art. His teachers recognized his talent for botany, but considered him unsuited to higher studies. A hearing disability might have contributed to this. Aguéli had frequently made drawings as a child and expected a letter from his father clearly giving him permission to begin studying painting; but his father refused to encourage a prospective artist, and sent his son from the island of Gotland in the Baltic, where Aguéli's desire to paint had first come to the fore, to Stockholm, to a school where he could learn a simple craft profession so as to be able to support himself. While still a teenager, however, Aguéli had read works by Ibsen, Strindberg, and Nietzsche;[3] within the next fifteen years he would learn some dozen languages, make advanced translations from Arabic into French and Italian, and write original essays in French about art, philosophy, and religions. He had been held back by his father's narrow-minded ideas about his future, and had accumulated a yearning for freedom and for a more comprehensive intellectual orientation.

Aguéli became interested in the unique form of Christianity of Emanuel Swedenborg, and this became his introduction to mysticism. "Swedenborg has given me the spiritual upbringing through which I have defended myself and liberated myself from all Protestantism and germanization," he later wrote.[4] Aguéli was also a family friend of the Boyesens, Adolph Boyesen being the first pastor at the newly established Swedenborgian church in Stockholm.

From the summer of 1889, Aguéli was working seriously with painting. At this time he met two Swedish artists representing the Artists' Association (Konstnärsförbundet), founded by the opposition movement against the official Royal Academy of Fine Arts

Figure 2.1 Ivan Aguéli, *Gotländskt landskap* (Gotland landscape) *c.* 1891. 27 x 32 cm. Collection of Sala Konstförening—Aguélimuseet. Full-color image available at www.aguelimuseet.se/2_1 and on the publisher's website.

(Kungliga akademien för de fria konsterna), and further discussed in Chapter 3. Karl Nordström (1855–1923) and Richard Bergh (director of the National Museum in Stockholm after 1915) saw Aguéli's first paintings, landscapes and portraits (see, for example, Figure 2.1), and gave him much-needed encouragement to continue his studies in France. Their friendship was to last throughout Aguéli's life.

1890: First Trip to France; Synthetism and Symbolism

When Ivan Aguéli finally gained his father's permission to study painting, he immediately went by boat to Le Havre, France, where he landed on April 15, 1890, and wrote to his mother the following day.[5] He attended the Académie Julian in Paris where he met other Scandinavian artists and started to make new friends. He visited museums and was invited to join groups of Swedish artists in the suburbs of Paris, St Ouen and Bois-de-Colombes. He longed to paint outside, in the country. In the summer he joined a group heading for Étaples in the department of Pas-de-Calais in northern France. On August 9, 1890, however, he wrote to his mother that he did not feel comfortable, was having difficulties painting in the company of other artists, and did not have enough opportunity to learn French.[6] He moved back to Paris, where literary symbolism, with its strong influences from Swedenborg's idea about correspondences, had been an inspiration for the poetry of Charles Baudelaire (1821–67), which captured Aguéli's interest. However, literary symbolism had reached its peak, and the theories of symbolism specifically for painting were yet to emerge.[7]

Synthetism as a primarily painterly practice is attributed to Paul Gauguin and Émile Bernard (1868–1941) in their work together in Pont-Aven, Brittany, in 1888. A decorative shallow picture space with non-naturalistic color in summarized surfaces, outlined with darker contours, was a statement against both impressionism and realism. Synthetism was also being practiced by Paul Sérusier (1864–1927), and was eventually to reach many Scandinavian painters by way of the Académie Julian in Paris.

Aguéli's thinking during the 1890s would develop in deeper agreement with the French than with the Swedish or German tradition.[8] French symbolism has its roots in Plato's philosophy of ideas as located beyond the apparent world, which in turn was manifested in the mysticism of Plotinus's Neoplatonism. Through intuition, love, and ecstasy, man could gain access to higher spiritual levels. Only love of philosophical knowledge could bring the soul closer to the only true Reality. For Plotinus more than for Plato, art was an appreciated form of spiritual activity. The creativity of the artist mirrored God's creative act. The artist had a unique ability to see the beauty radiating from the highest levels of existence.[9] These were ideas that appealed to Aguéli, who was already attuned to Swedenborg's thought.

Aguéli fully accepted symbolist ideas and applied them to his own painting:

For symbolism, I take the liberty to make a perhaps somewhat banal remark. That every color, sound in the music or language symbolizes profoundly different, usually opposed ideas. Moreover, it is more often the place in the composition which determines—so to speak, selects—what the matter in question means at the moment. Incidentally, within real symbolism, no arbitrariness is possible.[10]

Among French symbolist art theorists, Aguéli held Gabriel-Albert Aurier (1865–92) in highest regard. An essay by Aurier on Gauguin's art was published as "Le Symbolisme en peinture: Paul Gauguin" in *Mercure de France* in 1891,[11] and contains the essentials of the symbolist theories that appealed to Aguéli.

Aurier prioritized the Idea, and was strictly against both impressionism and realism. Art should be based on ideas, symbolist, synthetist, subjective, and decorative.[12] Aurier had in fact already met Émile Bernard in 1888 before Bernard and Gauguin's period of collaboration in Pont-Aven began.[13] Aguéli recommended Aurier in a letter to his artist friend, Richard Bergh: "You have to cultivate again the higher qualities of the soul. One has to become a mystic again. One must learn that love is the source of all understanding."[14] The esoteric symbolism of Aguéli's art saw in the artistic, creative process a path to self-realization on a higher level. The goal of the artist's endeavor was to uncover an already existing, hidden reality in such a way that the mind of the viewer would turn to the world of ideas or God. At the gallery of the art dealer known as "Père Tanguy" (Julien François Tanguy, 1825–94), contemporary paintings by Vincent Van Gogh (1853–90) and Paul Cézanne (1839–1906) were on display,[15] and Aguéli's earlier biographer, Axel Gauffin, supposes that it was at Père Tanguy's gallery that Aguéli was advised to contact Émile Bernard in his studio in Asnières and ask for guidance.[16]

Aguéli was well received. In 1890 Bernard and Gauguin had not yet broken with each other, and Aguéli gained the best introduction he could have had to the art of Gauguin, Van Gogh, and Cézanne. Bernard, a friend of Van Gogh, wrote about Cézanne in *Les Hommes d'aujourd'hui* in 1891.

1890: Early Studies; Art Theory and Practice

With encouragement from Bernard, Aguéli started by painting still life. It was probably also through Bernard that Aguéli was introduced to *The Grammar of Ornament* by Owen Jones (1809–74),[17] whose initial theses Aguéli copied by hand and circulated among his fellow artists.[18] The pursuit of simplicity, harmonious proportioning of colors, the importance of contouring, the tracing of the principles behind nature's forms, and the avoidance of imitation were essential features of Jones's theses. The book also had a pedagogical ambition: to improve the quality of European art through the study of the decorative arts of advanced foreign cultures. Aguéli paid several visits to the Paris museums. To learn more about the collections, he studied *Les Arts méconnus: Les nouveaux musées du Trocadéro* (The Unknown Arts: The New Trocadero Museums) by Émile Soldi (1846–1906) and he also copied the main contents of a work by Frédéric Portal (1804–76), *Des Couleurs symboliques* (An Essay on Symbolic Colors).[19] With Aurier's death in 1892 at only twenty-seven, following soon after Gauguin's departure the previous year for Tahiti, symbolist aesthetics were led back to a more conservative attitude toward intuition in the artistic process with the work of the painter and writer Joséphin Péladan (1859–1918).[20] Aguéli, however, did not follow him.

Bernard also introduced Aguéli to the Theosophical Society in Paris, and Aguéli was accepted as a member by Loge Ananta.[21] Much later, in 1939, Gauffin met the Lodge member Jacques Tasset, who told him that Aguéli's main focus had then been on Swedenborg and on Islam. Aguéli did not dwell on spiritism, Theosophy, or fin-de-siècle decadence, probably because he was not searching for a general spirituality, but rather for an individual path to God, and a language for his art.

1891–2: Painting in Stockholm and Gotland

Many new impressions came to Aguéli's mind as he painted in Gotland during the two summers of 1891 and 1892 after his first trip to France. In January 1892, he attended the Artists' Association's school in Stockholm.[22] In this same year he also frequently visited the National Library of Sweden (Kungliga biblioteket) in Stockholm. On March 11, 1892, he borrowed a copy of the Qur'an for the first time, and a week later the collected poems of Baudelaire.[23] Aguéli's suite of paintings of Stockholm's outskirts (see, for example, Figure 2.2) dates from this period. In them, one can follow Aguéli's composition method—his division of the canvas into separate color fields to create a complete harmony, a method inspired by stained glass windows—with dark blue outlines and the rhythm of arch lines in the skies. In the later paintings from this period simplification is far driven, and the contrast effect of the sensitive color tones builds the volume.

Figure 2.2 Ivan Aguéli, *Stockholmsutsikt* (View of Stockholm), 1892. Oil on canvas, 46 x 58 cm. Private collection. Photo courtesy of Stockholms Auktionsverk. Full-color image available at www.aguelimuseet.se/2_2 and on the publisher's website.

Figure 2.3 Ivan Aguéli, *Havsstrand Gotland* (Gotland Beach), 1889. Oil on canvas, 41 x 63.5 cm. Photo: Moderna Museet, Stockholm. Full-color image available at www.aguelimuseet. se/2_3 and on the publisher's website.

The Gotland landscapes (see Figures 5.2 and 5.3) remind us that for Aguéli the horizon had a special significance. This is visible from the very beginning in his first painting *Havsstrand Gotland* (Gotland Beach, see Figure 2.3) of 1889, perhaps as a fixed point for a longing to travel far away. Then, later in his life, it is more noticeable as "an ever-present eye" directed from object to subject.[24] In the Nordic landscape, Aguéli had observed the significant contrast of light. Shadows seemed opaque, and through the dim light, his gaze was drawn toward the foreground and the soil in front of him.

Paris 1892–4: Anarchist Sympathies; Aguéli Meets Marie Huot

Aguéli returned to Paris at the end of 1892. In the following year he met Marie Huot (see Figure 2.4), a French poet, feminist, and animal-rights activist. The letters Aguéli and Huot wrote to one another over the following twenty years testify to their sometimes stormy and painful relationship, but also to their mutual admiration. She was married to the founder of the weekly periodical *L'Encyclopédie contemporaine illustrée*, discussed in Chapter 3, and was thus in a position to give Aguéli an opportunity to work as a journalist.

Aguéli had probably already visited the Anarchist Club in London and met with Peter Kropotkin (1842–1921) before his return to Sweden in 1891.[25] He seldom

Figure 2.4 Olof Sager-Nelson, *La Dame du Silence* (The Lady of Silence, i.e., Marie Huot), 1894. Oil on canvas, 62 x 39 cm. Thielska Galleriet, Stockholm. Full-color image available at www.aguelimuseet.se/2_4 and on the publisher's website.

mentioned how deeply involved he was with the anarchists. He called himself a revolutionary, sometimes a "Swedenborgian anarchist," but also wrote that he longed to get away from Paris to get some rest from the intense discussions and politics and just find some peace of mind. He witnessed the Paris riots of July 1893 and described the dramatic impact they had on him, invigorating and perhaps also channeling his newfound liberation from the strict upbringing of his early years. An informative letter of October 10, 1893, to the painter Richard Bergh, translated later in this book, surveys the diversity of Aguéli's interests and studies. In the letter, well aware of the French censors, Aguéli uses pseudonyms for his anarchist friends.[26]

Imprisoned in Mazas Prison; Intense Studies

In April 1894 Aguéli was arrested as a member of a criminal association (*association de malfaiteurs*) of anarchists, on the basis that he was sharing accommodation with Charles Chatel (1868–97), the editor of the anarchist periodical *L'En Dehors* and then of the *Revue Anarchiste*, and had a letter from some Belgian anarchists in his possession.[27] This was part of a wave of arrests aimed at breaking up anarchist cells that had become increasingly problematic because of their use of bombs, ending in the famous "procès des trente" (the trial of the thirty). He spent four months in the Mazas Prison in Paris. He used this time well, however. Before his trial, scheduled for August 7, Aguéli had to work on his defense. His French was still deficient and he feared that he would be convicted. He maintained contact with Finnish symbolist painter Werner von Hausen and with Huot, who also supplied him with necessities for surviving the uncertain existence in the cell. Through his letters from prison, written to Hausen almost every day, one gets a unique idea of Aguéli's studies. He knew which second-hand bookshop, library, or bookstore could supply Hausen with the books he wanted. Among the many books he ordered were an anatomy book for medical students, Emanuel Swedenborg's *True Christian Religion* (Vera Christiana Religio), Saint John's Gospel in Arabic, the Qur'an, books on Arab art and Arabic literature, the Arabic alphabet and grammar, the Bible in Hebrew, and the Hebrew alphabet and grammar. In this period he developed a unique method of learning new languages. He proceeded from a translation of Saint John's Gospel, which opens with the words, "In the beginning was the Word, and the Word was with God, and the Word was God." Knowing the content well, he thus got an idea of what he called "the architecture of the language." In his dark cell, he formulated his essential thoughts on art and religion, initiated by his personal experience of the difference in landscape impressions: that a landscape can mirror a state of mind, that strong light leads the eye in the landscape toward the far distance and the skies, and thus evokes "the lofty and intimate principles" in the soul. This he calls the "monotheistic landscape." Light is, at an early stage in his development as a painter, a key symbol, and this statement of his also becomes his religion, his language as a painter.[28]

Aguéli's fear of conviction was uncalled for. On August 12, 1894, he was acquitted by the jury, with seven votes against five.

1894–5: First Trip to Egypt

After one month of freedom, Aguéli received some money from his mother and was able to travel to Egypt. He settled in Cairo, where Bernard was already staying. Being amidst the Egyptian and the Arab civilizations was inspiring. "One could advantageously study analysis in Paris, but synthesis in Cairo,"[29] the twenty-five-year-old Aguéli wrote to the friends he invited to join him. The Gotlandic light had never been as impressive as the overwhelming "monotheistic light"[30] that he experienced in Egypt. He made many drawings, and tried to capture the desert landscape with a sparse palette, with a lot of lead-white to re-create the light that so fascinated him. These paintings have a characteristic rhythm in the lines, a rhythm that the landscape impression gave him. They call to mind the Gotlandic painting sessions, when Baudelaire and Swedenborg's ideas about the correspondence between spirit and matter were on his mind.

1895–1900: Language Studies; Conversion to Islam; the Gunshot in Deuil

Returning to Paris, Aguéli immersed himself in his studies. He chose Sanskrit, Arabic, and Islam, and studied at the École pratique des hautes études (special school for higher studies). At the École spéciale des langues orientales vivantes (special school for living Oriental languages) he studied written and spoken Arabic, while he wrote art and literary criticism in *L'Encyclopédie contemporaine illustrée*, in which he was to publish forty-four texts on art and literary criticism between 1895 and 1913. For a long time after his first Egyptian period, Aguéli abandoned painting.

There are no traces of any sudden repentance; rather, over the years to come, a slowly maturing inner assurance that Islam's esotericism, Sufism, mediated by the great mystic theologian Muhyiddin Ibn 'Arabi, was the only religion that would allow Aguéli to stay true to himself. It may be argued that Sufism, like the mystical branches of other great religions, represents intimacy, renewal, and liberation from solidified forms: it is the heart and life of religious practice. Aguéli converted to Islam some time in 1898. In 1899 he made the long journey to Ceylon and India, staying at Islamic madrasas as a Muslim.[31] His experiences are documented in ten letters from his travels published in *L'Encyclopédie contemporaine illustrée*, testifying to a deep love for, and longing to return to, the desert and the Egyptian landscape. He compared his landscape impressions during his boat trip to Ceylon and regretted not combining his trip with a second stay in Egypt and Aden, which fascinated him. But at the end of 1899 he returned to Paris.

In 1900 he reported in *L'Encyclopédie contemporaine illustrée* on the great Paris Exhibition, also reviewing art and literature. In this year, Huot initiated Aguéli's violent protest against the introduction of bullfighting in the Spanish style into France. In Deuil, a northern Parisian suburb, Aguéli shot and wounded a matador and was arrested. Aguéli defended himself in court and was sentenced to pay a fine. The Spanish-style bullfighting initiative was abandoned in France. Huot wrote to Aguéli in

1909: "There is only one thing that you have done out of love for me and religion, and that is the gunshot in Deuil."[32] Following these dramatic events, he returned to Egypt.

1902–9: Second Trip to Egypt; Initiation in the Shadhiliyya Order; *Il Convito*

In Cairo, probably in the years following 1902, Aguéli was initiated into a Sufi order, the ʿArabiyya-Shadhiliya, by Shaykh ʿAbd al-Rahman ʿIllaysh. His name as a Muslim, ʿAbd al-Hadi, means "servant of the Guide," a name he had already used when he met Muslims in Ceylon in 1899. ʿAbd al-Hadi spent seven years in Egypt, translating and writing about the work of Ibn ʿArabi.

His first attempt to support himself financially in Cairo was to work as an editor on the Italian periodical *Il Commercio Italiano: Rivista quindicinale degli interessi Italiani in Oriente* (Italian Trade: Fortnightly Magazine of Italian Interests in the East)[33] from April 1903. Aguéli wrote under the pen name "Volontario." In the first issue, he published a short article on "La Coscienza Commerciale nell'Islam" (Commercial Awareness in Islam) followed by a longer article "La Coscienza Politica e Commerciale nell'Islam" (Political and Commercial Awareness in Islam). With the ninth issue, however, on June 2, 1903, *Il Commercio Italiano* closed.

The following year, from May 1904, Aguéli edited and wrote under a new identity, ʿAbd al-Hadi El Maghrabi or Abdul Hadi Agueli or simply Abdul Hadi, in *Il Convito/ Al-Nadi*,[34] published in Italian and Arabic. The significance and meaning of the titles *Il Convito/Al-Nadi* is discussed in Chapter 8. Initially, he co-edited the periodical with the Italian activist and agent Enrico Insabato, but ʿAbd al-Hadi was soon left solely responsible for everything. By the time the periodical temporarily closed in December 1907, ʿAbd al-Hadi had published several studies of Sufism, in particular translations and articles about Ibn ʿArabi,[35] and a series entitled "El Akbariya."[36] He also announced the founding of an Akbariyya society,[37] discussed in Chapter 13.

Aguéli was deeply involved in the struggle for Arab cultures to retain their uniqueness in their encounter with the modern European ideas that were quickly gaining entry with colonialism. An idealist and a bridge-builder with deep knowledge of both European and Arab cultures, he saw the great dangers in fanaticism, nationalism, and economic inequality. In 1909 he had to leave Egypt. With no further opportunity to support himself, he returned to Europe in October. Aguéli broke with Huot and, not wishing to return to Paris, spent the winter in Geneva. In March 1910 he returned to Paris, where a reconciliation with Huot took place.

1910–13: Sufism and Art; Aguéli's Essays in *La Gnose*

Back in Paris once again, Aguéli published reviews in *L'Encyclopédie contemporaine illustrée* and in a new periodical, *La Gnose*, from 1910 to 1913, under the name Abdul-Hâdi. His most intricate and complex articles, intertwining his experience of Sufism and art, were published in *La Gnose*, whose editor-in-chief was René Guénon, discussed in Chapter 13. Abdul-Hâdi was mentioned in the periodical for the first time in December 1910.[38] His translation from the Arabic of "Epitre intitulée *Le Cadeau* sur la manifestation du Prophète" (An Epistle Called "The Gift" on the Manifestation of the Prophet)[39] was published in 1910, followed by the essays "Pages dédiées à Mercure" (Pages Dedicated to Mercure), which included the seminal essay "L'Art pur" (Pure Art)[40] and "Pages dédiées au Soleil" (Pages Dedicated to the Sun),[41] "El-Malâmatiyah,"[42] "L'Universalité en l'Islam" (Universality in Islam),[43] "L'Islam et les religions anthropomorphiques" (Islam and Anthropomorphic Religions),[44] "L'Identité suprème dans L'ésotérisme musulman" (The Supreme Identity in Islamic Esotericism),[45] and "Les catégories de l'initiation" (Categories of Initiation).[46] Two of these articles are translated later in this book: "L'Art pur" as Chapter 18 and "L'Universalité en l'Islam" as Chapter 19.

An inspiration for Aguéli was Ibn ʿArabi's idea of recurrent creation, Henry Corbin's *création récurrente*, one of his key terms. Corbin describes Ibn ʿArabi's idea of creation as a process by which being is manifested at every instant in the innumerable forms of being; when God hides in one of these forms of being, He manifests Himself in another.[47] The precondition for perceiving the hidden unity of existence is a subtle, non-dualistic approach, an ability to experience simultaneous opposites: that God at one and the same time is the Hidden and the Revealed, the defined and the unlimited, both He and non-He. In a subtle dialog, God manifests Himself in *dhikr* (Sufi prayer ritual). In Aguéli's creative process, with his focus on the unity of opposites, and in his references to a place in the heart exclusively dedicated to the encounter with God, a parallel to the preconditions for the development of artistic creation in general may be seen. Aguéli in his essays in *La Gnose* attached great importance to distinguishing what he called cerebral (*cérébral*) from sentimental art:

> Every act of visual art consists in imposing one's passionate or enamored will upon three-dimensional Euclidean space by means of well-considered emphasis, in other words through drawing, through form-giving, in the widest sense of the word. Now, form indicates light, and light indicates colors, whether expressed or implicit. It is thus conceivable that, given a certain elevation of the spirit, the antithesis of line vs. color may vanish into luminous perfection. The identity of line and color is the criterion of accuracy of the *solar* or *mental perspective*.[48]

The representatives of pure art, he argued, were to be found mainly in the tradition originating from Jean Baptiste-Siméon Chardin (1699–1799) and Cézanne—the cubists.

In "L'Art pur," Aguéli expressed his new art theory:

> Cerebral art deserves to be called pure art, because the process of its perception is direct (*direct esthesis*), through its ability to impress without the intervention of any alien self or external object, solely by an inner apprehension, an internal sensing of the beating pulse of life itself, in other words by its rhythm … This is why the "dhikr" of the dervishes [Sufis] is an essential assimilation of certain initiate rhythms … whoever really wants to learn about it, need only study the world of

Muhyiddin ibn ʿArabi. If lacking the language skills, one may simply study Arab art. You need only consider why ancient monuments of purely Arab architecture, even the most modest, always appear to be larger than life. They seem to grow and expand as you gaze at them, a kind of spreading of wings or a fan being opened. However, in the absence of Arabic scholarship, one may just as well study the transformation that space always undergoes at the approach of death. One need only treat with artistic attention a moment of real and conscious mortal danger.[49]

His spiritual experience of the union of time and space was also fundamental to Aguéli in terms of art:

> We can sum it up neatly and succinctly by saying that rhythm is a sequence that unifies linear and dynamic contrasts … The Purists … pay more careful attention to the contrasts of dull and dark colors, far more important contrasts than those of greens and reds for instance, because they sometimes resemble a conflict between the active and the inert, or even between life and death.[50]

1910–13: Reviews in *L'Encyclopédie contemporaine illustrée*

In his reviews in *L'Encyclopédie contemporaine illustrée* between 1910 and 1913, Aguéli used his new identity, Abdul-Hâdi. In April 1910 he hailed Cézanne in his review of the Salon des indépendants, the first art exhibition he had seen in almost eight years. Cézanne, with his truthfulness and his discipline, appeared to Aguéli to be the unsurpassed master.

> What is the significance of Cézanne's influence? The person who copies Bonnat [Léon Bonnat (1833–1922), a classical realist painter, popular in Paris in his time] is only a worse Bonnat. However, one cannot copy Cézanne but only follow his path. And then one does not end up with Cézanne, but with oneself. Doing as Cézanne involves two things: 1) To tell the truth and nothing but the truth. 2) To impose a discipline that makes every lie impossible. This discipline is the "Simplisme," that is, the desire to express the subtlest emotions, the most intimate emotions, with the most unprocessed, resistant, and compact matter.[51]

Aguéli's reviews in *L'Encyclopédie contemporaine illustrée*, covering thousands of exhibited works, gave these artists a brief characterization and did not forget several talented women artists. Aguéli's stay in these years 1910–13 was at the height of the breakthrough of modernism in Paris. Among his many exhibition reviews were Le Salon de la Société nationale des beaux-arts (in May 1910), "Futurism in Italy" (in December 1910), and the first group exhibition of the cubists in the twenty-seventh Salon des indépendants (in April 1911). Among the 6,745 works in the fifty-nine halls were works by the cubists Albert Gleizes (1881–1953), Marc Chagall (1887–1985), Jean Metzinger (1883–1956), Fernand Léger (1881–1955), Robert Delaunay (1885–1941), and Henri Le Fauconnier (1881–1946).

1911–13: Back to Painting in Stockholm; Exploring Cubism in Paris

In 1911, Aguéli returned to painting after the long break. In the fall of that year, his friend the artist Carl Wilhelmson (1866–1928) offered him the possibility of studying without a tuition fee at his school in Stockholm. Not unexpectedly, Aguéli had some difficulty working in these conditions. The Artists' Association showed Aguéli's Gotland paintings from the 1890s in a Swedish collective exhibition in the summer of 1912, but he had left Sweden before the opening. This was the only exhibition of Aguéli's paintings during his lifetime.

In November 1912 Aguéli returned to Paris, and in his review of the important exhibition by the cubist group "La section d'or" at Galerie la Boëtie he formulated an original and personal analysis of cubism. Few Swedish artists knew about cubism. Aguéli's continuous contribution as a messenger of the new art movements to artist friends in Sweden was therefore of great value. According to Aguéli, the cubists had understood that the primary motif in a painting was space itself:

And because the "portrait of a space"—if I may say so—can only be carried out by precise proportions between distance, lines, and light, it follows that cubism is above all the stubborn architecture that works with the bright and obscure elements of the void. We see, therefore, that the unusual idea about cubism is to be found only in its boldness, it is nothing more than the strictest method known— at least today—to study the accuracy of the color hues and the precision of the drawing.[52]

In Aguéli's eyes, the widened perspective and the simultaneity of the cubist paintings also had an esoteric dimension: the whirling-dervish experience of a sky that opens up.[53] Aguéli is here unique in his path to understanding cubism, via Sufism. "Cubism, viewed as a teaching, is in fact the way that infallibly leads to the simple truth, that is, with maximum accuracy obtained with minimal means. It is the strictly personal vision expressed as briefly as possible."[54]

His last articles in *L'Encyclopédie contemporaine illustrée* date from 1913: "Sur les principes du monument et sur la sculpture" (Concerning the Principles of Monuments and Sculpture), and a review of the Salon des indépendants, testifying to his fatigue at the heat of sensational "news" in the art market: "The Salon des indépendants is not always what the name suggests. However, it is not their fault, but that of the wind; it depends on from where the wind is blowing at the moment. It is difficult to be 'indépendant,' and few people are so in reality."[55]

Aguéli joined the cubist circles in the spring of 1913, and won appreciation from the poet and critic Guillaume Apollinaire (1880–1918),[56] who invited Aguéli to become a contributor in an art book series. But just when it seemed as if he would "be successful" in Paris, Aguéli rejected Apollinaire's offer and made plans to leave the city—tired of the coteries, the bounders, of some artists and intellectuals. "Freedom, it cannot be obtained, or given, it must be taken with sacrifice. Freedom for free is of no value,"[57] he wrote as he moved out into the countryside.

1913–16: Aguéli's Last Painting Period

Aguéli's paintings from the late period are still based on Aurier's ideas, with the exception of his views on art as decorative. Aguéli had developed his own version of symbolism. Sufism, as he understood it, meant that man is closest to God when he is most himself:

> The artist is one for whom God seemingly has created a special Sun. It is by bringing into evidence the light of this Sun … that the artist reaches the heights of wisdom and character. I see nothing wrong in it if he likes to imagine that his *personal Sun* is really the only one existing in the Universe. It is more a matter of his inner awareness; perhaps his quirky preoccupation with this harmless obsession forms a part of his occupational hygiene[58]

The secret of Aguéli's esoteric symbolism is to be found in its rendering of light. The "solar" or "mental perspective"—or the emotionally moved spectator's perspective—speaks directly to the soul. The Renaissance perspective, and drawing in the horizontal and vertical picture planes, anyone could learn. Artistically, in Aguéli's opinion, this was a platitude.[59]

In his paintings between 1912 and 1917, especially in the Egyptian landscape (see for example Figure 6.1, Egyptiskt kupolhus [Egyptian Domed House]), he senses Unity and Light in a new way:

> The landscape is changing so fast that it hardly seems to be anything but a pretext for a solar demonstration or, if you wish, a cosmomorphic theophany … Everything—from perspective to the distances and interrelationships of objects—depends solely on the radiant star, which, as the absolute master of the horizons, sculpts the mountains as it pleases and arranges the masses of infinite space according to its swift architectural will.[60]

Aguéli's paintings from this time represent pure love for light, making all its dimensions visible in both an outer and an inner sense. Before Aguéli's eyes, the gap between the symbol and the reality to which it alludes ceases to exist. The character of the Egyptian landscape—the extraordinary quality of illusion, the impressive simplicity of the desert and its timelessness—created within him a feeling of deep peace, a sense of eternity. One can imagine Aguéli owning both an external observation of nature and an inner vision with what the Sufi calls the "eye of the heart" ('ayn al-qalb), the esotericist's most important organ of spiritual knowledge. It is with the eye of the heart that Unity makes itself known, looks back, as in Aguéli's experiences of the "ever-present eye of the horizon."

In the summer of 1913, Aguéli traveled to Touraine, near Tours. There he painted and experienced the stillness of the river landscape by the banks of the Loire, Seine, Oise, and Indre, where the reflection of the sky in the water expanded space. He also visited the house of the author, priest, and physician François Rabelais (1494–1553).

December 1913–January 1916: Last Trip to Egypt

When Aguéli had an opportunity to return to Egypt, he did not hesitate. In December 1913 he arrived, but in a troubled Egypt, marked by the impending world war and also by British colonial policy. He was determined to concentrate on his painting, to prepare for a possible exhibition in Paris. The employer for whom he had hoped to work dumped him. For the first time, Aguéli was also attacked and robbed while out in the countryside to paint. In some understandings, Islam does not allow realistic depictions of ensouled beings, and some Muslims who questioned Aguéli's activity persecuted him. In an undated manuscript written in French, in the Aguéli archive, "On the character and value of painting,"[61] Aguéli tries to explain to some of his Muslim co-believers that a high degree of abstraction in art can sanction figurative painting. By showing the high principles behind the Creator's works, the artist maintains his veneration for God's superior role as Creator.

Desperate letters, with pleas for money, were written when moving to different places and during rare moments of concentrated painting. Paradoxically, Aguéli now had one of his most productive periods. He wrote to Bergh in January 1915: "I work a lot outside of all theories … It is odd to see how one recreates one's artist's life every time one studies a new sky … I spontaneously and instinctively recall my first ideas from Gotland. The starting points in the paintings are the skies, for everything depends on them."[62]

In the heightened atmosphere that followed the outbreak of the First World War, the Egyptian authorities suspected Aguéli of being pro-Turkish, while the British suspected him of agitating among the Arabs. The Swedish consul offered to lend him money for the journey home, but Aguéli was concerned about not being able to take his eighty-one paintings and drawings and his other belongings with him. His return to Sweden was delayed. In January 1916, he was deported to Spain. He traveled in February to Barcelona, with a letter of recommendation from the consulate which enabled him to bring his artwork with him. In Barcelona, Aguéli started on translations from the Catalan of work by the Christian mystic Ramon Llull (*c.* 1232– *c.* 1316). Aguéli's painting sessions in the Catalan mountains were some of his best moments. He relied on his ruling method for painting and spiritual practice: that one is never accurate enough, simple enough, profound enough. And, he added, "never close enough to nature."[63]

Prince Eugen of Sweden (1865–1947), the brother of King Gustaf V (1858–1950) and himself a considerable artist and an admirer of Aguéli's art, sent money for the journey home, but Aguéli did not take the boat for fear that his paintings and documents might be seized by the British on the way. In January 1917, the Swedish consul in Barcelona appealed to the Ministry of Foreign Affairs in Sweden for Aguéli to be allowed to take the first boat to Sweden at the consulate's expense. In July, unrest increased; foreigners were particularly vulnerable. Aguéli wanted to leave Barcelona and move to some other place where he would find peace and possibility for work. He was not allowed to rent a room because he was a foreigner. His last letters to his mother, of June 28 and September 11, 1917, show that he had recently been harassed almost every day by people he did not know. He was at this time not involved in politics. On October 1, he was run over by a train at the village of L'Hospitalet de Llobregat outside Barcelona. He was fatally injured.

Aguéli's legacy—from Spain and from Huot's home in Paris—was returned to Sweden at Prince Eugen's expense. A memorial exhibition took place at the gallery AB Konstverk in Stockholm on January 26, 1920.[64] The critics gave him recognition as a pioneer in Swedish art of a more modern ideal. Despite the fact that Aguéli was unknown to much of the Swedish audience, the exhibition was a success. Anna Agelii received the proceeds of the sales.

There is a hadith that summarizes Aguéli's way of being in this world: "Be in this world as a stranger or a passer-by."[65]

Exploring the Territories of the Avant-garde: Ivan Aguéli and the Institutions of His Time

Annika Öhrner

The canonical idea of a late-nineteenth century modernist artist traveling throughout Europe is one of autonomy, individuality, and innovation.[1] This is mirrored in modernism's historiography since the canon creates a reciprocal and symbiotic relationship between cultural significance and scholarship.[2] Ivan Aguéli's established place in cultural history has followed this pattern: it is that of a lonely explorer of art and spirituality, a free thinking intellectual positioned outside institutions.[3] After his untimely death in 1917, Ivan Aguéli bequeathed to the world not only a fine collection of small paintings but also a wealth of mostly unpublished texts, in several languages, on art and on spiritual matters. This has inspired scholars to investigate the link between these two corpora, not least how his texts could help us understand his painting.[4] However, I will here suggest another approach to the topic: instead of making connections between his paintings and his theories, this chapter will focus on the strategic aspects of Aguéli's choices and paths.[5] They were, as I will argue, connected to specific parts of the historical avant-garde, a concept that will be examined further. I will position Aguéli's work in the space of European modernism, with an emphasis on cultural transfer and mobility. While doing this, I will highlight how he *made himself public*, that is, how and to which extent he appeared in publications, exhibitions, and public arenas of different kinds. Paying close attention to the public positions he took through his work and actions, as opposed to his authorial intentions, reveals an image of an artist deeply embedded in particular networks and institutions of his time.

Paris's dominant position in European cultural life is often accepted as natural, so that its impact for cultural production at times becomes invisible. This has been the case in connection with Aguéli, whose life and work have instead often been explained in terms of his more remote and unusual destinations—Egypt, Ceylon, and India. Aguéli first arrived in Paris as a 21-year-old in 1890, and before exploring his paths there as professional and social strategies, I will discuss the cultural situation that a move to Paris involved and the theoretical framework this suggests.

New art history has emerged in new geopolitical research fields that approach the concept of the dominance of Paris in alternative ways.[6] My work is linked to this historiographical project in that it underlines how one has to accept, as a material fact, that around the turn of the twentieth century numerous artists went to Paris from Europe and beyond. Instead of using the more frequent aesthetic sense of "avant-garde," David Cottington has proposed that the avant-garde be viewed as *formations*, thereby enabling a more detailed study of how thousands of young artists from all over Europe and beyond gravitated toward certain centers such as Paris, and how artists grouped together to protect themselves from the dominant tendencies in the art market as well as from the domination of the academies.[7] In the 1910s, the avant-garde formations comprised a large group that created what Cottington has called an alternative professionalism.[8] Thus, during precisely the period during which Aguéli was linked to Paris, certain structures and tendencies appeared in the space of art at points where they coincided with his presence—in periodicals, exhibitions, cafés, salons, and, not least, in the *académies libres* (free academies), that is, art schools that were as widely developed as the ones they opposed in the state academic system. These structures were echoed in other European cultural centers, including Stockholm.

Capitals are the nodes of cultural spaces, social spaces, and national institutions, and are also points of contact between nations.[9] In Paris, the number of institutions and the quantity of cultural production grew over time, thus reinforcing the city's cultural domination.[10] The main structure of this development was the struggle of an emerging avant-garde against the power of the traditional state-run art academy. Aguéli himself supported the view of this city's cultural domination in the modern world, underlining the importance of its unique equilibrium between tradition and nature.[11] Meanwhile, in Stockholm, new institutions and representations emerged simultaneously in ways in which Aguéli was to play a certain role, despite often being physically absent. In 1886, the Swedish Artists' Association (Konstnärsförbundet) was founded, demanding reformation of the Royal Academy of Fine Arts (Kungliga Akademien för de fria konsterna), its teaching, exhibition policies, and organization. Many in the generation behind this opposition movement had just returned to Sweden after several years of residence in France, and during the coming decades they would develop an alternative structure of exhibition platforms and art education, while ending up themselves, as mature men, in key positions on the cultural stage. It was to this "pole," the party of the "opponents," of the cultural field in Sweden that Aguéli was closely connected.[12] It is telling that the one exhibition in which Aguéli's paintings were shown during his lifetime (in his absence) was the Swedish Artists' Association's exhibition in 1912.[13]

The French historian Christophe Charle has established three types of cultural mobility between intellectual centers: transfer, circulation, and mobility.[14] This chapter will elaborate on Aguéli's mobility in terms of cultural transfer between artistic spaces. Aguéli devoted energy to cultural and artistic transfer between Paris and Stockholm; the tension and relations between the two positions marked his painting and his thinking, as well as his social networks. He was constantly traveling, oscillating between "centers" and "peripheries" within Sweden, in Europe, and beyond.

With exceptional perceptivity and eagerness, Aguéli explored different fields of knowledge as well as their related social networks. Later chapters in this book discuss, for example, Aguéli's network regarding the publication *Il Convito/Al-Nadi* during his seven-year-long second stay in Egypt (1902–9). In Paris he visited cafés and salons linked to a specific part of the modernist movement, namely, the avant-garde. He counted among his connections in the Parisian art scene painters such as Émile Bernard and Kees van Dongen (1877–1968) and the poet and art critic Guillaume Apollinaire, all prominent in the historiography of modern art, as well as lesser-known artists. In Stockholm, as I have emphasized, he was closely attached to a particular faction involved in the struggle between state-run and insurgent institutions, namely, the most prominent members of the Artists' Association, Richard Bergh and Karl Nordström. Aguéli mainly lived a bohemian lifestyle, appearing as typically avant-garde, living in poor areas, and dressed in unconventional clothes.[15] On his occasional visits to Sweden, he continued to act out his avant-garde identity in a way that appears to have gained attention there. For example, he cruised the streets of Stockholm during the winter of 1912 dressed in his "fur," which was in fact a large piece of white cloth in which he had cut a hole for his head. To keep warm, he kept one newspaper on his back, one on his front, under the cloth, with a cord around his waist to keep it all in place. With self-representations like that and "with his eccentric appearance, a mixture of Socrates and Zola, he attracted attention everywhere," as one eyewitness suggested.[16]

However, Aguéli was active in the art world in several other ways. Between 1896 and 1913, he published many essays and reviews which focused on Parisian art in the French weekly periodical *L'Encyclopédie contemporaine illustrée*, discussed below. His other written contributions to the periodical took the form of travel letters. On the other hand, his *paintings* were never exhibited in France, and they were only exhibited in Sweden once during his lifetime. As Christina G. Wistman has shown, Aguéli became known to a wider Swedish audience as an artist only after his death in 1917, more specifically in 1922, when his first retrospective was staged by his colleagues and mentors in Sweden.[17] In Paris, he was well connected in intellectual and artistic circles, and was assigned to write reviews and invited to salons and social events. Very few people there were acquainted with his painting, and he rarely painted in Paris. In fact, his painterly efforts were only known to a few of his fellow artists, not least the circle of Swedish artists in France. Further, very little of Aguéli's religious and art-historical writing was known or published in Sweden. Just one essay was published, and that after his death, despite the fact that he repeatedly asked his friends in Stockholm to find ways to publish his articles.[18]

Aguéli's journeys to France and beyond have often been seen as those of a lone seeker, yet they were part of a broad trend. Aguéli's early mentors had a clear tendency to adopt Parisian values, even though they had returned to Scandinavia in the 1870s in order to explore the Swedish landscape. Artworks by a large number of Swedish and Norwegian artists were on display in the Parisian salons between 1889 and 1908. Vibeke Röstorp has found 380 such artists, and when counting even all those who—like Aguéli—had not exhibited there, we can establish that a large cohort of Scandinavian artists belonged to the extended avant-garde formation in Paris to which Aguéli was connected.[19] It serves us well, I argue, to understand Aguéli's presence in Paris in terms of the alternative professionalism of the avant-garde, the notion coined by Cottington. I will, therefore, look at the various professional institutions, academic, but primarily avant-garde and anti-academic.

Aguéli and Paris

Aguéli moved in several avant-garde circles in Paris, some of which are now part of art history. Others had less cultural capital at the time, not enough to enter later discourses. It is well known that Paris was home to formations of artists and authors of the same nationality. The importance of the Swedish groups in Paris for the network that Aguéli built up should not be underestimated. His mentors, Bergh and Nordström, served to create contacts and relations of cultural and strategic importance for a new young artist in town in the form of recommendation letters and in other ways. The peers of his generation seem to have been ready to give him a helping hand in practical matters and in times of trouble.

Aguéli arrived in Paris on April 15, 1890. After a short bout of sickness, according to his letters home, he oriented himself within the intense life of Parisian art, visiting the Académie Julian and enjoying art exhibitions: "I have to see the exhibitions, the painting exhibitions, that they call the 'salons.' This is necessary, absolutely necessary for my development. I cannot do it for less than one franc (75 öre) a day. And all of May is Salon Month," he wrote, with feverish intensity, in a letter begging his mother for money.[20] He soon moved to *les banlieues* (the suburbs) to live with young compatriots and then moved further out and lived among the Swedish artists in Saint-Ouen and the coastal village of Étaples for a few months.[21] At that time, his ways were being guided by Carl Trägårdh (1861–99), a moderate impressionist who had promised Nordström that he would take care of Aguéli. Trägårdh and Nordström, along with August Strindberg and Emma Chadwick (1855–1932), had spent the summer of 1886 together at Grez-sur-Loing, a prominent international artists' colony.[22] In Étaples, Aguéli frequented Trägårdh and other Swedish artists.

That Aguéli was self-taught as an intellectual has been explored by scholars and is well documented, for example, in the registers of the National Library of Sweden (Kungliga biblioteket), which has records of the books he borrowed, as well as in the letters he sent from the Mazas Prison to Werner von Hausen requesting specific titles.[23] He would also repeat in letters that he preferred to paint in solitude. This has helped reinforce the false image of an autodidactic seeker, while the fact is that he was on the contrary very eager to expand his knowledge and artistic skills both in schools and in the *académies libres*. During his various sojourns in Paris, Aguéli also enrolled at religious, linguistic, and artistic institutions. In the following section, this inclination to visit these will be studied further.

Exploring the Avant-garde: The Salons

Aguéli saw the significance of some of the most important institutions for artistic exchange within emerging modernism, including the newly established salons designed to ensure the circulation of artworks independently from the state-financed Académie des beaux-arts (Academy of Fine Arts). Created in 1884 by artists who saw themselves on the margin of society, Le Salon des indépendants (Salon of the Independents) had as its founding concept that there would be no jury and no prizes. Together with smaller art galleries, it was the dominant site for the exchange of modern art. However, 1890 saw the creation of a new association, the Société national des beaux arts (National Society of Fine Arts), with the ambition of being international and jury-based. It was a salon for the modernist elite, situated in the Champ-de-Mars.[24] In 1891, the painter Puvis de Chavanne (1824–98) became its president, and the artists in charge of the salon represented an accepted, moderate impressionism and symbolism. The salon was also the site for the presentation of a wide range of portraitists representing different artistic directions. All of a sudden, a large group of international artists, including Germans from Munich and Berlin, and Scandinavians such as the Swede Anders Zorn (1860–1920) and the Danes Peder Severin Krøyer (1851–1909) and Frits Thaulow (1847–1906), came together in the Parisian art scene through these two salons, which became international. It is telling that Aguéli chose to reassure his mother by writing home about the apparent success of his compatriot Trägårdh, who exhibited some paintings at the new avant-garde salon in 1890. Aguéli must have mentioned this to calm her worries about his financial circumstances.[25] However he himself never exhibited his own painting there. His great interest in these salons is reflected in his art criticism.

Periodicals

In a letter to Hausen, Aguéli wrote: "I have started to write in a small French periodical, different articles on art, literature, theater. I am not allowed to do as I please, but I will send you some examples, chosen among the least changed by editing."[26] The 27-year-old Aguéli wrote his first art criticism in 1896 in the weekly periodical *L'Encyclopédie contemporaine illustrée: Revue hebdomadaire universelle des sciences, des arts et de l'industrie* (The Contemporary Illustrated Encyclopedia: A Universal Weekly Journal of the Sciences, Arts, and Industry). The title echoes the views on the avant-garde in society of Henri de Saint-Simon (1760–1825). Long before the term "avant-garde" was used at the end of the nineteenth century to distinguish one section of art from another, Saint-Simon was already claiming in the 1820s that the avant-garde comprised precisely of the artist, the scientist, and the industrialist, who together would drive cultural, social, and economic progress.[27] The periodical targeted, it seems, an educated middle class with entrepreneurial ambitions, and it published articles with an international outlook not only on the arts but also on scientific, industrial, and business matters. *L'Encyclopédie contemporaine illustrée* had a large section filled with reviews of literature, theater, and art. Thus, while not one of the more famous periodicals of modern art in the 1890s—*La Revue indépendante, La Plume, La Revue Blanche, Le Mercure de France* seem to have been at the center of attention in artistic milieus at that time—it still seems to have followed the cultural life in Paris with considerable knowledge and was read in cultural circles.[28]

The periodical was founded by the left-wing journalist Anatole-Théodore-Marie Huot (1843–*c*.1913), who ran it along with his wife, Marie Huot.[29] Marie Huot, a mesmerizing personality and a champion of animal welfare, ran her own salon and was to have an unrivaled impact on Aguéli's personal life as his close friend and partner over almost twenty years. Her invitation to him to publish in *L'Encyclopédie contemporaine illustrée* gave him the opportunity to develop his critical eye and establish a professional position in Paris. He published some literary criticisms and a long series of letters from India and Ceylon in *L'Encyclopédie contemporaine illustrée*. However, the larger part of his contributions in the periodical focused on art criticism of exhibitions in the salons, primarily between 1896 and 1900 and then again between 1910 and 1913. Aguéli signed these written pieces using various names: G. Ivan, Ivan, Abdul-Hadi, and Habdul-Hadi. He would also, from 1910 and solely under the name Abdul-Hadi, develop his theories on religion and art in articles published in René Guénon's *La Gnose*. Aguéli's written contributions to *L'Encyclopédie contemporaine illustrée*, however, are instructive for understanding his particular place in the avant-garde in Paris.

The two salons Aguéli followed in his function as art critic, Les indépendants and the younger Salon de la Société national des beaux arts (sometimes referred to in the periodical as Le Salon du Champ-des-Mars or the Salon des Champs-Elysées), were created by different factions, one liberal, the other ready to form a new, more offensive avant-garde art elite. Aguéli's critical eyes were, it seems, carefully trained on the individual artworks that he generally describes very clearly and neutrally, even though his own aesthetic judgments are sometimes visible. Aguéli rarely penned general conclusions or aesthetic theories in these texts, but the modernist credo is emphasized, for example in his 1897 review of the Salon des indépendants that represented his opinions just as much as his ideals: "Les indépendants always offer us the new and unexpected. It is a whole field of observation for those who think. It is among the isolated, the libertarians, the anxious, and those who are groping that one can see the art of tomorrow. It is the transportation of art of the natured against the decorative and the stylish."[30]

Aguéli's art reviews in *L'Encyclopédie contemporaine illustrée* are walks through the exhibition rooms, where he briefly remarks on the artists whom he feels deserve the audience's attention. He seems to make an honest attempt at actually viewing everything rather than promoting a specific thesis or following a famous artist. As Viveca Wessel has noted, he gave female and male painters equal attention.[31] His reviews also carefully covered both well-known and lesser-known artists, as well as artists from among his compatriots. Importantly, the opportunity to review art in *L'Encyclopédie contemporaine illustrée*, as we shall see, gave Aguéli a platform to expand his network within the Parisian avant-garde, which at that exact moment was going through a process of professionalization. But he also visited another important scene of the Parisian art life.

Les académies libres

In a letter to Hausen in 1892, Aguéli stated:

> I argue less with you as you feel you need the art schools. It would be ridiculous of me to do that. One knows one's own needs. But I repeat once again that Cairo is also very useful, if not necessary, for a painter's development. Because here everything is synthetic, and that is what we need, children of the 19th century … Paris is a perfect place to study analytics, but you ought to know that the pessimism that I suffer, as do you … is a local disease, typical of Paris.[32]

In contrast to this advice, Aguéli had himself had considerable experience of the *académies libres*. They were generally small institutions, more like art studios, where artists could work for shorter or longer periods, paying weekly or sometimes even daily. Often students could later claim that the importance of this training was meeting with young colleagues from all corners of Europe to discuss art and culture, rather than actual instructions from teachers. Aguéli briefly enrolled at schools such as the Académie Julian (April–May 1890), an academy that admitted female students. He also went to the Atelier Delécluse at rue Notre Dame des Champs, where Louis Delauce and Georges Callot (1857–1903), apparently two academic artists, taught. The Académie Humbert (September 1912) and the Académie Vitti (Autumn 1912) were other schools he attended. During Aguéli's prosecution after shooting a bullfighter in 1900, a letter written by his teachers and colleagues at the Académie Delécluse and its master August Joseph Delécluse was published in the press. This letter was signed by C. Martel, P. Viault, Guy H. Mitchell, A. Yule, E. Kiefer, Georges Willis, Back, E. Smith, F. Coleman, Georges Morand, and Edmond Socard, all of whom, it seems, were affiliated with the male department of the academy, the focus of which was otherwise on women artists.[33] Although a large number of Swedish and other Scandinavian artists were residing at Atelier Matisse in 1910–11, it seems that Aguéli chose other inspirations. However, when in Stockholm and in Gothenburg, he did visit the Swedish version of these academies, the Artists' Association's School (Konstnärsförbundets skola).

The Great Modern

Aguéli's encounters with some more canonical subjects of art history will serve as examples of his extended networks. Aguéli met Bernard during his first stay in Paris in 1890, and was introduced by him to the work of Gauguin and Van Gogh. Bernard also famously introduced the young Swede to Owen Jones's *The Grammar of Ornament* and to the periodical *Le Lotus Bleu*. This was before Aguéli returned to Sweden in 1892 and enrolled at the Artists' Association's School, where he disseminated some of these new ideas. He later journeyed to Gotland to paint landscapes.[34] He also frequented all kinds of informal gatherings and sought contacts with persons whom he thought were of interest. He was, for example, a frequent guest at the salons in the studio of Ida Molard (1853–1927) and William Molard (1862–1936) at rue Vercingétorix, where he occasionally slept and also met Gauguin, whose studio was on the floor above.[35]

As Axel Gauffin, Aguéli's early biographer, informs us, the artist received recommendations to present his work to Père Tanguy, the art dealer who counted among his patrons Van Gogh and Cézanne, whose paintings he exhibited alongside Japanese prints in his store.[36] Aguéli, whose French was still not that good, turned up at Tanguy's art supply store holding a collection of small, rolled-up paintings. This is, to my knowledge, the only confirmed attempt by Aguéli to approach a dealer to seek an opinion on his work, presumably in order to get it exhibited. The legendary Tanguy was not impressed, however, and advised him to look for Bernard and gave him his address. The source of what happened next is Bernard himself, who many years later wrote to Gauffin about the encounter. Bernard studied Aguéli's paintings, concluding to himself that he undoubtedly showed great talent but still

lacked enough confidence in himself. He offered Aguéli the opportunity to work
with him in his studio, whereupon Aguéli returned the next day, having walked
the long distance from Paris to Asnières. "I put Aguéli in my school. I had the best
intentions to bring order to his ideas about painting. I let him make simple things,
drawn with one stroke and colored in summarized gradations."[37] The two especially
discussed the art of Van Gogh and Cézanne. Aguéli was later given Bernard's two
essays on them, which the latter had published in the periodical *Les Hommes
d'Aujourd'hui.*[38]

Gauffin suggests, however, that something else could have affected Aguéli even
more. It was at Bernard's studio that Aguéli learned of Gauguin's plans to go to
Madagascar or Tahiti, after Bernard had discussed Gauguin's correspondence with
him. Aguéli later mentioned these travels in a footnote in his text "L'art pur" (Pure
Art) of 1917: "Gauguin went to Tahiti primarily to re-immerse himself in the primitive
world of simple feelings. In a way, this return to the origins was a bath of innocence.
Parisian critics could not comprehend that his journey was more of a displacement in
time than in space."[39] It is noteworthy that it was precisely in Paris, at Bernard's studio,
that Aguéli encountered the idea of an exotic, remote place where the purity of art can
be found, and this may have inspired his later travels.

Félix Fénéon was another personality with whom Aguéli connected. Fénéon was
a French anarchist, freelance journalist, and intellectual, with immense importance
for the establishment of the painter George Seurat (1859–91) and his circles, and
the theorist behind the concept of neo-impressionism. His style was brilliant, as was
his networking and role within avant-garde circles. Fénéon was the director of the
Bernheim-Jeune Gallery, thus among other things presenting the Italian futurists
outside Italy for the first time. In a letter to Bergh on October 10, 1893, Aguéli refers
to the French writer with much appreciation, and draws his portrait. He describes his
personality in a way that seems a role-model for Aguéli himself.

> I cannot resist the temptation to talk about a new-French type in formation, a type
> that is decent, simple, sober, completely free from snobbery and pose. Emancipated
> as a social creature, international to the limit of being antipatriotic ... He [Félix]
> is one of the best of this type I have seen. Superb and great critical intelligence. All
> ask for his advice, and it is so nice to see the unquestionable esteem everybody
> has for him ... I stand very high in his esteem, something which encourages me
> greatly.[40]

A year later both of them were imprisoned during the "procès des trente" (the trial
of the thirty), both serving time in the Mazas Prison. This trial was followed by the
Parisian bohemia, including the poet Mallarmé (Étienne Mallarmé, 1842–98), which
to a large extent supported Fénéon and the others.[41] The trial meant Aguéli's position
in Paris, even though he was in jail, became even more established.

Yet another example of when Aguéli's path intersected with those at the heart of
Parisian art circles coincided with the famous 1911 Salon des indépendants, which
inspired an intense and famous debate on cubism. Aguéli himself later contributed to
it, in an article in *La Gnose*, where he develops his theory on cerebral and sentimental

art, and claims that the French cubist Henri Le Fauconnier is among the young masters who will make a mark on the future of art.[42] In Aguéli's archive, an undated letter from Le Fauconnier invited Aguéli, together with Huot, to a soirée at the house of the painter and collector Conrad Kickert (1882–1965), who had asked Le Fauconnier to invite Aguéli on his behalf, together with some friends, to celebrate his purchase and hanging of Le Fauconnier's *Le Chasseur* (The Huntsman, 1911–12, now in the Museum of Modern Art in New York): "I have naturally been thinking of you, what has been written recently are such interesting reflections on modern painting."[43] Le Fauconnier had until then been quite a marginal figure in modern painting; his work had gained little prominence in the presentations of the museum collections where they were held. It was precisely at this moment in time that he was starting to be considered one of the Parisian art scene's leading cubist artists, and the originator of the cubist movement no less, and interestingly it is now that Aguéli connects to him.[44] This position was only later accredited to Picasso and Georges Braque (1882.1963), who at that time were contractually bound with their gallerists, Daniel-Henry Kahnweiler (1884–1979) and Wilhelm Uhde (1874–1947), not to exhibit in the salons but only to present their work upon request in their small art stores. They were simply less well known to the wider audience. Aguéli, whose view corresponded with these currents of thought, called Le Fauconnier in a 1913 article "one of the leading cubists and a master at that, maybe the most talented within the school when it comes to the monumental."[45] It was within the mainstream of cubist debate that he was positioning himself.

Aguéli commented on Le Fauconnier's work in several articles, for example, in "L'Art pur," where he established his position between tradition and modernity: "Le Fauconnier possesses all the magnificent qualities of the old primitives of France, in addition to his modernity."[46] This duality can also be found in the painting *Le Chasseur*, which was first exhibited at Les independents in 1912, and juxtaposes fragments of motifs of technical innovation and the individual. As Cottington has suggested, the ideas expressed in this painting "indicate a deepening of the painter's attachment to traditionalism, a pessimism in the face of modernization that ran counter to the simultaneous enthusiasm for urban dynamism … a sharpening, in sum, of the conflict between his painterly avant-gardism and the ideological purpose it served."[47] In another card, Le Fauconnier refers to Aguéli's articles in *L'Encyclopédie contemporaine illustrée*, indicating that he was building up his reputation among people who cared for the success of the avant-garde in the free salons and *academies libres*. We find him, as shown, in the field of the emerging modernist scene, creating an avant-garde position within a professionalized, alternative art scene.

Les grandes écoles

Finally, we must consider Aguéli's relation to institutions somewhat outside the artistic field, slightly off topic than from our main focus. In Cairo, Aguéli explored religious matters in great depth, as discussed in other chapters in this book. However, Aguéli had gone through thorough preparations for this. He visited various Western associations and institutions connected to his spiritual and religious search. In 1891, aged twenty-two, he became a member of the Theosophical Society. Around 1898, he began studying Buddhism and Islam. Yet his spiritual search was not limited to moving in lesser-known circles and being a member of unofficial societies. In the autumn of 1895, he began, according to Gauffin, three years of study at the École spéciale des langues orientales vivantes (special school for living Oriental languages), an institution that educated interpreters and administrators working in business and commerce. Aguéli studied Arabic and Hindustani there. The other school he attended was the École pratique des hautes études (special school for higher studies), founded in 1868 and still in operation today, as is the École spéciale des langues orientales. The students received a free education in the sciences and humanities, and those who passed an exam after a year were awarded the title "élève titulaire," which Aguéli acquired in 1896.[48] He then studied at two of the school's five sections: the historical and philological section, where he learned Sanskrit and Arabic, and at the religious sciences section, where he studied Arab religions, the Qur'an, and its exegesis. Between 1895 and 1900, he studied Ethiopian, Sanskrit, and ancient Egyptian, all these topics taught of course by highly skilled masters. The two schools were prestigious state-run institutions of higher education (*grandes écoles*), and this period of study gave Aguéli not only linguistic skills and cultural knowledge that helped his further travels. For his second trip to Egypt, he was extremely well equipped with a network, knowledge, and skills much more so than most European artists of his generation. He gained all this *in Paris*, not only in small intellectual gatherings, but at two of the most important institutions in their respective fields in Europe.

Transfer, Circulation, and Mobility

Returning to Charle's concept of cultural exchanges between intellectual centers, defined as transfer, circulation, and mobility, we see how Aguéli can be associated with these in various ways. Aguéli's chosen route was framed within the European avant-garde and its new, alternative, professional institutions. His important explorations of non-Western culture and religions were not made as such, they were made "through Paris." His painting, on the other hand, was not presented in these contexts in Scandinavia, Paris, or Cairo. Despite his eager suggestions to his mentors to help him publish his art criticism in Sweden, he never succeeded in this.[49] However, a more significant type of circulation of culture was when his mentors in their later careers created important new art at exhibition sites such as Liljevalchs Art Gallery, in Stockholm. They also asked Aguéli for advice about which living French artists to exhibit. Bergh was, during the last years of Aguéli's life, greatly occupied with recontextualizing the state collections at the Swedish National Museum, where he was the director, into a modern museum of European standards, and it happened that he took Aguéli's advice during the process.[50] Importantly, he also made very sure that Aguéli could be a part of this new, modern museum. In 1915 he persuaded Per Hallström (1866–1960), a friend of Aguéli from his youth, to donate his *Stockholm motif* (1913), to the collection, and he also deposited three of his own Aguéli paintings in the museum in the same year. Two of them were those exhibited in 1912 in Stockholm.[51] As we have seen, Aguéli's mentors never removed their protective hand from him, neither in Paris nor even after his death. They nurtured his artistic legacy, made it public, and reframed it within Swedish art history, where they possess a solid position even today.

How did Aguéli's broad intellect and spiritual search affect his painterly work? This is not the topic of this chapter, and it remains to be seen whether this question can ever be sufficiently answered. I would argue, however, for the importance of recognizing the deep importance of "Paris" for Aguéli. He digested it second-hand from his mentors when he was young, and then explored it in person at its very core. When Gauffin published the second part of his biography of Ivan Aguéli in 1941, it contained a catalog of 255 known paintings, mostly small canvases, maybe due to the artist's mobile lifestyle and lack of funds. A complete list would today include some more. His oeuvre is dominated by landscapes, while portraits and models are recurrent motifs as well; they are today mostly represented as part of prominent Swedish museum collections such as Moderna Museet and Prins Eugens Waldemarsudde, and in a dedicated Aguéli Museum in his birthplace, Sala. He had first become acquainted with the landscape and light of the island of Gotland in the Baltic Sea when sent there by his father to attend school. He returned to Gotland in 1889, and it was while tutoring a young boy in botany that he made his first attempts at oil painting. With its clear light, white chalk cliffs, green nature, historical buildings, and the sea, Gotland attracted many artists.[52] Aguéli's attempts at oil painting caught the eye of one of these artists, Bergh, who, according to Gauffin, found them to be "excellent."[53] Nordström, also on Gotland that summer, concurred. He kept Aguéli's sketches and paintings from that summer in his private collection. Thus, Aguéli was early on imbedded in his older colleagues' ideas of an emotionally charged landscape, informed by French modernism painting. The year after, Aguéli told his parents of his decision to travel around Europe and develop his artistry. He informed them that he had arranged passports for Germany, Russia, France, and the Netherlands.[54] In reality, the passport signed for him by the governor of Gotland only has one destination registered: France.

4

Ivan Aguéli the Esotericist, in Reality and Fiction

Per Faxneld

This chapter consists of two interrelated parts. Firstly, I will contextualize Ivan Aguéli's interest in Theosophy in relation to the Swedish artistic milieu in which he participated even while in exile. In conjunction with this, I will also briefly highlight some parallels between Aguéli's esoteric speculations and those in circulation in European artistic networks linked to Sweden. Secondly, I will discuss Torbjörn Säfve's 1981 novel about Aguéli, *Ivan Aguéli: En roman om frihet* (Ivan Aguéli: A Novel about Freedom), and how esotericism is depicted in it. This depiction will be compared to some of the contextualization in the first part, and I will also attempt to correlate it with the position esotericism has historically occupied in Sweden. The chapter thus attempts to show that Aguéli's approach to esotericism was far from unique among artists, and it dissects his use of esotericism *pour épater les bourgeois* and as a tool for cultural critique. Hereby, we can problematize the notion of esotericism as a form of "rejected knowledge," and arrive at a better understanding of the social multivalency that such a status implies. This, I will demonstrate, also has implications for how to understand Säfve's fictionalized account of Aguéli's life.

Rejection and Transgression

To begin with, we need to consider one of several scholarly attempts to define Western esotericism. Antoine Faivre's 1992 definition probably remains the best known,[1] but it is rivaled by Wouter Hanegraaff's more recent definition, which has had a significant impact in the academy. Hanegraaff, drawing on the 1970s work of historian James Webb, suggests we define esotericism as "rejected knowledge"—those ideas and worldviews that have been marginalized mainly by Protestant and Enlightenment historians and gatekeepers of "truth." It is thus a wastebasket category, the leftovers of the reformation and secularization, if you will. Said leftovers, then, are those things that do not fit within mainstream Christianity, positivist philosophy, and materialist natural sciences.[2]

Hanegraaff's definition has been criticized by several scholars, for example for being too broadly inclusive.[3] I will offer something in the way of a critique here as well, but I think Hanegraaff's concept can also help shed light on why Aguéli was so attracted to esoteric ideas. I would like to pinpoint this by highlighting what (with inspiration from Bourdieu and the musicologist Keith Kahn-Harris) could be called esotericism's *transgressive cultural capital*.[4] If we consider the biographical data at hand regarding Aguéli, it appears likely that his exploration of Western esotericism, primarily Swedenborgism and Blavatskian Theosophy, and Sufism for that matter, may have been partly motivated by a desire to shock the bourgeoisie (a common desire among avant-garde artists, and a strategy explicitly employed by, for example, French nineteenth-century writers like Baudelaire, whom Aguéli appreciated), and to stand out. More generously phrased, we could say he used esotericism and Islam as a form of cultural critique. It would be misleading to reduce them to having only this function, of course, but it is clearly a significant factor in much of his approach to spirituality, especially esotericism. Here, then, we have the transgressive cultural capital of esotericism being invoked. The image becomes more complicated, however, if we consider Theosophy's position in Sweden at this time, which makes clear it cannot as a whole be labeled "rejected knowledge."

Theosophy and Swedish Artists

The impact of Theosophy on Swedish art is yet to be the subject of a full-scale mapping, but its influence was certainly considerable. Among the educated Swedish population in general, Theosophy was a hot topic of discussion at least since the establishment of a Swedish branch of the Theosophical Society in 1889, and well into the first decades of the twentieth century.[5] This was not unique, and we must remember that even the famous Orientalist Max Müller (1823–1900) himself had found it necessary to refute Theosophical doctrines at length, thus attesting to it being taken seriously even by those who disagreed strongly with its tenets and interpretations.[6] The situation in Sweden was similar, if we look at reports and debates in Swedish newspapers at the turn of the century. Many figures from the cultural elite sided with Theosophy, while several others could be somewhat dismissive of it but still embraced certain of its ideas. A case in point is August Strindberg, an author Aguéli took an interest in—but seemingly not due to Strindberg's occult speculations.[7]

The esoteric current causing major ripples in Sweden before Theosophy was Spiritualism. It is in relation to Spiritualist notions of mediumship that we can situate Swedish artists who produced art they claimed was to some degree channeled from spirits. Examples include such high-profile figures as author Viktor Rydberg (1828–95, who stated that he had received a poem from a deceased French songwriter), and Ernst Josephson (1851–1906, who both received poems from spirits and produced paintings that he signed with the names of dead artists).[8] Outside of the public view, there was of course also Hilma af Klint and her circle of friends who worked with mediumistic art.[9]

Spiritualism never reached the level of respectability attained by Theosophy, and it could be decidedly dangerous for one's career to have publicly associated with it. Even so, many of its leaders were establishment figures, like geology professor (and later chair of the Royal Swedish Academy of Sciences) Alfred Elis Törnebohm (1838–1911). It is further notable that one of the most prominent mediums was also an artist, the highly successful photographer and portrait painter Bertha Valerius (1824–95).[10] The latter was very active in the Spiritualist group Edelweissförbundet (Edelweiss association), where Hilma af Klint was also briefly a member in 1896. Her main long-term esoteric source of inspiration was, however, arguably Theosophy.[11]

In this, she was far from alone. While Hilma af Klint toiled in semi-obscurity, one of the most popular mainstream Swedish artists, Carl Larsson (1853–1919), was also an avid reader of Theosophical literature—and some of the famous decorative patterns his wife Karin (1859–1928) produced for their home in Sundborn may have stemmed from this source.[12] Tyra Kleen (1874–1951), a fairly famous artist in her own time, was strongly influenced by Theosophy (e.g., its idealization of androgyny), and also exhibited at the Theosophical Society in Stockholm.[13] Gustaf Fjaestad (1868–1948) and his wife Maja (1873–1961) constitute a further example of a well-known artist couple holding strong Theosophical interests, with Gustaf also being a very active lecturer within the Theosophical Society.[14] As previously mentioned, authors like Strindberg were also influenced by Theosophy, even though Strindberg remained somewhat ambivalent toward it. Another figure that, like Larsson, might today seem a slightly unexpected enthusiast of Theosophy was the composer Wilhelm Peterson-Berger (1867–1942), in whose home ("Sommarhagen," on Frösön, Jämtland) are many Theosophical publications. And these are just some examples. In short, many of the main creative figures in Sweden at the turn of the century were deeply marked by the teachings of Theosophical guru Helena Blavatsky and her cohorts. The interest was reciprocated, we should note, with Swedish Theosophical periodicals often containing essays about art, and the Theosophical Society in Stockholm hosting art exhibitions. The close ties to the art world no doubt generated cultural capital for Theosophy, while a different type of prestige came from its links to royalty.

The Royal Connection

In a letter to his mother, Aguéli noted that "King Oskar [*sic*] is supposedly a Theosophist."[15] This is significant because Aguéli's patron Prince Eugen was the youngest son of the very same King Oscar II of Sweden (1829–1907), and because the king himself is supposed to have put in a good word for Aguéli with the French authorities after he was arrested as a suspected anarchist terrorist.[16] King Oscar did indeed have a deep and open interest in Theosophy. His library was filled with Theosophical books, he granted private audiences to Theosophical leaders like Henry Olcott (1832–1907) and Annie Besant (1847–1933), and even fired a cannon salute from the royal castle to welcome them.[17] When the Theosophical leader Katherine Tingley (1847–1929) visited Sweden in 1907, he met with her and subsequently gave her some of his land on Visingsö to establish a Theosophical center there. This unsurprisingly met with harsh reactions from the local representatives of the Church of Sweden.[18] A point here, then, is that Prince Eugen, though he at times chose to support artistic figures his father actively disliked, would not have found Aguéli's esoteric interests particularly bizarre. He was used to somewhat similar ideas from his own father. Such a context is at times forgotten when Aguéli is discussed. His esoteric pursuits were, in some sense, commonplace. This fact, however, may not have been much to Aguéli's liking. While no doubt an earnest spiritual seeker, he was also a devoted rebel and provocateur. A possible interpretation could hence be that in his efforts to transgress, Islam became a way of going much further away from anything mainstream and Swedish—a next step after an esotericism that was so widespread that even the king embraced it.

This speaks to esotericism's double position in Sweden, and many other places, at this time. It was a phenomenon that the king could support openly, and the Theosophical Society had a large portion of members from the Swedish nobility and upper classes. Yet, it could also attract figures like the radical socialist reformer Kata Dalström (1858–1923).[19] Many felt Christianity was intimately bound up with other power structures they wished to challenge, like patriarchy, colonialism, or even the current socioeconomic order in general. For this reason, Theosophy could function as an alternative, and a rallying point for dissidents, while paradoxically also having upper-class connotations.[20] For example, *Svenska Dagbladet*, one of Sweden's two main newspapers, sarcastically described it in 1894 as "an upper-class sect."[21] Theosophy thus offered both a cultural capital tied up with aristocracy and established (or in the process of becoming established) artistic elites and a transgressive cultural capital gained from its connections to anticolonialism, socialist reformers, etc. Aguéli was decidedly more attracted to the latter, but we must be careful not to over-emphasize this side of Theosophy in general.

The Masonic initiations that Aguéli received in Paris[22] also take on a slightly different character if we consider the somewhat special position Freemasonry enjoyed in Sweden. Unlike the typical situation on the European continent, where it was generally associated with anticlerical and republican values, the Swedish Order of Freemasons had the king himself as its grandmaster from the mid-eighteenth century until 1973, and many high-ranking officials in the Church of Sweden were also deeply involved.[23] The specific ("fringe") Masonic lineages Aguéli was initiated into were quite divergent from this, but being Swedish his (peripheral) involvement with Masonry still in a way fits better with something that was very much part of the establishment than one might think. However, Aguéli probably did not give this too much thought, as these were just some of a series of radically different initiations he went through around 1910 to 1911, including a Taoist one.[24]

A radical dimension of all types of Masonry, including the Swedish, is that this was a space where members from different social backgrounds met and became "brothers," more or less laying mundane titles and hierarchies aside. The same applies to Theosophy. We thus find wealthy aristocrats like Baron Victor Pfeiff (1829–1901) and Countess Constance Wachtmeister (1838–1910), as well as the poverty-stricken social democrat Axel Fritiof Åkerberg (1833–1901), occupying key roles in the movement.[25] In a way, this is similar to the trans-class nature of the artistic milieu, where a man like Prince Eugen could rub shoulders with middle-class artists like Aguéli. Analogous to the international artistic milieu, esoteric groups moreover offered transnational networks.

Aguéli's Esoteric Connections

Let us now look closer at some of Aguéli's specific esoteric ties. In France, esotericism was so prevalent in cultural life toward the end of the nineteenth century that (future) Nobel Prize laureate Anatole France (1844–1924) famously claimed that "a certain knowledge of the occult sciences becomes necessary to understand a great number of literary works of our time."[26] In the 1890s, Aguéli was quite involved with the Theosophical lodge Ananta in Paris. Later, he paid an extended visit to Olcott in Madras, and spent much time reading in the Theosophical library there.[27] Many of his close associates, like the poet Marie Huot, were active Theosophists, and he continued to associate with persons closely linked to Theosophy for most of his life. Notably, Islam was the major religion Theosophists took least interest in, so it might seem strange that a Muslim convert would continue to engage with Theosophy. However, as Mark Sedgwick suggests, Aguéli's later choice of Sufism as his preferred type of Islam was likely related to Theosophical descriptions of it as the esoteric form of Islam, that is: the highest form of Islam.[28] Even after Aguéli's conversion to Islam (around 1898), Theosophy—as well as Swedenborg—remained of key importance in his thinking.[29]

There are indications in Aguéli's letters that one of his reasons for continuously engaging with Theosophy was its usefulness as a tool in anticolonial struggles. But there was surely more to it. In an article published in 1907, he was still emphasizing that Sufism was compatible with Theosophy. Only a few years later, in his articles on Sufism in *La Gnose* in 1910, he represented a different position where he even questioned the existence of the Mahatmas (the mysterious "Hidden Masters" that Blavatsky claimed to be in communication with). A perennialist foundation remains in these articles, but with expressed skepticism against the Theosophical take on it, which was influenced by Hinduism. Nevertheless, there are, as Sedgwick notes, still significant traces of Theosophical ideas about hidden masters, in Islamized form. As Sedgwick points out, we can also observe a surprising absence in these writings of any actual Sufi *practice*, or references to the Qur'an, with the whole argument instead remaining firmly embedded in a Theosophical framework.[30]

While things like a lack of references to the Qur'an is quite odd for a Muslim writer, most of the comments we find in Aguéli's notes and letters on esoteric matters can on the other hand hardly be considered very idiosyncratic. For example, he connects natural science and esotericism in a manner typical of the so-called epoch of *occultism* in the history of esotericism, in which esoteric currents had to shift to new positions to deal with secularization of various kinds.[31] This was also emphasized in Theosophy, and very much in tune with the needs of the time (where many had difficulties reconciling faith and science).[32]

In Aguéli's letters, we also find an emphasis on *will* that is familiar from occultist figures like Éliphas Lévi from the mid-1850s onward, and which became further accentuated among the many esotericists who combined such notions with Nietzschean influences in the 1890s. Aguéli, we should note, expressed his dislike of Nietzsche.[33] This is not to say he would automatically have rejected all the occultists influenced by the German philosopher.

When Aguéli praises the Sufi master Muhyiddin ibn 'Arabi in a 1908 letter to Huot, he calls him "a Leonardo in the form of philosophy."[34] Leonardo had a very special standing among occultists of the time, and in the Parisian circles where Aguéli moved there was even a Rosicrucian order (run by Joséphin Peladan, 1858–1918) that had an initiatory degree centered around Leonardo. Aguéli was well-read in occult literature, and would probably have been aware of most major themes in contemporary occultism—like that of Leonardo as one of the great esoteric initiates.[35] As an example of his well-informed reading patterns, Aguéli asked a friend for books on "occult sciences" during his short term in jail in 1894, among them the 1889 edition of *The Key of Solomon* by Samuel Macgregor Mathers (1854–1918), the founder of the Hermetic Order of the Golden Dawn, which he requested specifically, indicating he had extensive and specialized knowledge of the esoteric literature on the market.[36] He also recommended the book *Traité méthodique de science occulte* (Methodical Treatise on Occult Science) by Parisian occultist Papus in a letter written around the same time.[37]

Several scholars have highlighted Aguéli's interest in Baudelaire, and his poem "Correspondences," linking it to Swedenborg (whom Baudelaire had become acquainted with through his reading of Balzac's highly didactic 1834 Swedenborgian novel *Séraphîta*).[38] It is worth pointing out that Baudelaire's poem may also have been inspired by his close collaboration with the influential Parisian occultist Éliphas Lévi. The two worked together on a piece of popular journalism, and were friends in private. Baudelaire's poem moreover shares its title with an 1845 poem by Lévi, and essentially treats the same subject.[39]

Though Baudelaire was obviously important to him, Aguéli does not seem to have given the pro-Satanic poems contained in *Les Fleurs du mal* (The Flowers of Evil) much thought. In fact, he actively repudiated Satanism, as can be seen in his comments about the French author Joris-Karl Huysmans (1848–1907) in an 1893 letter to Richard Bergh: "Huysmans has taken on, it would seem, a handsome work by fighting Satanism on behalf of sound mysticism and real spirituality."[40] In spite of this, there are many parallels in Aguéli's esoteric thought to a self-professed Satanist and one of the period's most influential art critics and networkers: the Pole Stanislaw Przybyszewski (1868–1927), who played a key part in the reception of Scandinavian artists like Edvard Munch (1863–1944) and Gustav Vigeland (1869–1943) in Germany as well as Central and Eastern Europe. Simon Sorgenfrei has highlighted how Aguéli wrote of "the artist in touch with his authentic self, and hence one of the initiated, the chosen."[41] This is very similar to Przybyszewski's concept of the "naked soul," the authentic, pure self from which all true art springs. According to Przybyszewski's widely translated, published, and discussed art-theoretical texts, the naked soul was reachable only for the elect few, a class of artists Przybyszewski claimed were the present-day inheritors of the magicians of old. This is a type of conflation of art and esoteric endeavors that was widespread at the time. There existed a great similarity between esoteric notions of elites with privileged spiritual insights, and artistic avant-gardes' ideas about how they constitute a special group with special insights about art and the world.[42] Unlike Przybyszewski, who was a purely theoretical occultist author, Aguéli was also himself (as we have seen) in concrete terms an initiate of both Eastern and Western esoteric lineages, alongside his affiliation with avant-garde cliques.

Where Przybyszewski connected artistic creativity to a heroic Satan, Aguéli connected it to God and Christ. To quote from one of Aguéli's letters: "Christ also bestows upon me the idea of the anthropomorph ability, that is, to give human form to ideas and emotions, an ability likely the result of an intense and harmonious love felt with the innermost depths of the soul, the artist's and creator's ability, which is related to the aesthetic sense."[43] The phrasings as such are strikingly similar to Przybyszewski's art-theory texts from the 1890s, even if Satan is nowhere to be found in them.

Erasing the Esoteric

In spite of Aguéli's esoteric ideas concerning art being part of broader contemporary tendencies, this aspect of his life was largely blanked out for a long time. The early reception of Aguéli, for example, in conjunction with the 1920 memorial exhibition at AB Konstverk in Stockholm, seems to have been positive toward his artistic achievements. His art's basis in Islam and esotericism did not then become a matter of any real discussion.[44] In general, esoteric connections were not a topic of much discussion in Swedish art criticism in the 1920s, having faded rapidly from memory (and public conversation) after an esoteric high-point in such contexts from the 1880s to the 1910s. This was in spite of it still having great significance for artists two decades into the new century, with figures like Gösta Adrian-Nilsson (1884–1965, better known as GAN) being heavily influenced by it at this very moment. He was at this time reading Theosophical books and attending lectures, resulting in works like *Livsstegen* (The Ladder of Life, or Life Steps), which illustrates Theosophical ideas. His 1922 art-theory work *Den Gudomliga Geometrien* (Divine Geometry) shows clear influences from Theosophy.[45] Moreover, the international Theosophical Society (Adyar) in fact had more members than ever in the 1920s.

Of course, GAN's esoteric abstraction had several precursors abroad. Ten years earlier, Wassily Kandinsky (1866–1944) had explicitly referred to Theosophy in his manifesto *Über das Geistige in der Kunst* (Concerning the Spiritual in Art), and other pioneers of abstraction like Kupka, Malevitj, and Mondrian were also influenced by Theosophy.[46] In Sweden, however, this dimension seems to have been even less acknowledged than in many other places. Perhaps this was because of how postwar Sweden combined a secularist dominance in much political and public discourse with a population at the same time retaining firm institutional ties to the Church of Sweden.[47] Whatever the reason, Swedish cultural memory has been peculiarly short when it comes to esotericism in the arts.[48]

Let us now finally turn to Säfve's fictionalization of Aguéli's life, *Ivan Aguéli: En roman om frihet*, published in 1981. Säfve has always cultivated an image as a radical freethinker and misfit in Swedish literature, and is known for several biographical novels as well as his fanatical interest in boxing. He has a background in Maoist circles, and has also described himself as "some sort of Anarcho-Stalinist in younger years."[49]

Säfve's novel downplays Aguéli's interest in Western esotericism, and instead brings anarchism and Sufism to the fore. Only around fifteen pages, interspersed through the book, deal directly with Aguéli's involvement with esotericism. It is clear, especially in more recent scholarship but also from Gauffin's book *Ivan Aguéli: Människan, Mystikern, Målaren* (Ivan Aguéli: The Man, the Mystic, the Painter), one of Säfve's sources on Aguéli's life, that esotericism in fact held a significance in Aguéli's life. So Säfve's downplaying of Aguéli's esotericism is a somewhat curious choice. Säfve himself identified very strongly with Aguéli. He became a Muslim and a Sufi while writing the book, but never himself held any sympathy for esoteric ideas, which perhaps explains this omission from the narrative.[50]

Säfve portrays Aguéli as very critical of Theosophy and occult ideas from the outset.[51] He lets Aguéli proclaim that he "stands apart from the [esoteric] carousel."[52] He is depicted as clearly unimpressed by his encounter with the Belgian artist Félicien Rops (1833–98), one of the foremost exponents of occult and Satanic motifs at the time, who shows him a séance table.[53] The fictionalized Aguéli talks of a friend who has "thank goodness seen through Sar Peladan's sick mystical symbolism," and later calls Peladan's notion of ideal art "humbug."[54] The novel's Aguéli, unlike the real person, is generally entirely dismissive of all esoteric ideas, summarizing the situation with the words "Paris is running a fever, and the quacks are making money [from it]."[55]

In 1981, the significance of esotericism to art was not fully on the radar anywhere, least of all perhaps in Sweden. This gradually began to change with the celebrated exhibition *The Spiritual in Art* in Los Angeles in 1986, which also heralded the international discovery of Hilma af Klint.[56] Knowledge had, however, begun to spread in Sweden of such connections already in the very year Säfve's novel appeared, 1981, when Peter Cornell's pioneering book *Den hemliga källan* (The Secret Wellspring) was also published. This was the first full-scale attempt in Swedish to tackle the topic, even if there had been monographs on specific artists published earlier, like Sixten Ringbom's important 1970 book *The Sounding Cosmos*, about Kandinsky and esotericism, and a couple of studies of Strindberg's occult interests. Nevertheless, there is but one single mention of esotericism in all the reviews of Säfve's book on Aguéli. The Swedish newspaper *Aftonbladet* commented that "Aguéli and Säfve rush forward in the maelstrom of ideas like Theosophy, anarchy, dawning war, cubism, futurism, and colonial events in Egypt."[57] That is all.

Seven years later, Säfve would himself write a review where he briefly touches on this topic. Reviewing Viveca Wessel's book about Aguéli, *Ivan Aguéli: Porträtt av en rymd* (Ivan Aguéli: Portrait of a Space) Säfve praises the chapter where Aguéli's article on "Pure Art" is analyzed: "There she places Aguéli's oft-quoted essay on the Pure Art in its esoteric context."[58]

If we move forward in time a couple of decades, the situation in Sweden looks very different. In the wake of the enormously successful Hilma af Klint exhibition at Sweden's leading museum of modern art, Moderna Museet, in 2013, one of the museum's most popular exhibitions ever, with more than a million visitors, the connection between art and esotericism has become well-established.[59] Swedish newspapers now overflow with essays and articles on the topic, and in relation to the 2018–19 Aguéli exhibition at the Thiel Gallery in Stockholm this was also a fairly clear theme in reviews.[60] We stand, then, at a point in time when this dimension of art history enjoys an unexpectedly high status. Now, therefore, is the ideal time to explore in depth what role esotericism played in the creative work and life of figures like Ivan Aguéli, and what the broader implications for cultural history are.

Conclusion

This chapter has aimed to contextualize Aguéli's esoteric ponderings, by relating them to similar ideas in circulation in European artistic networks and the Swedish artistic milieu. Aguéli connected esotericism and science in a way typical of Theosophy and the broader occultist current it was part of. He emphasized *will* in much the same manner that Éliphas Lévi and others did, and he made references to Leonardo that might be related to this artist's special position among French estericists. His view of artists as "initiates" is similar to what we find with esoteric art theorists like Przybyszewski and Péladan.

All this is quite natural, as Aguéli moved in the artistic circles where such ideas were discussed, and he had strong direct ties to esoteric currents. Since his youth, he was (just like his mother) an enthusiastic reader of Swedenborg. He was involved with a Theosophical lodge in Paris, his closest French associates were Theosophists, and he visited Olcott in Adyar. We have also seen that he was quite knowledgeable about some highly specialized occult literature available on the market. Even after his conversion to Islam, Theosophy and Swedenborgianism continued to mark his thinking.

One reason for Aguéli's long-term engagement with Theosophy seems to have been his view of it as strategically useful in anticolonial struggles. This brings us to the question of why esotericism was so appealing to him, aside from its potential to aid him in his spiritual quest. I have suggested that we should acknowledge the transgressive cultural capital of esotericism, where its status as "rejected knowledge" was attractive as a means to bolster one's credentials as a rebel against mainstream culture. The esoteric could thus be useful when portraying oneself as audacious and intentionally deviant. In some contexts, for example, among avant-garde artists, this type of transgressive cultural capital would have been highly desirable.

At the same time, esotericism was often much less "rejected" than this model definition suggests. This, then, may account for Aguéli taking his spiritual rebellion to the next level by moving beyond Theosophical perennialist appropriations of non-Western religion that had become socially accepted to some degree, and embracing an actual Eastern tradition, Sufism.

Considering the Swedish king himself embraced Theosophy (and was also the grandmaster of the Swedish Freemasons), as did much of Sweden's creative elite, esotericism held a considerable cultural capital in turn-of-the-century Sweden. In this sense, Aguéli's esoteric involvement was commonplace and mainstream. His conversion to Islam could therefore be seen as the next step in his constant attempts to rebel and go beyond Swedish respectability.

As a whole, it might be fair to say that esotericism often straddled the fence of cultural acceptance, holding something of a double position in Sweden and many other places at this time. Most of its manifestations were certainly not accepted by dominant

Christian churches or academies of science. Theosophy, while popular with royalty and the upper classes, simultaneously attracted many radicals critical of colonialism, patriarchy, and capitalism. Freemasonry, though associated with the well-to-do and having the king as its grandmaster, also held a radical egalitarian potential in its notion of brotherhood, where the king himself would be the "brother" of individuals of far simpler background.

Esotericism, then, is such a tangled and sprawling phenomenon, even if we only consider a specific current like Theosophy, that it is difficult to reduce it to being either "rejected knowledge" or socially accepted. Its status would have shifted between different contexts, and it often encompassed elements of both mainstream respectability and avant-garde/progressive credibility at the same time. Furthermore, I have argued that we need to take into account the strategic value of *self-chosen* marginal positions, that is, the transgressive social capital this generates.

By the 1920s, when Aguéli's art was increasingly gaining acclaim in Sweden, there seems to have been no discussion of his esoteric interests. In 1940-1, Gauffin's big, and still unsurpassed, biography of Aguéli was published, detailing these matters. This study provided the basis for Torbjörn Säfve's 1981 novel, which portrayed Aguéli as keeping his distance and being critical of all things esoteric from the outset—hereby contradicting the documentation provided in Gauffin's work.

It would appear Säfve at this point considered esotericism a type of rightfully rejected knowledge, which should remain rejected. Säfve here adheres to the dominant secularist and traditional Protestant narratives regarding esotericism. On the other hand, his own fascination with Sufism certainly seems related to its status as something alien and in a sense rebellious—in contradiction to the Stalinism and Maoism of his own youth as well as mainstream Swedish religious (i.e., the Church of Sweden) and secularist formations. Yet he does not seem to acknowledge the politically radical potential of esotericism, or its function as a form of cultural critique and transgressive cultural capital—perhaps because it was in his mind too closely associated with the leisure class.

When Viveca Wessel's epochal study of Aguéli appeared in 1988, Säfve seemingly changed his mind somewhat, enthusiastically praising its esoteric contextualization of one of the painter's essays. Things have continued to move in this direction, with reviews of the latest Aguéli exhibition in Sweden very much highlighting his esotericism. Presumably, this has to do with the abundant local (and international) discussion of Hilma af Klint's esoteric practice during the last few years, which has created interest and an open-minded attitude toward the influences of esotericism in Swedish art history.

5

Ivan Aguéli's Monotheistic Landscapes: From Perspectival to Solar Logics

Simon Sorgenfrei

Ivan Aguéli had a great ability to creatively synthesize his many interests and let landscape painting, philosophy of religion, and art theory inform and nourish each other in a symbiotic relationship. This chapter aims at analyzing such creative entwinements, focusing on two short but intense periods of painting, in the 1890s, and between 1913 and 1917. Considering the first of these periods, a closer analysis of Swedenborg's influence on his art theory and painting will be presented, while the later period will take into consideration also his reading of Sufi literature. Further, a greater focus on the importance of place and sensory impressions will nuance the strong emphasis given to theoretical aspects of Aguéli's development. Primarily the chapter examines how shifts in Aguéli's geographical whereabouts seem to combine with changes in his artistic view and painting techniques, as well as in changes in his religious interests.

In Paris Reading Swedenborg

After arriving in Paris, Aguéli immediately immersed himself in an impressive number of avant-garde religious, cultural, and political currents. A friend and colleague, the Swedish artist Arthur Bianchini (1869–1955), reported how Aguéli after just a brief time in Paris "had already managed to gain entrance to exclusive and radical circles that it would have taken decades for someone else to find out about. Sometimes he showed up and invited me to strange places with gypsy music and mysticism."[1] In relation to that same period, the Swedish artist Fritz Lindström recalled someone having "said … how in Aguéli's bureau drawer that there lay a pile of membership cards to the YMCA, the Theosophical Society, an anarchist club, some Swedenborgian society, etc." and, Lindström continues, "the story could quite possibly be true, if Aguéli ever had any kind of bureau drawer."[2] Both memories are telling, and evoke the image of a curious, hyperactive, and bohemian person, drawn to the subversive coteries à la mode.

Maybe the most important person for Aguéli during his first period in Paris was Émile Bernard, through whom Aguéli would not only be introduced to symbolism and synthetism, but also, among other things, to the Theosophical lodge, Ananta. Ananta, which was previously called Lotus Bleu, was a prominent Theosophical lodge during the 1880s and 1890s, and especially so under the leadership of Arthur Arnould (1833–95), who also moved within anarchist circles in Paris.[3]

Members of Ananta recalled how Aguéli was primarily interested in the study of Swedenborgism and Islam and that the fruits of such studies were his main contributions to the discussions at the lodge.[4] Precisely when he developed these interests is uncertain, but we know that Aguéli was already studying Swedenborg before moving to Paris, and that he was a reoccurring guest in the home of the (Swedenborgian) New Church pastor Adolph Boyesen during his time in Stockholm in the late 1880s.[5] When he first got interested in Islam is difficult to say, but it seems to have been around these years.

Religion was however not his only interest in those days and, like Arnauld, Aguéli was sympathetic to anarchism, which in a letter to his friend and colleague Richard Bergh he called "the most beautiful thing in our foul times."[6] His envolvement with anarchism and anarchists got him arrested in the spring of 1894, and he was sent to the Mazas Prison. In many ways the time in prison was an uncertain and horrific experience, but it also was a time of intense studies. In Gauffin's words, the prison walls meant a protection just as much as a hindrance. "In the silence of the prison cell his thought could blossom like never before. In the tranquility of prison he was given the opportunity for studies and self-reflection which he had yearned for."[7] At any rate, Aguéli wrote to Werner von Hausen, "It is less boring than Sweden."[8]

Through the letters Aguéli sent to friends from his prison cell we know fairy well what he was reading and what thoughts occupied him during these months. Of special interest is his correspondence with Hausen in which books and religion were discussed. Through these letters, we are granted a unique insight into Aguéli's religio-historical studies and the development of his thoughts during this period.

The Perspectival Logics

Even though Hausen's letters are lost, the replies suggest that he asked Aguéli about his views on religion in one of the early letters from April 1894. On April 24 Aguéli answers him:

> What my faith consists of. What is Christianity? First and foremost: monotheism, i.e., belief in and yearning for a single supreme being. A supreme locus of greatness and universality and a source of life. A creator, the only being who [possesses] an essential and substantial life and above all else comprehensible, the Creator who forms the heavens and the Earth out of nothing and who brings forth the light of the Word. Monotheism is the religion of those who hate the worship of fetishes and who possess the gift of being able to collect oneself in concentration.

> Belief in a supreme being which is above all else, Allah … Monotheism is
> the essence of Christ's teachings, so significant that the faithful Muslim is more
> Christian than most Christians.[9]

The above passage is telling: God as the absolute One transcends the boundaries that
separate the world's religions. To Aguéli, God is the *singularity* toward which all true
religions—in the plural—point. It seems here as if the monotheism of Swedenborg
attracted him—in a later letter to Marie Huot from March 18, 1908, he states that
Swedenborg saved him from "Protestantism and Germanization"[10]—and worked as
a bridge leading him to Islam. We might notice how already in these letters he uses
the Arabic word for God, "Allah," when talking about the God of monotheism.

The influence of Swedenborg in the letter, as well as in his interest in an Islamic
concept of monotheism, might be clarified by comparing the above-cited passage with
the fifth paragraph of Swedenborg's *True Christian Religion* (Vera Christiana Religio),
which Aguéli refers to as his daily bread.[11] Here Swedenborg begins the text not only
by formulating his rejection of the doctrine of the Trinity but also by celebrating true
monotheism as a universal religious trait: "Such is the Christian faith respecting the
unity of God … The other nations in the world possessing a religion and sound reason
agree in acknowledging that God is one; all the Mohammedens in their empires; the
Africans in many kingdoms of that continent; and also the Asiatics in their many
kingdoms; and finally the Jews to this day."[12]

It is telling, in relation to the above paragraph, that Aguéli during the months spent
in jail devoted his time to Hebrew and Arabic, to the Hebrew Bible and the Qur'an.
But most interesting for the purposes of this chapter is how these discussions of
metaphysics after some time merge with Aguéli theorizing about art and the painter's
gaze. An example might be found in a long and expressive letter from May 6, in which
painting, art theory, and the philosophy of religion seem to converge:

> Admit that a landscape can reflect a state of mind. The monotheistic landscape is
> very sunny, illuminated by a penetrating sun, a light strong enough to let the aerial
> perspective supersede the linear perspective. In it, light masters matter … Religion
> is decisive for the sun in the landscape within me. That is why I love monotheism
> and the Arab spirit … If the landscape is the soul's mirror, then the sky and *lointain*
> [the far distant] correspond to the lofty and intimate principles and the foreground
> to the lower principles. When one travels, one constantly sees the sky as unmoving
> while the level of the terrain changes unceasingly, the first every moment, the other
> less quickly, and the *lointain* almost not at all. Who finds a moral satisfaction, who
> a "sine qua non" for the inner equilibrium, his center of gravity, so to speak, in the
> objects on the first level, a near-sighted talent, given to fetish worship and facile
> pleasures, who goes from mistake to mistake, and when his idol has been crushed,
> which sooner or later is going to happen, will immediately be knocked down. Let
> us then break down our idols before they cause our fall.
> That is my religion in summary. Perspectival logic.[13]

Perspectival logic. For both Aguéli and Swedenborg, what is beautiful relates to what is true, good, and ordered. It therefore becomes a question of perspectives, as what is good becomes visible in relation to its opposite.[14] Swedenborg's view might be illustrated by the following paragraph from his *Sapientia Angelica de Divina Providentia* (Angelic Wisdom about Divine Providence): "For the nature of good is not known except by contrast with what is less good and by its contrariety to evil. All perceptiveness and sensitivity arise so; their quality is thence. All pleasantness is perceived and felt over against the less pleasant and unpleasant; all the beautiful by reference to the less beautiful and the unbeautiful."[15]

Aguéli was of course far from the first symbolist to be inspired by Swedenborg's teaching of correspondences—through Baudelaire much of the French symbolist movement came to be inspired by these teachings—but for Aguéli, it seems as if Swedenborg's influence also worked as a hermeneutical key to several interests, which Aguéli then could combine and have nourish each other. In a letter to Bianchini he wrote:

> Moreover, the more one studies symbolism and correspondences, the more one sees how sharply scientific and universal they are and how little about them is arbitrary, random, and conventional. I am absolutely convinced of the deep truth of symbolism. I doubt it as little as I doubt that I live. It is experience. The experience from both my deepest, most intimate thoughts, from my most serious meditations, investigations of my interior, conversations with myself in deserts of different varieties. As well as experience from history, art, the people, the positivistic sciences. I give you here this "confession of faith" because every honest conviction is a witness.[16]

Swedenborg, then, influenced his religious speculations as well and his art theory. But can such an inspiration be traced even in his art? Did theory transform into practice?

Art historian Hans Henrik Brummer has proposed the hypothesis that Aguéli's often layered skies—especially seen in his paintings from Stockholm done around 1890—could have been inspired by Swedenborg's teachings about heaven being divided into two kingdoms.[17] Art historian Niclas Franzén also detects influences from Swedenborg in Aguéli's skies of the time, but rather finds these to be three-layered, which could also correspond to Swedenborg's teachings: "There are three heavens, entirely distinct from each other, an inmost or third, a middle or second, and an outmost or first. These follow upon each other and are in relation to each other."[18]

Aguéli's first introducer and interpreter, Axel Gauffin, was impressed and bewildered by the colors and skies in these motifs, such as the painting *Stockholmsutsikt* (Stockholm View, Figure 2.2) "with its striking, full palette" which "possess an intense, suggestive power." He also notices the layered skies: "The strange arc in the sky that divides it up into two layers of one darker and one lighter blue is undoubtedly an excellent artistic effect but has naturally awakened wonder from the start."[19]

Maybe these skies were inspired by Swedenborgian theology, as Bremmer and Franzén held. Aguéli himself, however, when asked about these, reportedly answered: "You see, it is my pince-nez that makes me see things in this way."[20] Aguéli's laconic answer could of course be taken as an expression of his sense of humor, but should also remind us to be careful not to draw too far-reaching conclusions from such ambiguous material as an artwork. Regardless of whether or not Aguéli wanted to reflect Swedenborg's theological teachings in these paintings, I believe we may hold that several of the works from this period strive to depict the "monotheistic landscapes" he writes about in the letter to Hausen. In several of these, lustrous, distant skies are the focal point, and these are then accentuated by dark, base, and somewhat blurred vegetation in the foreground.

An illustrative example is found in one of the paintings entitled *Slätten* (The Field, Figure 5.1) from 1892, where the immense, luminous sky that takes up two-thirds of the painting is contrasted to the dark ground of the lower third. The correspondence between the theory advanced in the letter and the technique and choice of motif in the painting is even more striking if we look at the painting as if we were looking out a window of a speeding train, while remembering a passage from the letter quoted above where Aguéli describes his perspectival logics: "When one travels, one constantly sees the sky as unmoving while the level of the terrain changes unceasingly, the first every moment, the other less quickly, and the *lointain* almost not at all."[21] *The Field* could then very well be analyzed as a materialization of the ideas developed in Aguéli's letter to Hausen (which raises the interesting question of what comes first—theory or practice?) and in this context, be understood as an attempt of painting the principle of sovereign monotheism discussed in the same letter.

Looking closer at the skies which Aguéli painted in the early 1890s, there maybe yet further influence from Swedenborgian theology. Shortly after he painted the Stockholm motifs, he traveled to Gotland to paint some of his most well-known works, such as *Gotländskt landskap* (Gotland Landscape, Figure 2.1, one of several with the same name) or his *Motiv från Visby I & II* (Motif from Visby I & II, Figures 5.2 and 5.3). Gauffin sees the latter as typical for this period, "held in reddish yellow

Figure 5.1 Ivan Aguéli, *Slätten* (The Field), *c.* 1890. Oil on canvas, 23 x 40 cm. Photo: Moderna Museet, Stockholm. Full-color image available at www.aguelimuseet.se/5_1 and on the publisher's website.

Figure 5.2 Ivan Aguéli, *Motiv från Visby I* (Motif from Visby I), 1892. Oil on canvas, 50 x 90.5 cm. Photo: Moderna Museet, Stockholm. Full-color image available at www. aguelimuseet.se/5_2 and on the publisher's website.

Figure 5.3 Ivan Aguéli, *Motiv från Visby II* (Motif from Visby II), 1892. Oil on canvas, 51 x 79.5 cm. Photo: Moderna Museet, Stockholm. Full-color image available at www. aguelimuseet.se/5_3 and on the publisher's website.

with sharp shadows in blue, green and violet, and sky fading from yellow to blue-green with clouds in violet pink and pale green."[22] In these paintings, he continues, the result has "become something entirely different from the artist's paintings of Stockholm with their deep tones. The impression is in an indescribable way subtilized."[23] Gauffin interprets these paintings in the light of Charles Baudelaire's poem "Correspondances" and its symbol-laden depictions of nature: "In Aguéli's poems in color treating motifs from Gotland—I cannot provide them with any better name—in these visions with their mixture of calm loveliness and 'putrid fragrances,' we recognize something of the inconceivable eternity as well as of the seductive rush of the senses of which Baudelaire sings in 'Correspondances'."[24]

Even though we know that Aguéli brought the collected works of Baudelaire with him to Gotland,[25] perhaps these paintings are even more obviously inspired by Swedenborg than by Baudelaire? In the spring of the following year, on March 16, 1893, Aguéli writes to Bergh:

> A propos symbolism, I will take the liberty of making a perhaps somewhat banal remark. That everything—color, light in music or language, figure, number, etc.— symbolizes several widely diverging, usually diametrically opposed, ideas. It is usually the place in the composition that determines, so to say decides, what the thing in question means at the moment. Incidentally, within real symbolism, no arbitrariness is possible.[26]

The letter to Bergh also contains quotes from Frédéric Portal's study *Des couleurs symboliques dans l'Antiquité, le Moyen-Age et les temps modernes* (An Essay on Symbolic Colors: In Antiquity, the Middle Ages, and Modern Times), which Aguéli copied— most likely some time during the first few years of the 1890s. The Aguéli archive at the National Museum in Stockholm shows that he often copied books that he could not afford to buy. In his biography, Gauffin quotes several passages from Aguéli's copy of Portal's work:

> White is God's symbol, gold and yellow signifies the Word or the revelation and red and blue sanctification or the Holy Spirit.

> The color pink borrows its meaning from red and white. Red is the symbol for divine love, white for divine wisdom, the union of the two colors shall signify: the love of divine wisdom.

> —

> Each color has according to the principle we have established a double meaning, divine and hellish. The symbol of divine love becomes the sign for egoism, hatred, hellish love. The devil appears dressed in red, and the sacrificial fire has the fires of hell as its counterpart.[27]

Gauffin himself does not seem to have had the opportunity to study Portal's book, which he describes as a "very rare work (I have sought it in vain at the Bibliothèque

Nationale)."[28] Viveca Wessel, in her study of Aguéli, devotes a section to Portal's book and its influence, but does not seem to have come across it either: "It is a hard-to-find work, of Theosophical character, published in Paris in 1837. The copy is in the National Museum's archive, and the original, according to Aguéli's page references, should have spanned roughly 300 pages."[29]

Today, Portal's book is easier to come by, and it is clear that he partly based his study on Swedenborg.[30] "The doctrine I present here," he writes, "has been put forth by Pico de la Mirandola and fully confirmed by Swedenborg."[31] The transcript Gauffin presents in his book points to Swedenborg as well, and the part about "the color pink" is a direct paraphrasing of a passage from Swedenborg's *Arcana Coelestia* (Heavenly Mysteries):

and the color "white" signifies the truth which is of faith ...

"gold and silver" signifies good and truth in general ...

And crimson. That this signifies the celestial love of good is evident from the signification of "crimson" as being the celestial love of good. The reason why this is signified by "crimson" is that by a red color is signified the good of celestial love. For there are two fundamental colors from which come the rest: the color red, and the color white. The color "red" signifies the good which is of love; and the color "white" signifies the truth which is of faith. That the color "red" signifies the good which is of love is because it comes from fire, and "fire" denotes the good of love; and the color "white" signifies the truth which is of faith, because it is from light, and "light" denotes the truth of faith.[32]

These are also colors found in Aguéli's paintings from the time, for example in the Gotland-inspired motif that graces the wall of the Aguéli Museum in Sala, where the sky's strange cloud formations in purple simultaneously correspond with what seems to be a watercourse, or perhaps a rock formation, on the ground. Perhaps it is not only his layered skies that are inspired by Swedenborg but even the choice of color and that his paintings from the 1890s could be analyzed as a matter of a Swedenborgian style of painting, which may require further information based on these color schemes.

At the same time, theory and practice should not be confused to too great a degree. One cannot, as Wessel puts it, interpret Aguéli's painting in the same way that one solves a riddle.[33] Maybe it was just his pince-nez that made Aguéli paint those layered skies over Stockholm, and maybe the clouds over Visby shifted in purple, yellow, and white that summer of 1892. The above-analyzed material however suggests that Swedenborg's writing had a greater influence, also on his art of the 1890s, than earlier studies have shown.[34] And as we will see in the following, the "perspectival logics" he found in Swedenborg's teachings would later both correspond and contrast to a "solar logics" discovered in the Sufi texts which would occupy more and more of his interest in the 1900s.

In Egypt—Studying Sufism

Aguéli was released from the Mazas Prison in October 1894, and shortly thereafter made his first trip to Egypt, where he began publishing essays and translations on political and religious issues, and through these articles we can follow his growing interest in Sufism.

As discussed in Chapters 10 and 11, the Egyptian Sufi ʿAbd al-Rahman ʿIllaysh was important for Aguéli's orientation during these years. To what extent ʿIllaysh actually initiated Aguéli into living Sufism is, however, disputable.[35] Even so, it is probably safe to say that it was in this environment, under the influence of ʿIllaysh, that Aguéli put great effort into reading, translating, and commenting on the Sufi mystic Muhyiddin ibn ʿArabi and other Sufi writers influenced by Ibn ʿArabi.[36] He did however also continue to study Swedenborg, and further developed a growing interest in Taoism and other Asian religions. It seems he let texts from different traditions mirror and inform each other in a way common among Theosophists and other religious seekers of the time.[37]

In Egypt, he found not only new sorts of religious writings, primarily by Sufi scholars, which for the rest of his life would accompany and nuance his reading of Swedenborg, but also a different type of landscape, a different type of sunlight in which he read this new literature, and in which he painted new sorts of paintings.

The Solar Logics

In the Egyptian landscape, Aguéli found a stronger light than he had experienced on Gotland. In a text published in *Il commercio italiano* in 1903, he wrote about a land "where the wonderful and blinding light extinguishes the details and transforms proportions and planes."[38] It is an impression that would follow him for years to come, and that also came to resonate with his reading and own writing, as well as in his late art. The Egyptian sun and desert landscape stood in sharp contrast to the forests and fields of Sweden, and in these new monotheistic landscapes it was the unifying effect of sunlight rather than the contrasting perspectives which were in focus.

The experience of an all-extinguishing light also finds an echo in the Sufi literature which he was now studying. Over the last twenty years of his life, Aguéli translated a range of Sufi texts, and wrote some of his best-known articles on Sufism. Many of the theologians and theorists in whom he developed an interest had in common a philosophy of light. Light as metaphor for divine power and illumination has a long standing in Islamic tradition (as it does in many other religious traditions), and several Muslim thinkers have been inspired by the so-called Light Verse in the 24th chapter of the Qurʾan (al-Nur):

Allah is the Light of the heavens and the earth. The similitude of His light is as a niche wherein is a lamp. The lamp is in a glass. The glass is as it were a shining

star. [This lamp is] kindled from a blessed tree, an olive neither of the East nor of
the West, whose oil would almost glow forth [of itself] though no fire touched it.
Light upon light. Allah guideth unto His light whom He will. And Allah speaketh
to mankind in allegories, for Allah is Knower of all things.[39]

In an analysis of approaches and interpretations of the Light Verse, Gerhard Böwering
has shown how Sufi writers, other differences aside, display similarities in how the
light of the sun is generally considered to be a metaphor for God, and how God's light
illuminates and enlightens the various prophets—and through them human souls.
Within these traditions, Böwering holds, God's "light is the most exalted image by
which the invisible God can be represented in a visible and temporal world, and the
most powerful symbol by which the eternal God can be apprehended in the human
realm of sense perception and intellectual insight."[40] When God's light rises in the
soul, it lights up every corner and extinguishes all human capacities, just at the
light described in the Light Verse. These and similar images are popular within Sufi
literature to try to imagine the disappearance (*fanā'*) and remaining (*baqā'*) of the
individual self in God, what often is deemed to be the raison d'être of the spiritual
struggle.[41]

The idea of God as an animating and all-illuminating light is also visible in Aguéli's
own writings about Sufism, as well as in some of his translations from the time. In
1910, for example, he published a translation of a text, entitled "Le Cadeau" (The Gift)
in Aguéli's French translation, ascribed to Muhammad ibn Fadl Allah Burhanpuri
(c. 1545–1620). In his introduction to the text, Aguéli states that he chose to translate
the text because of its didactic nature.[42]

The treatise begins by stating that God is Existence itself, and hence does not have
either form or limit. But as Existence, God makes Himself manifest in the forms in the
perceivable world, without submitting to the limits of form. This first section of the text
ends with a quote from the Light Verse, stating that "Allah is the light of the heavens
and the earth" and in the second paragraph of the text, Burhanpuri holds that the
relation between God and forms and things created are like "light in relation to colors
and forms." All that is revealed to us are such colors and forms, but neither intellect nor
imagination can comprehend God/Existence in itself. The only way that humans are
able to approach God is through the extinction of all human attributes, to let all human
existence be drowned in divine existence, as the lamp in the niche was obliterated by
the divine light in the Light Verse.

The following year Aguéli published yet another translation, this time of a treatise
on absolute unity or totality of the Godhead, "Le Traité de l'Unité" (Treatise on Unity),
which he ascribed to Ibn 'Arabi. The text has, however, later been identified as a work
by Awhad al-Din al-Balyani (d. 1287/1288).[43] As the title indicates, this is a treatise
concerned with the Islamic doctrine of *tawḥīd* (oneness or Divine unity), and more
than anything else, the text insists on the absolute oneness of God:

> I do not mean that you are or possess this or that certain quality. I mean that
> you do not exist at all and that you never will exist, neither through yourself nor
> through Him, in Him or with Him ... You will see that your exterior is His, that

your interior is His, that your beginning is His and that your end is His, without any reservation or doubt. You will see that your qualities are His and that your inner nature is His, without you ever having become Him or Him become you, without any (transformation), diminution or expansion. "Everything will perish except His face."[44]

In Aguéli's translation of the text, light is connected both to initiation into the right understanding of *tawḥīd* and as the medium through which its truth is revealed— much like in Burhanpuri's text, where God is compared with the light which brings forth shapes and colors.[45] Light brings forth what seems to be existing, and extinguishes everything that seems to exist. This was also Aguéli's own impression of the Egyptian sun, as described in *Il commercio italiano* in 1903, and as related by the Swedish painter Yngve Berg, who recalled a discussion he had with Aguéli in 1910 about the Egyptian landscape. Here Aguéli seems to allude to Burhanpuri's text: "The sun shines with such an intensity that it eclipses the local colors and paints everything in its own color. It is the light which is foremost, the landscape changes in relation to the light and becomes unreal, as if it was only a pretext for revealing the sun."[46]

These impressions and inspirations also shine through in his own writing since the time of the publication of "L'Art pur" (Pure Art) in *La Gnose* in 1911, which is arguably his best-known essay.[47] Here Aguéli states that the study of art is a "graphology of the human soul" and "an excellent way of learning how to see, as well as of providing training in solar logic, knowledge of which is practically indispensable for being able to devote oneself to the metaphysics of form." Pure art is possible, he further holds, through the abstraction of the painter's individual self and his absorption into the universal life. The solar logics is then related to the "element of mystery in art" where "line and color ... melt together to form an impression of luminosity that gives a work of art its life and magic." In place of the emphasis on perspectives found in his earlier paintings, he now emphasizes unification of contrasts, an extinction in light which also seems to be a spiritual quest. What pure art, the solar logics, aims toward is "to progress towards God through the union of complementary contrasts in formal reality."[48]

Aguéli would later return to these and similar thoughts throughout his essays in *La Gnose*, whether the subject of his texts were art or Sufism. The two subjects clearly became intermingled. In "Pages dédiées au soleil" (Pages Dedicated to the Sun), his personal impressions of the African sun, Sufi literature and art merge in a dense essay:

It is the light which gives things their existence. The sun not only illuminates the world, but also gives the things their individual shapes. The Great Sun of down there [in Africa] ... shines so strongly that its light extinguishes the local colors, so that one only sees its own [colors], that is to say it and nothing but it. The landscape changes so fast that it barely seems to be anything but an excuse for a solar exhibition, or, if you wish, for a cosmomorphic theophany ... Everything from perspectives to distances and relations between things, is dependent on the brightly shining heavenly body, which, as absolute master of the horizons,

Figure 5.4 Ivan Aguéli, *Staden bland kullarna* (The City in the Hills), *c.* 1895. Tempera on canvas, 22.5 × 30.5 cm. Photo: Moderna Museet, Stockholm. Full-color image available at www.aguelimuseet.se/5_4 and on the publisher's website.

shapes the mountains at its own pleasure and distributes the masses of immensity according to its architectonic and whimsical will.[49]

Keeping his own initial impressions of the African sun, the texts on light mysticism, and the essays he wrote on light and art in mind while looking at his artwork during this time, one could very well see that it was such insights that influenced his paintings, such as *Kalifgravarna* (Tombs of the Caliphs, Figure 6.2) or *Staden bland kullarna* (The City in the Hills, Figure 5.4). In these paintings from Egypt, the above-related impressions of a unifying and extinguishing light all come together in an artwork where houses, palm trees, and sand dunes, even the sky itself, all seem to function only as projection surfaces for the sunlight, which would then be his primary motif.[50]

Conclusion

Viveca Wessel holds that Aguéli, to be able to make the synthesis he made between his different interests, had to make an "inner journey" that by far exceeded the ones he made in the measurable time and space of "reality."[51] Without dismissing Aguéli's intellectual efforts, however, the current chapter suggests that geographical shifts were of no less importance for his development. His travels in, and impressions of, "reality" seem to have been crucial for how he encountered and interpreted spiritual and philosophical literature. His intellectual and spatial shifts seem to have been very much entwined. If we analyze Aguéli's paintings from the different periods considered in the current chapter, in relation to his mediated impressions of the places he visited, the religious literature he read as well as to his writings on art and art theory, we can see how they all influenced each other. The source material even suggests that practice sometimes came first, and theoretical analysis followed suit. The theoretical stance presented in the letters to Werner von Hausen in 1894 seems in many ways to be the fruit of this intense period of painting, just as early impressions of the African sun are later interpreted and developed though the study of Sufi texts. During both the periods analyzed in the chapter, considerable overlaps of themes, metaphors, and motifs can be identified in his own writing and paintings, as well as in the literature he reads, translates, and writes about.

Aguéli is primarily conceived of in Sweden as an artist and a painter. Therefore, everything that kept him from his artwork—language studies and translations of Sufi texts, for example—has sometimes been regarded as a distraction which kept him away from his true calling. But as this chapter suggests, these activities were often closely intertwined for Aguéli himself, and philosophy of religion, art theory, and painting seem at these very intense periods of his (most often very intense) life to have nurtured each other. Hence, I argue, it is misleading to understand Aguéli primarily as a painter with an interest in languages and religions. Art, language, and religion were all part of the same quest and included in the same logical systems—whether perspectival or solar—and therefore follow a similar trajectory. If Aguéli in the 1890s painted perspectival motifs simultaneously inspired by the landscape of Gotland and by Swedenborg's theology, we might say that his late paintings from Egypt related to Sufi-Islamic conceptualizations of monotheism which he could also envision in the desert landscape outside of Cairo.

As Wessel suggests already in the title of her seminal book, *Portrait of a Space*, Aguéli wanted to paint the void. To some extent he was then moving in the direction of the all-white canvas, an idea realized (in a totally different idiom) by Kazimir Malevich (1878–1935) in his *Suprematist Composition: White on White*, the year after Aguéli's death.

Painting the Sacred as an Initiatic Path: Art and Cubism in the Eyes of Ivan Aguéli

Thierry Zarcone

In *La Peinture cubiste* (Cubist Painting), the leading French critic Jean Paulhan (1884–1968) wrote that the "cubist adventure resembled a religious awakening, with its adepts and enthusiastic proselytes who finally understand what God is and what the world means, who afterwards live in Truth."[1] Paulhan refers to Plato, who encouraged painters to base their art as much as possible on "geometrical forms," and to "escape from perspective," and quoted the Neoplatonist Plotinus, who suggested "avoiding any imitation," that is, to have no links with traditional painting.[2] So the cubists have broken with the symbolists, the impressionists, and the neo-impressionists.

Paul Cézanne, one of the precursors and inspirer of the cubists, regarded afterward as one of the "first cubists" with the emergence of a movement called "cubisme cézannien," affirmed that the forms of sphere, cone, and cylinder are the models for everything in nature, and that painters must try to get a clear understanding of what the simple figures are. It is obvious, as remarked by some authors, that if, at a later point in time, the term "cubism" was chosen for this trend, it also could have been called "cylindrism."[3] Geometry played a central role in cubism, as explained by the poet and art critic Guillaume Apollinaire, who was also convinced that geometry is "the science which has for its scope space, its measurements and its relations, and has been from time immemorial the rule even of painting." "Geometry," he added, "is to the plastic arts what grammar is to the art of the writer."[4]

Apollinaire then introduced an intriguing concept, that of the "fourth dimension." He explained that "painters no longer hold to the three dimensions of Euclidean geometry, and have been led quite naturally, so to speak by intuition, to preoccupy themselves with possible new measures of space" we can call the "fourth dimension." This fourth dimension "would show the immensity of space eternalized in every direction at a given moment. It is space itself, the dimensions of the infinite: it is this which endows objects with their plasticity."[5] In 1916, the painter Jean Metzinger wrote to the cubist painter Albert Gleizes:

Geometry with four dimensions is no longer a mystery for me … everything is number. The spirit hates what can be measured: all things must be reduced and made understandable … This is the mystery … The arts are no more than the mathematical expression of the relations existing between what is inside and what is outside, between the number and me.[6]

At the same moment, in Russia, as shown by Margareta Tillberg, the painter Mikhail Matiushin (1861–1934) also defended a direct connection between cubism and the fourth dimension through his reading of Gleizes, Metzinger, and some Theosophical authors, Hindu philosophers, and the esotericist P. D. Ouspensky (1878–1947), who introduced the concept of the fourth dimension in Russia in 1909.[7]

For all the reasons given above, the cubist painters were viewed by Ivan Aguéli as the followers of a hermetic and closed school of art, a cerebral and abstract art which is inaccessible to non-initiates. Aguéli, who was fascinated by this artistic movement, shared almost all their ideas, and considered in 1912 that "cubism doesn't fit with the esthetic habits of the masses."[8] Several among the cubist painters were members of occult secret societies such as Freemasonry, the Theosophical Society, or the Rosicrucians, all of which cultivate initiation, a process that cuts the initiates off from the masses, and others were associated more or less with the Traditionalist school of René Guénon. It is not accidental that the *Dictionnaire du cubisme* (Dictionary of Cubism), published in Paris in 2018, has an entry on "Cubism and occultism."[9] Cubism is the expression of a certain form of the sacred; in the eyes of Paulhan, it is a "kind of hierophany (*hiérophanie*)," that is, a manifestation of the sacred. For Paulhan, the sacred is opposed to the profane, the profane world being dominated by the interests and the habitus.[10] Hence, following Apollinaire and Gleizes, Paulhan claimed that cubism will be the "sacred painting" of the twentieth century.[11] Nowadays, in a foreword to an art book on the domed mausoleums of Sufi saints in Morocco, the well-known Moroccan novelist Tahar Ben Jelloun (born 1944) writes that "all spiritualities are an aesthetic of the soul. The aesthetic of the domed mausoleum [*marabout* in French] intimidates because it is stripped-down; its simplicity moves us and leads us back the metaphysic of our main concerns."[12]

This chapter is composed of two parts. The aim of the first one is to question the way Aguéli interpreted cubism as an "occult science" and an "esoteric art." Aguéli's ideas on cubism reflect neither what is cubism in general nor the current mainstream scholarly interpretation of cubism, but rather the interpretation of cubism by an artist immersed in Western and Islamic esotericism, in Swedenborg and Sufism. The second section investigates the place occupied by a particular theme—the domed mausoleum of the Sufi saint—that has pleased many Orientalist painters in Egypt and in northern Africa, cubists or not, among them Aguéli. The domed mausoleum is an architectural structure reduced to a cube and a half-sphere—obviously a very inspiring subject for cubists and for those among them who are gnostics. This second section is actually an extrapolation from Aguéli's ideas on esoteric cubism and its confrontation with the theme of the domed mausoleum. It will question the views of some French artists and painters interested in cubism, such as Gleizes, and the members of the Atelier de la Rose (Studio of the Rose), all of whom can be depicted as "cubist gnostics."

Cubism as an Esoteric Art and an Occult Science

The role played by Aguéli in the history of cubism is unusual. In general, cubism pivots on the metaphysics of the French philosopher Henri Bergson (1859–1941), as demonstrated by Mark Antliff,[13] but not in the case of Aguéli, who never cited or used Bergson, and developed his ideas on cubism separately from Bergson's philosophy, relying rather on Sufism and Swedenborg. Besides, although Bergson was influential on cubism and on Gleizes, he was fiercely opposed by Guénon,[14] who was one of the major intellectual references of Gleizes and of the artists of the Atelier de la Rose.[15] The influence of Bergson on these cubist artists is thus complicated in ways that have not been addressed by Antliff and other researchers. This question needs further study.

Aguéli considers two aspects of cubism. The first one offers a cosmological view in which the place of man and the path he has to follow in order to realize his full potentiality is obvious. This cosmology, though originally Neoplatonic—that is, inspired by the emanatic scheme—is based mainly on the theosophy of Muhyiddin ibn ʿArabi and, indirectly, on the mysticism of Emanuel Swedenborg. Both applied to several arts: painting, sculpture, architecture. The second aspect of Aguéli's view is his interpretation of cubism as a soteriological and contemplative exercise similar to the Sufi *dhikr* (prayer ritual), which will be discussed below.

Cubism, a Cosmology

The reality of things is hidden behind intermediaries, and the goal of those who want to see the essence is to travel up through these intermediaries; for the artist, the aim is to paint this reality in its simpler forms. Cubism can help an artist to do this since, Aguéli writes, it is "a path that leads us unerringly to the *simple truth*, that means utmost uncertainty and little means."[16] The philosophy of this path was explained by a critic in a journal published in 1913; the anonymous author considered, though with a touch of irony, that "matter is no more than a reflection and an aspect of universal energy. From the relations of this reflection to its cause, which is luminous energy, are born what are improperly called objects, and the non-sense of 'form' is established."[17] "Simplicism" and purism are other artistic trends that follow the same aim. For Aguéli, simplicism and purism are "not only the principle of any art but also of any activity of the spirit." Briefly, for Aguéli, "purism" permits one finally "to discover the secrets of ancient art, Greek, Arab, Gothic, and of the Renaissance."[18] In other words, a particular cubism can establish a link with the traditional arts.

Aguéli also thinks that art gives a better understanding of "immobile time" or of the "permanent presence of the extra-temporal and timeless self" (*actualité permanente du moi extra-temporel et immarcescible*). This time leads to the understanding of the fourth dimension and of its esoteric character.[19] At this stage, we must consider two actions of the painter; the first one is the act of painting. The second is the transformational process experienced by the artist. For Aguéli, the act of painting is "no more than an 'occult science'"; the artist must be aware of the "right proportions between distances, lines, and light." This pure art is really esoteric because, as he writes, "nothing can reflect the occult sciences like the complete transmutation of the natural form into the rational forms of Euclidean geometry. Isn't that an action of high sorcery when the concrete life is expressed by such abstract forms?" Here Aguéli compares this phenomenon with the "Great Work" of the alchemists.[20]

Cubism, a Soteriology and a Contemplative Exercise

More important, in my view, are Aguéli's thoughts about numbers and rhythm and their relation to art and cubism as a contemplative exercise. When distinguishing "cerebral" and "sentimental" art, Aguéli noticed that only cerebral art can reveal the "pulsatory movement of life" (*battement pulsatoire de la vie*). He explained that "pulsation means rhythm, that is an action of numbers"[21] and adds that "pure art, according to Gnosis, wants to link the concrete to the abstract, the quantity to the quality, space to time, through the extreme limit of the matter, that is numbers."[22] Aguéli had already drawn attention to the centrality of numbers in art in an article on Ibn 'Arabi published some years before in *Il Convito*.[23]

Elsewhere, Aguéli states that the artist sets up a "personal rhythm" as soon as he learns what are the proportions, that is, the relations between things and living creatures. This rhythm is a "manifestation of pure art, cerebral and esoteric, that is neither ancient nor new, neither Eastern nor Western, neither primitive nor civilized, but only art." Aguéli indicates that if this rhythm wants to manifest itself through a particular envelope, cosmomorphic, anthropomorphic, social, or otherwise, that are called intermediaries, this is hybrid art, sentimental art, exoteric art.[24] Let us mention here, by way of parenthesis, that Gleizes and Guénon also saw the origin of the whole of the arts in the science of rhythm.[25]

Aguéli then went further into his demonstration of the association of art and contemplation. He elaborated a link between the art of the painter and the ritual of the Sufi, especially the *dhikr*, both of which are based on rhythm: "Through the practice of *dhikr* the dervishes [Sufis] learn some particular rhythms. So *dhikr* is a kind of Hatha-Yoga."[26] "Rhythm during a psycho-physiologic movement is no more than numbers. This is why the *dhikr* of the dervishes is the vital assimilation of certain rhythms known by initiates only."[27]

Obviously, Aguéli was referring to elements of the *dhikr* which are based on numbers and rhythm: it might be either the number of repetitions of the names of God, or the varying number of the beats of the rhythmic movements, depending on the *ṭarīqa* (Sufi order), or also the minute regulation of the rhythm of breathing. The question of a possible link between art and rite or ritual was addressed several years later by Émile Dermenghem (1892–1971), a writer of the Guénonian Traditionalist school and an expert on North African Islam. Dermenghem writes in the conclusion of his book on saint veneration in Islam: "The rite, like art, on a symbolic level, brings us into contact with the Reality."[28] In another article, Aguéli reported that "mastery of art is similar to the state of grace in dervishism" and that "both [the artist and the dervish] are marked by a same sign: the sky which opens."[29] Aguéli alluded probably to the ascension of the soul to God and perhaps also to the *mir'āj* (ascension) of the Prophet Muhammad which symbolizes for the Sufis the path to unification with God.

The spiritual function of cubism, as expressed by Aguéli in the early twentieth century, was made clearer, some decades later, by Gleizes, also a member of the

Traditionalist school, and one of the leading theorists of cubism. In the eyes of Robert Pouyaud (1901–70), a post-cubist painter, sculptor, and friend of Gleizes, the "traditional school" of painting established by Gleizes comes from cubism.[30] According to Xavier Accart, Gleizes was convinced that the "traditional artist has represented with sensitive and adequate forms the principles he had contemplated thanks to intellectual intuition, instead of imitating the appearances of things." Besides, "The work of art serves as a support for contemplation; it permits the observer to find these principles in himself."[31] The sacred character of esoteric cubism is clearly demonstrated here and fits perfectly with the ideas of Aguéli. Furthermore, Gleizes and Pouyaud also emphasized the place of rhythm in traditional art.[32]

Esoteric Cubism and Sacred Architecture: An Extrapolation from Aguéli's Ideas

Aguéli was very interested in architecture and noted that "the Arabs, a simplistic people ... who have a perfect understanding of principles and of centralities, have preferred to cultivate music and architecture, primitive forms of art. From the combination of these two 'springs' of art arose all the others."[33]

Aguéli made numerous postimpressionist paintings of the Egyptian landscape, of certain religious buildings (mosques, mausoleums), and of people, some of which have

Figure 6.1 Ivan Aguéli, *Egyptiskt kupolhus* (Egyptian Domed House), *c.* 1914. Oil on canvas, 21.5 x 30.5 cm. Photo: Moderna Museet, Stockholm. Full-color image available at www.aguelimuseet.se/6_1 and on the publisher's website.

Figure 6.2 Ivan Aguéli, *Kalifgravarna* (Tombs of the Caliphs), *c.* 1895. Oil on canvas, 50 x 87 cm. Photo: Moderna Museet, Stockholm. Full-color image available at www.aguelimuseet. se/6_2 and on the publisher's website.

Figure 6.3 Ivan Aguéli, *Moské II* (Mosque II), 1914–15. Oil on canvas, 23 x 29.5 cm. Prins Eugens Waldemarsudde. Full-color image available at www.aguelimuseet.se/6_3 and on the publisher's website.

already been discussed in earlier chapters.[34] One of his paintings, *Egyptiskt kupolhus* (Egyptian Domed House), already discussed in Chapter 5, represents the domed mausoleum of a Sufi saint (Figure 6.1); this building also appears in Aguéli's other paintings (Figures 6.2 and 6.3). I do not know if Aguéli wrote any commentaries about the architecture of this religious building, composed basically of a cube and a dome (half a sphere), since this structure is a natural model par excellence for cubism.

The domed mausoleum has drawn the interest of many artists and photographers who have visited Egypt and North Africa.[35] This religious structure is first and foremost an essential element in the local landscape and a major holy place, along with the mosque; especially, it is emblematic of a certain understanding of Sufism. Secondly, its unusual shape and its beauty have fascinated Westerners, and for all these reasons it was painted by many artists who visited North Africa and the Middle East, including Eugène Fromentin (1820–76), Eugène Delacroix (1798–1863), Étienne Dinet (1861–1929), Auguste Chabaud (1882–1955), Paul Klee (1879–1940), Henri Matisse (1869–1954), and Victor Prouvé (1858–1943).[36] Matisse in particular was very attracted to this edifice at the moment when he was interested in cubism and in "pure art." Jade Cowart, who studied Matisse's paintings and drawings in Morocco, points to the role played by such architectural structures on the artist's vision of art and cubism in particular. We know several paintings and drawings of the domed mausoleum by Matisse; one—*Le marabout* (see Figure 6.4)—is a postimpressionist painting, a second

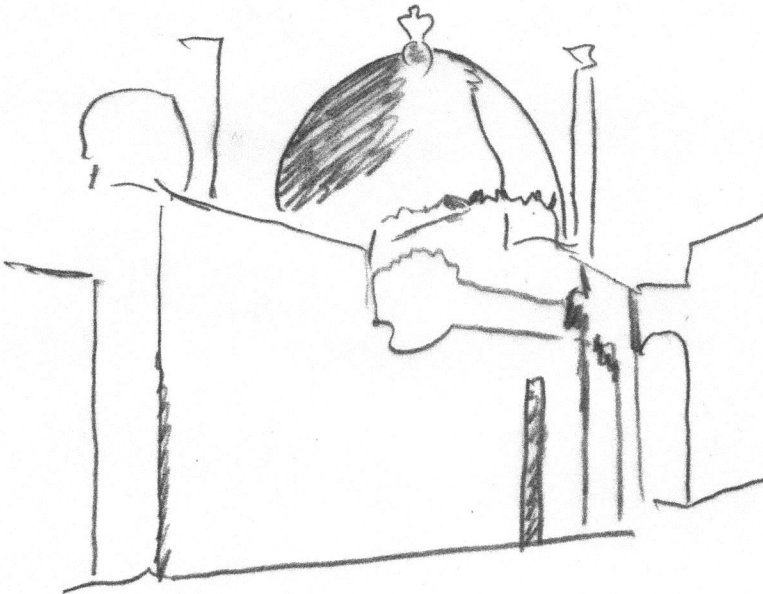

Figure 6.4 Sketch after Henri Matisse, *Le marabout* (The Marabout), 1912–13. Sketch by Thierry Zarcone.

one is a "realist cubist" drawing—*Casbah* (see Figure 6.5)—and another is a cubist painting—*Les Marocains* (see Figure 6.6). Cowart suggests that the structure of the domed mausoleum may have drawn Matisse to cubism. She writes:

> There is a more telling contemporary context, however, for the treatment of the compositional elements of this drawing of the *marabout* [domed mausoleum, Figure 6.4]: Matisse's evolving relationship to Parisian cubism. This 1912/1913 drawing announces a drawing and painting style (one of analysis, structure, and economy) central to Matisse's later work in 1914–15. In *Casbah: le marabout* [Figure 6.5] geometry prevails as white rectangles and triangles intersect project, recede. It is a kind of observed, rational cubism, more in the spirit of Cézanne than Picasso or Braque. The seeds for Matisse's cubist-period future seem to have been planted during his Moroccan experiences. Several years later he produced in a "cubist" mode a series of portrait drawings, still lifes, and large paintings not the least of which is the monumental *Les Marocains* [Figure 6.6].[37]

Figure 6.5 Sketch after Henri Matisse, *Casbah: le marabout* (The Kasbah: The Marabout), 1912–13. Sketch by Thierry Zarcone.

Figure 6.6 Sketch after Henri Matisse, *Les Marocains* (The Moroccans), 1915–16. Sketch by Thierry Zarcone.

The domed mausoleum in Matisse's *Les Marocains* (Figure 6.6) was painted in the cubist style compared to *Le Marabout* (Figure 6.4), which is postimpressionist, similar actually to the *Egyptian Domed House* of Aguéli (Figure 6.1). Besides, according to Cowart, the *Casbah: le marabout* (Figure 6.5) of Matisse reflects rational cubism. This rational cubism is expressed also by the Provençal painter Chabaud, who spent several years in Tunisia where he painted domed mausoleums (see his drawing *Tunisienne devant le marabout*, Figure 6.7).[38]

Whether it is painted by a cubist or a postimpressionist brush, the domed mausoleum theme is actually beyond the schools of painting; its compositional elements are simple and, as I show below, it is a natural model for esoteric cubism. A suggestive example could be the representation in 1908 by the cubist painter Georges Braque of the *Maisons à l'Estaque* (Houses of l'Estaque), near Marseille: the house here perfectly resembles a North African mausoleum with a conical dome instead of a cupola (Figure 6.8).[39] Even nowadays, the domed mausoleum is still an attractive model for a painter in search of simplicity and harmony, such as Mohamed Hamidi, who is regarded as "the master of cubism in Morocco." Hamidi says—like Aguéli decades before—that his "aim is to build a universe of architectural forms that will launch a search for harmony."[40] Some of Hamidi's paintings in the "form of a dome," actually a domed mausoleum (Figure 6.9), are regarded by art critic Farid Zahi as an "ascetic symbol" which, in his eyes, is not surprising since—he writes—the painter lives in Casablanca, not far from the city of Moulay Bouchaid, a well-known Sufi saint (*marabout*) buried in a domed edifice.[41] Zahi's analysis might suggest that Hamidi is a gnostic cubist.

Figure 6.7 Auguste Chabaud, *Tunisienne devant le marabout* (Tunisian Woman in front of the Marabout). Pencil on paper, 32 x 25 cm. Collection of Thierry Zarcone.

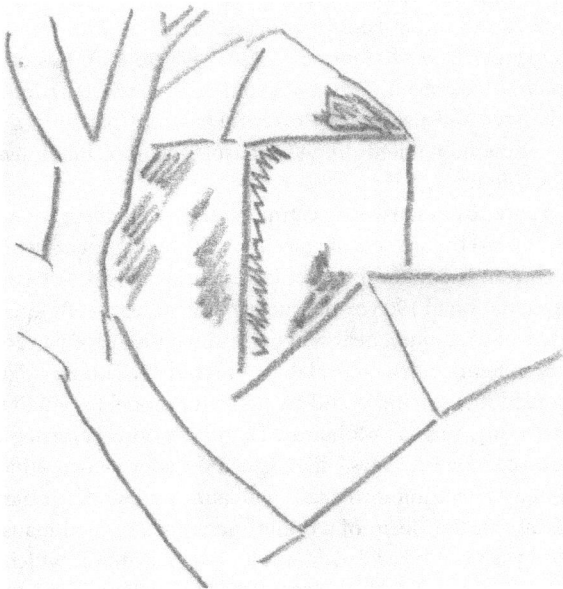

Figure 6.8 Sketch after Georges Braque, *Maisons à l'Estaque* (Houses of l'Estaque), 1908. Sketch by Thierry Zarcone.

Aguéli translated some chapters of the gigantic *Futuhat al-makkiyya* (Meccan Revelations) of Ibn ʿArabi but it is not known if he read the chapter of this book where the Andalusian Sufi has a discussion of the symbols of square and circle that links well (in my view)—Theosophically speaking—the ideas of Aguéli on esoteric cubism with the architectural and geometrical structure of the domed mausoleum. Ibn ʿArabi discussed the cubic nature of the heart, which also resembles the Kaʿba in Mecca. He explained that the heart has six faces or six spatial directions, corresponding to the six faces of a cube. Stephen Hirtenstein (who depicts Ibn ʿArabi as the original cubist) writes that "the heart through its faces encompasses God's manifestation to it in each face, and becomes wholly light."[42] He adds that "we may then conceive of our inner human consciousness as a cube, which faces outward into the six directions of the outer world … In other words, when the singleness of the six-faced cube is revealed, it becomes unified and spherical."[43] The idea that the heart has a central role in the spiritual path was well known to Aguéli; he wrote in the periodical *Il Convito* that the heart, as the center of life (*centro della vita*), is positioned between the higher faculty of

Figure 6.9 Sketch after Mohamed Hamidi, from a series called "dome-shaped structure," *c.* 2009. Sketch by Thierry Zarcone.

man and that of animality. The heart is no more than the sun which revives all things.[44] During one of his spiritual illumination that happened at Fez, in Morocco, in 1197, Ibn ʿArabi confessed that he had experienced in his body the reality of this translation from the square to the sphere. He wrote:

> I was leading a group of people in prayer in al-Azhar Mosque when I saw it as a light which was almost more visible than what was in front of me, except that I had lost all sense of behind [or in front]. I no longer had a back or the nape of a neck. While the vision lasted, I had no sense of direction, as if I had become completely spherical. Any sense of direction I might have had was simply hypothetical, not what I actually experienced.[45]

Conclusion

Aguéli was the first to attribute to cubism, in 1911, a transcendental and esoteric value.[46] Besides, he occupied an unusual place in Orientalist painting, both as an Orientalist who mastered Arabic perfectly and as a talented painter. As a theorist of art, he established the bases of an esoteric art deeply inspired by cubism and "pure art" that was later called "traditional art" by Gleizes and his French followers. There are two characteristics of this "traditional art," also named "esoteric cubism." The first one is cosmological, since the painter considers the universe as based on the emanatic scheme of the Neoplatonists, also reflected in Ibn ʿArabi's theosophy. Consequently, the art of painting consists of picturing the simplicity of the Being behind the forms (appearance). The second characteristic is soteriological: while painting, the artist practices an exercise based on the Sufi *dhikr* and on the Hatha Yoga; its results remind us of the illumination of Ibn ʿArabi in Fez in the thirteenth century. Regarding the domed mausoleum, which pleased Aguéli, we can propose that such a structure embodies both cosmology and soteriology. Ibn ʿArabi showed the link between the square/cube (the human) and the circle/dome (the perfect human) who is produced by the projection of the square.

Kill the Audience: Ivan Aguéli's Universal Utopia of Anarchism and Islam

Anthony T. Fiscella

We might imagine each person as a living jigsaw puzzle whose various pieces shift and flow into different shapes and configurations over time. Historians necessarily simplify this complexity with labels and stories that typically annihilate many of a person's "puzzle pieces" in order to highlight a few that they deem particularly important (often revealing as much about their own priorities and interests as their object of study). I shall do exactly that now by presenting a highly condensed (and necessarily distorted) version of the life of a child born in Sala, Sweden, on May 24, 1869, and given the name "John Gustaf Agelii." While associating his life with labels such as "anarchism" and "Islam" we do well to recall that these concepts, too, entail a wide variety of shifting parts. We examine but a few through his life. In general, this chapter aims to convey an image of Ivan Aguéli's anarchism and Islam as closely interwoven with both Theosophy and concern for animals.

Agelii's birth preceded that of Emma Goldman by one month and Mohandas Gandhi by five months. During his young adulthood he saw a world in rapid transition. In less than twenty years, between 1894 and 1913, at least thirteen heads of state in Europe, the Middle East, and the United States fell to (mostly anarchist) assassins. After the assassination of Austrian Archduke Francis Ferdinand in 1914, Europe exploded into war.

The turbulence of the late nineteenth century, marked by civil wars, anticolonial revolts, the Paris Commune, the invention of dynamite and telephones, etc., contrasted with that of small-town life in Sweden where Agelii could overhear animals suffering at the hands of his father, a veterinarian.[1] In his late teens, he frequented the home and fancied the daughter of a pastor in the Swedenborgian congregation of Stockholm, Adolph Boyesen. As Simon Sorgenfrei noted, Boyesen provided a "complete opposite" type of father-figure for Agelii. Rather than critical and disciplinarian like his father, Boyesen provided an example of love and reason.[2] Agelii, a distant relative to Emmanuel Swedenborg through his mother's side of the family, seemed to take Boyesen's (and Swedenborg's) teachings to heart. In 1889 Pastor Boyesen gave a speech at the annual gathering of Djurvännernas nya förening (the New Union of Friends of Animals), which Agelii might have attended. In this sermon, entitled "Hvarför är det Plikt att Behandla Djuren med Godhet" (Why it is a Duty to Treat Animals with Kindness), Boyesen buttressed support for animal rights with quotes from Matthew 25, where Jesus told his followers, "That which you have done for the least of my brothers you have also done for me." For Boyesen asserted that although animals have a lower "degree" of life than humans, their life stems from the same source as humans—God— and this makes them our divine kin.

> That which we call animal and that which we call human is in the Word of the Lord not described with any word other than life. That is the common expression for everything, both for the soul of humans and the soul of animals ... If humans had this conviction, that these are the Lord's lowest form of life, that what we do to them, we do to Him, then I am convinced that the heart of humans would be warmed by an entirely different love than the one that now moves within them and is the inclination and cause behind many of their bad actions against animals.[3]

In particular, Boyesen described the story of a large ox painfully dragged by a ring in his nose up a hill and toward a butcher. The ox shook from the pain and "fell down exhausted on his knees" whereupon he "veritably prayed to his executioners for mercy." Boyesen emphasized the reaction of the audience of people in the street:

> No one raised their voice against this cannibalistic behavior. The stupid crowd stood around him and laughed. They took delight in watching this big powerful animal fall down literally subjugated by the torture that these human beasts had prepared for it. I may as well ask each person who still retains a spark of feeling in their chest, is it not revolting to see such things take place? And what is worse is that it took place in a Christian country on a public street and no one raised their voice to oppose such cruelty ... For those who still bear human feelings, it is disgusting to see, that there is no justice for the poor defenseless animal, that people—with law and courts on their side—can both causally and publicly so cruelly display such heartlessness. This contributes to the annihilation of feelings of empathy in the heart of humans such that both young and old could, with mirth in their mouths, watch an animal overwhelmed by pain collapse at the hands of its human torturers.[4]

The now-depraved Christian world had lost its once perfect relationship to God and animals and forgotten how to find its way back to its utopian origins. Swedenborg's teachings would resolve this. Through "divine love" those with understanding would "raise their voice and ... strive to remove the sleep of death among those who have no sensation of pain except when it concerns their own skin."[5] For, while each human contains heaven and earth inside her, she only actualizes the image of God by allowing divine love and wisdom to guide "everything she does" and "exercises them in daily life ... That's how people were in the so-called golden age."[6] With a touch of millenarianism Boyesen struck an activist tone:

One must act so that others awaken from their sleep of death and, for once, get even these people to act for the liberation of animals from their misery and the pains for which they heave. Then a new day will have unfolded for humankind, then a new epoch will have begun, and then, we could say, a new sun will have risen in the sky of the human heart in the entirety of the infinite universe. A new era![7]

While the teaching of Emmanuel Swedenborg played a significant role in breaking ground for the later development of Theosophy and New Age movements, it played an even more significant and direct role on Agelii throughout his life (and, one could note, he later joined a Theosophical lodge in Paris).[8] As Sorgenfrei has written elsewhere, "Swedenborg is ever present like a handrail through all of Aguéli's diverse activities."[9] Holding on to this handrail, John Gustaf Agelii gradually transitioned into Ivan Aguéli as he ravenously began learning several languages, developed his painting skills, explored the Qur'an and the *Tao Te Ching (Dàodé Jīng)*, and consumed the works of Dostoyevsky, Turgenev, Baudelaire, Nietzsche, Ibsen, and Strindberg. Tolstoy, in particular, left a notable imprint on him. Later in life he said, "Except for Tolstoy and some young Russian writers, I have no desire for any novel writer or philosopher."[10] Here too he could find some familiar themes, from Tolstoy's vegetarianism and anarchism to the critically minded Friedrich Nietzsche. The latter wrote in 1874 that the "deeper minds of all ages have had pity for animals" and that "Nature" needs the artist, philosopher, and saint—all roles that Aguéli seemed to aspire toward. Of the last role, Nietzsche wrote, "In him the ego has melted away, and the suffering of his life is, practically, no longer felt as individual, but as the spring of the deepest sympathy and intimacy with all living creatures ... in whose light we understand the word 'I' no longer."[11] This echoed Swedenborg's admonition: "We are to undergo a process of annihilation, or becoming nothing."[12] Helen Keller (1880–1968), both a Swedenborgian and syndicalist, wrote "beneficence includes many gifts, but above all the power of going out of oneself and appreciating whatever is noble in man and wonderful in the universe ... We can now meet death as nature does, in a blaze of glory, marching to the grave with a cheerful step."[13] Aguéli himself later wrote: "I hardly care for my own pain and worry. For I—I *do not exist*! I *am not*. There is nothing more godless than crying: 'Me! Me!'"[14] This general theology seemed to remain with Aguéli throughout his life: "This is how I conceive a modern monotheist in terms of outer morality: fanatical toward oneself, tolerant toward others, an intense thirst for the infinite."[15]

Collective Oneness: From Anarchism to Islam

As anarchist ideas, writings, and practices swept across Europe, Aguéli moved along with them to France and even to London, where he met Peter Kropotkin. Although Aguéli met with Kropotkin in 1891 and did not formally convert to Islam until approximately 1898, his interest in anarchism and Islam grew simultaneously. As we have seen, he first borrowed the Qur'an from the National Library of Sweden (Kungliga biblioteket) in Stockholm in 1892. Also, his concern for animals rooted itself in his social life when, in 1893, he met vegetarian and fellow Theosophist Marie Huot. Huot had a prominent position in the Ligue populaire contre la vivisection (Popular League against Vivisection), founded France's first animal protection home, and once physically attacked a professor about to perform vivisection on a monkey.[16]

Anarchism attracted Aguéli in part due to its emphasis on direct action. He wrote that "only the anarchists are really moving the world forward … But socialists are arming themselves for seats in parliament."[17] In July 1893 he partook in riots in Paris and a few months later wrote to Richard Bergh:

> I have followed political developments rather intensively since the student unrest. I participated, of course. Contributed with heart and soul some material to the barricades … I have never in my life had such a good time … Our Lord initiated that revolution just in order for me to learn how a *real* revolution should be staged. Have had revolutionary fever since then. Have visited old anarchist friends, they wondered where I have been all this time. They live in the neighborhood, and we meet almost every day … It is a beautiful phenomenon, anarchism. It is for certain the most beautiful in our filthy time. Imagine a sunrise and a sunset at the same time. The dynamiters' superb, mindful, calm heroism; the revenge of the culture victims; the dreams of utopians, intuition, and artists—this may be a pale light, but it embodies the first rays of the new sun.[18]

During the same year, Swedish painter Olof Sager-Nelson (1868–96) portrayed him as "The Anarchist" (Figure 7.1).

However, he combined this apparent enthusiasm for social change with a strong dose of fatalism and wrote in a letter in 1894: "Why cry against an inevitable fate?"[19] It appears that he saw his actions and his commitments as tied to forces beyond his control and viewed hardship as opportunity embedded into the ebb and flow of life's challenges:

> Difficult circumstances, poverty, and the antagonism of enemies are only a lesson and lead to increased boldness externally and to a perfect closeness to God internally. … Praise is due to Allah forever! "After difficulty comes relief" (see the Qur'an, sura 94, 5–6). In actuality constraint and liberation lead to the same result for the one who is blessed, just as they lead to the same result for the one who is cursed.[20]

In 1894 French police arrested Aguéli on charges of belonging to an anarchist criminal association, and he spent four months in Mazas Prison awaiting trial where, among other things, he studied Swedenborg and Arabic literature. Whether reading anarchism, Islam, Lao Tzu, or Swedenborg, Aguéli found a radical egalitarianism that tied together opposites into a complementary whole. This opposition to social hierarchy fueled his rejection of clergy (a rejection shared by anarchists and Muslims). In an unpublished letter that he had written to the Swedish anarchist periodical *Brand* in approximately 1911, Aguéli disparaged "social democrats who utopianize into an imperial order," "anarchists whose individualism has blown into snobbery," and "the

Figure 7.1 Olof Sager-Nelson, *Anarkisten* (The Anarchist, i.e., Ivan Aguéli), 1893. Oil on canvas, 60 x 36.6 cm. Värmlands Museum, Karlstad. Full-color image available at www.aguelimuseet.se/7_1 and on the publisher's website.

clerical danger," while arguing that the solution to the apparent conflict between individual and community lay in first realizing their harmony rather than antagonism and secondly in solidarity that extends hierarchically from self-care to care for others and then to the world:

> As there exist many degrees of distinction between one and everyone, the question of harmony between the revolution of individuals and the general revolution will remain an ongoing problem that every age, every decade or century resolves, for the moment, in its own most appropriate manner. We have already received the solution of our generation. The union of individualism and solidarity has worked with tremendous impact right under our eyes for several years. This union is called syndicalism, and it is the only possible form of cooperation between socialism and anarchy. This is the secret of its enormous success and rapid spread.[21]

And what did this "syndicalism" entail that had captured the imagination of Ivan Aguéli? One might describe syndicalism as a sort of worker-run communism that bypasses the state. The movement started in Europe in the late 1800s and took particularly strong hold among unions in Spain and France. While many socialists saw the parliament or political revolution as a means to take over the state, syndicalists felt that workers themselves needed to organize in order to run all aspects of society directly. They would use union-organizing, cooperatives, collectivization of industries, direct action, and the general strike as means to gradually assume power. Even at the grassroots level, the principles of syndicalism contrasted with pro-state socialists.[22] As Rudolf Rocker wrote, the "organisation of Anarcho-Syndicalism is based on the principles of Federalism, on free combination from below upward, putting the right of self-determination of every member above everything else and recognising only the organic agreement of all on the basis of like interests and common convictions."[23]

As soon as he left prison, Aguéli set sail toward Egypt for the first time and arrived in September 1894. Anarchists seemed to have the tide of the times with their cause as hundreds of thousands of people joined the struggle against state and capital. In some cases anarchists engaged in revolts taking place in predominantly Muslim countries. For example, Errico Malatesta (1853–1932) from Italy joined the 1882 'Urabi revolt in Egypt against the British; Macedonian-Bulgarian anarchists known as Gemidzhi (the "Boatmen of Thessaloniki") resisted Ottoman occupation in 1898–1903 (through planned and actual attacks on post offices, railway, ships, banks, and the sultan); and Belgian anarchists such as Edward Joris (1876–1957) assisted Armenian revolutionaries in the attempted assassination of Ottoman Caliph and Sultan Abdülhamid II in Constantinople in 1905 as a response to the massacre of tens (if not hundreds) of thousands of Armenians.[24] In Egypt, Shibli Shumayyil (1850–1917) wrote perhaps the first Arabic text on contemporary anarchism in 1898.[25] As Anthony Gorman described the period during which Aguéli lived in Egypt:

> In the fifty years before World War I an anarchist community emerged in Egypt sustained by an expanding Mediterranean network of migration, labour mobility, communications and transport. Initially taken up by elements in the resident

Italian community, it was gradually embraced by members of other communities who shared a radical view of social emancipation ... In the decade and a half before World War I anarcho-syndicalism, typified by the "international" union, was a leading force in the organization and development of a militant labour movement. Calling for international solidarity among all workers, it adapted with little effort to a society characterised by ethnic and religious pluralism and articulated an anti-capitalist, anti-nationalist discourse as it did battle with nationalist and other forces in seeking the support of the popular classes in Egypt.[26]

Although he identified as an anarchist (except when questioned by police in 1894), Aguéli did not seem to spend time with anarchist workers in Egypt who organized themselves into unions in the printing, tailoring, transportation, and cigarette industries.[27] Nor did he seem to have contact with (or interest in) the anarchist-organized Free Popular University in Alexandria.[28] Rather, his anarchist vision seemed closer to an "Islamic aristo-democracy," as he would later term it, led by an elite of humble yet principled pauper-mystics committed to the all-embracing principle of *tawḥīd* (oneness or Divine unity).[29] Indeed, his friends described his lifestyle as minimalistic: living on dry bread, figs, and water in a tiny apartment about two and half square meters with no furniture—only books (upon which he slept).[30] He did not seem to lead a social life like most anarchists or Sufis, but lived more like an ascetic, an outcast, or a hermit.

As reported earlier, Shaykh ʿAbd al-Rahman ʿIllaysh initiated him into the ʿArabiyya-Shadhiliyya[31] and Aguéli began to write under the name Abdul-Hadi. Significantly, ʿIllaysh introduced Aguéli to the writings of Muhyiddin ibn ʿArabi, who would come to profoundly inspire Aguéli who seemed to draw his model for social organization from what Ibn ʿArabi idealized as "the Malamatiyya" (the blameworthy— not the Sufi *ṭarīqa* or order of the same name—although the two certainly overlap to some degree). Aguéli translated Ibn ʿArabi's description of them into French in *La Gnose* in 1911: "Their rule obliges them not to show their merits and not to hide their faults." Among their further attributes we find "voluntary poverty," "constraint of passions," and "obedience to the prophetic tradition."[32]

His particular theology not only saw a complementarity between individual and collective but annihilated the gap between them at an esoteric and practical level. In other words, through a literal interpretation of *tawḥīd*, all various forms of existence unite in a single manifestation which only *appear* separate and distinct. In this way, Aguéli united an empirical oneness of existence (not necessarily bound to—and potentially independent of—theology) with conceptions of *tawḥīd*. In "L'Universalité en l'Islam" (Universality in Islam), published in *La Gnose* in 1911 and translated as Chapter 19 in this book, he wrote that to understand oneself in an esoteric sense entailed releasing attachment to one's desires, body, and personality and "following one's destiny *obediently and consciously*, which means to live, to live one's entire life, which is that of all lives, that is to say, to live the lives of all beings."[33] In order to understand humility we must therefore understand existential oneness and the fact that life "is not at all divisible."[34] He lingered on this topic in order to help the reader grasp its gravity:

Let it be said right at the outset that the term altruism is an empty word; it should be banned from metaphysical discourse, because that "other" does not exist. There is not the slightest difference between you and the others. You are the others, all others, all things. All things and all the others are you. We are only mutual reflections of one another. There is but one life, and all individualities are only inferences of the destiny that radiates in the crystal of creation. The identity of self and non-self is the Great Truth, just as the realization of this identity is the Great Work. If, in the case of a robbery, you cannot understand that you are the robber at the same time as you are the robbed; that, in case of murder, you are simultaneously the murderer and the victim; if you do not blush from shame or guilt at the account of a monstrous, novel, and inconceivable crime that you have never in your life been tempted to commit; if you do not even minimally feel that you had something to do with the earthquake in Turkestan or the plague in Manchuria, then you had better give up your esoteric studies, because you are wasting your time.[35]

This understanding of the oneness of all existence did not preclude an understanding of difference and distinction which, due to gradation, disguise fundamental unity.[36] Abdul Hadi also emphasized animals and their role. First, "it is more perfect, more pure, to give to one who appears weak or inferior than to one who is on an equal footing, or more powerful." Second, from "an esoteric point of view, to give to a species far removed from one's own is better than giving to one's fellow [human]." Third and lastly, a "taste for the exotic, a love of animals, and a passion for the study of nature are such indications of an esoteric disposition … Good done to an animal draws us even closer to God because our egoism is less invested in this, at least in ordinary situations."[37] Nonetheless, compassion for animals only constituted a first step: "True charity begins at the level of the beast; it continues on to that of plants."[38]

Still, animals figured strongly in his personal life. Farid Nur ad-Din wrote, "At almost every stage of Abdul Hadi's life, be it in Paris or Cairo, he nearly always had a number of street cats in his care."[39] In particular he had taken care of a "starving, one-eyed, toothless, and pregnant street-cat" in Colombo in 1899 whom he named Mabruka ("the blessed one;" see Figure 7.2) and whom he took with him on his long journeys. He began (but apparently never finished) a translation of medieval writer Ramon Llull's *Llibre de les bèsties* (The Book of Beasts) which, like *Animal Farm*, described the unjust exploitation of animals by humans while also using animal relations as metaphors for human relations.[40] Both books also seemed to draw inspiration from Arabic renditions of Indian folk tales: Epistle 22 by the Ikhwan al-Safa (Brethren of Purity) and *Kalila wa Dimna*. Certainly, when reading the Qur'an, he would have found numerous verses expressing concern for animals and their part in God's plan including verse 55:10 stating that God assigned the earth (*waḍa 'ahā*) "to all living creatures" (*li'l-anām*).[41] And he may also have found similar themes in his conversations with Kropotkin prior to the latter's publication of *Mutual Aid* wherein Kropotkin wrote: "Happily enough, competition is not the rule in the animal world or in mankind … Better conditions are created by the elimination of competition by means of mutual aid and mutual support … natural selection picks out of the ants' family the species which know best how to

Figure 7.2 Ivan Aguéli, *Liggande katt* (Reclining Cat), 1890s. Oil on canvas, 40 x 38 cm. Photo: Moderna Museet, Stockholm. Full-color image available at www.aguelimuseet. se/7_2 and on the publisher's website.

avoid competition as much as possible."[42] Although Abdul Hadi did not ever publicly discuss his vegetarianism or write a manifesto advocating animal rights (or liberation), his concern for animals clearly permeated his daily life, his ethics, and one of the most decisive public stances he ever made. When Spanish bullfights took place in Paris in 1900, he felt compelled to act.

Kill the Audience: From Passion to Action

Spanish bullfights (in contrast to French bullfights) entail killing the bull at the end. The last portion of the nineteenth century saw several attempts to introduce Spanish bullfighting in France, yet many French—especially among the elites—opposed it. Prominent French personalities, including Napoleon III, a strong supporter of the Société protectrice des animaux (Society for the Protection of Animals), had opposed the practice for years.[43] When Aguéli heard about the plan to introduce Spanish bullfighting in Paris, he interrupted his stay in Ceylon and returned to Europe.[44] When the day came for the bullfight in Deuil, just north of Paris, on June 4, 1900, Aguéli, Huot (dressed exotically in Renaissance attire), and other protestors attended. While others blew whistles in protest at the event, Aguéli pulled out a revolver and fired two shots at the matador, who sunk his head at the very moment the shots went off, sending the bullets into banderillero Ramón Laborda (but did not seriously wound him). Security forces (*gendarmerie*) wrestled Aguéli to the ground and the show continued.

Later, when police questioned Aguéli after the attack, he declared unapologetically: "I have through my actions wanted to express the deep disgust that the Spanish bullfighting awakens in me ... They are a school for cowardice and brutality. They mark the fateful development towards the downfall of a nation."[45] When the police interjected that he did not come from France, Aguéli responded enthusiastically: "That doesn't matter. My fatherland is the universe. If I have shot at the matadors it is because I could not shoot the most guilty, that is, the audience. I had in fact no more than two francs and eighty centimes, and I would have needed at least five francs to enter the circus building."[46] His startled interrogators continued, "So you would, if you had come in, fired your revolver on the general public?" "Without a doubt," Aguéli replied (as if channeling the fury of Boyesen's condemnation of the crowd who gleefully watched a tortured ox).[47] While in jail between the fifth and eleventh of June, 1900, Aguéli continued to justify his action:

> If I had allowed the performance of this evil act to take place within the scope of my vision, without doing anything about it, I would have to answer before God as an accomplice to a criminal. I stake no claim to influence the order of things directly, either in great matters or small. I am not a tool of fate. I would find such a claim to be silly, if not blasphemous, in light of the unchangeable order of things. A [person] can only act according to the law of [their] conscience and [their] innermost being. I have done this. But the success or failure of things belongs to God alone.[48]

While not quite approaching biocentrism, Aguéli came close to it when he expressed an anthropocentrism clearly limited by responsibilities in accordance with its privileges. According to Aguéli, humans, with a status above animals, have an obligation to care for all lower forms of life because, as difficult as it may feel to see ourselves in other humans, it proves all the more difficult to recall in relation to plants and animals, whom we kill and eat, that we "are simultaneously the murderer and the victim" (as cited above):

> Bullfighting leads undeniably to a nation's downfall ... I confess completely openly that these animals were of more concern to me and infinitely more beautiful than

the mob around me. They suffer like us, maybe more, their minds are a mystery for us. But they certainly knew that they were victims while the others were not aware that they were executioners. There is no high crime against humanity in my act. [People] who deny their own humanity sink lower than animals precisely because they stood above them ... She [humanity] could not have sunk so low if she had not previously stood so high. Theologians and philosophers are of this same opinion, even the wise of the nations agree. I repeat that the bulls and horses in the amphitheater are closer to my heart than the satanic executioners with human faces who torture and kill them or who, with pleasure, stand and watch. The latter of these are particularly sickening. It is these people, not me, who have committed a crime against humanity. I have proven my humanity by protesting against those possessed [as if by demons]. I have confirmed humanity's nobility and royalty by defending those lower than me from my equals.[49]

When told that, regardless of his ostensibly noble intent, he had no right to shoot at people, Aguéli responded: "As far as I am concerned, they are not humans, they are bloodthirsty sorts whose human rights ought to be denied."[50] Amazingly enough, the judge felt swayed by Aguéli's unapologetic defense of his act and sentenced him only to probation.[51] Aguéli, perhaps for the only time, had the masses behind him, and the government banned Spanish bullfighting.[52]

Yet his stardom remained short-lived as did his enthusiasm for the anarchist movement. Within a decade, anarchists whom he admired seemed to have left the cause and he felt betrayed by his close anarchist friend Enrico Insabato who, as a secret agent for the Italian police, supported Italian colonization of Libya.[53] He also felt isolated from the anarchist movement in general, writing "I have always locked horns with these men and they have played several pranks on me personally when all I did was attack their business ... the stupid anarchists want me to be the brunt of their jokes, and freely at that."[54] Again, he seemed to accept this fate, writing: "Freedom cannot be *received* or *given*; it has to be *taken* through sacrifice. Freedom without cost is a joyless enterprise."[55] His isolation from the movement, however, would seem to cost him his life. In 1916, the British expelled him from Egypt as a suspected opponent of their war effort, and he settled down in Barcelona where the newly started Spanish anarcho-syndicalist union Confederación Nacional del Trabajo (CNT) had huge support. They prepared for revolution yet instead of merging with the syndicalists whose ideology he shared, Aguéli felt harassed and described a class hate toward him by the locals. While Europe raged with war, local workers seemed hardly impressed by a painter living on family money. They more likely saw him as a spy. After a group attacked him, he wrote: "Either I will be forbidden from painting out in the open or I will be killed by the mob."[56] In Russia, the Bolshevik Revolution would change the world in a matter of weeks. Yet Ivan Aguéli/Abdul Hadi would not live to see it. On October 1, 1917, he breathed his last breath when a train mysteriously hit him in the early morning. It might seem like a miserable end or even a failure. Yet, from the perspective he described of the Malamatiyya, he succeeded phenomenally in living without ever selling his soul, without celebration of his merits, and dying as humbly as those whose lives he defended.

Concluding Thoughts: From Life to Legacy

As we have seen, Ivan Aguéli/Abdul Hadi's anarchism, Islam, and defense of animals did not manifest separately but intertwined with one another as well as with his Theosophy, Swedenborgian influence, and personal relationships, from Boyesen to Kropotkin, from his mother to Huot. Like a living jigsaw puzzle, each of these aspects interconnected with others even while they shifted and changed somewhat during his life. During certain phases, some elements took center stage. Later, other elements or personalities would figure larger. Yet, throughout his life, Aguéli crafted—mostly in ways not visible or obvious in his well-known artwork—his own particular blend and evolving balance between them behind the scenes. His personal visions of syndicalism and Islam hardly reflected those of the majority of his syndicalist or Muslim contemporaries yet they remain at the cutting edge of contemporary issues. Beyond models of integration, accommodation, segregation, or jihadi pursuit of an "imaginary *umma*," he sought to set age-old Sufi values and internal *jihad* (struggle) at the heart of societal transformation of both East and West. And rather than leave syndicalism dependent upon international union-organizing, he saw the potential for civilization-critique and the personal austerity of an enlightened elite to lead by example toward an egalitarian society with the universe as its nation and with all existence—not just humans—as its citizenry.[57]

At the core of his worldview lay a profound commitment to existential oneness. Unlike many mystical and philosophical conceptions of oneness, his vision necessarily implied a social program, direct action, defense of animals, and a commitment to act without attachment to (or expectation of) results as a concrete response to interdependence. As Lori Gruen wrote: "We are entangled in complex relationships and rather than trying to accomplish the impossible by pretending we can disentangle, we would do better to think about how to be more perceptive and more responsive to the deeply entangled relationships we are in … Being aware of our place in a web of life matters."[58]

To some degree—primarily through the work of Mark Sedgwick and Robert Carleson—Aguéli has received recognition for his pioneering work and role in the early development of contemporary Traditionalism.[59] Yet, Aguéli/Abdul Hadi's radical defense of animals and his blend of anarchism and Islam (as early as that of Isabelle Eberhardt [1877–1904] if not earlier),[60] which long preceded Peter Lamborn Wilson (aka Hakim Bey), have not received much recognition.[61] Not only have most works related to this period completely ignored him (works related to European anarchism in the region, histories of animal rights in Islam, etc.), Wilson could barely remember his name when talking about him,[62] the English *Wikipedia*'s entry on Aguéli completely ignored his direct action against bullfighting, and an entire issue of the Swedish scholarly journal *Aura* devoted to Aguéli in 2017 mentioned his commitment to animal rights only twice in passing.[63] A lack of translation may have played a role. In Sweden, Aguéli has influenced fellow Sufi-syndicalist Torbjörn Säfve (who, like Wilson, joined the Ibn 'Arabi Society), well-known poet and blogger Mohamed Omar (now Eddie Råbock) who named his publishing company after Aguéli, and an apparently non-

Muslim, anarcho-primitivist Earth Liberation Front activist, Jonatan Strandberg, also known as Jonatan Agueli, behind the blog *AgueliAgainstCivilization*, with the motto: "If my life is one of struggle then maybe my grandchildren's life will be one of cleaner water and at least a few cities in ruins."[64]

Aguéli/Abdul Hadi apparently never described anarchism in Islamic terms nor Islam in anarchist terms. The closest instance came perhaps when he wrote: "The man who realizes that the Great Powers shall judge him as he judges weaknesses will no longer need a spiritual guide. He is definitely on the right path, on the way to becoming himself the universal Law as an incarnation of destiny itself," a theology that anticipated Wilson/Hakim Bey's conception of "anarcho-monarchism" and "imam-of-one's-own-being."[65] Yet this sort of anarchist perennialism (as one might call it) has certainly persisted and appeared in slightly different variations over time, from the implicit example of Leo Tolstoy[66] and the more overt example of Wilson/Hakim Bey to the quite explicit version that Paul Cudenec expressed in *The Anarchist Revelation*.[67] The type of "spiritual anarchism" that they share highlights common beliefs: rejection of priesthood, receiving truth and insight from various traditions, and affirming the "kingdom of God within."

This process, however, can carry colonialist baggage whether intentionally or not. In *Rethinking Ibn ʿArabi*, Gregory Lipton critiqued a "thinly veiled universalist elitism that presupposes a unified tradition underlying all religions" which "may at first appear to acknowledge and celebrate diversity" but in actuality expresses a type of exclusivism "through which all meanings must conform" and which thereby "calls into question the Western ideal of religious universalism" revealing "the historically constituted and situated nature" of its advocates.[68] As Susanne Olsson and Simon Sorgenfrei observed, Aguéli/Abdul Hadi's life conformed to a pattern of people from Europe who adopted individualistic interpretations of foreign traditions that enabled them to both challenge and escape Western norms while remaining unhindered by the conventional boundaries and restrictions (through a shaykh, guru, sensei, family, or local community) that people who grow up in those traditions typically experience.[69] Yet, as his utopian worldview remains incomplete, subjective, and partial, so too does this story of *him* (or, from his *tawḥīdī* perspective, *us*).

Part Two

Ivan Aguéli the Sufi

)

Ivan Aguéli's Second Period in Egypt, 1902–9: The Intellectual Spheres around *Il Convito/Al-Nadi*

Paul-André Claudel
Translated by Nathalie Senné

The second period during which Ivan Aguéli resided in Egypt, from 1902–9, was a decisive one on his personal and spiritual path. While in Cairo, Aguéli began his initiation into Sufism, developing closer ties to Shaykh ʿAbd al-Rahman ʿIllaysh, frequenting al-Azhar, studying and translating the texts of Muhyiddin ibn ʿArabi, and even collecting rare manuscripts of the work of great Arab mystic.[1] Aguéli was also active in an ambitious editorial project: with the Italian doctor Enrico Insabato, he coedited the periodical *Il Convito/Al-Nadi*. He devoted himself completely to this endeavor from May 1904. As he wrote in a letter to his mother, "Three-quarters of the periodical is my work."[2]

Its articles were written in Italian and Arabic and published in Cairo. While the periodical is well-known to specialists and often cited, it is rarely studied in detail,[3] no doubt due to the barrier posed by its bilingualism, and the difficulty of rebuilding its tortured editorial history.[4] Still, it is an unusual publication that well deserves deeper study, as it reveals a particular facet of Aguéli who, as coeditor of the periodical, explored Sufi and Islamic spiritual topics over the course of about forty articles.[5]

This chapter offers an overview of the thirty-six issues of this periodical and attempts to deepen our understanding of several questions: Who was the intended audience of *Il Convito/Al-Nadi*? What did Aguéli's tastes, ideas, and ambitions reveal about him? Also, importantly, which intellectual circles developed around this periodical over the course of nearly four years?

From a few scattered clues—signatures present at the end of articles, periodicals cited by editors, books received—we will attempt a reconstitution of the different cultural worlds Ivan Aguéli tapped into as editor of *Il Convito/Al-Nadi*: Italian Orientalist circles to begin with, but Spiritualist, libertarian, and anarchist circles as well, and, of course, those pertaining to Islam and Sufism. Before exploring these varied spheres, some more specific data about this periodical and its complex editorial history must be presented.

A Telling Title

Printed in Cairo from 1904 to 1907, with two additional issues in 1910 and 1912, *Il Convito/Al-Nadi* was without doubt a unique publication. For nearly four years, this bilingual periodical, written half in Arabic and half in Italian—enriched by pages in Ottoman Turkish for one and a half years—was conceived as an "Italian-Islamic"[6] periodical, to serve the dialog between "Islam and the West," and also the interests of Italian foreign policy.

The double title chosen by Insabato and Aguéli has never been the subject of particular commentary, but is worth some consideration. How one should interpret the choice of words *convito* and *al-nadi*, which are not exactly a translation of each other, and how they must have resonated for a turn-of-the-century reader is intriguing. The Italian term *convito*, derived from the Latin *convivium*, designates a sumptuous meal offered to chosen guests: this "banquet" in the antique mode elicits Platonic associations (it is the term traditionally used, in Italian, to translate Plato's *Symposium*). It contains the idea of a table laden with food and offered, but also the quasi-religious ritual which sublimates nourishment into a shared mystical experience. The metaphor is transparent: the periodical itself is conceived as a place of offering and communion (it presents spiritual nourishment, of which the readers partake). In keeping with these images, the word also invokes the New Testament, adding an initiatory and sacred dimension: "il sacro convito" is the Last Supper offered by Christ to the Apostles, the eucharistic banquet, again evoking sharing, but also sacrifice and transfiguration.

One might add that the name chosen for the periodical has a long literary heritage: in Italian cultural memory, the word *convito* brings to mind *De Amore* by Marsilio Ficino (1433–99), the Florentine Neoplatonic bible openly inspired by Plato's *Banquet*, and particularly *Convivio*, the "feast" imagined from 1304–7 by Dante (died 1321), whose monumental work was presented precisely as "nourishment" in the vernacular, and offered to his contemporaries, according to a metaphor much loved by Dante,[7] and which Insabato and Aguéli certainly had in mind. It is no accident that the pseudonym "Dante" comes up a dozen times to designate one or both of the editors.

The concept of the sacred table is familiar to Islamic culture, as evidenced by *sura* (chapter) 5 of the Qur'an, *al-Ma'ida*, generally designated as *the sura of the table spread*.[8] The Arabic term chosen as the counterpart to *convito*, *al-nadi*, however, is a bit different, as it has no connection with a meal and at first glance has more worldly connotations: *al-nadi* designates a circle, league, or association. It might have been an attempt to translate "symposium." But *al-nadi* above all implies the idea of a rallying around a singular cause, be it intellectual or political, in the way of a party. At the end of the First World War, for example, *al-Nadi al-'arabi* (the Arab Circle) was the name of an important Palestinian political association, created in Damascus, in semi-clandestine and militant fashion, for an independent Syria-Palestine region. Thus, it is less a simple "club" than a privileged social place, suggestive in this context of the Arabic term chosen by Insabato and Aguéli.

The semantic divide between the Arabic and Italian terms thus creates a surplus of meaning: the two words cause the *secret* (*al-nadi*) and the *sacred* (*il convito*) to confront one another. Given the contents of the periodical, the double title takes on a prophetic dimension. The "banquet" announced on the first page is not a banal celebration destined for a circle of friends, but an exchange of exalted ideas intended for a select society. Thus, one is already disposed to read the periodical from both an elitist and a spiritual perspective.

A Brief History of the Periodical

Based on copies of the periodical which have been found, it is doubtful that the editorial vicissitudes of this intellectual "banquet" can possibly be wholly reconstructed. However, one thing is certain: the date of birth of the periodical can be established as May 1904 while the adventure came to an end in December 1907 (the two subsequent issues, in 1910 and 1912, are to be considered as a separate set). In the interval, one can see a slow metamorphosis, with several parameters.

To begin, from 1904 to 1907 there was a progressive drop in the frequency of the publication: the weekly (1904) became bi-monthly (1905), then monthly or less (1906), and finally almost quarterly (1907), before subsisting through sporadic publications (two issues published in 1910 and 1912). In addition, suspensions in publication introduced "blanks" in the continuum. As issues became infrequent, they also become larger: one can observe that the number of pages inflated over time, as the number of issues fell.

To be exact, *Il Convito/Al-Nadi* first appeared as a newspaper (*jarīda*) of four pages (Figures 8.1 and 8.2), in the first eighteen issues printed between May 22 and October 30, 1904. It then became an eight-page periodical for eleven issues, from November 20, 1904, to June 25, 1905, in a slightly smaller format. This physical change was related to a major novelty at that time: the advent of Turkish as the periodical's third language of publication.

June 25, 1905, marked a break in publication, and *Il Convito/Al-Nadi* did not reappear for eleven months. Thus, nearly a year went by until a new issue of the periodical can be found. Exactly three issues, published in the spring and summer of 1906, then constitute a distinct group[9]: the format and use of Italian, Turkish, and Arabic were unchanged but, emblematically, the editorial was entitled "Ricominciando" (Starting again).

This renewal was short-lived, with a second interruption of about ten months, after which four issues were published during the year 1907, forming a new group[10] and indicating a fundamental change: the notion of newspaper was cast aside in favor of a real journal (*majala*), bound and covered (Figure 8.3). The articles in Turkish disappeared. The number of pages increased once more: 64 pages in the first two issues, then 128 in the next two, split equally between Italian and Arabic. These four issues of 1907 marked the end of *Il Convito/Al-Nadi's* existence as a journal associated with regular publication: after December 1907, just two isolated issues appeared (in 1910 and 1912) at a time when Ivan Aguéli, in any case, had already returned to Europe.[11]

Alongside this slow evolution from newspaper to journal, the content of the articles underwent a profound transformation. The first issues published were those of a

Figure 8.1 *Il Convito* as a newspaper. Author's photo.

weekly paper on Islamic studies focused on spirituality, but mindful of the current political situation in the Mediterranean and written as an editorial opinion piece (the periodical defended the Arab people and the Ottoman Empire against the greed of the

Figure 8.2 *Al-Nadi* as a newspaper. Author's photo.

great powers, especially in relation to Macedonia, Crete, and Armenia). From the first issues published in 1907, this balance changed. The focus of the publication shifted quite clearly toward religious studies, backing away from the immediate present: the texts chosen were not so much articles on current events as essays seeking greater understanding of Islamic spirituality, namely in the philosophy of Ibn ʿArabi.

Figure 8.3 *Il Convito/Al-Nadi* as a journal. Author's photo.

Pathways to Italian Political and Intellectual Spheres

In which intellectual circles did this unusual, half-political, half-theological periodical take root? Which minds did it hope to engage? What readers were meant to read it? It is difficult to say precisely who Insabato and Aguéli were targeting, as, clearly, it depends on whether one is considering the sections in Italian or in Arabic. Still, one can attempt to reconstruct a certain number of networks within which *Il Convito/Al-Nadi* could be said to have resided, including Italian-, French-, Arabic-, and Turkish-speaking circles.

Enrico Insabato and the Italian Diplomatic Circles

Il Convito/Al-Nadi was the materialization of a political strategy developed by Enrico Insabato, the "direttore-proprietario" (owner and director) of the periodical.[12] Insabato was officially a physician in Cairo. However, behind the scenes, he was also an agent of the Italian government, in direct contact with both the Director General of Public Security Giacomo Vigliani (1862–1942) and more importantly, the Minister of the Interior and Prime Minister Giovanni Giolitti (1842–1928).[13] Italian Public Security maintained a network to spy on Italian anarchists abroad, who were a significant security threat, and the French historian Daniel Grange suggests that Insabato might have originally been part of this network, sent to penetrate Italian anarchist circles in Cairo, which would explain his connection with both the Ministry of the Interior and the Ministry of Foreign Affairs.[14]

The archives of the Italian Ministry of Foreign Affairs contain a document[15] that is essential in understanding Insabato's plans when he first arrived in Egypt. Entitled "1903: Studi Insabato" (1903: Insabato Studies), it contains four "studies" penned by the physician and transmitted to Foreign Affairs about extending Italy's influence in the Arab countries, especially in Egypt.

In the fourth study, Insabato recommends, among other things, founding an Italian-Arabic periodical, considered crucial in attracting members of Arab-language circles. *Il Convito/Al-Nadi* would be the realization of this idea. Insabato believed such a periodical would have several effects: establishing Italy as a "friendly" and "trustworthy" nation among educated Egyptians; presenting it as the only European power able to aid in a cultural *Risorgimento* of Islam; more deeply, extending Italy's sphere of influence south of the Mediterranean, establishing a space between France and England, and thus opening new economic and commercial opportunities for Italy.

With such aims, it is not surprising that the periodical was looked upon favorably by Giolitti, the most influential politician in the period 1900–1914, with whom Insabato had good relations: Giolitti went so far as to ask his Minister of Foreign Affairs, Tommaso Tittoni (1855–1931), to assist the diffusion of *Il Convito/Al-Nadi* throughout the Mediterranean region via consular channels.[16]

In Egypt, the periodical had the support of the Italian emissary, Marquis Giuseppe Salvago-Raggi (1866–1946), even if other diplomats were more cautious. Augusto Medana (1857–1907), Italian Consul in Tripoli, slowed the diffusion of the periodical in Libya, resulting in being the subject of thinly veiled criticism in the tenth issue of the periodical.[17]

Alongside his editorial activities, Insabato actively sought out contacts with elites in the region, from whom it was hoped he would receive support for Italian objectives.[18] His key contact in Cairo was Muhammad ʿAli ʿAlawi (1872–?), the son of an Egyptian army colonel and a member of the Sanusi *ṭarīqa*.[19] ʿAlawi had for some years already been the intermediary between the Sanusis and the Italian mission, where he had been appointed Second Dragoman, a post which was in part that of an interpreter and in part that of a diplomat, and was the highest rank which could be held by someone who was not an Italian citizen. Through ʿAlawi, Insabato was in contact with Sanusis in ʿAsir (now part of Saudi Arabia but then part of the Yemen) and in Cyrenaica (now part of Libya): the former relationship proved more effective, as it cemented the Italian alliance with Muhammad ibn ʿAli al-Idrisi (1876–1920),[20] a Sanusi shaykh in ʿAsir who led an anti-Ottoman revolt with Italian support (in money and arms).[21] This improved the Italian position in a region of strategic importance, given its proximity to Eritrea, which Italy had occupied in 1889. Al-Idrisi and ʿAlawi, it can be assumed, felt that Italian assistance against the British could serve the interests of the Muslims and the Arabs, even though they were doubtless also well aware of Italian imperial ambitions. Insabato's negotiations with the Sanusis in Cyrenaica, in contrast, were less productive, as the Sanusis there ultimately resisted rather than supported the Italian invasion of 1911, even though they had seen Italian assistance as possibly useful before 1911, when the major threat still came from the French.

Through the intermediary of Alawi, Insabato also came into contact with other regional notables, including Sharaf al-Barakati,[22] a representative of the Sharif Husayn of Mecca (1853/54–1931), the northern neighbor of al-Idrisi in Arabia, who later also led an anti-Ottoman revolt, though with British rather than Italian support. One meeting with al-Barakati was documented by a formal group photograph (see Figure 8.4), in which ʿAlawi sits in the front with al-Barakati, with the back row made up (from left to right) of Aguéli, Insabato, and al-Barakati's servant ʿAbdallah. ʿAlawi is wearing the elaborate Arab dress that he also wore for another formal photograph. Insabato is also wearing Arab dress. Aguéli, in contrast, is wearing the Moroccan-inspired clothing that he normally wore in Cairo, similar to the clothing he is wearing in the only other known photograph of him from this period.[23]

In the view of Eileen Ryan, the basic message that Insabato wanted to convey to Arab readers of *Il Convito/Al-Nadi* was that Italy was the protector of Islam, and thus preferable to the British and the "reforms" that they were sponsoring—to serve their own interests, not those of the Muslims. The complementary message that he wanted to convey to the periodical's Italian readers was that the Arabs who could best be trusted were old-fashioned, religious ones, a view he was still pressing on Vigliani in 1911.[24]

One document shows how Enrico Insabato identified with his Italian-Arabic periodical and considered it a central instrument of the perspective which he calls "propaganda": in an undated letter addressed by Insabato to the then prime minister (at that time not Giolitti), in which he reviews his actions:

Since 1901, I have had the honor of presenting to His Excellency Giolitti, then prime minister, my project of settling in Cairo to launch the publication of a periodical with the aim of making its writings the center of all information of a political nature and all initiatives which, as we understand, could not be taken on by the legation in Cairo.

My choice of Cairo was determined by the fact that this city is the vital center, I dare say the cerebrum, of the entire Muslim world ... In terms of the actions I have been able to develop around the periodical, I do not hesitate for an instant to say that they are vast and more than useful. I have in fact been able to inform my government of all hydraulic and rail works undertaken by the Anglo-Egyptian government in Sudan, on Lake Tana, at Kassala, at Marsa Matruh and even the project of canals on the Euphrates and Tigris prepared by England with the aim of removing all political value from the German railroads through Asia Minor and Mesopotamia. I have revealed the Anglo-Egyptian shenanigans at the border of Tripolitania and Egypt and the back country of Tripolitania; I have entered into contact with the Sanusis of Cyrenaica and the sultans of central Africa, and even had the opportunity of offering musical instruments to the Sultan of Wadai; I have foiled complex Anglo-Egyptian schemes to our detriment of two English agents, Hag Idriss al-Hersi and shaykh al-Adaui in Italian Somalia; I am in close relations with, and able to dispose of aid from, the sharifs of Hejaz and Mecca, the sharifs of

Figure 8.4 Group photograph in Cairo with Aguéli and others, *c.* 1904. Made by Studio of Bernard Edelstein, Cairo. Original in the Picture Archive of the National Museum, Stockholm. Photo: National Museum.

Yemen, who I wrested from the influence of Lord Cromer, of the amir Ibn Rashid of Negd, and nearly all the leaders of Arabia are favorable to me; the Sultan of Constantinople sent me an invitation to come to Constantinople by way of one of my publishers; I have disciplined Somali and Eritrean students from the Azhar University in Cairo, also bringing them financial support, as I did to the Bektassis in Albania and numerous revolutionaries. These are the primary channels that describe the widespread actions I have been able to conduct.[25]

The list is dizzying: it is difficult to comment on all the "sensitive" information Insabato proudly mentions in this letter, but it must be said that he certainly succeeded in establishing a multitude of contacts with religious authorities in Africa and the Middle East, far more than achieved by any Italian diplomat. In response, he was considered by career diplomats as quite a difficult figure. As early as 1905, Insabato's presence in Cairo was poorly tolerated. Salvago-Raggi's successor as Italian emissary in Cairo, Giacomo De Martino (1849–1921), determined to stop Insabato's independent activities. He dismissed 'Alawi and requested the recall of Insabato, which was granted in 1907;[26] by then, the British-guided Egyptian authorities were also pressing for Insabato's expulsion.[27] Aguéli visited the new Italian emissary to plead 'Alawi's case, but to no avail.[28] With the departure of Insabato, *Il Convito/Al-Nadi* ceased publication.

Il Convito/Al-Nadi and Italian Intellectuals

Insabato used his newspaper for political and diplomatic purposes. But for an Italian reader *Il Convito/Al-Nadi* had the basic appearance of a journal of Oriental studies. Insabato and Aguéli were well-informed about all subjects related to the Orient and Islam, with commentaries on the latest works on the Orient published in Italy appearing regularly. Thus, one finds a report on the book by Lodovico Nocentini (1849–1910), *L'Europa nell'Estremo Oriente e gli interessi dell'Italia in Cina* (Europe in the Far East and Italian Interests in China), a critique of two papers by Enrico Catellani (1856–1945) concerning the situation in the Balkans, and a commentary on the upcoming publication of *Atlante d'Africa*, an ambitious encyclopedia of Africa edited by the geographer Arcangelo Ghisleri (1855–1938).[29] Among the editorial priorities of these years was the launch of *Annali dell'Islam*, a study on the origins of Islam in ten volumes directed by Leone Caetani (1869–1935)[30] that was central to the history of Italian Islamology. This was followed a few weeks later by an enthusiastic review of this monumental work, considered a symbol of "a new era in Oriental studies."[31] Under the pseudonym Abdul Hadi el-Maghrabi, Ivan Aguéli also devoted two articles to the Italian Orientalist Italo Pizzi (1849–1920) and to discussing the opinion on the work of Pizzi of the respected Italian Orientalist Carlo Alfonso Nallino (1872–1938).[32]

Despite its peripheral location in Cairo, through these literary reviews, *Il Convito/Al-Nadi* appears to have been a periodical in direct contact with the world of Italian intellectuals. Also, there were other means for Insabato and Aguéli to establish a learned dialog. One issue thus featured a letter by the ethnographer Antonio Baldacci (1867–1950) on its front page, encouraging the ideal of brotherhood between the

Orient and the West, as defended by the editors.[33] Another responded to a missive addressed to the periodical by the anthropologist Giuseppe Sergi (1841–1936) about the Turkish repressions in Macedonia and Armenia.[34] A third was even prouder to show a letter by the linguist Alfredo Trombetti (1866–1929) on its first page, in which he responded to a philological question posed in the previous issue.[35]

This fleeting appearance of the theoretician of the doctrine of the primitive unity of language—particularly respected at this time—was far from innocent, as it revealed one of Aguéli's own centers of interest during this period. We know that Aguéli, a reader of Trombetti, had dreamed of writing a universal dictionary of languages while in Cairo, inspired by the great Italian philologist.[36] One of Aguéli's articles in the Italian section, *Il Convito*,[37] presented just this idea of a linguistic root common to all of humanity, directly influenced by late-nineteenth-century theories of a "mother language." Clearly, Aguéli was struck by the idea of a common ancestral language, situated in the origins of history and containing a concentrate of all other languages derived from it. This dream of linguistic unity may well be linked to his beliefs concerning a Theosophical matrix in an original spiritual unity hidden within the variety of earthly religions. In any case, Trombetti's presence behind several articles brings to light a little-studied facet of Aguéli's reflections during his years in Egypt.

Libertarian Thought and French Networks

Far from all cultural provincialism, *Il Convito/Al-Nadi* thus constructed relationships with well-known Italian intellectuals, entering into dialog with their ideas. However, the periodical also had a more political side, especially during its first three years, through articles devoted to international events. In this respect, French-language periodicals were the most often cited sources, from the *Revue des deux mondes* to *L'Europe coloniale*, from *Le Figaro* to *Le Temps*, but among those most cited, *Le Cri de Paris* comes to the fore most significantly.[38] This weekly periodical, founded by Alexandre Natanson (1867–1936), was well known in France for its irreverent tone and satirical articles.

To see *Le Cri de Paris*, the incarnation of a certain libertarian and internationalist thinking, cited in the pages of *Il Convito/Al-Nadi* is revealing: Insabato and Aguéli were no doubt pleased to find scathing judgments of French foreign policy, in keeping with the anti-colonialist position of their own periodical. Several texts in Italian written by Aguéli under the pen name Abdul Hadi El Maghrabi, such as "I nemici dell'Islam" (The Enemies of Islam), translated as Chapter 17 in this book, or "Quando governeranno i levantini ... " (When the Levantines rule ...)[39] developed a very critical opinion of Western exploitation and of the awful state of the Levantines, archetype of the uprooted individual who has abandoned his culture and given in to Westernization.

It is in this same critical perspective that certain essays appearing in France were identified by *Il Convito/Al-Nadi*: one article reiterated the opinions expressed in a work that was very critical of British policy in the Orient, *Les Anglais en Égypte. L'Ossature de la trahison* (The English in Egypt: An Anatomy of Betrayal) by Auguste Tollaire, whereas another editorial is dedicated to *La Vérité sur l'Algérie* (The Truth about Algeria) by Jean Hess (1862–1926), which launched a real indictment of French colonialism.[40]

If France and the UK were the target of the most trenchant articles, all other European nations—Germany, Austria, Russia, and Spain—were also the object of cutting commentary by the periodical. From 1904–6, *Il Convito/Al-Nadi* had a militant and anti-Western dimension designed to emphasize, in comparison, the special position of Italy, seen as the only nation that could create sincere links with the Muslim people. An "Italian-Islamic" brotherhood appeared possible, in the name of a community of destinies (Italians and Muslims were long subjugated by foreign peoples), but also common interests, as through this alliance, Italy could help Islam regain its moral and spiritual supremacy.

Huot, Grolleau, Dupré

Alongside its integration into a heritage of protest and anti-imperialism, a few small clues, lost among the mass of issues, inform us of another type of contact cultivated by Ivan Aguéli in the Parisian microcosm. They highlight the persistence of certain friendships in "alternative" spheres of the artistic and literary world.

Looking closely at the periodical, tucked in the corner of one of its pages, one thus notes a very familiar name: Marie Huot. One article from January 1, 1905, signed Abdul Hadi el-Maghrabi, is dedicated "A Maria Huot, la grande combattente illuminata" (To Marie Huot, great enlightened warrior).[41] It was dedicated to a comparative historical sketch of religions based on the conception of sacrifice across several civilizations. Two and a half years after this homage, the June 1907 issue offered to its readers four poems by Huot, preceded by a brief introduction.[42] It is interesting to note that, practically at the same time, Huot dedicated a collection of her poems, *Le Missel de Notre-Dame des Solitudes* (The Missal of Our Lady of Solitudes), to Aguéli. Published in Paris in 1908, the title page of the work is inscribed with the dedication: "To my brother in arms, to the fervent artist Ivan Aguéli (Abdul Hâdi in religion)."

Huot's presence in *Il Convito/Al-Nadi* was very discreet: her only direct participation (in addition to the four poems published in 1907) was a brief review she did of the collection of poetry *Reliquiae* by Charles Grolleau (1867–1940).[43] This mention of the collection by Grolleau—a mystic poet close to the esoteric Papus—may seem minor, but it is not unimportant: Grolleau was very close to Aguéli when the latter was in Paris.[44] *Reliquiae* also contained a poem dedicated by Grolleau to Aguéli, evidence of the link between the two.

It thus becomes clear that during his time in Cairo Aguéli stayed in contact, even from afar, with the most active members of the Parisian bohemian scene, who represented a certain social and intellectual marginality. After all, he did live for a time in Cairo with Eugène Dupré (1882–1944), a fervent mystic who was also part of the same esoteric network as Grolleau, and who was also linked, like Grolleau, to René Guénon.[45] The resilience of these friendships demonstrates the spiritual and mystical vein that sometimes surfaces in *Il Convito/Al-Nadi*, and which is not totally erased by the subject of Islam, though the latter dominates. Here one must consider the numerous esoteric periodicals cited in the section "Libri e riviste" (Books and reviews) of the periodical, such as *Luce e ombra* (Light and Shadow, a "spiritual sciences" review), and *Ultra*, "The Theosophical review of Rome," or even the strong homage in *Il Convito/ Al-Nadi* paid to Henry Olcott, co-founder of the Theosophical Society, on his death.[46] These elements allow a glimpse into Aguéli's persistent centers of interest, linked to esoteric and Theosophical spheres in France, and can explain an orientation that is *islamosophical* rather than *islamological* in certain parts of the periodical.

A Curious Anarchist

Besides this Parisian network, the name of one periodical contributor seems especially intriguing, as this time it relates to Aguéli's background as an anarchist. We refer to the journalist and political militant Romolo Garbati, who signed an article published in 1907.[47] With a career rich in exploits, the appearance of such a figure from the Egyptian world of journalism in this context should come as no surprise. Born in 1873, Garbati spent his youth in Sardinia, where he edited several periodicals engaged in the cause of the working class. Threatened by a lawsuit, he left Italy suddenly during the summer of 1902. Arriving in Egypt at the end of the year, he managed to make a living from various journalistic activities, before landing for a time in *Il Convito/Al-Nadi*, essentially as typographer and proofreader.

Garbati's involvement in Insabato's and Aguéli's project makes sense, given his libertarian sympathies, namely his close ties with the anarchist Icilio Ugo Parrini (1850–1906), who Enrico Insabato also knew; in 1903, Parrini and Garbati founded the Italian-language periodical *Il Domani* in Cairo, to which Insabato contributed. This is a reminder that a certain number of rootless political exiles also gravitated around the two editors, namely from Italian anarchist circles.

The discovery of Garbati's name, however, presents another point of interest: at the end of his life, Garbati published a unique work of memoirs, *Mon aventure dans l'Afrique civilisée* (My Adventure in Civilized Africa).[48] This text, written in French, constitutes an extraordinary testimonial on the press in Egypt, specifically *Il Convito/ Al-Nadi*. In his memoirs, Garbati provides a lively description of the main members of the editorial team, with whom he had worked for several months. Here is an example of the way he presented Aguéli:

> Of the editorial staff at *Convito*, especially for the part in Arabic, was one hugely energetic and highly unusual person ... This person, who I saw smiling as he read the contributions to the periodical (in Insabato's home or at the printing press) in a turban, wearing ostentatious robes which tended toward a Moroccan style, huge boots, and a large white cloak, was ... a Swede named Aguéli ... Insabato met him in Bologna, then ran into him again in Paris and in Egypt. He was, to say the least, a unique man, with a highly alert mind and an extraordinary faculty for assimilation. He already knew several languages and was trying to learn Persian. An Arabist might have had something to say about his style, but Aguéli didn't put too much stock into Arabists.[49]

A few pages further, Garbati evokes the day-to-day experiences he shared with Aguéli while living in the same poor neighborhood in Cairo:

> I was the only European living in Bab al-Wastani, that is, in a shack that leaned more than the Tower of Pisa, where a Swede named Aguéli also lived, and who belonged, in his own way, to the Islamic world … Up there in Bab al-Wastani, either I would visit Aguéli in his ramshackle place, or he would come to mine. Two miserable bodies together rarely bring solace, but the Swede was physically resistant like me; on top of it, it was just him, and he could survive on just bread and a little jam. He even had a store of jam in pots and plenty of good humor … Then, whenever we managed to pull together a few piastres, we would go down to Midan al-Suq, to buy fish from the Nile, fried. The poor natives stared at me, because I was the only European who would come to the neighborhood, and showed a certain deference for my converted companion. Everyone knew him. All along the way, the shops and shopkeepers, all *salams* and smiles and pompous phrases, would generously serve us their merchandise.[50]

The reminiscences furnished by Garbati are hard to date precisely. However, this testimony is very instructive, as it unveils Aguéli's simple and ascetic life, recognizing his integration into the Muslim population around the city. A few lines later, Garbati reveals a more mischievous side, pointing a finger at some of his companion's eccentricities:

> When Aguéli received a few pounds, he would disappear from home. He was the least regular of practicing Muslims. With some money in his pocket, he would resume his Nordic habits of eating ham, drinking beer and strong liquors, depleting his resources in just a few days with his mistress, a beautiful local girl, an ironic and carefree creature who must have had heaps of fun relating the strange eccentricities of her master.[51]

These slightly sarcastic observations need to be confirmed—no other source mentions Aguéli's deviations from the dietary prohibitions of Islam which seem quite surprising, nor the local "mistress" that Garbati refers to. Still, this portrait no doubt contains revealing elements—namely on the bewildering character, for more humble Muslims, of this turban-clad Swede determined to live peacefully among them.

Egypt and the Muslim World

This reference to Aguéli, living on the outskirts of Bab al-Wastani, in the neighborhood of the Citadel, reveals, far more than other commentaries, his almost fusional efforts to integrate into the Muslim world. This ideal is the same as *Il Convito/Al-Nadi*, as it undertakes to dialog with Islam, embracing a *Weltanschauung* rooted in the Egyptian religious and political context.

It would be interesting to have a more precise notion of exactly what role the editors in the Arabic-language section may have had in the periodical. The question of the periodical's integration into its Egyptian environment is clearly central: the very legitimacy of the intellectual project carried by Insabato and Aguéli relied on collaboration with figures in Middle Eastern society and, even more, with Islamic religious authorities, so as not to appear a foreign initiative, external to Arab realities. Thus, it is interesting to consider whether the Arabic sections of *Il Convito/Al-Nadi*, in the eyes of Arab-speaking readers, seemed to be written "from inside" the Muslim world, rather than by "foreigners" settled in Egypt.

The name of 'Illaysh, an Azhari shaykh and authority on Islam, clearly acted as an intellectual and moral guarantee for the periodical. 'Abd al-Rahman 'Illaysh, who is discussed further in Chapters 10 and 11, was the son of Muhammad 'Illaysh (1802–82), himself an Azhari shaykh, who was known as a hero of the revolt against the khedive and the British at the end of the nineteenth century. When Insabato and Aguéli moved to Cairo in 1902, 'Abd al-Rahman 'Illaysh was covered with exceptional glory, for his piety, his years in exile from Egypt, and the tragic destiny of his father (with whom he is often confused). If we follow the testimony of René Guénon,[52] 'Abd al-Rahman 'Illaysh was head of the Maliki *madhhab* at al-Azhar and the shaykh of a Sufi *ṭarīqa* linked to the Shadhiliyya. Is this testimony reliable? Guénon is to our knowledge the only source which grants him such a function. He appears in any case to have been a respected person in Cairo and even a spiritual guide, if only because of the aura surrounding his father.[53]

The shadow of 'Abd al-Rahman 'Illaysh discretely traversed the pages of Insabato and Aguéli's periodical, his name mentioned now and again—there is even a text signed by him in *Il Convito/Al-Nadi*: a homage to Ibn 'Arabi. The text was first published in Arabic in the June 1907 issue, with the title *al-Imam al-qutb al-kabir wa al-kawkab al-dhiaw fi kulli zaman munir* (Imam, Great Pole, the Planet That Forever Illuminates).[54] It then appeared in an Italian translation under the title "Il Principe della Religione, il Gran Polo spirituale, la Stella brillante in tutti i secoli" (The Prince of the Religion, the Spiritual Grand Pole, the Shining Star in All Ages).[55] A second text by 'Illaysh featured in the columns of *Il Convito/Al-Nadi*: a *fatwa* on slavery published in the Arabic-language pages of issue 24, among other texts dedicated to "Slavery, its legitimacy and its regulation." The Italian version can be found in the preceding issue.[56] Without doubt, the patronage of 'Illaysh, skillfully brought to the fore by the editors, gave credit, symbolically, to the opinions published by the periodical.

Through the support of 'Illaysh and contacts made in religious circles, Insabato and Aguéli made *Il Convito/Al-Nadi* a periodical well-anchored in the Arab world: its legitimacy to speak not only *of Islam*, but also *in the name of Islam*—with the same legitimacy as other periodicals in the Middle East—never seems to have been really questioned.

In fact, it is noteworthy that the editors made contact, on several occasions, with the local press. The periodical *Arafate*, edited by attorney Mahmud Salim, first published in Cairo in 1904, at nearly the same time as *Il Convito/Al-Nadi,* was thus referred to regularly and in positive terms.[57] That said, the editorial line of this "monthly Islamic review," written in French, was not without parallels with the "Italian-Islamic" periodical of Insabato and Aguéli. There are even regular references to *al-Manar*, the reformist periodical edited by Rashid Rida (1865–1935). In the latter case, however, the editors engaged quite soon in a debate with Rida, both over the question of the caliphate and the Islamic "nation," as well as a construction project for a mosque dedicated to King Umberto of Italy, supported by Aguéli but judged "heterodox" by Rida.[58]

One may wonder who precisely were the contributors for the periodical from the Arab world. Certainly, Aguéli signed a certain number of contributions in Arabic under the name of ʿAbd al-Hadi, but he was not alone. One can see that two other names often recur. The first is Muhammad al-Sharbatli, who contributed mainly on religious subjects, taking on the publication of five articles on the subject of *tasawwuf* (Sufism or mysticism) in the summer of 1904. A brief presentation of the author in an issue from 1907—"L'Ulema sceik Mohammad Scerbatly, egregio nostro collaboratore ed amico" (The *ʿālim* Shaykh Muhammad al-Sharbatli, our dear friend and collaborator)[59]— suggests that he was a Muslim theologian, probably linked to a *ṭarīqa* at al-Azhar. In any case, the name of al-Sharbatli is given as coeditor of the newspaper *al-Umma*, also printed in Cairo, which was very critical of the English, especially after the Denshawai Incident (June 1906).[60] The second is Yusuf Kamal al-Bukhari, who made seven contributions on questions of politics and diplomacy, but who we have unfortunately been unable to identify. Other names appeared more fleetingly. We must highlight that there is a central group related to al-Azhar: ʿIllaysh, of course, but also al-Sharbatli and the theologian Muhammad Farid Wagdy (1875–1954), who wrote a text published in Italian in the June 1907 issue.[61]

Reading the articles in the Arabic part, we can see that *Il Convito/Al-Nadi* was grounded in traditionalist Islamic spheres, developing a conservative type of discourse. We can identify four themes that characterized the editorial line of the periodical: firstly, constant references to the religious circles of al-Azhar, presented as the "authentic" voice of Islam; secondly, eulogy of the Sanusis, seen as those who best knew how to preserve religious traditions;[62] thirdly, a call for a union of Muslims in a supra-national perspective (the "Egyptian" cause is never defended explicitly from an angle that would be nationalist);[63] fourthly, an increasingly strong distrust of religious reformers. An article written by Aguéli in 1907 expresses the position of the newspaper on this subject: Rida is presented as the spiritual son of Jamal al-Din al-Afghani (1839–97) and Muhammad Abduh (1849–1905), trying to subject the Muslim religion to what Protestantism did to Christianity. Rida is described as the representative of a "gang" (*banda*) that, under the pretext of modernizing Islam, will make it lose its soul.[64] All these elements contribute to a form of ideological traditionalism, far from any "modern" and "liberal" model.

This is an unusual perspective: for a long time, the French Orientalist movement— which in the nineteenth century was underpinned by the aim of introducing Oriental peoples to the virtues of "civilization"—sought to enter into dialog with "moderate" Islam.[65] The same was true for Italian Orientalism, whose aim was to encourage a path of reconciliation with scientific and technical modernity. For their part, Insabato and Aguéli proposed another path, that of greater dialog with the representatives of the religious world and a defense of positions skeptical about the notion of European "progress:" *Il Convito/Al-Nadi* intended to encourage a return to a more traditional Islamic identity, which was considered under threat by the West.[66]

Turkish Connections: Abdullah Cevdet and *İçtihad*

The inclusion, from November 1904 to July 1906, of a section in Ottoman Turkish brings to the fore a final set of questions linked to the networks mobilized by Insabato and Aguéli within the Turkish-speaking community to enable this new facet of the publication. It is clear why the editors adopted a third language of publication. First, it allowed them to favorably develop their own image by expressing the pro-Ottoman position of the periodical directly in Turkish. In addition, it ensured a readership in the territories of the Sublime Porte, fulfilling a much-reiterated wish of Insabato. If a justification of this decision is easy to grasp, the specific way it was put into action still begs analysis, namely as to how Insabato and Aguéli entered into contact with editors, translators, or typesetters in Cairo able to master Ottoman Turkish and enrich its pages. Clues are few and far between, but fortunately, Garbati's testimony sheds a bit more light on the subject.

In a passage from *Mon aventure dans l'Afrique civilisée*, Garbati wrote of an editorial decision to move to a new print shop: "When Insabato came back, after wandering from printer to printer, it was determined that *Convito* would be entrusted to Doctor Djeveret, who published *Le libre examen* in Turkish and French. A Swiss medical doctor, he had taken refuge here to escape capital punishment, to which he had been sentenced in Turkey under the paternal government of Abdülhamid."[67] While the passage may seem anecdotal it is also very revealing, as "Doctor Djevert" is none other than Abdullah Cevdet (1869–1932), a major figure on the Turkish political scene of the early twentieth century: a trained doctor, this politician of Kurdish origin was also a writer, philosopher, translator, journalist, and editor. His reformist stance under the Ottoman powers, at the time led with an iron fist by Sultan Abdülhamid II, resulted in multiple convictions and a long exile far from his country: Cevdet led a rootless existence between Libya, France, Austria, Switzerland, and Egypt after 1896. His presence in Cairo is proven from 1905 to 1911, when he returned to Istanbul.

In his text, Garbati also refers to a French title of the famous review *İctihad*: *Le libre examen* (Free Inquiry), partially written in French. Cevdet directed this literary and intellectual periodical in defense of freedom for over thirty years. He devoted all of his energy—and nearly his whole fortune—to this editorial effort. Thus, certain trilingual issues of Insabato and Aguéli's periodical were printed by Cevdet, in the same press that produced *İctihad*.

How such a link could exist between a progressive and reformist Turkish militant, who was not only very wary of religious institutions but favorable to the decentralization of the Ottoman Empire and its different Arab peoples, and Insabato and Aguéli, who favored a far more traditionalist and unifying position vis-a-vis Islam,[68] is counterintuitive and a question deserving of deeper study. Was their arrangement purely economic? This may be an possibility. Was this rapprochement due, quite simply, to the personal sympathy which linked Insabato and Cevdet? Cevdet was a doctor like Insabato, convinced of the importance of the dissemination of ideas between Europe and the Ottoman world. We can assume that, despite the two editors' divergent views on the interpretation of Islam, they found common ground in their defense of anticolonial politics.

Conclusion

Often reduced a bit too hastily to an Insabato-Aguéli duo, the contributors to *Il Convito/ Al-Nadi* each organized their work within a far more complex web of relationships than that which is readily apparent. From Cairo, the "beating heart" and "brain" of the Muslim world,[69] the periodical wove its web, multiplying contacts, cultivating an ever-greater exchange of information, eliciting dialog with other periodicals, as much in Italian spheres as in Islamic communities. This effort of openness was vital in ensuring the legitimacy of a periodical that saw itself as an interface between two cultural universes and two geopolitical systems (Europe/Arab world): only the wealth of the networks established by the editors guaranteed that they would escape any form of culture "lag."

From this point of view, the results obtained by Insabato and Aguéli seem equal to the task at hand. Balanced between several linguistic domains (Italian-, French-, Arabic-, and Turkish-speaking), the periodical skillfully located itself at the interstice of different spheres of influence: European scholars with whom the editors established contact through interposed articles; spiritual, literary, or anarchist circles; Islamic or Sufi circles; and Turkish political exiles represented by Cevdet.

This diversity was both social and ideological—far from the homogeneity of the mental horizons of most European Islamic reviews of the time, especially in academia. This made for the extraordinary richness of the periodical imagined by Aguéli. From this point of view, *Il Convito/Al-Nadi* illustrated a particular moment in an itinerary where politics intersected with mysticism, with the dream of producing, via this "Italian-Islamic" review, a transformative energy, capable of changing mentalities.

Sufi Teachings for Pro-Islamic Politics: Ivan Aguéli and *Il Convito*

Alessandra Marchi

The periodical *Il Convito/Al-Nadi*, discussed in Chapter 8, is a valuable source for investigating the ideas and knowledge of Islam promoted by its editors, and can also help in understanding Italian colonial and anticolonial literature and politics. My central aim in this chapter in analyzing *Il Convito* (the Italian section of *Il Convito/ Al-Nadi*) and Ivan Aguéli's contribution to it is to provide a deeper understanding of religious conversion to (Sufi) Islam within a social and political framework, trying to answer the question of how the spiritual and the sociopolitical dimensions intertwine and shape the new, or renewed, identity of European converts, notably among intellectuals. The intellectual and spiritual itinerary of Aguéli is similar to other "radical" conversions of the time, such as those of the French artist Valentine de Saint-Point (1875–1953) and the Italian anarchist Leda Rafanelli (1880–1971), whose life as a Muslim has been often considered as "heterodox" in many aspects.[1] This chapter will thus propose one view of Aguéli's Islam; alternative views will then be proposed in Chapters 10 and 11.

This chapter will examine some aspects of Aguéli's life to understand to what extent his conversion corresponded to a radical political and social engagement, along with his deep personal motivation for his spiritual quest. It asks if and how a process of political consciousness has been at the root of conversions to Islam as a personal choice to transform society, and how anticolonialism or other political ideologies thereafter pushed people to adopt the Islamic religion as a different way of living.

As we have seen in previous chapters, Aguéli began reading the Qur'an around 1892, converted to Islam some years later,[2] and in 1902 moved to Cairo, where he was initiated by Shaykh 'Abd al-Rahman 'Illaysh, further discussed in Chapters 10 and 11, and helped Enrico Insabato, already discussed in Chapter 8, with *Il Convito/ Al-Nadi*.[3]

Some less-known aspects of Aguéli's life as a Muslim were reported in the book *Mon aventure dans l'Afrique civilisée* (My Adventure in Civilized Africa), published in 1933 in Alexandria by the Italian anarchist Romolo Garbati, who also wrote for *Il*

Convito and other periodicals in Egypt.[4] In his book, Garbati described Aguéli's house in the Bab al-Wastani district of Cairo, where they both lived. According to Garbati, Aguéli was a well-loved and respected person, a "peculiar man, very smart and with an extraordinary ability for learning." He knew many languages, including Arabic, Italian, and Persian, and also Ethiopian and other Semitic languages that he had studied with his "master," Professor Joseph Halévy (1827–1917).[5] Garbati also wrote, however, that Aguéli "was the least regular of practicing Muslims. With some money in his pocket, he would resume his Nordic habits of eating ham, drinking beer and strong liquors, depleting his resources in just a few days with his mistress, a beautiful local girl."[6] This report is not contradicted by other reports, as there are no clear details of Aguéli's everyday ritual practice, or whether he fasted during the month of Ramadan. Indeed, there are some references to consumption of alcohol, and he is known to have painted human figures and female nudes,[7] so that it is possible that his obedience to Islamic precepts was flexible or heterodox. On the other hand, this might be a way for Garbati to reconcile Aguéli's anarchist background with Islamic principles and lifestyle. Similar remarks have been made about other converts, as it has about others at the time who also shared common interests in politics and social justice as well as in Theosophy and (Oriental) spiritual traditions, to compose an idiosyncratic religiosity.[8]

Radical Ideas and Lives

The cosmopolitan cultural milieu of Cairo was common to other Middle Eastern cities in the nineteenth and twentieth centuries, when new ideas about anarchism, socialism, esotericism, and art were circulating. These ideas often went hand in hand with the quest for a universal truth and the need to change the sociopolitical order imposed by Western imperialism. According to Ilhan Khuri-Makdisi:

> Those who embraced such ideas expressed them in articles, pamphlets, plays, and popular poetry (in Arabic, but also in Italian, Ottoman Turkish, and Greek) … disseminating radical thought through educational, cultural, and popular institutions … Radicals in Beirut, Cairo, and Alexandria forged a culture of contestation in which they challenged existing and emerging class boundaries, redefined notions of foreignness and belonging, and promoted alternative visions of social and world order.[9]

It needs therefore to be asked to what extent Aguéli and other converts to Sufi Islam were part of this kind of "radicalism," a radicalism which is generally described as a set of disparate ideas, including anarchism. Several historical factors were at the root of a potentially common "language" linking anarchism and Islam, including resistance to oppression, contestation of human or centralized authority, and commitment to egalitarianism, universalism, and solidarity, as Anthony Fiscella has also argued in his *Varieties of Islamic Anarchism*.[10]

Occasionally, we can find in Aguéli's words what Fiscella called an "overlap in his Western and Eastern paradigms,"[11] a juxtaposition between the East (often identified with Islam) and Europe, seen as two different worlds. Fiscella noted that Aguéli usually wrote about Islam and anarchism without connecting them to one another, but it is possible to presume their relation under the umbrella of Sufism, as such a relationship has been observed in the case of other converts, for example, in the case of Rafanelli,[12] based on an understating of Sufism as less restrictive than "orthodox" Islam. According to some scholars of anarchism, she might have converted to Islam as a form of rebellion against the Western world, of which she criticized the political and military hegemony over the colonized countries, as well as from a cultural perspective. Her "anarchist islamicity" has also been deduced from her lack of attachment to material things, her very poor lifestyle, the number of her lovers, and other aspects of her life.[13] According to Fiscella, "a potentially common 'language' between Islam and anarchism" might be better found in "a language of resistance to oppression and skepticism to human authority but also commitment to egalitarianism, universalism, and solidarity."[14]

Similar characteristics were often found among other European converts, even if not anarchists, such as Saint-Point, who was close to René Guénon during his years in Cairo, where she lived in hardship after 1924. In Cairo she also published the periodical *Le Phoenix. Revue de la Renaissance orientale* (The Phoenix: Review of the Eastern Renaissance), clearly contesting European colonialism.[15] Another example was the artist Henri-Gustave Jossot (1866–1951), who converted in 1913 in Tunisia, and was known for his anticlerical and anticolonial satirical cartoons. Jossot's conversion has been seen as a symbolic and political act, an "anticolonial performance," in a context where his engagement stood with the religion of the subalterns.[16] Like the other converts mentioned here, Abdul Karim Jossot engaged in the denunciation of the perverse mechanisms of cultural colonization.

Political and symbolic dimensions, then, are also often intertwined in the life of converts. Rafanelli was extremely clear on this point, not far from Aguéli's position: she considered the East and the West as two worlds apart, separated by an "abyss" existing between them in every action of life. She saw Africa and Islam as opposed to Europe and modernity, and identified herself with the "pure and instinctive Africa."[17] She tried to rebuild the East in her home in Milan by creating a "small *harem* room," decorated with symbols and Arabic calligraphy, which she learned and taught for decades in her "illusionary" place, where she also worked as fortune teller. She met Mussolini and introduced him to Islam, notably between 1913 and 1914, but ended up identifying him with the Western oppressor. The distance she felt from the West was once more put into words in her books and writings, where she repeatedly condemned European— colonialism, military intervention, and more broadly Western culture and societies.[18]

It is therefore important to look at how deeply religious conversion and spirituality contributed to shaping political ideas, and conversely, how much political vision and activism influenced and inspired conversion to Islam and to Sufism specifically. Conversion to Sufi Islam can be seen as a militant and political choice, a way to challenge the Western (imperialist) social order.

Against Islamophobia: *Il Convito* between Anticolonial and Pro-Islamic Politics

The European press in Egypt flourished during the decades before and after the turn of the twentieth century, with a number of newspapers and periodicals published in Italian, French, Greek, English, and other languages. The issues covered by the European press were quite varied, from politics to society, trade, art, and literature, to religion and spirituality. Social and cultural engagement was openly declared by many Italians and Europeans in Egypt; thus their press became a major instrument for spreading political ideas too.[19]

As we saw in Chapter 8, before the invasion of the Libyan provinces in 1911, Italy undertook what has been inappropriately called a strategy of "peaceful penetration" in its territories, with a series of programs for economic development and cultural propaganda that aimed to present Italy as a benevolent European power, far from imperial ambitions. Insabato's writings and political action shed light on the strategy of cultural penetration. The claim of a pro-Islamic attitude was shared by Aguéli in many articles, written in Italian and Arabic, for *Il Convito/Al-Nadi*, published from 1904 to 1910.[20] Under his Muslim name, Abdul Hadi El Maghrabi, or simply Abdul Hadi, Aguéli collaborated closely in editing the periodical, which covered issues of Italian and international politics and Islam in the Middle East, the Balkans, Russia, and China. Several issues were dedicated mainly to Sufism, the teachings of Muhyiddin ibn 'Arabi, prejudices against Islam, and also to medicine and justice, to women and feminism in Islam, and related topics.

From the very first edition of *Il Convito*, Insabato and Aguéli stressed their lack of prejudice against the Muslim religion, unlike the prevailing general ignorance and misunderstanding in Europe. Aguéli—introduced as an "expert" on the subject of Islam (but never as a convert)—was asked by Insabato to write a section about "The Enemies of Islam" (translated as Chapter 17 in this book) and on "Why Muslims are hated," with the aim of explaining Europeans' disdain for Islam.

For Aguéli "Islam should not be confused with Muslims"[21] (it is said, in response to an article published on June 23, 1904, by *Arafate*, a francophone weekly published in Cairo). Both Insabato and Aguéli often underlined this difference in their writings, with a view to "de-culturalizing" Islam, considered as a faith and religion, separate from cultural behavior in various societies. That might also explain why, when writing about Sufism, Aguéli "leaves out … the Quran, and Sufi practice."[22]

Aguéli distinguished between Islam and Muslims and attested that "in Europe there are people who hate Islam and Muslims … there are [others] who love both … like the director of this periodical"; others, Aguéli suggested, do not even consider contemporary Muslims as real believers.[23] *Il Convito* did not want to create confusion but to offer accurate information on Islam, the editors stated, as its aim was to encourage the Italian government to improve "pro-Islamic policies" and "achieve an effective action on the Islamic world, to attract its sympathy."[24] As Insabato said in the same issue, it was necessary to "leave aside all wishes of imperialism and violent colonization, to be replaced with a single Islamic action, valid for every country and every stratum composing the Islamic world."[25] But he continuously stressed the character of the Italian civilizing mission, which had to be achieved through economic and commercial expansion first and subsequently on a cultural level as well.[26]

Insabato borrowed his language from the positivist vocabulary of the time, showing the permanence and the evolution of an Orientalist framework, which has been reproduced since the Liberal Age, notably during the nineteenth century, when interest in Islam became part of the Italian political agenda and propaganda, and until the Fascist regime.

From the first issue of *Il Convito*, Insabato encouraged the exchange between "East and West" (with "East" generally understood as the Muslim countries, especially Arab ones, and "West" generally meaning Europe), against those who still wanted "crusades, wars, and aggressive conquests," as the editors stated: "We do not consider the East as a wild region to be colonized like Central Africa, but we consider it as a country of huge moral and intellectual richness."[27]

At the same time, the editors tried to demonstrate the meaning of the universal Islamic tradition, together with its inherent openness and adaptability. They wished to let people know and understand its structure, so that Italy could benefit (also economically) from being a major political ally, and "make Rome great again," due to its benevolent attitude and admiring judgment toward the Muslim civilization.

It is possible that Insabato and Aguéli adapted their knowledge and purposes to each other: the detailed analysis of the spiritual, religious, and cultural dimensions of Islam could go hand in hand with the aim of improving the political and commercial interests of the Italian government. Even if the editors denounced the violent colonization of the European countries, the concept of "the Orient" as essentially different from the West, the idea of a civilizing mission and of economic markets to conquer, are also present in *Il Convito*. But at the same time, the way in which *Il Convito* informed its readers about Islam and politics in that period is interesting and unusual. Even the concept of Islamophobia, which the social sciences have quite recently started to study, was mentioned by Aguéli in relation to European ignorance of Islam, and it is possible that it was used here for the very first time. In the section "Notes on Islam" in 1904, Aguéli stated that the concept of Islamophobia (*Islamofobia*) was linked to the theory of inferior races which was present among Germans to justify the rights of the Aryan people. He also wrote about other cultural origins of Islamophobia (English, Levantine, Russian), but more generally, clerical European people—literally "I clericali europei," notably secular Catholics, but also Protestant Christians—were defined as Islamophobic, so that especially artists and wise men (and many Israelites among them) had the duty to inform their readers properly.[28]

In the section "Miscellanea" in the first issue of 1907, including a summary of the Arab pages, Aguéli commented on the attacks on Islam of the British agent, Lord Cromer (1841–1917) and his "Islamophobic statements," described as a mixture of principles "imagined [!!] more than a thousand years ago, to lead a primitive society."[29] Insabato and Aguéli wrote:

> We also want to make the liberals of Europe understand how Islam is fundamentally democratic and liberal, both for its prophetic vein, the last beautiful Semitic

gesture, and for its prohibition of usury and the complete absence of any clergy. We also believe that the spreading of Orientalist and Muslim knowledge will have a beautiful mission against fierce materialistic dogmatism, the last link in the chain of slavery imposed by the Germans and against which Islam will be a valid answer.[30]

Even though Aguéli and Insabato aimed to join East and West, notably by an "alliance" of the Eastern (Muslim) countries with Italy,[31] the two are still frequently placed in opposition to each other in their spiritual and cultural meanings.

The way the social and the spiritual dimensions converge in a renewed order is very interesting to see, as it can shed light on the kind of society those converts aimed to realize. In such a society, the specific place of Sufism can be also examined as a combination of aesthetics and harmony, to which Aguéli aspired.[32]

> We are against the Europeanization of Muslim countries: the system has given bad results and we consider so-called "progress" as a huge fraud that we must unmask. It is nothing but stupid and useless vandalism: it means the destruction of harmonies and of sentimental and architectural orders that we want to preserve at all costs, at least in the name of aesthetics ... The Easterner who ceases to be Muslim is a rogue.[33]

So, Muslims should remain Muslims and education in Islam should be reinforced and "must be Muslim: that is to say, sentimental and aesthetic."[34]

This is why *Il Convito* attached great importance to "Muslim Sufism," "since in the East Sufi aspirations are the Art of personality."[35] But Sufism is important on a political level too, while they attributed lesser importance to Pan-Islamism, which they did not consider a "peril," but rather an opportunity.[36]

Sufi Knowledge of East and West

In such a period of strong opposition between Europe and the colonized countries, anarchists, socialists, and spiritual seekers such as European Muslim converts tried to overcome divisions in many ways. Muslim converts tried above all to transform themselves individually, to change and shape their society; the external and internal dimensions, the Sufi *bāṭin* (esoteric) and *ẓāhir* (exoteric), are very much present in the pages of *Il Convito*. Aguéli and Insabato dedicated much space to illustrating the expressions and forms of Sufism, its tolerance, virtue, and orthodoxy. As it "integrates every aspect of life," it could "improve and fortify men, develop their consciousness and deeper feelings."[37]

Among the instruments helping to achieve this consciousness was the knowledge of Muslim mystics, introduced in *Il Convito* in 1907:

> We wish to introduce you to three Arab mystics who are well known by European Islamophiles, but who have never been studied by Orientalist scholars ... We will

write about Sidi ʿAbd al-Qadir al-Jilani …, about Muhyiddin ibn ʿArabi, known as "the greatest shaykh," and about the poet Rabiʿa al-ʿAdawiyya, who every mystic writer can cite. We will start with M. Ibn ʿArabi because he is the typical representative of Islamic mysticism. Muslims who follow him are our friends and partisans. In each number of this periodical we will give ample space to meditation on his writings, which has been our collaborator's [Aguéli's] favorite study for many years.[38]

The *Futuhat al-makkiyya* (Meccan Revelations) was chosen among the most important of Ibn ʿArabi's works.[39] Aguéli translated two pages for his readers, accompanied by several notes, where he introduced two fundamental ideas of Ibn ʿArabi: the purification of the causes at the basis of men's actions and the concept of universality. According to Aguéli, "It is astonishing how men can perfectly recognize themselves in Ibn ʿArabi's immense thought even today. And everyone can find in it something related to their culture." Once again, he underlined Ibn ʿArabi's Arab background and also his "insistence on the universal," and noted how far it is from Persian "intellectualism."[40] The contrast between Arab and Persian (meaning between "theism" and "pantheism") is also related to the fact that "he was born in the west, he died in the east: his life is symbolic in itself."[41]

Il Convito announced the creation of a society for the study of Ibn ʿArabi in Italy in 1907, called the Akbariyya, after the Arabic title of Ibn ʿArabi, *al-shaykh al-akbar* (the greatest shaykh):[42]

In the last hour, we have learned that a society for the study of Ibn ʿArabi was founded in Italy and in the East, similarly to the English one for the study of Omar Khayyam, the Persian poet and philosopher, and the German one for Gobineau. The new society, which has taken the name of Akbariyya, proposes to:

1. deepen and spread the exoteric and esoteric teachings of the Master, with editions, translations, and commentaries of his works and those of his fellows, as well as with conferences and meetings;

2. gather, as far as possible, all the friends and students of the Great Master to create in this way, if not a bond of brotherhood, at least a rapprochement based on the intellectual solidarity between the two elites of the East and the West;

3. help materially and morally all those who today represent the Muhyiddinian tradition, above all those who, by word and acts, work for its spread and development. The work of this society will also extend to the study of other masters of Oriental mysticism, such as… Rumi, but the main subject will remain Ibn ʿArabi.

The Society will not be concerned with political issues, whatever they are, and will never emerge outside the philosophical, religious, or theosophical circle on which it is based.

Members must swear they do not belong to any anti-Islamist association.

One can therefore be atheist and Akbari together, but one cannot be a Jesuit. A Christian from the East cannot be admitted, except by special invitation, while the confession of a European Christian, as that of a Jew, Eastern or European, cannot be an obstacle to acceptance.[43]

The exclusion of Eastern Christians (but not Arab Jews) from the Akbariyya is not explained, but may be understood in terms of Aguéli's strong prejudice against "Levantines" (Armenian and Arab Christians), described elsewhere as having an "instinctive and ferocious hatred for all that is beauty, generosity, or mysticism" and being interested only in money. Anti-Semites see Eastern Jews in this way, Aguéli noted, but they are wrong.[44]

No trace of an Akbariyya Society has ever been found in Italy, though a group was later established in Paris, as we will see in Chapter 13.

It is interesting to note the way in which *Il Convito* promoted its knowledge, even in relation to the building of the King Umberto mosque in Cairo, to which the publication dedicated some articles. This mosque, it is said, was built by the will of Shaykh 'Illaysh near the al-Azhar mosque, and was dedicated to the memory of King Umberto I, who represented the "Islamic element" that the editors of *Il Convito* call Akbari,[45] which—it was explained—is very far from Wahhabism, described as the most rabid adversary of Ibn 'Arabi. The article discussed the legitimacy of such a mosque. Despite the exceptionality of naming a mosque after a non-Muslim, the response of many Muslims was positive, according to Aguéli, except for Rashid Rida, who edited *al-Manar* and was described in *Il Convito* as "the intellectual and scientific leader of the contemporary Islamic reformist and rationalist movement," successor of Muhammad 'Abduh and of Jamal al-Din Afghani, classed by Aguéli as among the "Calvinists of Islam."[46]

The (Anti)colonial Message and Mission

Il Convito was one of the rare European voices stressing the universality of the Muslim Sufi message and the importance of knowledge of it among a wider public. The will to spread spiritual Sufi teachings was closely related to the "civilizing mission" attributed to Italy. Building alliances with Sufi leaders was a major step to achieving this goal.

Many pages of *Il Convito* were dedicated to the Sanusiyya *ṭarīqa* and its presence "from Morocco to China."[47] Insabato, who as we saw in Chapter 8 was engaged in political negotiations with Sanusis in both Cyrenaica and 'Asir, considered the Sanusiyya a "civilizing force," fundamental for the stability in the region, whose deep roots in the Libyan territories clearly showed its role (albeit a rather instrumental one) as a potential ally in Italian expansion projects and ambitions.

Italy's main role was to replace the "feudal European politics in the East," as Aguéli wrote in *Il Convito*.[48] He was against the general prejudice about Eastern people considered incapable of having public opinion: he witnessed instead their "deep social sense," as far as they always did and still do politics. He attributed to Italy the important role of having broken with the European tradition of modern crusades and to the Italian people having spontaneously recognized the rights of natives, with the help of many Italo-Islamic periodicals,[49] proving that Italians understood the value of the Easterners' public opinion. He also wrote about the bad opinion the Eastern people had about Europe and its hypocrisy, aggressiveness, and cruelty.

Aguéli also understood the opposition of East and West in socioeconomic terms:

The same scientific, industrial or other kinds of progress, under such conditions, seems like good sorcery created only to crush the weak and strip the poor for the benefit of the rich. It has been a long time since I saw how the hate of Muslims against Europeans is more a hate of caste or social class than religion. Religious fanaticism is not to be taken seriously and when it appears, very rarely, it serves mostly to cover other feelings.[50]

European culture was attacked in many articles, with "radical" language, for having been for too long "the master of every event in the East,"[51] destroying everything and rarely acting for good.

Aguéli stressed the fact that, apart from its beauties and virtues, Europe was unfortunately known for its "fanatical monks, colonial regiments and customs officers." On the other hand, some rare good ideas coming from Europe to the Orient—like the development of the sciences, humanitarianism, and art—were not often appreciated, as a consequence of European economic and political corruption and conquest in the East, and were instead opposed by the anticolonial and anticlerical movements.[52]

In the last issue, in 1907, Aguéli spoke about contemporary "anti-Sunni" men.[53] He depicted them in comparison with the opponents of mystical and aesthetic Catholicism in Europe, such as the enemies of the symbol, gnosis, and spiritual nature; those who made religion a fruitless moral system. He distinguished religious practice within Protestantism in its several forms—"Lutheranism, Calvinism, Buddhism, Wahhabism, Muʿtazilism, Khawarijism, positivism, materialism, socialism"—from Muslim religious practice, responding to a noble spiritual need for good and beauty, meaning the love of God, which would encourage the development of a "second nature" in each Muslim.

In the twenty-first issue of *Il Convito*, in 1905, Aguéli dedicated the article "The Sacrifice of Humanity" to his friend and "enlightened intellectual," Marie Huot. He tried to explain the evolution of the concept of sacrifice in different religions and cultures, citing examples such as the bullfight in Spain, the Armenian genocide, the "German heresy of Christianity," the "Slavic deterioration of the Semitic ideal." He referred to both cultural differences between Northern people and Muslims and their way of staying in this world.

There is nothing more unlike a German or a Slav than a Muslim. It is therefore almost certain that the true primitive ritual of sacrifice, lost, forgotten in the hands of the barbarians and damned, must find itself in Islam. And that is how it is. However, it no longer keeps the name of sacrifice, but the name of the sacred and intense effort on the way to God: it is called the Holy War, jihad … All the arenas of human activity are its battlefield: it can be the effort for centuries in the way of civilization and culture, or the firing of weapons in a battle: it is the struggle against oneself and against the enemies of God.[54]

According to Aguéli, the concept of "holy war" does not represent the root of the movement, but rather its fruits or goals: social agreement and harmony within Muslim societies.[55] He was not interested in looking for homogeneity and similarities, but insisted that "Islam cannot change," and that everything has to be "Islamized."

Reading his pages in *Il Convito* we have the impression that they translate Aguéli's double sense of belonging, as part of both worlds (and prejudices). He compared the conduct of a real Muslim to the conduct of an honest freethinker in Europe: one who believes in justice and freedom, but who knows how to avoid sectarianism. He then expressed his pessimism on the idea of "Northern internationalism," which consisted in many members without real solidarity. But he insisted on looking for "equilibrium and agreement," "order, harmony and measure" among all things. It becomes evident that only Islam could satisfy this quest for harmony and freedom, also allowing libertarian tendencies, which "have always been present in Islam."[56]

Conclusion

We can now ask whether Aguéli's interpretation of Islam came from inside or outside the Muslim world he described; if radical ideas were shaped by Islam or vice versa. His quest for a renewed society corresponded to a period of deep spiritual and social crisis experienced by Europeans. In the nineteenth and twentieth centuries, the encounter between the Muslim "East" and "European modernity" encouraged a number of conversions to Islam as a response to this crisis.[57] The attraction to Oriental spiritual traditions among Europeans and their quest for orthodoxy or for universal spirituality have been revealed by research, but this encounter also involved tensions and conflicts which could hinder access to the spiritual benefits of what Traditionalist scholars such as Patrick Laude term "the Tradition."[58]

Thierry Zarcone observed that Ibn 'Arabi's thought attracted "certain heterodox Sufi orders and several mystico-political movements on the margins of Islam," suggesting that his writings "authorize several interpretations that are not in conformity with the spirit of the Islamic tradition, and that promote deviations."[59] We can of course discuss what is meant by "deviation" and what is meant by "orthodoxy," and we can of course state that many converts actually lived Islam in a flexible manner; they "settled" in their chosen tradition—as Guénon used to say—instead of adopting the new religion rigidly or speaking about conversion explicitly. Laude noted the status of "outsider" which has characterized the Western seeker and scholar, while guaranteeing strong independence of the contemporary community of believers.[60]

The outsider position is also very interesting when considering conversions to Sufi Islam, if we look at them as forms of cultural resistance to the new political order established in Africa. In this respect, the Gramscian insight about the "acquisition of consciousness of one's own historical personality" is also very useful for analyzing conversions to Islam as a continuing process of knowledge and transformative action.[61] This chapter has read the lives and writings of Sufi converts like Aguéli as forms of cultural resistance to the new political order established in Africa and the Middle East by European colonization. It has tried to understand if and how anticolonialism and other political ideologies and social struggles influenced the adoption of the Islamic religion and vice versa. We can also see this as a mutual process in which adhesion to a spiritual or religious tradition goes together with the acquisition of a political consciousness, which can be individual and collective. The creation of a new religious and anthropological subjectivity can be linked with the kind of solidarity of a new community of faith and culture under the name of Islam, but further research is to encourage in this direction.

We do not know how many readers *Il Convito* reached,[62] but in it, Insabato and Aguéli developed their political, religious, and spiritual perspectives, to be realized in the future society they imagined. The circulation of ideas through the international press developed during the nineteenth century contributed to shaping the sense of a larger international and cosmopolitan community, and possibly to the development of a civil society where people can live as free citizens, at least for those people in quest of such a society.

During the time Aguéli spent in Cairo, he was probably surrounded by humble people "oppressed by social injustice."[63] These so-called subalterns are fundamentally opposed to bourgeois and colonial power in every society, so even the way in which radical ideas and pluralistic social discourse spread can be seen as a way of resisting both imperialism and nationalism, as was the adoption of Islam for so many people. For Aguéli, Islam represented "liberation."[64] In this attempt, Islam could have played a role as an ideology of redemption or of rebellion: a radical choice, maybe improved by the embrace of Sufi spirituality in several contexts, as Aguéli's writings in *Il Convito* demonstrate.

In one of the last issues of *Il Convito* published,[65] there are no articles by Aguéli, and Sufism is no longer present. In Insabato's editorial, "Starting again" (*Ricominciando*), the role of Italy in connecting East and West is newly stressed, with almost messianic terms about "the spirit of ancient Rome," its humility and honesty.[66] The dominant narrative of Italy's benevolent mission toward Africa, passed down by various media, broadcast the need to recall great events of the Italian past, under a glaze of holiness, illustrating violent actions as if they were good ones and creating the myth of the "good Italian people." Fascism would then exaggerate this juxtaposition and create several Orientalist institutions to spread this kind of imperialist message.[67]

After the fall of the Fascist regime, Insabato still spoke about Fascist colonial policies, especially as regards the "sense of dignity, security and responsibility" shared by all officials, from ministers to governors and residents, and the "righteous" regime in Libya. New strategies for building alliances with the Sanusi elites discredited his work, until finally Italy resorted to military action before definitively "pacifying" Tripolitania and Cyrenaica.[68] At some point, Insabato even joined the Italian antifascist resistance movement in Rome. Nonetheless, he worked incessantly to accomplish his aim of union and collaboration with the Islamic world until his death in 1963, as is witnessed by his many posts. Insabato was president of the Mediterranean Center (Centro Mediterraneo) from 1950; secretary of the National Union of African Action and Italo-Arab-Islamic and Mediterranean collaboration (Unione Nazionale d'Azione Africana e di collaborazione italo-arabo-islamica e mediterranea) from 1951; director of the Center for Italo-Arab Relations (Centro per le Relazioni Italo-Arabe) from

1952 to 1955; and director of the Islamic-Catholic Center (Centro Cattolico-Islamico) in Rome, from 1955. He also continued to write about and promote Italian-Arab cooperation.[69] Since the pioneering studies of Gotti Porcinari and Anna Baldinetti, however, little work has been done on his activities and influence on Italian-Libyan relations until recent years,[70] and on its possible influence on the spread of Sufism among Europeans.

10

Ivan Aguéli and the Islamic Legacy of Emir ʿAbd al-Qadir

Iheb Guermazi

"I would consider myself as the last of all idiots until I learn Arabic."[1] With these words, Ivan Aguéli tried to convince his close friend and colleague the Finnish artist Werner von Hausen to provide him, while in prison, with more books in Arabic. The list of volumes that Aguéli required included a manual of Arabic grammar, a book on Islamic theology, the *Arabian Nights*, and the Qur'an. The Swedish painter who was accused and jailed for his affiliation with Parisian anarchist groups immersed himself during his detention in the study of non-European languages and religions. His notes show the traces of a slow, thorough, and perseverant project to study Arabic, Hebrew, Sanskrit, and Mandarin. Aguéli, who—according to many of his contemporaries— had an obvious talent for understanding the internal mechanics of every language he learned, was also versed in the study of the major religions associated with these languages. Books on Hinduism, Judaism, Taoism, and Islam were consequently at the center of his researches.

The study of foreign languages did not merely aim to facilitate his understanding of foreign spiritualties by enlarging the array of books he could consult. Aguéli saw a clear correspondence between the spiritual core of religions and the language they used to express themselves. His interest in Islam was thus coupled with, if not preceded by, an admiration for the Arabic language. To Hausen he wrote: "This is a language not like others. It has a way of considering things like someone who is all penetrated, saturated with an instinctive science of correspondences."[2] Aguéli identified what he meant by "correspondences" as the inner basis of a language that is expressed in "proverbs, locutions, slang expressions that prove they are in no way arbitrary but universal and submitted to natural laws."[3] His quest for universality was thus sustained with a steady project to find "universal and natural laws" in and between languages and religions. Islam and Christianity would remain at the center of this project throughout his life.

Aguéli's letters from prison demonstrate both his newfound admiration for Islam and also his attachment to a Swedenborgian Christianity. The two traditions needed to be merged and the conceptual category that permitted Aguéli to perform such bridging was that of "monotheism." And for the purpose of his argument, Aguéli often reduced monotheism to its purest essence and defined it as "the belief and aspiration towards a supreme unique being. A universal superlative other."[4] As one might expect from a young anarchist in jail, this monotheism had a modern twist: "This is how I understand a modern monotheism: fanatical towards oneself, tolerant towards others. Taking vitality and harmony as criteria of the 'real,' having as the goal of all actions conformity with oneself. It is a balance within the self and not outside of it. Whoever has his center of gravity exclusively in exterior things is a fetishist."[5] And since Aguéli's monotheism transcends exoteric religious manifestations, he wrote in the same letter that "monotheism is the essence of Christ's teachings, so essential that the faithful Muslim is more Christian than most Christians."[6]

This idea of Islam as an alternative path to Christianity on the way to the atemporal truth of monotheism was thus manifest in the writings of Aguéli since his days in prison in 1894. Four years later he converted to Islam, and in 1902, he was dressed like a Maghribi Arab (see Figure 8.4), strolling the streets of Cairo and following closely the instructions of his Sufi master, the Egyptian Shaykh ʿAbd al-Rahman ʿIllaysh; the man who would accompany Aguéli in his intensive study of the medieval Sufi mystic, Muhyiddin ibn ʿArabi. In one of his letters to Marie Huot, Aguéli described his relationship with his spiritual master in these words:

> You know the affection that Shaykh ʿIllaysh has for me. Now, Shaykh ʿIllaysh was the closest friend of Emir ʿAbd al-Qadir, the Algerian. The Shaykh himself bathed his dead body and buried him next to Ibn ʿArabi in Damascus. Both were the possessors of the secret doctrine of the Great Master. The Shaykh has always called me Muhyiddin, which was one of the names of Ibn ʿArabi, and this was before I became one of his disciples.[7]

Ivan Aguéli, or Abd al-Hadi, positioned himself within a *silsila* (spiritual lineage) that contained him, his direct shaykh (ʿIllaysh), and the Emir (*amīr*, commander) ʿAbd al-Qadir al-Jazaʾiri. All are described, in more or less clear terms, as heirs of the Akbari[8] doctrine of Ibn ʿArabi. This affiliation to an Arabic and Islamic religious and intellectual milieu was clearly important for Aguéli. Yet it has been overlooked in the studies dedicated to the Swedish painter, who has often been described as yet another link in a chain of European esoteric thinkers. When studying Western converts to Islam, intellectual histories point to a modern Western disenchantment, an Orientalist interest in Islam, or to the modern movement of translation that allowed European readers to get acquainted with non-biblical religions. This is the approach to Aguéli taken by many chapters in this book. Such interpretations, while accurate, represent Islam, at least implicitly, as a placid, static entity deprived of any agency. They are about the Westerners who wanted to become Sufi Muslims but rarely about the Sufi Islam that wanted these Westerners to convert. The conversion of Aguéli to Sufism was also, as this chapter will argue, the product of a Sufi Muslim interest in attracting and recruiting young, Western, free spirits.

When Aguéli arrived in Cairo, the city was already witnessing the birth and development of different intellectual responses to problems imposed by an invasive and intrusive Western modernity in largely Muslim societies. One trend saw possible salvation through an esoteric rapprochement with Christianity and promoted dialog with all Westerners who were critical of their European culture, of modernity and materialist philosophies. This school of thought was first developed, as noted by Aguéli in his letter to Huot, by the Algerian warrior and Sufi mystic, Emir ʿAbd al-Qadir al-Jazaʾiri.

The Universalism of a Warrior

ʿAbd al-Qadir[9] was born in western Algeria in 1808 to Muhyiddin al-Hasani (1776–1834), a prominent Sufi leader of a religious family allegedly descending from the Prophet Muhammad. He followed a traditional Islamic education, and at the age of eighteen he accompanied his father on his pilgrimage to Mecca, a trip to the east of the Arab world that would take the young ʿAbd al-Qadir several years. Father and son returned to their home country in 1827, a few months before the tensions between the French consul and the Dey of Algiers started, leading to the French invasion of the country in 1830. Some of the first attacks perpetrated against the French army were organized around the Sufi circles of ʿAbd al-Qadir's family. The young emir started one of the first major Islamic rebellions against a modern Western colonial power.

It is during this period that the early interest of ʿAbd al-Qadir in Christianity appeared. We have little knowledge of the emir's early (pre-1830) understanding of Christian texts and practices aside from what the Qurʾan and other Islamic sources had to teach him about the topic. We can only assume that he encountered Christian groups during his early visits to Iraq and the Levant between 1825 and 1827. It was definitely after the French invasion of Algeria that he could meet and rigorously discuss theological matters with Christian clergymen. One of the main encounters that revealed the early ecumenical interests of ʿAbd al-Qadir was his relationship to the French Catholic priest Father Jacques Suchet (1795–1870).[10] This was an early and unique example of a meeting between a Muslim shaykh and a Christian priest discussing theological matters under the umbrella of colonial struggle. Father Suchet, who was one of the delegates of the French colonial power to the emir, narrates here the discussion he had with ʿAbd al-Qadir after the release of French prisoners:

> He said to me, indicating the Christ that he saw on my chest: "Is that the image of our lord Jesus?" "Yes," I told him, "it is the image of Jesus Christ, our God." "What is Jesus Christ?" "He is the Word of God." And after a moment of silence I added, "and this word has made himself man to save all men; for our God is the Father and the God of all men, Muslims as well as Christians." "But you have only one God like the Muslims?" "We have but one God in Three persons." Then I gave him some explanations on the mystery of the Holy Trinity. He remained contemplative for a moment then he continued: "What is the mission of Catholic priests?" "As you might know, especially now that there is a Bishop in Algiers, our mission is to continue on earth the mission of Jesus, to do good to all men, who we consider our brothers, no matter what is their religion." "But if your religion is this good, and this benevolent, why don't the French observe it? If they followed it, they would be better people."[11]

To this last question the priest simply replied that Muslims also do not practice their religion, for the same reasons perhaps the French do not observe theirs. Father Suchet reported that the emir was interested in a longer and deeper conversation with him, but the interpreter apologized arguing he was unable to translate a discussion on such complicated theological matters. He then asked a second favor from the emir: that the Bishop of Algiers send a priest to the Christian prisoners "to give these poor sheep the help of our holy religion."[12] The emir agreed. Later that night, 'Abd al-Qadir told Suchet "he had so many things in his heart, he wanted to tell him,"[13] and wished they did not need a translator.

'Abd al-Qadir ultimately lost his war against the French and his family and companions were held captive in France for five years. His captivity ended when he moved to Bursa in Turkey. After the emir's military power was neutralized, the image of 'Abd al-Qadir as an amiable man of peace quickly replaced that of the Algerian warrior, and stories of his humanist interests started spreading.[14] This was rapidly actualized into a formal invitation that the French Asiatic Society sent to 'Abd al-Qadir requesting his affiliation to the newly created institution and asking him to write an essay on a topic of his choice, as a sign of his fellowship with the academic organization. This collaboration produced one of the first major intellectual works of the emir, a book he entitled *Dhikra al-'aqil wa tanbih al-ghafil* (Reminder to the Intelligent, Warning to the Indifferent).

Written in the form of a letter, the text combines historical and philosophical insights all in support of rational and scientific thinking. His critique of imitation (*taqlīd*) and his call for a new interpretation of Islamic texts (*ijtihād*) offered 'Abd al-Qadir a good conceptual and legal support to call for a new framing of the relationship between Muslims and Christians.

The *Dhikra* is one of the earliest examples, and perhaps the most important, of a Muslim dignitary addressing a European colonial power in a letter in which he explains what he thinks is the core of the religion of the colonized. It could be considered as the beginning of a "universalist" thinking of the emir where Sufism will increasingly take an important role over the years. "Religion is one," he wrote, "and it is so by the agreement of the prophets. For they differ in their opinions only regarding certain details and rules. Indeed, they resemble men who have the same father, each of them having a different mother. To accuse all of them of lying or accusing one of lying but believing another, amounts to the same thing: it is to thoughtlessly transgress the essential rule of religious duty."[15]

The message of an Islamic ecumenism founded on a perennial brotherhood between monotheisms appealed to a French public that found in that a possible "reconciliation," necessary for smoothing a nascent colonial project. This is at least what Gustave Dugat (1824–94), a prominent French Orientalist of the nineteenth century and a member of the French Asiatic Society, wrote in the preface to his translation of the emir's text in 1858:

> The impression made by reading the work of 'Abd al-Qadir is that the moral and religious ideas of peoples are not as opposed as is commonly imagined; they do not appear as divergent except through the prism of ignorance and prejudice. What is

it that most often has been lacking in them to arrive at conciliation, if not that they needed to know one another, hear one another, and establish between them the interchange of intelligence?[16]

ʿAbd al-Qadir's insistence in this early treatise on the veracity of all prophets' teachings was at the discursive brink between Islamic belief in other Abrahamic messages and, on the other side, the act of giving a thorough and clear legitimacy to *all* monotheisms. The step between them, while sounding trivial, is, in Islamic theology, tremendous. ʿAbd al-Qadir was naturally aware that classical Sunni theological texts do not consider the differences between monotheisms to be minor. While insisting on the common spiritual ground between Judaism, Christianity, and Islam, the major schools of *fiqh* give primary importance to Shariʿa as a defining element of Islam in relationship to other monotheisms. Implicitly considering Shariʿa as an ensemble of "details and rules," as ʿAbd al-Qadir did, is rare enough to be noted here. In his *Dhikra* he deliberately avoided putting Prophet Muhammad in a position of superiority and simply talked about "prophets" in general, and *all* their books, including Torah, Gospel, and Qur'an. In this same text, ʿAbd al-Qadir put himself at the center of this effort to transcend the religious differences toward a spiritual brotherhood between Muslims and Christians. In the second chapter of his book, he bluntly asked the French to position him at the heart of a modern and quasi-prophetic project of reconciliation: "If the Muslims and the Christians had wished to pay attention to me, I would have made them cease their quarrels; inwardly and outwardly they would have become brothers."[17]

After two years spent in Turkey, ʿAbd al-Qadir requested from the French powers permission to relocate to Damascus. He arrived in Syria in 1856, was received with pomp, and met with popular jubilation. For months, he received the visits of Damascene notable families, local scholars, and dignitaries, and also foreign consular officials, writers, and travelers. In Damascus, ʿAbd al-Qadir dedicated most of his time to reading and studying. His entourage was primarily composed of young scholars that he supported financially and who, in return, were responsible for the education of his eight children. It is around the Damascene circle of ʿAbd al-Qadir and his disciples that the universalist interest of the emir, his opinions on modernity, and his critique of Westernization emerged in the form of a new Sufi school: a Sufi modernity that was undeniably inspired both by his encounter with European imperial superiority and with the new reality of a failing Islamic empire; a modern, elitist, and—to the extent that the Shariʿa permits—humanist and Universalist Sufism. This school would constitute the theoretical framework around which Ivan Aguéli, René Guénon, and others will form their own metaphysical variations.

The Esoteric and Exoteric Rapprochement

Emir ʿAbd al-Qadir proposed a *spiritual* harmonization between Christianity and Islam, and with that hoped to "prove" the compatibility of his religion with the requirements of modernity. The school of ʿAbd al-Qadir was based on an emulation of the material and scientific productions of Europe that was to be paralleled with an esoteric rapprochement between the two sides. The difference between an esoteric and exoteric truth developed in his *Dhikra* was further developed in Damascus, but his new conclusions were already mature before his arrival in the Levant: the intellectual achievements of the West should be mirrored in the Muslim world, a step that is only possible if Christianity and Islam are understood as one single monotheistic unity. The emir depicted science as a global and human exercise that should remain indifferent to religious divergences—and consequently could be easily copied. The nature and scope of science are foreign to spiritual matters and after all, as he claimed, "The prophets did not come to argue with the philosophers nor to do away with the sciences of medicine, astronomy, or geometry."[18] 'Abd al-Qadir reduced the mission of all prophets to its most spiritual core and placed the scientific achievements of modern Europe within a more global landscape of reason. "The productions of ideas cannot be limited," as he argued, "the free use of reason is an infinite exercise."[19] For 'Abd al-Qadir, the followers of the same prophets should also be united under the same umbrella of modern scientific progress.

This ecumenical approach to modernity needed a *ta'ṣīl* (rooting) in Islamic tradition, and the main ground upon which 'Abd al-Qadir based his approach was the work of the most prominent medieval Sufi mystic and scholar: Ibn 'Arabi. The stories of the two Sufi masters hold numerous similarities. Ibn 'Arabi, like Emir 'Abd al-Qadir, was also born in a Western Islamic world in times of political upheavals and witnessed the unfolding events of the Reconquista. For both men, the questions of jihad, the integrity of Islam, and its relation to other faiths surrounded their mystical paths. Both spent their last days in Damascus. They died there and were buried next to each other. It will be in the metaphysical doctrines of Ibn 'Arabi that 'Abd al-Qadir will find an *antecedent* to his own variety of an intra-monotheistic brotherhood.

The *waḥdat al-wujūd* (unity of being) is one of these numerous philosophical principles sketched by Ibn 'Arabi and used by 'Abd al-Qadir. It affirms that only God truly, and in absolute terms, exists. Everything else "is" due to the divine existence—a form of a Muslim pantheism that acknowledges the plurality of other "existing" entities and transforms the possible unity with the divine into a necessary goal for humans. "Becoming one with the One" emerged as the cornerstone of Akbari Sufi metaphysics. A first conceptual ramification of Ibn 'Arabi's philosophy of unity is what one might call his proto-universalism, probably best illustrated in these famous verses from his *Tarjuman al-ashwaq* (The Discloser of Desires):

My heart has become capable of every form:
it is a pasture for gazelles and a convent for Christian monks,
And a temple for idols and the pilgrim's Ka'ba
and the tables of the Torah and the book of the Quran.
I follow the religion of Love: whatever way Love's camels take, that is my religion and my faith.[20]

The universality of Ibn 'Arabi is also expressed in his *Futuhat al-makiyyah* (Meccan Revelations) where he states: "Created beings have formed various beliefs about God, and for me, I believe everything they have believed."[21]

In that sense, the Sufism of Ibn ʿArabi was a "new" Sufism, with a relatively explicit and clear sense of universal brotherhood based on divine love. This aspect of Ibn ʿArabi's thought is one of several things that seem to have attracted ʿAbd al-Qadir.[22] It is also necessary here to notice that when the emir arrived in Damascus, the city had already experienced a renewed interest in the work of Ibn ʿArabi with Shaykh ʿAbd al-Ghani al-Nabulusi (1641–1731), Shaykh Khalid al-Baghdadi (1779–1827), and their disciples. Well into the eighteenth century, Ibn ʿArabi's ideas on God's mercy (that reaches non-Muslims) and the oneness of existence were often discussed, supported, or rejected in Sunni circles.[23] Ibn ʿArabi thus remained a controversial figure and it was perhaps due to his unconventional views that a formal *ṭarīqa* (order) was never constructed around him. Spiritual affiliation to the Shaykh was nevertheless preserved and secretly transmitted from one Sufi to another. Emir ʿAbd al-Qadir himself received the Akbari affiliation from his grandfather, who in turn received it from the Indian-born Shaykh Murtada al-Zabidi (1732–90),[24] whom he had met in Egypt on his way to the Hajj.[25]

It is therefore a man who was born in an al-Andalus at war, and who spread his doctrine of "unity" in the eastern cradle of Islam, that ʿAbd al-Qadir chose for a spiritual master. This is how the emir described the influence Ibn ʿArabi had on him: "The Shaykh Ibn ʿArabi is our treasure from whence we draw that which we write, drawing either from its spiritual form or from that which he himself writes in his books."[26] ʿAbd al-Qadir is alluding here to the spiritual apparitions and visions he received from Ibn ʿArabi himself. These manifestations of the Shaykh al-Akbar happened through dreams that the emir narrated in his writings.

The Akbari views of ʿAbd al-Qadir were best expressed in his *Mawaqif* (Book of Stages), a book composed of seemingly aleatory text passages with no titles, each depicting a specific topic related to Sufi metaphysics. The material of the book was collected by the students of ʿAbd al-Qadir after his arrival in Damascus in 1856, with a first edition published twenty years after the death of the emir. The composition and style of some of these texts belong to a Sufi category of literature where the author goes through a semiconscious mystical experience during the writing process. The book ends with transcribed answers that the emir gave to his students on questions related to Ibn ʿArabi's terminology and concepts. There, and in one of his ecstatic ecumenical statements, ʿAbd al-Qadir explained: "We all obey God and believe in him, and there is no absolute denier of God in the world … all the infidelity in the world is but relative."[27]

The main trait of ʿAbd al-Qadir's Akbari thought is an implicit and constant emphasis on the idea of polysemy: God's attributes are diverse, the paths leading to him are infinite, no vessel can encompass alone the divine presence, God is beyond human collective truths, and the Qur'an is a book of infinite meanings and symbols. The polysemy of the divine message was the cornerstone of the Sufi modernization that ʿAbd al-Qadir undertook. The emir writes: "No one knows him in all of His aspects; no one is ignorant of Him in all His aspects. Therefore each person necessarily knows Him in a certain respect and worships Him in the same respect. Consequently, error does not exist in this world except in a relative manner."[28] Muslims are right, others are not wrong, and the proof is both taken from an intellectual contemplation of the world and from a particular reading of the Qur'anic text.

The Damascene school of 'Abd al-Qadir considered European modernity as potentially threatening if not paralleled with a "Sufi refinement." The threat of an untamed modernity penetrating unprepared Islamic lands is present in 'Abd al-Qadir's texts. He relates in his *Mawaqif* a vision he had where Ibn 'Arabi was presented to him in the form of a lion who commanded him to put his hands in his mouth. The emir complied and Ibn 'Arabi turned into a *majdhūb* (one attracted by God), confused and uttering incomprehensible sentences. Ibn 'Arabi repeated that he would perish; he then fell on the ground. For 'Abd al-Qadir, the confused Great Master fainting and predicting his perishing was nothing but a visual metaphor of a decaying and troubled Islam.[29] For him, the new and troubling reality of a Muslim world under threat provoked the anguish and disappointment of all Muslim saints represented here by Ibn 'Arabi. This dramatic outcome could, at least partially, be addressed through a Sufi pacification of an otherwise aggressive and invasive European modernity.

Blindly mimicking European nations or categorically shunning their projects would then be equally problematic. An esoteric rapprochement as key to modernity was what 'Abd al-Qadir hoped for, metaphysics as an underground passage to the twentieth century is what he proposed: a hybrid model where a scientific rationalism is bound to a Sufi esoteric rationale. Emir 'Abd al-Qadir readapted Ibn 'Arabi's theosophy to construct proper answers coping with the undeniable Western military and technological supremacy that he had witnessed in his native Algeria and during his exile in France. Islam without a proper revision would be at the brink of perishing, as predicted by his vision of a troubled Ibn 'Arabi and modernity without Islam would be reduced to an aimless and blind materialism with no soul.

Emir 'Abd al-Qadir spent the first months of the year 1883 in his palace in Dummar suffering from a urinary retention that caused the deterioration of his health until his death on May 26, 1883. The day after, the body of the Algerian military leader and shaykh was taken to the Umayyad Mosque for the funeral prayer, then to the Salihiyya district where he was buried under the dome of Ibn 'Arabi's shrine, next to his spiritual master. Emir al-Hashami recounts the death of his father in a letter he sent to Marie d'Aire:[30] "At sunrise, the body of the emir was transported to Damascus in the omnibus that Napoleon III gave him. A large crowd gathered and the consuls of all powerful nations were there. Shaykh 'Abd al-Rahman 'Illaysh, his equal in sanctity, as well as his nephew, the pious Sid Ahmad ibn al-Makki, washed his body."[31]

'Abd al-Qadir, the 'Illaysh Family, and Ivan Aguéli

Shaykh 'Illaysh, described here by the son of the emir as nothing less than "equal in sanctity" to his father, was responsible for bathing and preparing the body of the dead shaykh for burial, a mission that is often reserved to the family of the deceased or to his closest friends. Shaykh Muhammad al-Hafnawi (1850–1942), in his biography of 'Abd al-Qadir that he claims to have collected from "the most reliable sources,"[32] also reported that 'Illaysh was responsible for organizing the burial ceremony of 'Abd al-Qadir, adding that the Egyptian shaykh was the guest of the emir at the moment of his death. If 'Illaysh was indeed hosted by 'Abd al-Qadir, then he would have been so for a relatively short period and in very special circumstances. By the end of the year 1882, Shaykh Muhammad ʿIllaysh, the great Maliki mufti of Egypt, was imprisoned with his son ʿAbd al-Rahman, due to their support for the ʿUrabi revolt.[33] The father died in jail very shortly after, and his son was sent into exile, traveling to Damascus where he was hosted by ʿAbd al-Qadir, an old friend of his father.

The traceable relationship between ʿAbd al-Qadir and Muhammad ʿIllaysh dates back to 1844, when the emir asked the scholars of Cairo to formulate a *fatwa* (legal opinion) on the hostile position the Moroccan Sultan took against the Algerian colonial struggle. The latter, after supporting and even hosting the rebellion of ʿAbd al-Qadir, had turned against him following French pressure[34] and expelled him from Moroccan territory. Shaykh ʿIllaysh, grand Mufti of the Egyptian Maliki school, declared the acts of the Moroccan king unlawful and contrary to the Shar'ia.[35] The exchange between the emir and Muhammad ʿIllaysh was not restricted to this fatwa and took other forms over the years. In the manuscript of ʿAbd al-Qadir's famous letter *Husam al-din li-qat' shubah al-murtaddin* (The Religion's Sword Cutting the Claims of the Apostates) one can find in the final pages what is described as "an exchange of letters and fatwas with Shaykh Muhammad ʿIllaysh al-Maliki"[36] that dates back to 1847. The relationship between ʿAbd al-Qadir and Muhammad ʿIllaysh was old and this helps explain how Abd al-Rahman ʿIllaysh was a student of ʿAbd al-Qadir in Damascus, along with other famous young Damascene scholars such as ʿAbd al-Razaq Bitar (1837–1917) and ʿAbd al-Majid al-Khani (1847–1900).[37]

After ʿAbd al-Qadir's death, and toward the last decade of the nineteenth century, ʿAbd al-Rahman ʿIllaysh finally returned to his native Egypt where he would live until his death in 1922.[38] When Ivan Aguéli arrived in Cairo, ʿIllaysh was there, and like Emir ʿAbd al-Qadir, the Egyptian Sufi master had an interest in Western audiences and in pursuing the project of a Sufi modern renewal. Ivan Aguéli adhered to this endeavor and later became the main protagonist of an Akbari ecumenism in the West.

Aguéli, who was increasingly dissatisfied with life in Paris, kept, upon his departure to Cairo, only a few contacts there. In a letter to Marie Huot, he asked her to propagate and nurture the legend that "he had left a longtime ago with Dervishes, probably to Yemen" and that he "had become more and more savage, and all relationship with him were interrupted."[39] After settling in Cairo, he informed Huot that he was now poorly dressed, wearing white cotton clothes, and was required to shave his head. Judging from this description, Aguéli was going through a relatively rigorous Sufi training in Cairo,[40] contrary to the view of Romolo Garbati reported in Chapter 9. And this was under the guidance of Abd al-Rahman ʿIllaysh. The young Swedish artist manifested much love and respect for the Egyptian shaykh, as is clear in his letters to Huot. In different instances, Aguéli described his spiritual master in glorious terms and even invited his correspondent to come visit him and the Sufi saint in Egypt. Although the visit never happened, it remains clear through this long-running correspondence that ʿIllaysh and Huot knew of each other through Aguéli. Responding to a letter of Huot where she inquired about ʿIllaysh's health, Aguéli wrote: "Shaykh ʿIllaysh is doing very well and was delighted to receive your greetings," adding immediately after, as a reminder of the high stature of the man Huot was receiving greetings from, "He is the current representative of Ibn ʿArabi, that is to say his school." Aguéli ended his letter describing to his friend his desire to come back to painting and the reluctance of 'Illaysh, "The great man" he wrote "will first take me through an 'isolation.'" He was referring most probably to a *khalwa*, a Sufi exercise of solitary retreat that a master could require from his disciple.

Conclusion

Although 'Illaysh was a Shadhili Madani Sufi[41] it was mostly the Akbari doctrine that the Egyptian shaykh was transmitting to his Swedish disciple—an Akbariyya that, according to Aguéli himself, was transmitted to 'Illaysh by Emir 'Abd al-Qadir, the "heir of Akbari sciences"[42] as described by his contemporaries. By introducing a European artist and Theosophist to the work of Ibn 'Arabi, 'Illaysh was still perpetuating the tradition of 'Abd al-Qadir: an esoteric rapprochement between spiritual circles from the Christian world and Sufi Islam through the study of Ibn 'Arabi. And while 'Abd al-Qadir, father of this approach, was interested in states and large institutions such as the French Asiatic Society, 'Illaysh turned to particular individuals to whom he ascribed the role of understanding, translating, and spreading the thought of Ibn 'Arabi in the West. Ivan Aguéli fitted within this category.

The admiration that Aguéli had for Ibn 'Arabi is visible in his letters to Huot. He described him as superb and staggering, compared him to Edgar Allan Poe (1809–49) and Auguste Villiers de l'Isle-Adam (1838–89), and added that "he is in art and in emotions absolutely similar to Swedenborg."[43] For Aguéli, Ibn 'Arabi appears as a resurrected hero who was able to reform modernity. "While reading him," he wrote, "you feel he is a man of our times, with the breadth of his ideas, and with his warmth and elegance of which we lost the secret a long ago."[44] Aguéli did not limit himself to the work of translation and analysis he initiated. He thought of himself as the heir of the Akbari secret, the true spiritual successor of Ibn 'Arabi after 'Abd al-Qadir and 'Illaysh. The legitimacy of this claim did not rely simply on the work he was doing for the Akbari cause. It was also "spiritual." He says in one of his letters: "14 years ago, I saw an unknown man in a dream. When I read the biography of Ibn 'Arabi that one of our Arab collaborators made, I recognized him. I never talked about my dream to anyone for the simple reason that it was a mystery for which I did not have an explanation yet. Something particular about his eye, the color of the clothes he usually wore, the exact nuance of his hair and his carnation. All was in there."[45]

To Aguéli, there was an authentic spiritual connection that linked him to Ibn 'Arabi: a special bond that was not only proven by the visions he had, but also by what he considered a special, unparalleled giftedness he showed in understanding the words of the medieval mystic. He wrote to Huot, "I haven't read much of the master [Ibn 'Arabi], but I could guess it all. And all the thought I developed about him turned out to be all perfectly correct. I have now translated all my articles on Ibn 'Arabi in Arabic (they are now in press). The rare persons of our time who understand the master recognize that I perfectly understood him, but in an absolutely novel manner."[46]

Novel yet authentic, rooted in the Akbari tradition and open to the upheavals of modernity. This is how Aguéli evaluated his own interpretation of Ibn 'Arabi. And one cannot avoid discerning the spirit of Emir ʿAbd al-Qadir in his work. Ivan Aguéli was directly involved in the project of an Arabic and Islamic modernity and could comfortably be positioned within a list of other thinkers that would include Muhammad ʿAbduh, Rashid Rida, and, of course, Emir ʿAbd al-Qadir. But Aguéli is also more than that. He was a multifaceted character who, as has been argued here, belonged to more than one tradition, but subtly retained many enigmas around his life, choices, and character. We will end with a final note that perhaps sums up the mystery around him: "I finally found the philosophy of disguise successful: it is to believe it yourself. No one doubts my Islam for that simple reason. That I don't doubt it myself."[47]

11

Ivan Aguéli's Humanist Vision: Islam, Sufism, and Universalism

Meir Hatina

This chapter analyzes Ivan Aguéli's humanist vision, with a focus on his understanding of Sufism, based mainly on his writings in La Gnose[1] and Il Convito/Al-Nadi.[2] A number of issues will be dealt with: How did Aguéli turn Islam and Sufism into an ecumenical vision that crosses borders and nations? To what extent was his humanism also nurtured by the anarchist philosophy of the late nineteenth century, which was largely anti-clerical, perceiving any authority or hierarchy as suppressing individual freedom, while promoting a just and egalitarian society? Did Aguéli reconcile the anarchist perception of human beings as free and rational creatures with the Sufi perception of their total submission to a Sufi master or shaykh?

Aguéli, both through his writings and his activities in civic associations, played a prominent role in the European–Muslim rapprochement of the early twentieth century that emerged under the shadow of colonialism and against the background of a growing dissonance between Islam and the West. In this sense, Aguéli can be depicted as an involved public intellectual, striving to introduce an ethical value system in the lives of both communities he lived in—the European and the Muslim.[3]

Aguéli, who converted to Islam in 1898 and called himself 'Abd al-Hadi al-'Aqili, was affiliated with the 'Arabiyya-Shadhiliyya ṭarīqa (Sufi order) in Egypt. He was also involved in the publication of the bilingual Italian/Arabic periodical Il Convito/Al-Nadi, which addressed issues relating to Islam and Sufism, the Ottoman Empire, and the European powers, mainly England and France. Il Convito/Al-Nadi, in spite of its Italian sponsorship, was both part and reflection of a flourishing printed culture of periodicals, books, and publication houses in the Middle East, which also responded to a growing readership and attested to a vivid public sphere in which key issues of imperialism, reform, and renewal were debated.[4]

In his writings Aguéli advocated a tolerant and pluralistic version of Islam, with Sufism and its icon, Muhyiddin ibn 'Arabi, used as a main lever.[5] Sufism was presented by Aguéli as a spiritual philosophy that, like other "Eastern" religions, dealt with the understanding of the universe, liberated man from his materialism and selfishness, and bestowed on humanity compassion, mercy, and social solidarity.

Despite the fact that Aguéli wrote within an Islamic-Sufi framework, his ideological mindset synthesized Western Marxist-anarchist values and Islamic-mystic values. As opposed to the Italian Enrico Insabato, his coeditor on *Il Convito/Al-Nadi*, Aguéli was essentially an intellectual and man of thought.[6] He had no connection to any official institution. He did not advance anyone else's political agenda, nor did he engage in promoting imperialist interests,[7] even though he was suspected by the Egyptian authorities of being pro-Turkish and by the British as pan-Arabist. Nevertheless, he remained a dissident, diverting his defiant views into writing and cultural activities. He continued to challenge a decadent, patronizing, racist, and imperialist Western civilization, and posed before it a mirror and a recipe for rehabilitation.[8] It seems that his anti-Western orientation was clearly reflected also in his views on gender relations, discussed in Chapter 12, when he argued that liberty and emancipation in the European sense of the terms would only cause harm to women's merits and morality.

Defense of Islam

Aguéli, in contrast to other Western Sufis of his time like Léon Champrenaud (1870–1925), Isabelle Eberhardt, and Leda Rafanelli demonstrated a deep and genuine approach to Sufism and converted to Islam in his late twenties. His admiration for Sufism also involved defending the good name of Islam and that of its believers. In his *A New Science: The Discovery of Religion in the Age of Reason*, Guy Stroumsa found that eighteenth-century enlightened views of Islam adopted a more positive and open attitude than did earlier views, motivated by intellectual curiosity about the civilization of the "Turks."[9] However, this modern development in the study of Islam did not significantly alter or transform the negative traditional perception of Islam as a religion of violence and lust and of its founder Muhammad as an impostor.[10]

It was this biased public and scholarly Western climate in which Aguéli and his colleagues operated and which they sought to change by fostering a tolerant, pluralistic, and pacifist version of Islam. In this context, *Il Convito/Al-Nadi* in its opening edition of May 22, 1904, declared that it aimed to address the people of the East in the language of humanity, compassion, and solidarity, and to serve the truth and history and unite hearts.[11] In a similar vein, the introduction to a volume of the periodical's first-year essays stated clearly that:

> human beings are all one family, and therefore have social rights which are mutual and must be placed above all religious, scholastic, and political disputes so as to preserve the sacred brotherhood. Human beings must recognize the proximity of blood lineage to other human beings just as they recognize the affinity to their family, tribe, and nation. The affinity between people, despite their distribution and the multiplicity of their communities, goes back to one root—the humanity represented by the first human being.[12]

Il Convito/Al-Nadi's declared humanist mission of advocating solidarity and morality in the world, and of siding with the colonized and oppressed people of the East, was ingrained in Aguéli's worldview. He often displayed contempt for European Orientalists, whom he accused of arrogance, racism, and Islamophobia.[13] This defiant mood was reflected also in Aguéli's portraits of men, women, and children he painted during his time in the East and Egypt, which were devoid of exotic and sensual features that otherwise characterized illustrations of nineteenth-century European travel literature of the Orient.[14] Aguéli's portraits were dignified, projecting respect, sensitivity, and empathy toward his characters. On the intellectual level which concerns us here, he declared, "Our Orientalists do not know Muhyiddin's true place in Sufism, nor Sufism's place in Islam."[15]

The main lever for Aguéli in promoting human solidarity, in which the big and the strong should also look after the little and weak, was Sufi teachings, with an emphasis on the philosophy of Ibn 'Arabi. With the blessing of his shaykh, 'Abd al-Rahman 'Illaysh, Aguéli saw himself as an advocate of Islam and Sufism, whose aim was to correct historical injustice against Islam and Sufism by clarifying their meaning to the Western public.[16] This mission was intertwined with another mission that Aguéli took upon himself, namely to present via the Arabic sections of *Il Convito/Al-Nadi* to the Muslim public a normative image of Sufism as in harmony with the Shari'a and to position Sufism at the heart of the Muslim consensus, as against the vigorous attempts by ideological rivals to exclude it.

Aguéli's humanist project was built on two related stages: firstly, dilution or softening of the legal aspects of Islam, in favor of placing mysticism at its center; and secondly, reframing Sufism as a universal philosophical and moral system, while minimizing problematic practices such as extreme asceticism, the cult of saints, or noisy *dhikr* gatherings.

Softening Legal Islam

For most Christian Europeans who turned to Islam, it was Sufism rather than Islamic norms as embodied in the *fiqh* (jurisprudence) literature which proved attractive. Judicial Islam was perceived as too dogmatic and scriptural, which also sharpened the divides between peoples and cultures. It was not so different from the Catholic Church and monasteries depicted as fossilized and oppressive institutions. The negative image of Islamic norms was reinforced with the emergence of Islamic protest movements, which emphasized puritanism and politics. In contrast, Sufism was seen as a flexible, inclusive culture devoted to the spiritual elevation of the believer. These Westerners traced in Sufi themes such as internal purification (*safā'*) or social altruism (*ihsān*) a lever to upgrade the individual's moral quality and to promote universal solidarity. Their attraction to Sufism reflected not only intellectual curiosity but also resentment against the capitalist modernity of the West. This attraction–resentment interplay was also embodied in the thought of Aguéli.

Aguéli was careful to show respect for the revealed, exoteric dimension of Islam— that is, the regular rites of religion—and to define it as a pillar of Muslim culture. He and other authors of *Il Convito/Al-Nadi*, for instance, depicted the Shari'a as one of the lofty systems of law, characterized by judicial flexibility and based on the principles of justice and freedom, especially in its capacity for eradicating crime and corruption. While defying the demonization of Islam in European discourse, these writers also criticized Muslim governments (especially in Istanbul) that did not do enough to enlighten European observers as to Islam and its laws. According to Aguéli, adopting an unbiased stance toward Islam would reveal a tolerant and pluralistic creed— illustrated by a multitude of different *ṭarīqas*, each led by righteous people and based on a different conception of Sufism. Another example was to be found in the existence of four legal schools (*madhāhib*),[17] all of which were legitimate and demonstrated no animosity toward those who lived according to another school. The reason for this was that there was a consensus (*ijmāʿ*) between these schools regarding the roots of Islam, even though they were based, through legal reasoning (*ijtihād*), on different laws that preserved the genuine objectives of the Shariʿa (*maqāṣid al-sharīʿa*). Thus Muslims disagree only about the practical ways of realizing faith. Moreover, these legal disputes did not (as Europeans mistakenly believed) result in sectarian fanaticism that might jeopardize public order. The ideal picture that Aguéli described did not prevent him from urging Muslim jurists to put an end to legal disputes and to formulate common rules of religious interpretation. Thereby he also would refute European allegations that they were fanatics.[18]

Another example of the humanist face of Islam as traced by Aguéli and his Muslim colleagues writing in *Il Convito/Al-Nadi*, such as Muhammad al-Sharbatli and ʿAbd al-Rahman ʿIllaysh, was the issue of slavery. For these writers, selling people into slavery was permitted only in wartime, and only from among the inhabitants of lands conquered by the Muslims. Moreover, this was only one of several options the Muslim ruler could consider, such as the release of prisoners without compensation, payment of money by their families, exchange for Muslim prisoners held by the enemy, or prisoners becoming "subjected people" (*ahl al-dhimma*), that is, people entitled to freedom of worship and communal autonomy and whom it was forbidden to enslave.[19] The issue of slavery and *dhimmīs* were closely related to the question of Islam's attitude toward non-Muslims. Aguéli and *Il Convito/Al-Nadi* emphasized that the emergence of Islam in the seventh century heralded the end of an era of oppression and the beginning of an era of justice. This was reflected in three legal institutions: the *jizya* or poll tax where only the Imam or his deputy were authorized to tax their subjects, as it was for public purposes and did not include women, children, and the insane; the protection of life (*amān*) in the case of foreign residents in Muslim countries; and an armistice (*hudna*) in times of war, which could last up to ten years and was nullified only in case of violation by the other side. Softening the legal Shariʿa dimension of Islamic thought left intact sensitive legal imperatives, yet still subjecting them to standards of justice and humanism.[20]

Aguéli did not ignore the image of the Prophet Muhammad, who in his personality mediated between unity and diversity, between the common people and the aristocracy, and between spiritualism and religious law. The Prophet achieved this without the need for coercion and violence. Thanks to his endeavors, the norms of justice, unity, and cooperation in the Arab tribe spread throughout the universe.[21] The word "Islam" derived from the causative verb *aslama*, that is, to give, to deliver oneself to God. Hence it was the destiny of man to be universal and devote his life to humanity. Islam abolished the culture of selfishness and, instead, nurtured the art of altruism (*l'art de donner*), based on asceticism (*zuhd*).[22]

No wonder, Aguéli pointed out, that Islam was able to foment perfect solidarity among its believers—despite the ethnic differences between Sudanese and Persians, Turks and Arabs, Chinese and Albanians.[23] For him, the altruistic theme of giving, charity, and compassion means living humanly in relation also to nature and animals, to which he dedicated an entire treatise in the Italian section of *Il Convito/Al-Nadi*, as Chapter 7 has discussed. Responsibility is a measure of nobility, Aguéli concluded. The more generous and noble a person is, the more responsible he is toward others and his surroundings.[24]

Aguéli's elaborate discussion of giving and compassion provides a further prism to his aesthetic sensitivity toward nature, landscapes, animals, and of course human beings on the one hand, and the grave dissonance toward materialistic European civilization dominated by social Darwinism, leaving the weak inferior and helpless.[25]

According to Aguéli, the exoteric intertwined with the esoteric was the driving force of Islam, while separation between them would cause decline and decay. Hence, it was impossible to talk about Sufism apart from the Shari'a, as the two were closely related. Aguéli rejected, unlike the Theosophists, some Eastern religions like Buddhism and Taoism, since they only focused on esotericism, while renouncing any link to law and practice. He also accused them of religious persecution, citing the Muslim minority in India as an example. It seems that at the background for Aguéli's criticism of Buddhism was his own personal experience when he was harassed by Buddhists while in Ceylon in 1899.[26]

Although he focused on the integration of legalism and mysticism in Islam, Aguéli stressed that only Sufism could ensure Islam as a lofty and viable creed. Without it, the fate of Islam would be like that of European Christianity. "When a religion declares with all seriousness that its rituals have neither a sense of mystery nor of the hidden world, it makes a public profession of superstition and needs to be sent to a museum of antiquities."[27]

Indeed, it was the spiritual language of Islam which captured Aguéli's imagination and reflected also his artistic soul. In 1894 he wrote to a friend: "You, on your part seek a religion. I [seek] a language."[28] Legal rules and precepts were important, but were confined to a preliminary level in the attainment of gnosis. This statement, according to which Sufism was the beating heart of Islam and the focal point of its encounter with the surrounding world, signaled the second stage of Aguéli's humanist project: that is, reframing Sufism as a cosmopolitan universal philosophy. Aguéli argued that the essence of Sufism did not lie in rituals and in veneration of saints, but in philosophy and texts.[29]

Reframing Sufism as a Universal Philosophy

The image of Sufism in Aguéli's writings was idealized. The goal was to position Sufism at the heart of the Islamic consensus, but no less importantly to present it as a moral ideal for Westerners and as a cultural bridge between diverse religions, between East and West. Aguéli defined Sufism as a spiritual philosophy that deals with the understanding of the universe, liberates man from his selfishness, and bestows on humanity compassion, mercy, and social solidarity. In contrast to monastic orders in Christianity, Sufi followers were not required to totally commit to the order, such as by retiring from society or suppressing their human needs. The essential difference between *ṭarīqas* and monastic orders, Aguéli stated:

> is the difference between freedom and freedom of choice and between coercion and suppression of personal will and restriction of human feelings. Every Muslim can be associated with or leave the order, can pay allegiance to the shaykh or withdraw from it in favor of another shaykh—all according to his own judgment and principles.[30]

As to the human fabric of the *ṭarīqas*, Aguéli insisted that Sufi leaders and followers possessed moral virtues, and any compression between them and Christian monks was unjustified and showed total ignorance.

> Some say that the *ṭarīqas* aimed only at making profits from the public and that their people beg just to satisfy their hunger. For this reason, some scholars perceived the Sufis as the counterparts of Christianity. Nevertheless, observing the monks will reveal that they are fat as if they had no other work than to fill the stomach. As for the dervishes [Sufis], they are slim and chronically ill. This indicates that they are preoccupied with things other than eating and drinking, i.e., taming the soul and doing good deeds that elevate the soul to the proximity of God.[31]

Aguéli's assertion as to the intertwinement between impoverished life (*iftiqār*) and spiritual elevation being the driven force of the Sufis was in some way a reflection of his own personal circumstances. Often he depicted the hardships he had to tackle in his life, but assured his readers with a sense of pride that this only made him more determined to pursue spiritual perfection and to come closer to the divine. "Predicament would always be preceded by salvation," was his motto.[32]

In Aguéli's view, the formation of the soul (*tarbiyat al-nafs*) and the love of God (*maḥabat Allah*) in Sufi rituals, as reflected in the *dhikr* ceremonies, should be guided by a pure intention to come closer to God, while maintaining the principles of religion. Otherwise it was the work of the Devil and a deviation from Islam. It is interesting to note that Aguéli hardly mentioned the veneration of saints or visits to their tombs (*ziyāra*). He did refer, however, to the issue of miracles (*khawāriq*), but claimed that there was no prohibition against or religious retribution for it.

While coloring Sufism with a humanist, intellectual, and normative hue, Aguéli also highlighted the interest and respect it aroused among European scholars and philosophers, who perceived Sufism as a spiritual science dealing with the human soul.[33] He even translated parts of their writings to put a different, more empathic face on the European discourse about Sufism, thereby also emphasizing its global outreach. However, the pinnacle in Aguéli's humanistic approach is embodied by Ibn

'Arabi, who became a cultural icon and a symbol of the continued vitality of Sufism throughout the ages.

Surely, Aguéli did not forget his Muslim audience, to whom he pointed out that Ibn 'Arabi was one of the purest scholars guided by divine inspiration (*ilhām*), which includes all the prophets of Shem, and whose culmination is Muhammad, the servant and messenger of God. Ibn 'Arabi moved away from heresy (*zandaqa*), whose members wear the garment of faith outwardly, and from those *ṭarīqa*s, mainly in Asia (as in Iran and Turkey), which adopted extreme asceticism (*ghulū*), a total monastic way of life and meaningless ecstatic cries (*shaṭaḥāt*). In contrast, Ibn 'Arabi sanctified the absolute oneness of God (*tawḥīd*), adhered to the path of the Prophet, and combined the rational and imaginal, Shari'a and *ḥaqīqa* (transcendent truth) or *'irfān* (gnosis). In other words, Ibn 'Arabi was a true and pure monotheist. He reached the highest spiritual levels, or in Sufi terminology stations (*maqāmāt*), including capturing the secrets of the universe, and looking at hell and heaven and their inhabitants.[34]

Aguéli's arguments about Ibn 'Arabi's orthodoxy corresponded to those of other Muslim writers in *Il Convito/Al-Nadi*.[35] The underlying aim was to refute Muslim puritans' accusations against Ibn 'Arabi and his contemporary followers as heretics upholding the concept of *waḥdat al-wujūd* (unity of being), according to which God is transcendent, and in essence immanent in creation. Notably, it was the Hanbali Ibn Taymiyya (1263–1328) who marked *waḥdat al-wujūd* as worse than unbelief, since it meant that no distinction could be drawn between God and the world.[36]

Aguéli rarely used the term *waḥdat al-wujūd*. When he did so he shifted its literal meaning away from the idea that everything is God and any thing is an object of adoration to aspiring to comprehend God's creation in order to glorify Him. Aguéli's preferred term in explaining Ibn 'Arabi's thought was *tawḥīd* (unicity), which is associated with the basic Muslim understanding of the total oneness of God. Relying on Ibn 'Arabi's writings, Aguéli carefully explained that for Sufis, *tawḥīd* did not mean complete unification with God in soul and body, but rather a state of profound spiritual nearness (*qurba*) with the divine.[37]

Still, as part of constructing Ibn 'Arabi's humanistic image, it was essential for Aguéli also to highlight Ibn 'Arabi's righteousness (*istiqāma*) and moderation (*i'tidāl*), and hence to show clearly that "a person who distinguishes between faith and just conduct is a heretic. Such a man denies the religious law which in essence is based on justice and morality."[38] In this context, Aguéli presented Ibn 'Arabi as a scholar who was demanding in his own religious conduct, but displayed understanding and restraint toward others, even though he was aware of their wrongdoing. Ibn 'Arabi did not think that evil could be rooted out, but believed that it could be limited. He also did not seek compliance and power, and used the term *siyāsa* not in the widespread political sense of seeking power and greatness, but in the sense of giving advice and guidance. Lack of religious fanaticism and earthly interests, Aguéli concluded, stemmed from the elevated virtues and spiritual perfection of Ibn 'Arabi.[39]

In addition, Aguéli placed Ibn 'Arabi into a glorified lineage that included two other, much-admired figures: Rabi'a al-'Adawiyya and 'Abd al-Qadir al-Jilani.[40] Ibn 'Arabi was also ranked higher than Abu Hamid al-Ghazali (1058–1111), who was described by Aguéli as a great expert in theology and logic, but without real experience on the Sufi path, which largely turned his Sufi writings into a mere intellectual exercise. In contrast, Aguéli argued, Ibn 'Arabi was blessed with divine illumination and served as a lamp (*miṣbāḥ*) and a compass for all deviants, including atheists and ungodly men (*mulḥidūn*) who fell into the abyss of the *dahriyya* (materialistic-hedonistic) school of thought, which denies resurrection and future life in the other world. Aguéli noted with a sense of triumph that the burial place of Ibn 'Arabi in Damascus eventually became a pilgrimage site for those seeking knowledge and divine grace.[41]

Nevertheless, Aguéli's attention was mainly directed to a Western audience, among which he sought to propagate the translated teachings of Ibn 'Arabi. Aguéli mentioned Ibn 'Arabi's prolific and clear writings on both spiritual and rational sciences. He also noted that Ibn 'Arabi's philosophy relied on three key elements: first, loyalty and pure devotion (*ikhlāṣ*) to God's worship devoid of selfishness and lust; second, striving for a comprehensive outlook (*kulliyya*), namely to praise and sanctify everything that existed in the universe, objects and creatures alike, attributing their existing to God; and third, faith in God based on love (*maḥabba*) and not on the fear of hell and a desire to reach paradise—the latter perception characterizes the common believers. Aguéli perceived these elements as having the great potential for Islam to carry out a universal civilized vision of the world. He also mentioned the fact that Ibn 'Arabi was born in the west (Spain) and died in the east (Syria), and thus embodied both the seminal encounter between East and West and religious tolerance.[42]

Ambivalences and Contradictions

As a cosmopolitan intellectual Aguéli absorbed anarchist elements into his humanist vision, such as individual freedom, equality for all without discrimination, public education, social justice, and empathy for the weak. Such ideas, common in global anarchist networks, were also present and loudly aired in Aguéli's Egyptian milieu by a vibrant anarchist movement which articulated the demands of the working classes via the press and educational institutions.[43] As we saw in Chapter 9, he was in close contact with the Romolo Garbati, who was involved in anarchist circles in Cairo and Alexandria.[44] In Aguéli's writings one recognizes expressions of political defiance of state structures of oppression, hierarchy, and domination. In his perception, a moral society based on mutual aid and mass education was a sine qua non in an age where the universal moral compass became indifferent and fatalist. In line with anarchist thinking, Aguéli also ruled out militarism and wars, and preached universal brotherhood.[45]

What about religion? Classical anarchism of the nineteenth century tended to reject any flavor of religion, as embodied in the writings of Pierre-Joseph Proudhon (1809–65), Mikhail Bakunin (1814–76), Louis Michel (1830–1905), or Peter Kropotkin. These founding fathers of anarchism sought to replace supernatural theology with a secular system of ethics. But, as shown by some recent studies, anarchist thinking was more diverse, and alternative approaches targeted only institutionalized (often Western) religious beliefs and institutions, or insisted on religion as a private matter.[46]

Aguéli did not defy divine authority; he rather seems to adhere to a softer version of anti-clericalism, comprising a profound criticism of the Christian Church, both Catholic and Protestant. He did not deny the existence of God or His absolute oneness. On the contrary, he was a committed advocate of monotheism, which may explain also his aversion to the Christian doctrine of the Trinity.[47] His writings also did not include explicit statements against the Sunni establishment, arguing that it lacks centralist and hierarchy structures. In one place he positioned the 'ulama as the third pillar of the Muslim community, alongside the *ṭarīqa*s and the sultanate.[48] Nevertheless, Aguéli certainly shared the anarchist concept according to which the principles of morality were not to be enforced; rather they were an expression of humans' free will. He spoke out against intermediation between the believer and God, arguing that the sky is like nature: it always responds when one's prayers or requests are done in a good manner.[49] He also stood against all missionary activity, Christian or Islamic, and called upon local Muslim authorities not to employ men of religion of any creed in administrative posts.[50]

Admiration for Sufism and the spirituality of the East as a recipe for saving humanity from degenerating into materialism also highlighted inner contradictions and intellectual elitism in Aguéli's humanistic outlook. This was so on at least two levels: the relationship between the disciple and the Sufi master, and the relations between the masses and the educated elite.

Sufism allows believers a rich religious experience, but it also requires them to acquire teachers and mentors on the path of spiritual perfection. The obligation to yield to the absolute authority of the shaykh is reflected in the term *ṣuḥba* (companionship) and the latter's superior morality is embodied in the institution of *baraka* or *karāmāt* (blessing, divine grace), which he passes on to his family members or close circle of followers. The two other circles, the shaykh's disciples (*murīdūn*) and the common people, are required to comply with his rulings. In Sufi history *ṣuḥba*, *baraka*, and *karāmāt* became an important lever in cementing the religious authority of Sufi shaykhs and the establishment of aristocratic Sufi families in Muslim society.

Aguéli did not deny the Sufi theme of intermediation in the achievement of thorough knowledge and a solid faith. In one place he made it clear that those disciples who seek to acquire spiritual experience and to develop their supernatural faculties outside the *ṭarīqa* are naive and attacked by spells. The reason that some of them do not fall into intellectual or moral derangement is because God has shown mercy on them.[51]

Aguéli identified the Sufi masters with the highest degree of divine illumination. Formalism and law, he stipulated, were the province of the "average man" (*l'homme moyen*) while the esoteric knowledge of God was the privilege of the elevated ones.[52] In fact, this perception contradicted the anarchist ideal of a free and volitional human society that does not resort to the use of force, hierarchy, or authority, and is characterized by solidarity and mutual assistance. Even if we classify Aguéli as following Kropotkin's model of communist anarchism, which seeks to accommodate individual autonomy and collective interests or needs, we can still argue that at the focus of this model lay the concept of the human being as a free and rational creature.

Another related contradiction in Aguéli's thinking can be found in the relations between the common people ('*āmma*) and the elite (*khāṣṣa*). The anarchist view protests against the enslavement of the masses and against bringing them under the control of a handful of privileged individuals. Aguéli preserved this distinction between the common believers and the Sufi shaykhs. Though emphasizing that Sufi masters upheld morality and justice, he still perceived them as a select and chosen group due to their intimate knowledge of the secrets of the universe and the Creator's intentions.

Aguéli affirmed the Sufi view that the spiritual masters have the second and third types of knowledge. The first type of people dealt with religious laws, their observance and their dissemination. They were experts in the realm of the revealed, of jurisprudence. The second type of people was those who were close to God and whose divine grace was manifested in their external conduct. Members of the third type belonged to the Malamatiyya, the perfect ones or the trusted men of God (*awliyā'*), to whom Aguéli devoted an entire essay in *La Gnose* based also on Ibn 'Arabi's treatises, as noted in Chapter 7. He described them as a group of great initiates who bow and humble themselves in front of God's greatness, and who are devoid of any claim to any reward whatsoever in this world or the other. They constrain their passions and adhere to voluntary poverty, indulgence toward others, and discipline of speech, not only by silence but also by the obligation to speak according to the permission of God. Thus the people of the Malamatiyya reached the highest levels of concentration and closeness to God (*proximité divine*), and possess supreme knowledge, wisdom, foresight, and the art of judging the intimate nature of persons and objects according to external signs. But God is too jealous of them to let them reveal their exalted merits to the world. So He gives them the appearance of ordinary knowledge. They observe religious laws and lead an ordinary way of life. Nevertheless, their interiors remain in continued connection with the truly divine.[53]

Aguéli never really reconciled the basic anarchist perception of human beings as free and rational creatures with the Sufi perception of their total submission to a Sufi teacher or shaykh, although he pointed out that such allegiance is voluntarily and stems from inner conviction of the shaykh's higher spiritual status. Nor did Aguéli relinquish social divisions or hierarchy based on the parameters of knowledge and moral superiority, which were the province of a chosen elite benefiting from intimate encounters with God. Such contradictions reveal Aguéli's multifaceted worldview, which intertwined rationalism and esotericism, egalitarianism and elitism.

Conclusion

Was Sufism for Aguéli merely a venue for promoting a cosmopolitan outlook according to which all cultures were equal, with no *a priori* preference of Islam? The answer is not equivocal. The impression we get from his writings is that Aguéli's conversion to Islam certainly derived from intellectual curiosity and conviction and that he deeply believed in Islam's credo and the elevated status of its prophet, Muhammad. He identified himself as a Muslim and when addressing a European audience often referred to Muhammad as "our Prophet" (*notre prophete*). Aguéli strongly upheld the unique contribution of Sufism—depicted later by Seyyed Hossein Nasr as the "heart of Islam"[54]—to the modern human experience. He also acquired an early and excellent knowledge of Islam as a religion and a culture, which he upgraded during his Egyptian phase (1904–10, 1913–16).[55] In contrast to other European Sufis of his time, such as Champrenaud, Eberhardt, and Rafanelli, whose Sufi identity was largely artificial and eclectic,[56] Aguéli did perceive Sufism as an integral part of Islam and as the sole framework for embarking on cross-cultural interaction.[57]

Yet, it may be argued that Aguéli's intellectual profile remained largely hybrid, while his Islamic identity was not definitely inclusive. As can also be inferred from his eccentric travel biography, he was in many ways a cosmopolitan person who was at home in different milieus and who had wide interests and networks across cultural and national boundaries. Addressing universal human predicaments and compassion to the deprived were ingrained in his personality and writings.

Although Aguéli turned against those Muslims who abandoned the Shari'a and adopted Western ideas and manners,[58] he himself continued to express an interest in non-Islamic traditions and ideologies (such as Chinese Taoism and Italian Futurism), was in constant contact with artists and Theosophical circles, while his religious observance on a daily basis was obscure. On the one hand, it was argued in Chapter 10 that he went through a "relatively rigorous Sufi training" but on the other hand he continued drawing human images (including female nudes) despite the prohibition of this in Islam and, as we saw in Chapter 9, Garbati, who was acquainted with Aguéli in Cairo, also alleged that he continued to eat pork and drink alcohol.[59]

Aguéli's mission was not only to bridge East and West, but also to prevent the moral deterioration of Western society because of its alleged hedonistic philosophy.[60] In his writings Aguéli consistently avoided portraying Muslims as being superior to Christians. He did, however, perceive Muslims as catalysts for the reshaping of Western thought. In one of his letters he stated: "Monotheism is the essence of Christ's teachings, so significant that the faithful Muslim is more Christian than most Christians," thereby, as argued elsewhere by Simon Sorgenfrei, attempting to clarify that Christians should return to the true path of Jesus by rejecting the doctrine of Trinity.[61] However, such a statement, which featured in Aguéli's later statements during his Islamic phase, was meant also to urge Christians to reinstate the balance between materialism and esotericism, which, he observed, was severely disrupted in modern times. Aguéli placed the lifeline of the West in Sufism.[62]

Saving the West went hand in hand with the deconstruction of Islam and Sufism by the creation of a soft model of faith—inclusive, humane, and universal, and whose true essence did not lie in religious services, rituals, and prohibitions, but in merits and texts. Aguéli, much like Guénon in the 1930s, sought to highlight Islam's spiritual components, thereby turning Islam into a universal philosophy that had much in common with other world cultures. These cultures, he observed, have different exoteric orthodox frameworks and different symbols, but share a similar esoteric path which addresses the individual human relationship with God.[63]

Positioning Sufism as a philosophy rather than a social practice had the effect of sterilizing it and reshaping its image. No wonder, then, that Aguéli, like many later Europeans and Americans who turned to Islam for comfort and inspiration, had limited impact on the Arab-Muslim milieu, where many considered them to be hypocrites (*munāfiqūn*) at best, and at worst agents of cultural imperialism. The impact of these Europeans was most tangible in the Western milieu by contributing to the inner debates over Western modernity and its flaws.

Feminism and the Divine Feminine: An Exploration of Female Elements in Ivan Aguéli and Subsequent Traditionalist Thought

Marcia Hermansen

This chapter takes off from two of Aguéli's articles each entitled "Femminismo" (Feminism) published in *Il Convito* in 1904 and 1907,[1] as well as certain other of his brief writings, assessing how his presentation of feminism and the feminine engages the progressive political, social, and cultural currents of *fin-de-siècle* Europe and the Middle East at the same time that it invokes Islamic and Sufi notions of the role of women and feminine expressions of the divine.

It is clear from his writings that Aguéli is not a feminist in the current sense of the term, and that today's language of female emancipation or women's rights might seem futile or alien to him. However, this discomfort seems to be due to skepticism or cynicism regarding the state or some outside power being able to grant these rights to females rather than due to any intellectual or other shortcoming on the part of women themselves. This ambivalence, it will be argued, is not alien to the Islamic tradition and even to the works of Muhyiddin ibn 'Arabi, who formed such a powerful influence on Aguéli as well as later Traditionalists. We do find in Aguéli a stronger political awareness of the importance of the role of women in society along with more explicit admiration of, as well as advocacy for, their achievements than we encounter among later Traditionalists. It is clear that for Aguéli women's education and female achievements were a given, and that he did not view women as inferior, although he may have viewed them as "different" in some essential way.

In order to illustrate the distinctive elements of Aguéli's discussion of feminism when compared with the "feminine" as conceived among later Traditionalists including René Guénon, Frithjof Schuon, and Seyyed Hossein Nasr, this chapter will briefly present some of their positions on this topic. I will thus consider Ivan Aguéli's views on women and feminism according to his writings,[2] while addressing some of the tensions within "Western" Traditionalist Sufism around the construction and performance of gender roles. Most Western Traditionalist Sufis, while criticizing modernity and promoting a return to traditional metaphysics and ways of life, are still very much socially located in societies where male and female interactions follow modern Western expectations. The intellectual challenges of how to respond to these competing frameworks on gender have persisted over the twentieth century and until our own moment, a century after Aguéli's death.

The fact that Aguéli operated within such diverse contexts during his brief and dynamic life alerts us to the complex negotiations of overlapping and, in some cases, conflicting political resonances of his positions. A topic such as feminism serves to point this out.

Other chapters in this book and the growing body of scholarship on Aguéli allow us to appreciate his originality and uniqueness as an artist, political activist, spiritual adventurer, and esoteric thinker. Situating him solely as a traditionalist Sufi seems increasingly problematic, and this is not to be taken as detrimental to his contribution. While this originality is of course Aguéli's own unique gift, it also helps us to appreciate its historical situatedness and perhaps this is some of the fascination that Aguéli exerts, increasing, rather than fading over time.

A number of summaries of Aguéli's life and thought mention his "feminism."[3] Upon reading and analyzing several of his articles related to women in Islam and "feminism" it appears that these are certainly not feminist manifestos, at least in the current sense of activism toward obtaining equality for women in all spheres. It must also be noted that these writings are journalistic, brief pieces, rather than extended theological reflections.

Aguéli is both a pioneering "Western" Sufi and a pioneering "modern" Sufi. While exposed to and influenced by diverse currents in contemporary spirituality including esotericism, Swedenborgian thought, Theosophy, and late Ottoman Sufism, as we have seen in other chapters, Aguéli is certainly not fettered by what these currents were or what they later became. Those situating Aguéli within Islamic and Sufic currents have at times used indigenous Sufi concepts for which he himself had a demonstrated affinity, such as *malāmat* (seeking out blame)[4] and *fardiyya* (singularity) to capture his uniqueness, if not eccentricity, and also to an extent to validate it. In classical Sufism this readiness to be blamed was valorized as a form of spirituality that inculcated humbleness, patience, and also a certain freedom from the conventions and strictures of the surrounding community and society. This throwing off of the fetters of convention finds a resonance with both the anarchism that Aguéli embraced during his years in France and some of the new and radical artistic currents of his era.

Aguéli's position on women's equality to men is evidenced by a brief quote from a letter written in 1894 during the period when he was imprisoned in France for anarchist ties wherein he declared, with respect to Strindberg, "It is the landscape artist or the impressionist who interests me, not the worshipper of Nietzsche or the idiot who said that women are inferior to men."[5]

Aguéli and Feminism

It is often thought that critical intellectual interest in gender and gender studies is relatively recent, emerging among second-wave feminists in the 1960s and 1970s in the wake of certain successes of first-wave feminist initiatives to ameliorate the position of women in society in practical matters. The end of the nineteenth and the early twentieth centuries mark the beginnings of important struggles for women's rights, not only in Europe but also in many other parts of the world, even in societies that were still under the yoke of European colonialism. In some Arab countries, indigenous criticisms of segregating women and denying them access to education were emerging at this time, initially among males in more progressive circles but also among political and literary female activists.

The secondary literature on Aguéli has characterized him as a feminist,[6] apparently on the basis that he published an article, "Femminismo,"[7] on this topic in Italian in the periodical *Il Convito* in Cairo in 1904.[8] This brief article ran for several print columns (some 1000 words) in the second issue of the periodical. While this chapter takes off from that piece, its content has been supplemented by several other writings by Aguéli for *Il Convito* that refer explicitly to the topics of women, the feminine, and Islam. In fact, a second article under the same title "Femminismo" that was published in 1907 features more explicit discussion of European feminisms, even briefly comparing what the author terms Anglo-Saxon and neo-Latin (French and Italian) feminisms[9] in order to illustrate how the cultural context of Muslims needs to be taken into account in understanding how local factors shape attitudes and practices relating to gender. For example, his assertion that the women of the South have a more developed "feminine faculty" than their Northern sisters[10] may either be regarded as essentialist or as anticipating the more recent ideas of third-wave or "cultural" feminisms, in that cultures may set their own priorities and styles for what is valued by women. Perhaps it is in this light that we may take Aguéli's rather blunt declaration: "We see that there is no need for Western[-style] feminism in the East."[11]

Context

The 1904 article appeared in the Italian section of *Il Convito/Al-Nadi* and probably reached a relatively small audience. As for the title, scholars of feminist history have explored early uses of the term "feminism" and what it connoted in diverse cultures and contexts. The term itself may derive from the French coinage *féminisme* circa 1837, and it was first recorded in English in 1851. However, the term originally simply meant "the state of being feminine." While one source stated that its usage in the sense of "advocacy of women's rights" begins after 1895,[12] an authoritative study of European feminisms more precisely states: "It was in the 1890s that numerous neologisms expressing departures in female aspirations began to appear. The term 'feminism' started to become familiar to wider audiences, having appeared as part of a feminist conference in Paris in 1892."[13] Therefore, it is fair to assume that the *Il Convito* articles were explicitly engaging political currents relative to the status of women.

Probing Aguéli's background for an interest in feminism one could expect to draw on developments in Sweden and France. Beginning in the late nineteenth century, many European countries were engaged in intellectual and social debates about "the woman question." Women were more and more present in the public sphere and in Europe the first females were admitted to institutions of higher education only in the 1870s. Undoubtedly Aguéli's anarchist, artistic, and progressive friends and mentors would have been interested, and in some cases directly engaged in projects of female emancipation. The bohemian, anarchistic, and progressive artistic circles in Paris and Stockholm that he frequented undoubtedly contained women who flaunted the conventions of their era. It is well known that Marie Huot, the Parisian patroness and muse of Aguéli, was a strong and independent woman involved in various activist projects including anarchism and animal rights.

But why publish a piece on "feminism" in *Il Convito*? We have seen in Chapter 9 how *Il Convito/Al-Nadi* generally took positions opposed to Muslim reformists and modernists and supposedly closer to Sufi and traditional elements.[14] One might therefore imagine that "feminism" would be a topic to avoid. Meir Hatina has observed that *Il Convito/Al-Nadi*'s portrayal of both the Shari'a and Sufism as essentially progressive enabled the paper to refute Western criticisms of reprehensible practices associated with Islam.[15] Defending the status of women in Islam and Muslim societies could perhaps be construed as an intervention that would garner support in certain Muslim circles. His two articles on feminism demonstrate both Aguéli's personal and *Il Convito/Al-Nadi*'s editorial stance of defending Islam and Muslims against Western colonial stereotypes. Indeed several years after his initial article on feminism, Aguéli returned to the topic in *Il Convito,* this time under the rubric of the regular section entitled "Notes on Islam."[16] While Aguéli's writings do not constitute apologetic pieces about the status of women in Islam, as were, for example, being produced at that time by Muslims such as India's Syed Ameer Ali (1849–1928),[17] the fact that the topic of women in Islam was addressed under the title "Feminism" is intriguing.

As for the local Egyptian milieu, the emergence of Egyptian feminism is dated from the late 1800s until the turn of the twentieth century. For example, *Tahrir al-Mar'a* (Emancipation of Women) by Qasim Amin (1863–1908) was published in 1899 and his *al-Mar'a al-jadida* (The New Woman), advocating for European-style progress for females in Arab societies, appeared in 1900. During this period we increasingly find Arab and Egyptian males and females who were writing in the press articulating new ideas about female education, women's public roles, and marriage.[18] In addition to intellectuals and literary figures, Islamic modernists from the religious class such as Muhammad 'Abduh could also be viewed as supporting causes such as female education and advancement.

The Text of "Femminismo"

The 1904 article "Femminismo" can be read as a polyvalent text with regard to the topic of women, due to both multiple positions taken by the author and its complex historical and political situation. Perspectives on many aspects of women, the feminine, and feminism can be extracted from this brief text. I will explore these by presenting some translated excerpts, highlighting and commenting on what they might indicate about the author's positions.

The Exceptional Woman

The opening sentences of the earliest article, "Femminismo," mention the famous scientist, Marie Curie (1867–1934), and her discoveries:

> The greatest discovery of our era in chemistry is that of radium, only comparable to that of Roentgen rays in physics and that of the wireless telegraph by the Italian Marconi[19] in the field of applied electricity.
>
> Radium was discovered by the Curies, both French, and according to the admission of Mr. Curie himself, the credit for this discovery should be equally given to Mme. Curie,[20] for without her scientific cooperation radium would still be unknown.[21]

In 1904 the recent (1894–5) inventions of wireless telegraphy by Marconi and the discovery of radium in 1898 by the Curies were certainly high in public awareness. In fact, in 1903 the Curies jointly received the Nobel Prize for this invention.

Also notice that in the opening "hook" paragraph of the article we find a confluence of Italy (by mentioning Marconi), France (the Curies—although Marie Curie was originally Polish), and Sweden (implicitly through the Nobel Prize). It is noteworthy that all three were roughly contemporaries in age to Aguéli. In terms of feminism, Aguéli notes that even Marie Curie's husband acknowledged her vital contribution to their joint scientific breakthrough. In fact, in 1911 Marie Curie was to receive the Nobel Prize for Chemistry on her own.

Aguéli introduces in this opening passage a theme that is taken up elsewhere in the article—that of the *exceptional* or talented female. This trope was part of nineteenth-century debates on "the woman question" and continues to haunt discussions of the status of women in general and also that of women in Islam, for example, why are there not many famous women chefs despite the fact that females do most of the world's food preparation; does the fact that we have an Indira Gandhi or an Angela Merkel mean that effective women's political leadership is possible in generality, or is it still limited to a rare handful of females?

But the *exceptional* woman is not the standard for all women, as we learn later in Aguéli's essay.

> If we take the word "liberty" in the European sense of the term, I repeat that it is absurd to give this "freedom" to woman because this liberty[22] should not be given and it would be a very bad gift like [putting] a weapon in the hands of a child. I do not see any problem, however, if an *exception*, be made in the case of a woman worthy of enjoying this freedom because of her merits and her intelligence, because then she will certainly make good use of it.[23]

What is implied by this paragraph is provocative if not definitive. Giving women "liberty" or "freedom" is analogized to letting someone unprepared by skill or wisdom wield a powerful tool. This hardly suggests "feminism" in the contemporary sense. However, at least some women are felt to be worthy of such emancipation.

The Feminine as Associated with Sentiment, Feeling, Intuition [as Female Qualities]

> Even if nothing were to be conclusive, we could still always say that in almost all the developments of the great souls of the West, there was always a determinative feminine influence that guided the male towards the pinnacle of his intelligence. Let's consider that in all the spiritual spheres, the collaboration of the two poles of the soul, sentiment and reason, is necessary and only this is able to achieve great works and unite and balance them.[24]

This passage accentuates difference between the sexes, probably difference in terms of "complementarity"—since it is stated that collaboration of the two poles is necessary and that maleness cannot fully achieve perfection without a "feminine" influence. The passage appears to be characterizing the influence on a male of an actual female, rather than that of an internal feminine "anima" figure, for example, as is postulated in Jungian thought.

In a further assertion by Aguéli, regeneration or rebirth in the case of the East needs to occur through the advancement of females as well as of males: "The rebirth of the female must occur simultaneously with that of the male but through slightly different means. Woman is like nature; she always responds justly to anyone who knows how to interrogate her so we should never despair from that side."[25]

We find in the second sentence cited here woman being equated or associated with nature, matter, or the world as is quite usual in traditional and Traditionalist systems. The reference to woman responding justly to whoever knows how to interrogate her could be rather troubling from a contemporary feminist standpoint as it seems to deprive females of agency.

The duality of reason and sentiment or intuition is foundational in many systems of religious and philosophical thought, both traditional and modern. In an era of feminist theology, a struggle continues around whether to emphasize ideas of equality and sameness, or alternatively to assert "equity" while maintaining that there are essential differences between the sexes. For example, concepts such as "gender complementarity" may be espoused by those who wish to stop short of endorsing full "equality" in all spheres, including some Muslims, since equality as sameness would conflict with the gendered nature of certain Islamic laws and practices. While complementarity is not explicitly presented as being Aguéli's position, variations on it are the preferred configuration among later Traditionalists, and the passage cited above does seem to suggest essentially different or at best complementary roles and natures for the sexes.

The Feminine as Muse/Inspiration

Aguéli writes in another passage: "In Europe the influence of religion is almost nil. Fortunately this has been partially replaced by the influence of the female that inspires the male to elevated thinking, to pure and noble emotions, and to honest and generous conduct."[26] Thus Aguéli seems to find at least some positive aspects related to the rise in women's status and to modern developments in Europe despite an overall decline in religiosity.

In contrast, the elimination of religion in modernity as being a major factor in the spiritual "fall" of humanity is a major trope of Traditionalist thought in Europe. Thus we find Traditionalists standing "Against the Modern World," as the title of Mark Sedgwick's work on Traditionalism[27] encapsulates, echoing the title of Julius Evola's book: *Revolt against the Modern World.*[28]

In other twentieth-century critiques of the role of religion, a "masculinization" of culture and religious symbolism, especially in Protestant Europe, together with a concomitant devaluation of the "feminine principle," is seen as a root symptom, if not actual cause, of this decline.[29] Joan Chamberlain Engelsman, a Jungian scholar writing on Jung and the feminine, argues that the lack of attention to the feminine in the concept of the divine raises profound psychological questions and, even though psychotherapists have been raising this issue for generations, "theologians have avoided comment on either the absence of the feminine in the Judeo-Christian tradition or the distortions of the feminine which do appear."[30] Engelsman cites Carl Jung in this context, stating that he "appears to believe that if the feminine is not restored to its archetypal place in Western religion the results might be catastrophic."[31] In contrast we observe that for many Traditionalists it was secularization, which they view as a rebellion against heaven on the part of males, that opened the door to females agitating for greater independence and equality—in other words, this modern decline in traditional practice and thought is symptomatic of a disturbance in the natural sacred order.[32] It may therefore be seen as original and in contrast to these currents that in the passage cited above, Aguéli seems to find a highly positive or restorative aspect to women as muses and as inspirations to males, in some cases replacing those traditional functions of religion itself.

In another passage Aguéli briefly mentions "Mary" as a feminine ideal in the phrase, "She may be an absolutely superior woman, a true image of the Virgin Mary,[33] while making spelling errors and not knowing a basic word of physics, chemistry, or philosophy,"[34] which would be an odd assertion in a Protestant context, but not in an Islamic or Traditionalist one.

Women, Men, and Power

In another excerpt from "Femminismo" Aguéli states:

> She must know that she is made to reign over the spirits and that her image alone must suffice to drive out demons.
>
> Above all she must have the science of the heart, then the art of having a certain power over her husband through a beauty that is more spiritual than physical. A woman of heart and spirit is always beautiful whatever her age and will always hold the affection of her husband. True feminine intelligence is a magic, which can even take control over time;[35] literary, artistic, psychological, and even historical knowledge is extremely useful up to a certain point, rather in this case almost essential.[36]

The above passage seems to locate the sources of female power in self-knowledge, spiritual beauty, and "feminine intelligence." The references to "reigning over spirits" and "driving out demons" seem rather cryptic here. Feminine intelligence as "magic" is an intriguing formulation. Later Traditionalists have associated the feminine with the principle of *maya* in South Asian religious traditions,[37] that is, the power of the cosmic illusion that makes us think that this world is real and ultimate and that is, in fact, the source of creation itself, so perhaps this is the implication of a female "controlling time." Since Aguéli was interested in temporality, succession, simultaneity, and the relationship of time and space, this association of female power and temporality may constitute an aspect of this musing about the power over time exerted by "female intelligence."

Women's Emancipation and the State

Aguéli states rather sarcastically: "We do not believe that any governmental proclamation of the emancipation of women would have any influence, like a nice word, or a toast, or some more idiots receiving public honors. It is all progress; only those who know the East will certainly enjoy a laugh that day."[38] As an anarchist Aguéli resisted the encroachments of the state on individual choices and freedoms. Here he appears to be highly skeptical of official government sincerity and efficacy in addressing the situation of females.

Female Education

Education of women likely with particular reference to the Egyptian context, is endorsed by Aguéli, but with some equivocation. He says that it should be voluntary (chosen). The idea of choice and spiritual liberty in the development of an individual's destiny is in his view one of the highest forms of spiritual development. Again he clearly prefers the exceptional to the collective, here as elsewhere:[39]

> We have only to make her conscious of her mission, her strength, and her rights and duties. She needs education rather than instruction, and also that this education is chosen.
>
> She needs emotional and religious education which is the one suitable for her attitudes. It is necessary that she comes to know God, his Prophet, and herself.
>
> I previously stated that the education of the woman is more important than instruction, but scientific knowledge is not to be disdained, while we must not exaggerate its value from the moral point of view.[40]

It was during Aguéli's coming of age that women began to make inroads into institutions of higher education in Europe. In 1873 women were finally allowed to study at Swedish universities. Likewise in France, early feminist initiatives were being undertaken at this time.[41]

Meanwhile in the Egyptian context female education in the late nineteenth century was largely delivered by missionary schools. One statistic of 1893 reports thousands of girls in these schools compared to only 242 in state schools.[42] Those in Egypt who did advocate for female education saw it as making women better homemakers and mothers or as a step in the reformation of society, along modernizing Europeanizing lines.[43]

While, as already noted, Aguéli does see women as having an important role in societal regeneration, his specific focus on her education more broadly, as opposed to her instruction, is on the religious component and seems to primarily align with his idea of individual spiritual cultivation.

In the later 1907 article on "Femminismo," the topic of female education in the East is addressed more directly and with some skepticism, as least toward such education as might be promoted by Europeans or by Muslim government reformists. In the concluding paragraphs of this reflection, Aguéli opines:

> Education must [first] be reformed before introducing educational reform. What until now has been imparted to men does not constitute an ideal and has produced rather negative results. Poisoning women as men have poisoned themselves, under the pretext of feminism and gender equality, would seem to me a cruel irony. It would not be proper [for me] to expound here a program for the use of girls' schools in the East. I have only to recommend that you not approach the question of women in the East except with a lot of tact and perfect knowledge of Islam and the Muslims of our day. Without this preparation you will run the risk of appearing ridiculous.[44]

Islamic References in the "Femminismo" Articles

It is noteworthy that Islamic references are relatively sparse in the 1904 article. Perhaps one reason for this is that this article is in Italian, and therefore we may assume directed to a European, Western, audience rather than a Muslim public. There is, however, a brief mention of the Shariʿa giving freedom to women and thus Aguéli is contesting the colonial trope of women being kept back by Islam: "We will not say anything about freedom of women because we consider it to be an absurdity, whether in form or in essence. In the first place the woman has never been a slave in Islam, her freedom is found in the Shariʿa."[45] More explicit in this regard is the further assertion that the Muslim woman is not "inferior" to the Western woman; "In the first place we should not conclude that the Muslim woman is inferior to the European woman. In general she, like the male, is suffering the consequences of the disorder; intellectual, religious, and moral, that reigns in almost all of the East; now we need her contribution for regeneration."[46]

Aguéli seems to imply a need for female participation in order to effect the necessary regeneration of Muslim societies. This contrasts with the idealized portrayals of static "traditional" gender roles typical of Traditionalist idealizations of the East. However, in his later article on feminism and, in fact, more broadly on Muslim and Eastern women, Aguéli strikes a somewhat more idealizing tone, declaring that "in the East, the condition of women is better than in Europe and that is despite the decline."[47] He acknowledges that there are deplorable conditions impacting Muslim women but notes that these are caused by overall decay, rather than anything specific in Islamic teachings, after all the Qur'an is explicitly addressed to both believing males and believing females. "In the era when art and science were still cultivated in the Orient, women cultivated them equally with men."[48]

Since the 1907 article is more directed to explaining basic teachings and practices of Islam, we can find in it more explicit and extensive discussions of topics such as veiling, segregation of the sexes, women's rights in marriage, abortion, and so on, all elaborating and reflecting positively on Muslim practices.

The "Feminine" in Traditionalist Sufi Thought

Insofar as Ibn 'Arabi was the major Sufi intellectual influence on Aguéli as well as on later Western Sufi Traditionalists, we can expect some commonalities across their views of the feminine. Ibn 'Arabi's thought does discuss the feminine principle in an abstract and metaphysical way and this, as well as the role of women in his biography, has been extensively studied.[49] In fact, Ibn 'Arabi's and subsequent Sufi understandings of the feminine principle have become sources of diverse currents in contemporary theological reflections on gender relations in Islam. For example, the perspective of gender complementarity as espoused by Traditionalists is reflected in works such as Sachiko Murata's *The Tao of Islam: A Sourcebook on Gender Relationships in Islamic Thought*. Following the Traditionalist view of gender, Murata holds that hierarchy and gender roles are defined by God. Thus, "In the Islamic perspective, the revealed law prevents society from degenerating into chaos. One gains liberty not by overthrowing hierarchy and constraints, but by finding liberty in its true abode, the spiritual realm."[50] In contrast, taking a more progressive, egalitarian stance to gender roles and relations, Sa'diyya Shaikh's *Sufi Narratives of Intimacy: Ibn 'Arabi, Gender and Sexuality* seeks sources for gender equality and female empowerment in the life and thought of Ibn 'Arabi including his legal rulings and his encounters with female Sufi teachers. For Shaikh, "The realm of spirituality is intimately linked to issues of social and legal equality."[51] Her observation that "Ibn 'Arabi's Sufi works, like so much in the Islamic legacy, reflect the tension between patriarchal formulations and gender-egalitarian impulses"[52] could also resonate with some of the conflicting currents within Aguéli's reflections on feminism even if Aguéli, who was deeply immersed in the works of "the greatest Shaykh," does not seem to be directly drawing on Akbarian thought in his articles.

James S. Cutsinger, a scholar who wrote sympathetically about the perspectives of Schuon and other Traditionalists, lays out their concept of gender complementarity as follows:

> The supreme complementarity is duplicated on every plane of existence, whether angelic or astrological, human or animal, vegetable or mineral. Masculine and feminine are embodied, moreover, not only among the kinds or species of creatures, but in various created forces and natural laws, and in certain pairs of

human faculties: in "contraction" and "expansion," "geometry" and "music," and "knowledge" and "love." We should note that in both of these first two respects, whether we consider the polarity as within the Principle or as within its manifestation, the two poles or qualities are complementary, reciprocal, and symmetric. They are, as it were, horizontally equal.

It should come as no surprise, however, that a metaphysics as hierarchical as the perennial philosophy also stresses certain vertical applications of this fundamental pair, nor perhaps is it surprising to discover that in most such instances—I do emphasize "most"—the feminine is subordinate to the masculine.[53]

This view is further articulated by the contemporary Traditionalist thinker, Seyyed Hossein Nasr, as follows:

Both man and woman were created for immortality and spiritual deliverance. Below that level, however, there are differences between the two sexes whose reality cannot be ignored in the name of any form of egalitarianism ... The female is at once Mary who symbolizes the Divine Mercy in the Abrahamic traditions and the beatitude which issues from this Mercy, and Eve who entices, seduces and externalizes the soul of man, leading to its dissipation ...

The revolt of the female sex against the male did not precede but followed upon the wake of the revolt of the male sex against heaven.[54]

It is thus clear that Traditionalists reject contemporary feminist ideas of gender equality while not accept critiques based on the social and historical construction of gender, and that they take positions that are more essentialist than those of Aguéli, despite drawing on some of the same Sufi intellectual sources.

Conclusions

This brief engagement with Ivan Aguéli's writings on feminism has allowed us to make a few general observations about his somewhat ambivalent position, between feminist and Traditionalist currents. The "women question" has not been an easy one for Traditionalists. Some, like Julius Evola, definitely wish, at least in theory, for women to remain at home and to achieve their highest position through selfless devotion and sacrifice to the male.[55] Female demands for rights and equality are presented as a modern aberration, provoked by the feminization of males and symptomatic of the disorder than ensues when the traditional hierarchy is not maintained. Later Traditionalists, like Frithjof Schuon and Seyyed Hossein Nasr, construe ideal female power as mysterious and veiled as in terms of a Marian purity, warning against the dangerous other side of female potency which—rather than "a magic that conquers time"—may bear the negative deceptive quality of *maya* or Eve. Such femininity needs to be contained.

The positionality of being the "Swedish Sufi"[56] points to the complexity of the diverse elements that Ivan Aguéli was processing in his views, including those on women. G.

Rocca, editor of the French collection of Aguéli's articles and translations from the periodical *La Gnose*, comments on Aguéli's recognizing in the East his ideal adoptive homeland, even at the exterior level, despite its exotic traits and signs, "in a certain sense, he felt, on the part of his interior nature, more Oriental than Occidental. But his thought, understandably, was not, nor could it be, also spontaneously Oriental."[57] Thus we find in Aguéli's feminism and approach to the feminine as well as to actual women, elements drawn from his European sensibilities, including the social and political currents that he encountered and embraced in Europe which he combined with his studies in Sufi thought up to that point, thereby articulating as do contemporary Muslim theologians of gender, rich resources and appreciations of actual women as well as abstract philosophical and theological concepts of a "feminine principle."

Part Three

Ivan Aguéli and Traditionalism

The Significance of Ivan Aguéli for the Traditionalist Movement

Mark Sedgwick

The Traditionalist movement, as explained at the start of this book, is based on the writings of the French philosopher René Guénon, who Ivan Aguéli met in Paris in 1910–11, during a brief return to Paris from Cairo, which had become his primarily domicile in 1902. Aguéli wrote for Guénon's journal, *La Gnose* (Figure 13.1).

As we have seen in earlier chapters, ʿAbd al-Rahman ʿIllaysh introduced Aguéli to the work of Muhyiddin ibn ʿArabi, the preeminent mystical writer of the Sufi tradition, about whom Aguéli then wrote at length in *Il Convito/Al-Nadi*, the bilingual Italian-Arabic publication for which he was largely responsible, developing a Sufi universalism that had origins in Swedenborg and Western esotericism, in anarchism and progressive Western political thought, and also in Islam and, as has been argued by Iheb Guermazi, in the Sufi universalism developed by the Amīr ʿAbd al-Qadir al-Jazaʾiri. ʿIllaysh also accepted Aguéli into a branch of the Shadhili *ṭarīqa* (Sufi order).

In 1907, as we learned in Chapter 9, the Italian section of *Il Convito/Al-Nadi* announced the formation of a society for the study of the work of Ibn ʿArabi in both the East and Italy as a basis for a rapprochement between the Orient and the West, to be called the Akbariyya, a reference to the epithet "al-Shaykh al-akbar" (the greatest shaykh), often applied to Ibn ʿArabi. The only record of any activities by the Akbariyya is a note of one single meeting, in Paris, in 1911, attended among others by Guénon.[1] Even so, as a leading French Traditionalist and Sufi shaykh of the later twentieth century, Michel Vâlsan (Shaykh Mustafa, 1911–74) noted in 1953, the whole Traditionalist movement was in some ways the fulfillment of Aguéli's plan of 1907.[2]

Aguéli affected the development of Traditionalism in three ways, which this chapter discusses. Firstly, he had an impact on Guénon through personal contact. Secondly, his articles and translations in *La Gnose* between 1911 and 1912 had an impact on Guénon and on other Traditionalists, at the time and through reprints in Guénon's second and more important journal, *Le Voile d'Isis* (The Veil of Isis), later known as *Etudes traditionnelles* (Traditional Studies), between 1933 and 1946. These articles were further reprinted after Guénon's death in 1951, though only one was translated into English,[3] limiting Aguéli's impact on international Traditionalism. Thirdly, he

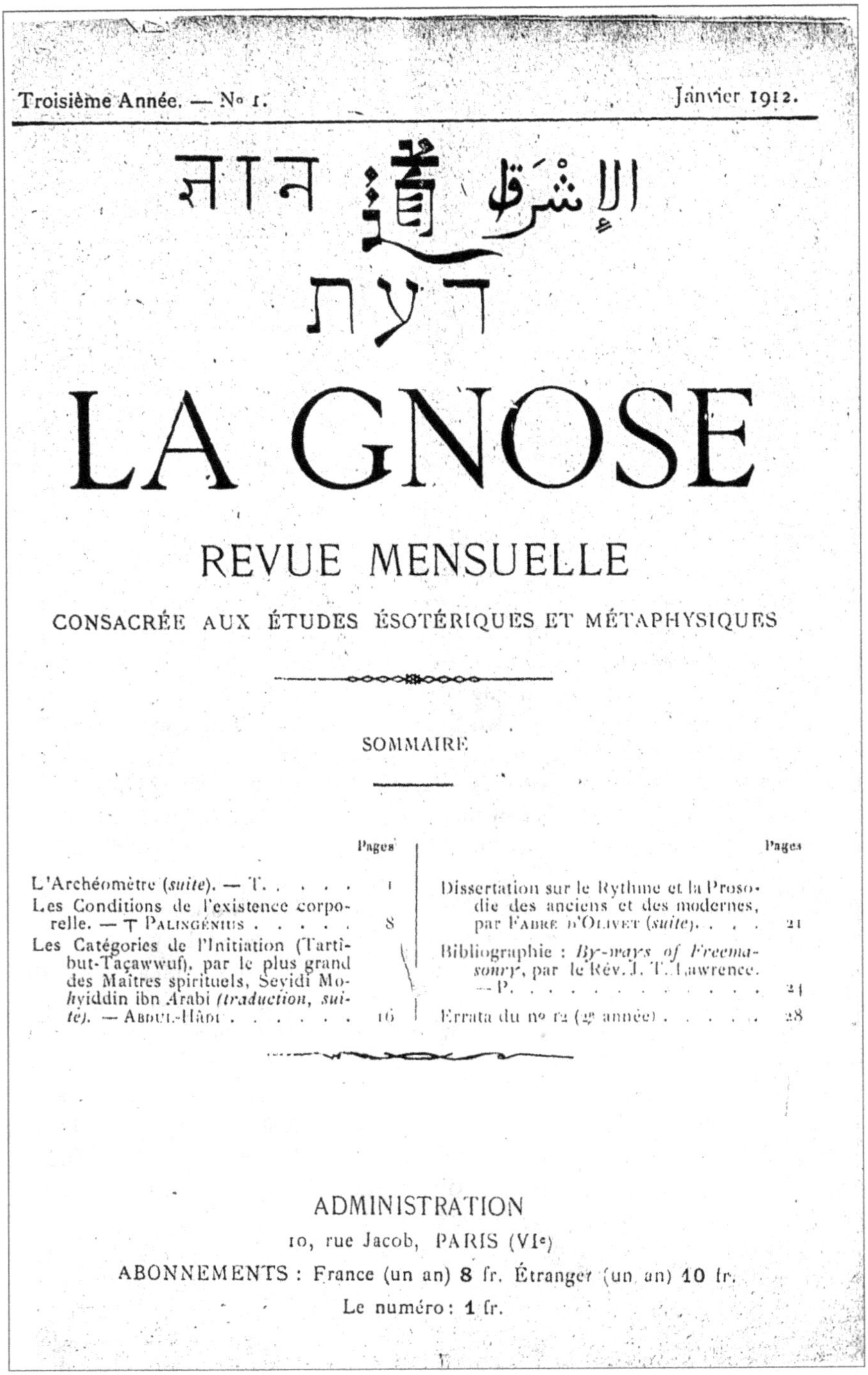

Troisième Année. — No 1.   Janvier 1912.

जान 道 الإشرق

דעת

LA GNOSE

REVUE MENSUELLE

CONSACRÉE AUX ÉTUDES ÉSOTÉRIQUES ET MÉTAPHYSIQUES

SOMMAIRE

ADMINISTRATION

10, rue Jacob, PARIS (VIe)

ABONNEMENTS : France (un an) **8** fr. Étranger (un an) **10** fr.

Le numéro : **1** fr.

Figure 13.1 The journal *La Gnose*. Author's photo.

had an impact through the part that he played in the "sacred history" or "myth" of Traditionalism, the understanding of the origins of Guénon's work that developed after his death. This chapter will deal with each of these three impacts in turn.[4]

Aguéli and Guénon

In 1911, Guénon was one of those who attended the only known meeting of Aguéli's Akbariyya, where, according to Aguéli, Guénon converted to Islam, taking the name 'Abd al-Wahid. Some others followed suit, probably including Guénon's friend Léon Champrenaud, who became 'Abd al-Haqq.[5]

This conversion to Islam was of major importance for Guénon, but its importance was initially latent. After Guénon moved from Paris to Cairo in 1930, he lived as a pious Muslim under the name that Aguéli had given him, but between 1911 and 1930 there are no reports of him following Islamic practice of any variety in Paris, or indeed even of him ever self-identifying as a Muslim. That Guénon spent the last twenty years of his life as a Muslim and a Sufi, then, was not just because of Aguéli; it was also because of events in Egypt after 1930. It was, however, the fulfillment of what had happened in Paris in 1911.

Beyond this, very little is known of the personal relationship between Aguéli and Guénon. It seems, however, that the two never became close, as Guénon knew little of Aguéli's background. The earliest reference to Aguéli by Guénon is in an introductory note in *La Gnose* in December 1910, in which Aguéli is presented as "an Islamic student, Abdul-Hâdi," who "knows nothing of Christianity or Judaism, nor of the Hindu and Chinese traditions. He only knows Islam, or rather a single Islamic school, that of Muhyiddin ibn 'Arabi, the Malamatiyya, and 'Abd al-Karim al-Jili. But he knows almost all European languages and the so-called Semitic languages."[6]

Even if Guénon knew little of Aguéli's background, he did know of Aguéli's shaykh, 'Illaysh, to whom he dedicated his 1931 book, *Le Symbolisme de la Croix* (The Symbolism of the Cross): "to whom is due the first idea for this book."[7] *Le Symbolisme de la Croix* was a development of an article published in *La Gnose* in 1911 that itself developed a discussion in an earlier article, "La prière et l'incantation" (Prayer and incantation),[8] that does not refer to 'Illaysh or Abdul-Hâdi by name, but reflects an understanding that would fit comfortably with a verbal description by Aguéli to Guénon of the nature and functions of Sufi *ṭarīqa* and of *dhikr* (Sufi prayer ritual), an understanding that Aguéli might well have ascribed to 'Illaysh. At least one discussion with Aguéli, then, was visibly important for Guénon. It can be safely assumed that other discussions, of which no trace remains, were also important; many of the ideas that are later central to Traditionalist thought echo those developed in *Il Convito/Al-Nadi*, and, more broadly, Islamic understandings. They also, however, echo other ideas that Guénon might have encountered independently.

At some point during the 1930s, possibly from someone he met in Cairo, where he was then living, Guénon learned that Abdul-Hâdi was also a Swede called Ivan Aguéli;[9] he wrote to a collaborator in 1938 that Aguéli was "born in Sweden, or more precisely in Finland, but he was of Tartar origin," and that his original name was probably "Aquileff" or "Aguileff."[10] This seems to have been an attempt by Guénon to reconcile his original understanding of Abdul-Hâdi, a Muslim, with later information that identified him as Ivan Aguéli, a Swede. Both "Aquileff" and "Aguileff" are plausibly Russian names that fit with the Russian first name "Ivan." Russia has various Muslim minorities, most notably the Tartars, so a Russian might be a Muslim. Finland has been both Russian and Swedish, so a Russian Finn might also be a Swede. Guénon, however, was evidently shaky on the details of Finnish history, as Finland had in fact passed from Swedish to Russian hands in 1809, sixty years before Aguéli's birth. In 1910, when Guénon met Aguéli, someone born in Finland would thus have had to be at least 101 years old to have ever been a Swede.

Aguéli in *La Gnose, Le Voile d'Isis*, and *Etudes traditionnelles*

La Gnose was Guénon's first journal. It was published monthly for a little more than two years, starting in November 1909 and ending with the issue of February 1912, and was printed and sold by the Librairie du Merveilleux (the Bookstore of the Marvelous), a well-established Paris bookstore and publisher specializing in occultist works. Most issues were twenty-four pages long, and the journal had an unknown, but probably small, circulation. It started as the *Official Journal of the Universal Gnostic Church*, its original subtitle, the Universal Gnostic Church being a small occultist organization that Guénon had recently joined, which included Champrenaud among its members. It quickly became *A Monthly Journal Devoted to the Study of the Esoteric Sciences*, however, losing its connection with the Universal Gnostic Church, along with some of its original contributors, during 1910, before Guénon met Aguéli, although Guénon continued to publish under his "ecclesiastical" name, Palingénius, until the last issue.[11] During 1911, ever more articles were written by Guénon and Aguéli, until there were finally no new articles by anyone else, at which point the journal closed.[12] It is not known whether loss of readers led to the loss of contributors, or whether conflicts within the occultist community led to the loss of contributors, and thus also of readers. Both are possible.

Many of the ideas that later became central to Traditionalism were first developed in Guénon's articles in *La Gnose*, and some of the titles of books that Guénon published in the 1920s and 1930s are taken from the titles of articles in *La Gnose* from 1911.[13] In a short article in the second issue of *La Gnose*, Guénon identified gnosis with knowledge, and knowledge with "the orthodox Tradition contained in the sacred books of all peoples, a Tradition which in reality is everywhere the same, in spite of the various forms which it takes to adapt to each race or each era."[14] Toward the end of 1910, another article distinguishes clearly between "Tradition" as "primordial Doctrine," which is "Truth," and religions, sects, and systems built around individuals, especially messiahs and saviors, which are "parasitic vegetations ... which embrace [the primordial doctrine's] trunk, and which, while living on its own substance, try to suffocate it."[15] The true Tradition is "constantly honored and practiced" in "the Orient," "while in the modern West the vast majority are completely ignorant of it."[16] Here, in a nutshell, are the central elements of Traditionalist doctrine: perennialism (primordialism), a respect for Oriental traditions, and a critique of modernity and the West. In this second article, by "the Orient" Guénon meant principally Taoism, as explained by "our Master and collaborator Matgioi,"[17] "Matgioi" being a name used by Albert de Pouvourville (1861–1939), a translator into French of the *Tao Te Ching* who was also been a member of the Universal Gnostic Church, along with Guénon and Champrenaud. In a later article, Guénon drew on the Vedanta,[18] which became the main source on which he based his mature work.

Aguéli also refers to Matgioi's understanding of Taoism in his first major article in *La Gnose*, in which he argues that "the esoteric doctrines ... of the Arabo-Islamites" are remarkably close to the "primordial Tradition" and to Taoism.[19] This, he concludes, cannot be explained in terms of historical contacts; rather, he suggests, "the two schools resemble each other because they reached the same depths of the human consciousness." He does not deny the "unity of the primordial Tradition," he adds, or "the spiritual genealogy of the initiates," but "certain parts of the chain [of initiation] may be on an extra-temporal plane."[20] Elsewhere, Aguéli proposes the possibility of two chains of initiation: one passing through an authorized living shaykh, as in Sufism, and one direct, which he calls "Marian initiation" as this is the initiation that the Holy Virgin received, and which he asserts is often found in Europe.[21]

Aguéli's identification of Islamic esoteric doctrines with the primordial tradition proved crucial to the later development of Traditionalism, as although Guénon drew mostly on Vedanta in his writings, the path that he and most later spiritual Traditionalists followed was not Vedanta but Sufism, and spiritual Traditionalism thus became a primarily Islamic phenomenon. Guénon's move to Cairo in 1930 was also a major reason for this development, but without Aguéli's articles in *La Gnose* in 1911, Traditionalism would probably never have become primarily Islamic. Aguéli's concept of "Marian initiation" may also have been important, as direct initiation from the Virgin was central to the experience and teaching of Frithjof Schuon, the Traditionalist who established spiritual Traditionalism as a worldwide movement; that Schuon's *ṭarīqa* was called the Maryamiyya was a result of Schuon's own Marian initiation.[22]

Other arguments of Aguéli's in *La Gnose*, however, did not become part of mature Traditionalist doctrine. The discussion that he touches on, of quite why esoteric traditions resemble each other, is a difficult one, and not one that later Traditionalists have attempted to resolve. Most of Aguéli's articles in *La Gnose* were in fact translations from Arabic: the first was of a classic introduction to Sufism, *Al-Tuhfa al-Mursala ila Ruh al-Nabi* (The Gift Addressed to the Spirit of the Prophet) by Muhammad ibn Fadl Allah Burhanpuri,[23] the second was of the *Risalat al-Malamatiyya* (Treatise on the Malamatis) of Abu ʿAbd al-Rahman Muhammad al-Sulami (937–1021),[24] and the remaining two were of works attributed to Ibn ʿArabi, *Risalat al-ahadiyya* (Treatise on Unity), actually by Awhad al-Din al-Balyani, and *Tartib al-tasawwuf* (The Classification of Sufism).[25] In addition, Aguéli published a long article on "L'Art pur" (Pure Art), translated as Chapter 18 in this book, a discussion of subjectivity and reality entitled "Pages dédiées au Soleil" (Pages Dedicated to the Sun),[26] an article on "L'Universalité en l'islam" (Universalism in Islam), translated as Chapter 19 in this book, and a short note on Islam and anthropomorphism.[27]

Just as Guénon's articles in *La Gnose* were later developed in Guénon's later journal, *Le Voile d'Isis/Etudes traditionnelles*, and in Guénon's books, so Aguéli's translations and some of his articles were republished in *Le Voile d'Isis* and *Etudes traditionnelles*, thus becoming part of the Traditionalist canon. *Le Voile d'Isis* started in 1933 with two of his translations,[28] then with "L'universalité en l'Islam" in 1934,[29] and with two more translations and "Pages dédiées au Soleil" in 1935 and 1936.[30] At this point all Aguéli's articles and translations had all been republished save for his first article, on Islamic esoteric doctrines and the primordial tradition, which was republished in 1946.[31] Only the short note on Islam and anthropomorphism, which was really just a response to comments, was never republished.[32]

Guénon later sometimes cited Aguéli in his own writings, though not as often as he celebrated another (later) collaborator, Ananda Coomaraswamy. The impact of Aguéli's writings on Guénon's own, however, is hard to assess, as Guénon did not generally footnote his sources.[33] That a writer is not cited by Guénon, then, does not mean that he is not important, as we have already seen in the case of "La prière et l'incantation," where Aguéli's understandings can be sensed, but are not directly referred to; only the oblique reference to them in the dedication to *Le Symbolisme de la Croix* twenty years later makes clear Guénon's debt to Aguéli.

Although the readership of *La Gnose* was probably small, the readership of *Le Voile d'Isis* and *Etudes traditionnelles* was wider, and was initially synonymous with the Traditionalist movement. This ceased to be the case when Traditionalism expanded beyond France to become an international movement, as although Guénon's articles and books were all translated into English and other languages, articles by other contributors to Guénon's journals were generally not translated. What was translated instead was the works of the second-generation Traditionalists, the contemporaries of Schuon, and then the works of the Russian political Traditionalist, Alexander Dugin.

Aguéli continued to be read by Francophone Traditionalists, however. His contributions to *La Gnose* were republished in one volume in 1988,[34] and were again republished in 2009, when the entire run of *La Gnose* was made available in e-book form by Les éditions de l'Homme Libre (Free Man Press),[35] a specialist in neo-Nazi works that also published the Italian political Traditionalist, Julius Evola.[36] As was noted earlier in this book, while spiritual Traditionalists often have no interest in politics, political Traditionalists are often interested in spiritual Traditionalism.

The *Risalat al-ahadiyya*, first translated into French by Aguéli in 1911, was re-translated more accurately by a later French Traditionalist and scholar of Ibn ʿArabi, Michel Chodkiewicz (1929–2020) in 1982.[37] Chodkiewicz had followed the *ṭarīqa* (Sufi order) of Shaykh Mustafa (Vâlsan), as had a number of other French Traditionalists who became respected scholars of Sufism, including Denis Gril.[38] Aguéli's example in translating classic Sufi texts into French, then, was important not just for Traditionalism, but also for French scholarship on Islam.

Aguéli in the Sacred History of Traditionalism

Although very little was actually known about Aguéli's relations with Guénon, these relations were clearly important, and they have consequently been much discussed. For some, Aguéli played a key role in the transmission to Guénon of a mission entrusted to him by unknown "masters," a mission of which the Traditionalist movement was the result. This "myth of origin," however, was increasingly challenged during the 1970s and 1980s, leading to the general disappearance of Aguéli from the "sacred history" of Traditionalism.

These two different understandings of Aguéli are linked to two different understandings of Guénon himself. As the Traditionalist Jean Robin (born 1946) put it in 1978, there are two ways of understanding Guénon's work: as a developing synthesis of pre-existing work, or as a "mysterious body that … no study of sources can account for, and that one is obliged … to accept or refuse as a whole, as an inseparable and invariable whole from the beginning, pre-existing in its entirety."[39] Non-Traditionalist scholars are naturally inclined to the former view, seeing Traditionalism as one intellectual movement among others, and Guénon as one theoretician among others, as someone who drew on identifiable sources, many of them secondary, in the normal way. Traditionalists, including Robin, were for a long time inclined toward the latter view, according to which Traditionalism is a coherent whole derived exclusively from primary sources, and probably an oral transmission. This was the view of André Préau, writing in 1934, for whom Guénon was "the very rare instance of an author writing in a Western language whose knowledge of Oriental ideas is direct, that is to say, due essentially to Oriental masters; it is indeed to Oriental oral teaching that René Guénon owes his knowledge of the doctrines of India, of Islamic esotericism and of Taoism."[40] Préau, as we will see, later changed his mind about this, but others still followed his 1934 view, which is crucial to understanding the development of the myth of Aguéli. It is also crucial to understanding much of the subsequent growth of Traditionalism, as what later Traditionalists generally thought they were accepting was an authoritative exposition of Oriental metaphysics, not the personal theories of one particular French esoteric philosopher.

'Illaysh and Aguéli as Oriental Masters

The myth of Guénon starts with a biographical article in the memorial issue of *Etudes traditionnelles* published immediately after his death in 1951. This was "La vie simple de René Guénon" (The Simple Life of René Guénon) by Paul Chacornac, the publisher of *Le Voile d'Isis* and *Etudes traditionnelles*, and also of many of Guénon's books. Aguéli is barely mentioned.[41] 'Illaysh, in contrast, is given an important role. Chacornac identified the period 1909–10 as the one in which Guénon's writings changed direction, and ascribed this to "direct contact with the authorized representatives of [Hindu, Chinese, and Islamic] traditions." He admitted to having no information about the representatives of the Hindu and Chinese traditions, but identified Guénon's Islamic "initiator" as 'Illaysh, in 1912, citing the dedication to 'Illaysh in *Le Symbolsme de la Croix*,[42] which is dated 1329–49 AH (Hijri, the Arab-Islamic dating system). Chacornac had converted 1329 AH to 1912 CE, an error, as 1329 actually corresponds to 1911, the year in which Guénon attended Aguéli's Akbariyya. Chacornac evidently supposed that Guénon had been initiated by 'Illaysh, in 1329 AH. He said nothing of 1349 AH, the second date that Guénon gives, which corresponds to 1930, the year in which he arrived in Cairo (by when 'Illaysh had been dead for eight years so the two men could never have actually met).

Chacornac was even more interested in Guénon's supposed "direct contact" with the authorized representatives of the Indian tradition. This is unsurprising, as Hinduism is what Guénon mostly wrote about, not Sufism. It is also unsurprising, as Indian emissaries had been repeatedly emphasized during the nineteenth century, from the mysterious and hidden "Mahatmas" of Helena Blavatsky and the Theosophical Society to the rulers of Agarttha, an alleged subterranean utopia described by Alexandre Saint-Yves d'Alveydre (1842–1909), a successful French writer with an interest in the occult. Indian emissaries were also thought to have contacted Yvon Le Loup (1871–1926), an occultist and member of the Gnostic Church who wrote as "Paul Sédir," and whose successful *Le Fakirisme Hindou et les Yogas* (Hindu Fakirisim and the Yogas) had been published by Chacornac. In fact, Chacornac suggested that Guénon might have been the third person to be contacted by unspecified Indians who aimed at influencing the spiritual development of the West, in succession to Saint-Yves and Sédir.[43]

The importance of 'Illaysh was further emphasized in *Etudes traditionnelles* two years later, in 1953, by Vâlsan, who, as a Sufi, was more interested in Guénon's contacts with the Islamic tradition than with the Hindu tradition. In "L'islam et la fonction de René Guénon" (Islam and the Function of René Guénon), Vâlsan dealt first with the general question of the relationship between Guénon's work and Islamic "orthodoxy," referring often to Ibn 'Arabi, and then moved on to 'Illaysh. The agreement between Ibn 'Arabi and Guénon that he had demonstrated, he wrote, was not just because both were great metaphysicians, but because Guénon "received his Islamic initiation from a master who was himself nourished by the intellectuality and the universal spirit of the Shaykh al-akbar [Ibn 'Arabi]": 'Illaysh. For this initiation, Vâlsan cited Chacornac's article and the dedication of *Symbolisme de la Croix*. He then connected 'Illaysh with an important point in Guénonian orthodoxy, a point that was important to Vâlsan personally as it had been central to a painful dispute between him and Schuon: the importance of placing the esoteric within an appropriate exoteric orthodoxy. He cited a letter from Guénon in which Guénon noted that 'Illaysh "was the shaykh of a Shadhili branch, and at the same time, in the exoteric order, he was the chief of the Maliki *madhhab* [school of interpretation] at al-Azhar" (a post that had in fact been held by 'Illaysh's father, not by 'Illaysh himself), and noted that this showed simultaneous exoteric and esoteric competences and authority in Guénon's master. He also noted that 'Illaysh was interested in Freemasonry, as Guénon had once spoken of him to Vâlsan as pointing out the Masonic symbolic significance of the Arabic letters that spell the name "Allah."[44]

As well as replacing hidden Hindu masters with Ibn 'Arabi and 'Illaysh, Vâlsan also explained at length, for the first time, who 'Illaysh actually was. For this he drew on several issues of *Il Convito/Al-Nadi* which he had obtained. He also identified Aguéli, who he called "Abdul-Hâdi Aguili," as the "most remarkable" among the "traditional contributors" to *Il Convito/Al-Nadi*, but did not identify his nationality or origin, nor give many details about him.[45]

Vâlsan attributed to the "spiritual advice" of 'Illaysh the formation of the Akbariyya as an association for the study of the exoteric and esoteric teachings of Ibn 'Arabi in Italy and the Orient, a move which he later admitted seemed not to have had many consequences, perhaps because of the outbreak of the First World War.[46] Vâlsan translated the objectives of the Akbariyya, the second of which was to bring together "all the friends and disciples of the great Master [the Shaykh al-akbar, Ibn ʿArabi], thus to effect ... a rapprochement, based on intellectual solidarity, between the elites of the Orient and the Occident," and noted the similarity between this project and Guénon's own project.[47] He was right to point out the similarity between the objectives of the Akbariyya and the objectives of Guénon. To what extent these objectives were those of ʿIllaysh or those of Aguéli is hard to say, but Iheb Guermazi has argued in Chapter 10 that they derive ultimately from ʿAbd al-Qadir. Equally, it is hard to say whether the observations about the Masonic symbolism of the letters that spelled "Allah" really came from ʿIllaysh, or from Aguéli.

Both Chacornac's view of Guénon as implementing the project of Hindu masters and Vâlsan's view of Guénon as implementing the project of ʿIllaysh and Ibn ʿArabi were soon challenged by more prosaic explanations. At about the same time that Vâlsan's article was published, there appeared a critical study of Guénon by Paul Sérant (1922–2002), a journalist and writer, which in an introductory biographical note emphasized the influence on Guénon of Champrenaud and Pouvourville (Matgioi).[48] The following year, Préau, who had evidently rethought and reversed the position (quoted above) that he had expressed so eloquently in 1934, went further than Sérant, suggesting that Guénon's unidentified "Oriental masters" might actually be Champrenaud (as ʿAbd al-Haqq), Pouvourville (as Matgioi), and Aguéli, identified as "Abdul Hâdî (the Russo-Finn)." Préau observed that for Guénon "it was ... the traditional attachment, not the local, national or racial factor, that counted. One may wonder, then, whether he did not also consider Oriental initiates as Orientals."[49] Préau may well have been right in this.

These revisionist views were rejected in *Études traditionnelles* in 1955 by Marcel Clavelle (1905–88), a close collaborator of Guénon and the editor of *Études traditionnelles*, writing as "Jean Reyor."[50] His argument was repeated by Chacornac in a book-length biography of Guénon,[51] also called *La vie simple de René Guénon*, which was published in 1958 and became the standard biography in Traditionalist circles, subsequently translated into English, Spanish, and Italian. In this book, Chacornac provided, for the first time, detailed information about Aguéli, who was identified as a Swede rather than a Tartar or a Russian Finn. Chacornac had somehow found the standard Swedish biography of Aguéli by Axel Gauffin, *Ivan Aguéli: Människan, mystikern, målaren* (The Man, the Mystic, the Painter).[52] *La vie simple* thus gave the first full account of Aguéli's life to be published in a language other than Swedish, based mostly on Gauffin.[53] Chacornac's book also provided a full account of ʿIllaysh, drawing on Vâlsan. He identified Aguéli as the *muqaddam* (representative) of ʿIllaysh, and— for the first time—as the likely intermediary through whom Guénon received his initiation from ʿIllaysh.[54]

Chacornac was evidently not entirely happy with the key role now assigned to Aguéli, however. He noted that "Abdul-Hâdî's career ... leaves a disconcerting impression, at least for a man who, in certain respects, can be qualified as spiritual."[55] It is not made clear what aspect of Aguéli's biography Chacornac was most disconcerted by; perhaps it was the anarchism. He suggested three solutions to this problem. First, "a certain esoteric knowledge is not necessarily accompanied by outside 'sanctity' or even simply exemplary conduct." Secondly, as Guénon had taught, the individual and the function are not the same thing. Thirdly, "The fact of holding a position in the esoteric order does not confer authority in areas that are not directly related to the exercise of that function."[56]

The Eclipse of Aguéli

Both the view of Guénon's work as deriving from Hindu masters or 'Illaysh via Aguéli and the view of it as deriving from Champrenaud, Pouvourville, and Aguéli were challenged by the first non-Traditionalist scholarly study of Guénon, by Jean-Pierre Laurant, who in 1975 published his groundbreaking *Le sens caché dans l'oeuvre de René Guénon* (Hidden Meaning in the Work of René Guénon). This was based not only on interviews with many surviving Traditionalists but also on extensive reading in French occultist literature.

Guénon's works, argued Laurant, remained faithful to the idea of "a hidden truth beyond the realm of the written word and sciences founded on reason," presenting his life as "an investigative mission entrusted by Oriental Masters."[57] Despite this, Laurant demonstrated, Guénon had drawn on many sources, including Albert Leclère (1867–1920), Ferdinand Gombault (1858–1947), Frédéric de Rougemont (1808–78), and, especially, Saint-Yves.[58] These were the sources that mattered, not hidden masters or living associates, but books. Given this, Laurant was not particularly interested in Guénon's Oriental contacts, and dealt with Aguéli and 'Illaysh only briefly, and not always accurately.[59]

Just as the revisionist versions of Sérant and Préau had been resisted by Reyor and Chacornac, so Laurant's book was resisted by Robin.[60] Robin also engaged with Préau, summarizing the "excellent" response of Reyor. He concluded that while "the most total uncertainty" reigned over Guénon's contacts with Hinduism, his contacts with Islam were known: Aguéli as *muqaddam* of 'Illaysh, who was "nourished by" Ibn 'Arabi. That it was only Guénon's contacts with Islam that were clear, however, did not mean that it was only these that mattered; Hinduism should not be forgotten.[61] Robin, then, attempted to reestablish Chacornac's understanding, though without presenting Guénon as the tool of someone else's mission.

Robin did not, however, succeed in reestablishing the old orthodoxy. The next treatment of Guénon was by another non-Traditionalist scholar, Marie-France James, who systematically considered Guénon's various sources: Hindu, Far-Eastern, Gnostic, Sufi, and Masonic.[62] The French Gnostic and Masonic sources proved the most significant. The Sufi sources considered were Champrenaud, Aguéli, and 'Illaysh. These she treated at greater length than Laurant, drawing on Vâlsan as well as Chacornac.[63]

Later Traditionalist works on Guénon thus necessarily retreated from Chacornac's and Robin's positions. Robin Waterfield (1914–2002), in the first biography of Guénon written in English (published in 1987), introduced Champrenaud and Pouvourville, Aguéli and 'Illaysh, before noting that although "Guénon always claimed that he received his teachings orally from Hindu and other masters and there certainly were Hindu teachers in Paris about this time ... it has not been possible to establish from which, if any of them, Guénon actually received his teaching, although there is no reason to doubt the truth of his statement." He then referred to the influence of Sédir and Saint-Yves, emphasizing the importance of Saint-Yves, apparently following Laurant.[64]

In 1988, G. Rocca, an Italian Traditionalist, in an introduction to the first reprinting of Aguéli's writings since 1946, went even further, noting that although the encounter between Aguéli and Guénon in the context of *La Gnose* was clearly important, "an analysis of all the factors that were at play in this relationship would, however, be too long and circumstantial." He therefore restricted himself to Aguéli's biography (correcting, in a footnote, Chacornac's mis-conversion of 1329 AH as 1912 CE, supplying the correct date of 1911).[65]

A similar but even more radical approach was taken by Harry Oldmeadow (born 1947), an Australian Traditionalist and follower of Schuon, who in a 1995 biographical introduction to a new English edition of Guénon's *The Reign of Quantity* observed that there was controversy about the years 1906–12, and therefore determined to leave them aside. It was unclear how Guénon had come to "a serious study of Taoism, Hinduism and Islam," but it might have been through his involvement in an occultist group, or perhaps "contact in Paris with some Indians of the *Advaita* school." Neither Aguéli nor 'Illaysh is mentioned, and Guénon's initiation into Sufism is placed after his 1930 arrival in Cairo,[66] not in 1911. Oldmeadow reused parts of his 1995 text in a 2004 book on Western encounters with non-Western religions,[67] still making no mention of Aguéli or 'Illaysh.

One explanation for this may be that it had become too difficult to maintain the "inseparable and invariable whole" position once the hidden masters had vanished, defeated by the scholarship of Laurant and James. Another explanation may be that Oldmeadow was personally more committed to Schuon than to Guénon,[68] and Schuon had varied parts of Guénon's teaching, which could thus no longer be inseparable and invariable. Aguéli, as precursor of Guénon, was important to Guénonian Traditionalists from Chacornac to Robin; for Schuonian Traditionalists like Oldmeadow, Guénon became a precursor of Schuon, and Aguéli was no longer needed. Schuonian Traditionalists tend instead to refer to Guénon and Coomaraswamy, a pair that has the further advantage that Coomaraswamy was not Muslim, which fits with the reduced emphasis on Islam of later Schuonians.

Oldmeadow's version, ignoring 'Illaysh and Aguéli, came to form a new orthodoxy. In 2019, a short biography of Guénon by Oldmeadow that follows this approach was to be found not only on the website of World Wisdom Books,[69] which is aligned with the Maryamiyya, but also of Counter-Currents Publishing,[70] which is aligned with the radical right. With Oldmeadow, then, Aguéli vanished as surely as Chacornac's hidden masters once vanished.

The Survival of Aguéli

Although Oldmeadow removed Aguéli from much Traditionalist myth, Aguéli is still mentioned in passing as Guénon's initiator into Sufism in many Wikipedia entries on Guénon, most importantly in French, English, Russian, and (of course) Swedish. At the time of this writing, however, he was not mentioned in the equivalent Wikipedia entries in Spanish, Italian, or Romanian; nor was he mentioned in the many shorter entries on Guénon in smaller Wikipedia languages such as Arabic.[71]

Aguéli has also survived in some Islamic Traditionalist myth. An account of Aguéli, for example, was provided by Jean Foucauld, evidently a follower of the *ṭarīqa* of Shaykh Mustafa (Vâlsan), published in a French Traditionalist journal, *Vers la tradition* (Towards Tradition), in 1998. This discussed only the Islamic aspects of Aguéli's life, and was something of a hagiography, for example, presenting Aguéli as "perfectly acclimatized to the traditional way of life, thinking and writing in Arabic," and as possessing "an admirable contempt for danger and indomitable courage through all the vicissitudes and obstacles raised by his enemies." For Foucauld, Aguéli had a "traditional mission" as "initiate" and "precursor," and he achieved it, establishing the Akbariyya and initiating Guénon.[72] Like Chacornac, Foucauld evidently found some aspects of Aguéli's biography disconcerting, as he noted that Aguéli's "'eccentricities,' his revolt against his family and his environment, his seemingly 'anarchist' reactions, [and] his maladjustment to the school system" were explained by the fact that he was born "alien to ... the pseudo or anti-traditional European mentality." "The apparent quirks of his behavior are beyond the facile decoding of a certain modern tendency which knows only to reduce the spiritual to the psychological."[73]

A similar account was provided in 2011 by a French Traditionalist working in English, Patrick Laude (born 1958), in a comparative study of Guénon and Schuon on the one hand, and of the great French academic Orientalists Louis Massignon (1883–1962) and Henry Corbin (1903–78) on the other. Laude noted that they all had in common that their understanding of Islam was not only derived from books but also from "the direct transmission of a knowledge imparted to them by living and authoritative representatives of the intellectual and spiritual traditions of Islam." In the case of Guénon, Laude names Aguéli, 'Illaysh, and 'Abd al-Halim Mahmud (1910–78), a prominent Egyptian scholar and Sufi who Guénon knew in Cairo.[74] Like Foucauld, Laude does not mention possible Hindu or Taoist masters, and there is no mention at all of possible occultist sources such as Sédir and Saint-Yves. In a later publication, containing the first ever translation of a text by Aguéli ("Universalism in Islam") into English, Laude again emphasizes 'Illaysh in his introduction, resurrecting the role assigned to him by Vâlsan. In this account, *Il Convito/Al-Nadi* is founded "with the blessing of Shaykh Illaysh," and Aguéli travels to Europe on the instructions of 'Illaysh to "spread Islam through the Sufi teachings of Ibn 'Arabi," as a result of which Guénon "became his loyal student and confidant" and Aguéli initiated Guénon into the Shadhili *ṭarīqa*, after founding an Akbariyya in Paris in 1911.[75]

Conclusion

The significance of Ivan Aguéli for the Traditionalist movement is, as we have seen, threefold. His personal impact on Guénon was major, as it was at his hands that Guénon converted to Islam and became 'Abd al-Wahid, though Guénon did not actually begin to follow Islamic practice and self-identify as a Muslim until after he moved to Cairo in 1930. Guénon's Islamic practice and identity, then, were not solely the result of his participation in Aguéli's Akbariyya in 1911.

Aguéli's impact on the intellectual development of Traditionalism was partly through his discussions with Guénon and partly through his articles in *La Gnose*, later reprinted various times. The only visible example of discussions changing Guénon's views relates to incantation, and this is clear only because of an indirect reference many years later (the dedication of Le *Symbolisme de la Croix* to Shaykh 'Illaysh), but there must have been other such examples. These may have been very important.

Aguéli's articles in *La Gnose* established an understanding of Sufism as Islamic esotericism, and of Islamic esotericism as a pure expression of the primordial tradition, alongside Taoism and Vedanta. That spiritual Traditionalism later became primarily Islamic also has other causes, but without Aguéli's articles, this might never have happened. Aguéli's discussion of "Marian initiation" may also have been important for Schuon, whose *ṭarīqa*, the Maryamiyya, was so named as the result of a Marian initiation. Finally, Aguéli's publication of translations of Ibn 'Arabi and of Sufi classics from Arabic started a trend that later French Traditionalists followed, a trend connected with the presence of accomplished Traditionalist scholars in French academia in the late twentieth and early twenty-first centuries.

'Illaysh and then Aguéli also played roles in the "sacred history" or "myth" of Traditionalism as "Oriental masters." This started with Chacornac, who wrongly supposed that Guénon had been in direct contact with 'Illaysh, and was developed by Vâlsan, whose work was then used by Chacornac, who adjusted his account of Traditionalism's origins to make Aguéli the intermediary through whom Guénon had been in contact with the Islamic tradition. This adjustment left him slightly uncomfortable, given that Aguéli's life was not exactly that of a saint.

This "myth of origin," however, was increasingly challenged, first by skeptical Traditionalists like Sérant and Préau, and then during the 1970s and 1980s, by scholars like Laurant and James. This led to the disappearance of Aguéli from the sacred history of Traditionalism, as later Traditionalists such as Waterfield mentioned him without attaching great importance to his role, and as Schuonian Traditionalists such as Oldmeadow ignored him entirely, making Guénon the precursor of Schuon, rather than Aguéli a precursor of Guenon. Only a few Muslim Traditionalists, such as Foucauld and Laude, now emphasize Aguéli.

As this chapter has shown, however, even if Aguéli was not an Oriental master or the emissary of Oriental masters, he was still a Sufi who knew Ibn 'Arabi and had learned much else from 'Illaysh, and he was very important for Guénon and the development of Traditionalism. Without him, Traditionalism might have remained focused on Taoism and Vedanta, and Guénon might never have followed the path of Islam after 1930. Perhaps Schuon would not have received a Marian initiation. The history of Islam during the second part of the twentieth century, especially in the West, would then have been different.

What Is Esotericism in Art?: Ivan Aguéli's Art versus the Traditionalists' "Traditional Art"

Patrick Ringgenberg

Ivan Aguéli met René Guénon in about 1910, before Guénon—initiated into Sufism thanks to Aguéli—became the founder of the so-called "Traditionalist school" and inspired the concept of "traditional art" in the works of three other major Traditionalists, Ananda K. Coomaraswamy, Frithjof Schuon, and Titus Burckhardt. While it would be anachronistic to evaluate an author according to later notions, the situation of Aguéli—a man initiated into Sufism, but also involved in the visual culture of his time—can inspire reflections on the relationship between metaphysical intellectuality, spiritual commitment, and aesthetic style. Seen in the light of "Traditionalist thought" Aguéli presents the paradox of a thinker generally considered as a "pre-traditionalist" author, but whose paintings and ideas on art are "non-traditional" according to the later criteria of Guénon, Burckhardt, and Schuon.

What Is "Traditional Art"?[1]

As a Sufi, Freemason, and supporter of the metaphysical doctrines of Vedanta, Guénon was interested in art only in terms of symbolism and craft initiations. In *L'ésotérisme de Dante* (The Esotericism of Dante), he offered an interpretation of the symbolism of the *Divine Comedy*, but his first article truly devoted to the arts, "L'initiation et les métiers" (Initiation and the Crafts),[2] is mainly in line with his concerns of the time—namely, to lay the foundations for an intellectual and spiritual development of the human being, rigorously based on an initiation given in a regular and traditional organization, whether Freemasonry or apprentice-brotherhoods (*compagnonnage*) in the contemporary West, or Sufism in the Islamic world.[3] Guénon thus considered the traditional—pre-industrial—arts and crafts as an initiatic path, based on symbols and rituals. However, he confessed to having little interest in aesthetics: his rare words on visual arts or literary works focus only on the adequacy of their symbolism.[4] Though he could appreciate the ideas and theories of Albert Gleizes on Western art and civilization, or of Antonin Artaud (1896–1948) on theater, he refrained from any aesthetic evaluation, although it is known that he disliked the style of some paintings by Gleizes.[5] Even Coomaraswamy, whose early writings show an eclectic interest in aesthetics,[6] focused on symbolism in his 1930s work, which was influenced by Guénonian metaphysics, and only considered the question of aesthetics in terms that would be described as "scholastic."[7] The art historian Luc Benoist (1893–1980), author of an *Art du monde* (Art of the World) and strongly inspired by Guénon, was a specialist in eighteenth century and romantic sculpture. He emphasized aesthetic appreciation, but his thinking on the arts was in no way part of the dogmatic vision that gradually asserted itself in the works of Coomaraswamy, Schuon, and Burckhardt.[8]

It is therefore Schuon and Burckhardt who, from the 1940s onward, synthesized the concept of traditional art in its triple aspect of symbolism, canonical aesthetics, and its ritual or initiatic and spiritual requirements.[9] An art is "traditional" if it is based on, or at least derived from, a tradition or a religion of nonhuman origin ("revealed" or "inspired"), and to the extent that it expresses—through a precise order of symbols and an aesthetic corresponding to an operative contemplative paradigm—the principles, values, or hermeneutics of a metaphysical and spiritual order. Coomaraswamy wrote mostly on Hindu art and the Buddhist art of India, which he understood as the symbolic and contemplative expression of a traditional doctrine. In his *Principes et méthodes de l'art sacré* (Principles and Methods of Sacred Art), Burckhardt wrote of Hindu temples, Romanesque and Gothic architecture, Orthodox icons, Islamic art, Buddhist figurative art, and Chinese landscape painting. The attachment to Islam and Sufism of Schuon and Burckhardt, and Burckhardt's books on Islamic arts (*Art of Islam: Language and Meaning*) and Morocco (*Fes. Stadt des Islam* [Fez: City of Islam]) have led many later authors, both Muslims by origin (Seyyed Hossein Nasr, Nader Ardalan, Laleh Bakhtiar [born 1938]) and converts to Islam (Martin Lings [1909–2005], Jean-Louis Michon [1924–2013]), to favor the Islamic arts, interpreting architecture, calligraphy, and geometric-based ornamentation as the vehicle or reflection of an inner wisdom, of a metaphysical perception of the world, and of an awareness of divine Unity.[10] Considering medieval art as the proper and normative expression of the Christian spirit, many authors (Burckhardt, Schuon, Jean Biès [1933–2014], Jean Hani [1917–2012], Henri Stéphane [1907–85])[11] have also taken up the theses of the Russian theologians of iconography (Léonide Ouspensky [1902–87], Vladimir Lossky [1903–58]), and, following them, have considered the icon, Byzantine and Russian, as the sacred and contemplative manifestation of Christianity par excellence.

For Guénon and his followers, traditional art also possesses a ritual character (in the sacred art of temples or icons, for example) or, at least, an initiatory or spiritual dimension (in the crafts). The practice of "traditional" arts and crafts is thus linked to a spirituality, given by a religion and more specifically by the affiliation to an initiatic organization conveying a cosmological knowledge (hermetic or alchemical). Artists and artisans must perpetuate motifs and aesthetics defined by tradition or by a spiritual authority, as these forms have a symbolic value and a spiritual quality that transcend individual intelligence and imagination. They can therefore express their personality only in the frameworks defined by tradition, and in a style that, without being "academic," more or less excludes subjective imagination, which would break the symbolic paradigm and/or the aesthetic cosmology of the traditional society.

The traditional arts are ultimately connected to the esotericism of a given tradition, and esotericism has a universality that connects traditions to each other, beyond the differences of their exoteric symbols, rituals, spiritualties, or ethics. This is how the Traditionalists rooted the supposed universality of their concept of traditional art in universalist metaphysics. And they justified the possibility for them to judge objectively the traditional adequacy of all the arts, inasmuch all aesthetic and symbolic motifs and forms, both Western and Eastern, can be deciphered and understood within the intellection of a universal metaphysics, esoteric hermeneutic, and spiritual perception—that is, through an esoteric intellectuality actualized by an initiatic method and rooted in the "primordial Tradition" (Guénon) or in the "*Sophia perennis*" (Schuon).[12]

For all the founding authors of Traditionalist thought, art was traditional in the West until the end of the Middle Ages. It was also traditional in all premodern civilizations, with the exception of Hellenistic and Roman antiquity, in which the authors generally see the beginning of a "non-traditional" conception and creativity. They see the development of naturalism in painting and sculpture as an anomaly, contrary to traditional aesthetics based on stylization and symbolic synthesis. According to these authors, the Renaissance inaugurated a break with the "real" principles of art; the cult of individualism, the use of naturalism, and the development of profane or worldly motifs were a deviation from the Christian tradition. Thus, alongside a virulent critique of the modern West—which Guénon developed in three books[13]—they have generally judged modern and contemporary Western art negatively, perceiving it as non-traditional or anti-traditional, even though Schuon could appreciate the qualities—anyway partial, according to him—of Paul Gauguin or Van Gogh.[14] Schuon showed an interest in the practical question of contemporary aesthetics, but without going into details. In 1954, he wrote that while sacred art must fully respect traditional canons, contemporary artists, in the "profane" field of their creativity, can "combine the valid experiences of naturalist and impressionist aesthetics with the principles of normal and normative art."[15] But Schuon never developed this idea, nor illustrated it with concrete examples, and he never mentioned the paintings of Aguéli.

Aguéli's Art and Theories, and Traditionalist Conceptions of the Arts

Many aspects of Aguéli's life match the intellectual and existential positions of the Traditionalist authors: his attachment to Sufism, and therefore to a traditional and regular initiatic path; his interest in Muhyiddin ibn 'Arabi; his universalist ideas and his quest for Oriental doctrines. On the other hand, both the theories of art and the pictorial work of Aguéli lie outside any traditionalism of art, as Guénon and especially Coomaraswamy, Schuon, and Burckhardt defined it. Both in his subjects (landscapes or portraits) and in his postimpressionist style, Aguéli is outside the norms of "traditional art," as they are disconnected from any symbolic or visual language rooted in a tradition, patronized by a religious or esoteric authority, legitimized by a spiritual filiation.

Modern in his painting, Aguéli is also modern in his theories on art. He saw in cubism a spiritual or initiatic path, as discussed in Chapter 6, but no modern aesthetics were considered traditional by Guénon and his followers, despite occasional qualities or potential. The ideas expressed in Aguéli's article "L'Art pur" (Pure Art), published in *La Gnose* in November 1910 and February 1911 and translated as Chapter 18 in this book, are very far from the concepts, the approach, and even the language that one will find in Burckhardt's or Schuon's texts about the arts, and far from Guénon's insistence on symbolism and initiation. Aguéli makes a distinction between "cerebral art" and "sentimental art,"[16] adding that the former "impresses directly, without any kind of intermediary, by the material, albeit inner, sensation of the pulsating beat of life."[17] He wrote that art "is passion doing mathematics,"[18] and he summarized his thought by saying that "the goal of the scrupulous artist is a personal style, by the combination of the loving and personal study of nature with the intelligence and taste developed by the study of the artistic past. Art is the balance between nature and tradition, not only in alchemy, but also in aesthetics."[19]

Traditionalist authors distinguish between a sacred or traditional art and a secular and worldly art; they consider symbolism as a founding element, rejecting any idea of subjective passion and sentimentalism, personal imagination, or subconscious inspiration in the creation of a traditional art; and they evaluate aesthetics according to medieval and premodern historical models. Moreover, the painters that Aguéli quotes in support of his presentation have been ignored by the Traditionalists: ancient painters like Tintoretto (1518–94)[20] or Jean-Baptiste-Siméon Chardin[21] who belong to periods and styles perceived as mundane or profane, or contemporary painters, such as Paul Cézanne[22] (who Aguéli sees as an heir to Chardin), Picasso, Henri Le Fauconnier, or Fernand Léger.[23]

Aguéli speaks of "the unconscious (or subconscious) esotericism of purist painters," mentions the Wisdom (*ḥikma*) which is "the art of setting everything in its place";[24] but these words serve to shed light on the deep intentions of a "purist" pictorial current, seeking "truth in the precision of light," and which expresses "an intense, personal theory, and an art of frankness and perspicuity."[25] These ideas would be refuted by all Traditionalists. For Guénon, an esotericism cannot be "unconscious," as an esoteric path is the actualization of a metaphysical consciousness; and if Traditionalists would agree with Aguéli about Wisdom, they would not accept that this concept serves a personal theory on art, arguing that Wisdom comes ultimately from a transcendental realm and determines an art far from any subjectivity. It can be noted here that Guénon was very critical of the thinkers or Spiritualist movements that influenced Aguéli in his youth: whether the Theosophical Society, of which Aguéli became a member in Paris, but that Guénon condemned as a non-traditional and pseudo-spiritual current of thought[26]; or Swedenborg, about whom Guénon mainly expressed reservations, noting in particular that the often problematic work of the visionary scientist is devoid of any truly initiatic or metaphysical character.[27]

Traditionalists would also condemn Aguéli's "eclecticism," which led him to quote in the same paragraph "the extraordinary Hispanic-Arabic thinker Muhyiddin ibn

'Arabi" and the "admirable Celtic writer Villiers de l'Isle-Adam,"[28] or to talk about a "Saint Rabelais" in an article about the "universality of Islam."[29] Aguéli also wrote that "thanks to purism [*purisme*] we will be able to discover the secret of ancient, Greek, Arab, Gothic, and Renaissance art," mixing traditional arts (Arab, Gothic) and arts that are—according to the Traditionalists—more or less apart from the tradition (Greek, Renaissance).[30] Admittedly, here and there, one can spot ideas that will more or less be shared by the Traditionalists. Aguéli's admires the Arab, African, Malaysian, and Polynesian arts[31]—all "traditional" arts, according to Burckhardt's and Schuon's criteria. He also insists on respecting the characteristics specific to a given technique (painting is flat, sculpture is three-dimensional),[32] and stresses the need for aesthetic stylization by simplifying forms—even if Aguéli cites Cézanne, whose works of "high cerebrality" (*haute cérébralité*) he praises,[33] but in which Schuon only saw imaginary metaphysical qualities.[34] In short, whether in his ideas or in the vocabulary he used, Aguéli does not develop or even foreshadow the Traditionalist concept of "traditional art."

To evaluate the cultural and human complexity of Aguéli according to later Traditionalist thought obviously makes little sense, but confronting the "Aguéli case" with the main theorists of Tradition may have a certain relevance. Aguéli's life and work contradicts first of all the quasi-dogmatic coherence between metaphysics, spirituality, and aesthetics postulated by the Traditionalists. The lack of developed reflection on the articulation between tradition/religion, society, symbolism, and aesthetics constitutes, in fact, along with a superficial epistemology of knowledge, is one of the blind spots of Traditionalist thought on the arts. Aguéli's texts demonstrate a deep concern with the material quality of art, the sensual and psychological impact of aesthetic choices, the visual construction of an image and the use of light in paintings, in other words very practical considerations, that we will hardly read from Schuon or Burckhardt, who always tended (for convenience?) to remain on a very theoretical, abstract, and general level.

Aguéli's cultural context also reveals an Orientalist, Spiritualist, post-impressionist milieu, the same matrix from which the Traditionalists came: be it Guénon, rooted in nineteenth-century occultism, Orientalism, and Freemasonry, or Schuon, whose ideas on art are at the crossroad of Romanticism, postimpressionism, and Guénonian metaphysics and universalism. In fact, the Guénonian or Schuonian point of view saw in Aguéli a kind of metaphysical precursor, while regretting the irregular nature of some of his ideas; conversely, Aguéli illustrates the modern Western paradigm underlying traditional thought, a paradigm that Guénon and his followers wanted to ignore or repress by the geometrical clarity of a metaphysical doctrine presented as perennial and universal. In other words, it is not so much the crystalline doctrine of a Guénon or a Schuon that reveals the limits of an Aguéli, torn between too many tendencies that they would consider contradictory, between Swedenborg and Ibn 'Arabi, between Sufism and postimpressionism; it is rather Aguéli who reveals how much Guénon and Schuon were modern Westerners ignoring their own cultural modernity, and how much their antimodernist and universalist notion of a "primordial Tradition" (Guénon) and of a "perennial Religion" (Schuon) constitutes a similarly modern and Western construction by its logic, radicalism, and idealism.

Aguéli's Cultural Complexity *versus* Traditionalist Dogma

Sufi, metaphysician, Orientalist, Theosophist, polyglot, anarchist, painter, postimpressionist, traditional feminist, occasional animal rights advocate, Aguéli was a multiple personality; a specifically modern and Western profile, and therefore a reflection of a society in turmoil and open to a world complicated by cultural encounters and political tensions between East and West. Thanks to an imperialist and colonialist West, to ethnographic museums, to the flourishing of Orientalism, to the aesthetic upheavals brought by impressionism and subsequent trends, Western thinkers and artists could discover or deepen their knowledge of extra-European aesthetic forms—African, Oceanian, Islamic, Indian, etc. Aguéli's eclecticism belongs indeed to the spirit of the times. So also do the cultural profiles of Coomaraswamy, a Sinhalese who emigrated to United States and "converted" to the metaphysics of the French Guénon settled in Cairo,[35] and of Schuon, a child of a German-French culture, painter, poet, metaphysician, impregnated with Romanticism. Although Guénonian metaphysics structured his discourse, Schuon combined in his work various interests, from Vedanta to Native Americans and Islam (especially that practiced in the Maghreb), which denotes, as with Aguéli, an eclecticism typical of the nineteenth and early twentieth centuries. It is by confronting the pictorial activity of Aguéli with that of Schuon that we will be led to reflections on the question of the spiritual in art and art in spirituality in contemporary culture.

Son of the Swiss sculptor Carl Burckhardt (1878–1923), Titus Burckhardt practiced drawing,[36] but Schuon—who worked in his youth as a textile designer—is the only founding author of the Traditionalist current to have produced any significant pictorial work. Especially after the 1950s, his paintings mainly depicted themes relating to the culture of Native Americans (White Buffalo Calf Woman, naked or half naked Native Americans, Native Americans and teepees) as well as—often semi-nude—"celestial women" (very personal representations of the Virgin Mary, of *yoginis* and *devis*, of Hindu mystical women like Akka Mahadevi or Lalla Yogshwari).[37] Unlike Aguéli's works, the subject matter of the paintings is explicitly symbolic and religious or spiritual; and Schuon's technique—which often tends more toward an illustrative style than a pictorial expression—also has little in common with Aguéli's aesthetic coherence and depth, borrowing his elements from postimpressionist painters as well as from Christian icons, Hindu aesthetics, or Japanese screens. On the other hand, what brings Schuon closer to Aguéli is the connection to a fully Western and contemporary aesthetic. We may not be surprised at Aguéli, but we can only be surprised regarding Schuon, insofar as he theorized a traditional doctrine of art that was in practice in conflict with his own paintings. Neither the aesthetics he used (sometimes a heterogeneous mixture of modern Western and revisited Oriental styles) nor the themes (scenes of Native Americans, or the syncretistic "Celestial Virgins" supposed to be at the same time Hindu, Christian, Islamic, universalist), nor even the status of these works (which are not sacred art, nor even traditional art in the sense that Schuon himself has defined them) correspond even to a broad definition of "traditional art."

What Schuon's pictorial works reveal is a gap, a dissociation, even a dichotomy between the "dogma" of traditional art and the concrete situation of contemporary creativity, and beyond that, between metaphysical interest and cultural linkage, between the concept of a traditional civilization and the historical realities of these civilizations, between the rigor of an initiatic process and the complexity of life trajectories. In this perspective, Aguéli hardly appears as a pre-Guénonian author, who could not logically obey a coherence of thought in the metaphysical and artistic domains (based on the assumptions that there should be an influential relationship between the two). As for Schuon, he appears as a modern Westerner, thinking in terms of a metaphysical and esoteric universalism (his "*Sophia perennis*"), but whose artistic creativity manifests a kind of syncretism between Romanticism and Orientalism, and demonstrates an eclecticism and a liberalism specific to the very modern West.

In the constellation of authors inspired by Traditionalist thought, another example can illustrate the difficulty of a contemporary metaphysical or spiritual aesthetics. The co-author of a famous book on the "Sufi tradition in Persian architecture," *The Sense of Unity*,[38] the Iranian-American architect Nader Ardalan evoked in an article published in 2000 the Islamic and Persian symbolism of the garden as paradise, quoting abundantly from the Qur'an and from Sufi writers like Rumi and Ibn 'Arabi. At the end of his article, he discussed the contemporary applications of these concepts, including one of his achievements: the ADMA–OPCO Headquarters in Abu Dhabi, built in 1991–4, whose atrium contains a vertical garden resembling, in his words, a classic Iranian carpet representing the Garden of Paradise.[39] However, the building is not traditional in the sense of taking inspiration from premodern architectural elements, but on the contrary, is in line with the trends of contemporary international architecture, disengaged from any symbolist or traditional intention. In other words, the use of Sufi authors essentially serves to give meaning, even legitimacy, to aesthetic forms whose modernism is rejected by all Traditionalist authors as nontraditional. But the question is then: If premodern metaphysics can give a hermeneutic value to contemporary aesthetics, why should this aesthetics be considered as "nontraditional"? Should we understand that some modernist creations have metaphysical potential, which may even not be recognized by their creators, but that philosophers spiritually formed in a metaphysical tradition can reveal and use? One may also wonder if the privilege of modernity—which an antimodernist metaphysics probably has difficulty seeing—is not to have created the cultural conditions favorable to the exploration of new aesthetics, likely to express other spiritual horizons or to offer new formulations of old ideas.

The inability to inspire an art that meets a metaphysical ideal undoubtedly reflects the over-theoretical, dogmatizing, and abstract nature of Traditionalist thinking on art. Aguéli's work shows in any case that, contrary to what the Traditionalist and highly questionable concept of "normal" or "normative" art might suggest, the notion of a traditional art is not self-evident. In fact, it results from a certain interpretation of ancient arts and traditions, willingly ignoring the sociocultural and political complexity necessary for the creation of the arts and erasing the details of historical developments. In any case, it cannot be deduced (as the Traditionalists suggest) "naturally" or "necessarily" from an understanding of a metaphysics or of a given tradition, even a regular or orthodox one, according to Guénon's criteria.[40] Above all, it highlights what Aguéli's work already showed or suggested. Spirituality, like art, has many dimensions and languages, and does not submit to a "hermeneutic" or "universalist" prejudice or motto. Artistic inventions are also made without or (sometimes) against any theory, and theories are most often retrospective formalizations that generate little contemporary creativity, and announce or inspire even fewer future developments. Last but not least, the cultural conditions of modernity, far from the supposed homogeneity of some so-called traditional societies, imply a complexity that makes it difficult to create or even theorize a spiritual art that could express metaphysical principles in a modern (but not modernist) way.

The traditional art wanted by Guénon and his followers is a retrospective vision of the past, which could not give the key to a fruitful understanding of modernity, nor an access to a living and contemporary creativity. A proverb of the ancient Greeks says that one must observe ancient laws, but eat fresh food. In a sense, this is what Aguéli did, not creating or re-creating a traditional art—assuming he had any idea of doing that, or even of the Guénonian notion of a "traditional art"—but immersing himself in centuries-old wisdom found in the East, while participating fully and with great talent in the aesthetics of his time and in the frame of his native European culture.

One can find in Aguéli's texts the reason for, or at least one of the meanings of, his cultural approach. The Swedish Sufi proposes a conception of the spiritual way that does not annihilate the personality, but on the contrary enhances the core of it, allowing the combination of different cultural horizons. He wrote, for instance, in 1911 that "the ideal tradition would be the one that develops individuality by all the means of ancient wisdom," and that the spiritual master, in Islam, is the one who "develops the *murīd* (the aspirant) according to the will of God, that is, who restores you to yourself, and enlarges your own self."[41] Unlike Guénon, who insisted on the transpersonal nature of traditions and described a somewhat disembodied initiatic method, Aguéli attached value to the spiritual path as a key to affirming one's deepest personality, and therefore one's most irreducible and individual (individualist?) originality. In this perspective, Aguéli's alleged eclecticism may be understood as the intimate and profound coherence of a multitalented man, trying to bridge and even unite East and West in a world that was gradually being transformed by the globalization of the West.

Concluding Remarks—Is It All about Hermeneutics?

Since the nineteenth century, from Nazarene painters to Kandinsky, from Romanticism to the New Age, many painters have wanted to rediscover a symbolic language of art, reinvigorate symbolism, and explore the paths of an aesthetic of interiority.[42] Aguéli and Schuon, about one generation later, are both heirs to a quite similar cultural configuration, made up of modernism, Orientalism, globalization, and spiritualism. Guénon and his followers have sought to establish their metaphysical and esoteric perspective as a potentially ultimate worldview and hermeneutic, capable among other things of defining degrees of orthodoxy and—in artistic matters—the degrees of "traditional" validity of creativities. But despite decades of books and articles, no significant art movement has emerged from the theoretical works of Schuon, Burckhardt, and their emulators. The scholastic and non-historical conceptions of traditionality in arts have only served to support the perpetuation, sometimes quite academic, of so-called traditional arts, as at the Prince's School of Traditional Arts in London.[43]

At another level, at a time of deep transformations and crisis of the historical religions, of the flourishing of new religious trends and syncretisms, of spiritual individualism and secular spiritualties, one can wonder what a "modern spiritual" art might or would be. According to what criteria and cultural backgrounds can we imagine it, recognize it, evaluate it, appreciate it? Is the re-founding of a traditional art even possible in the cultural conditions of the present times, where artists have deconstructed the very notion of art and scholars the concept of tradition, and where the cultural fragmentation of audiences makes it increasingly difficult to create a sacred or spiritual art which as many people as possible in a community can understand? Aguéli's case may suggest, as well as Schuon's paintings (yet in a quite paradoxical way, given the theoretical position of this author), that a spiritual art today, in the context of a kaleidoscopic (post)modernity, mainly (and sometimes even only) consists in a certain personal and unique inner relationship that the artist finds with the world and with a transcendence.

Ultimately, the arts and concepts of Aguéli and the Traditionalists raise fundamental questions about the hermeneutics of works of art, and, among other issues, about the relationship between intention and expression, between subjectivity and objectivity, and the cultural and intimate conditions of a philosophical and/or spiritual interpretation of visual arts. Assuming there to be "esoterism" or "esotericism" in art, what does it consist of? Does it reside mainly in the symbols used, borrowed from a given religion and/or from an esoteric or philosophical current? Or is it the aesthetics that must express first and foremost that particular esoteric tradition? Just representing a symbol does not suffice, since the genuine way of imagining it and expressing it visually must correspond to a specific intelligibility likely to touch an equally defined form of cognition and contemplation. And granted "esotericism" or "esoterism" be therein, what should we know in order to be able to understand it? Does the esoteric work of art require a certain state of mind, a particular spiritual awareness, a specific contemplative intellection, in order to be understood, or is it accessible to anyone who has been initiated in the hermeneutical life and/or aesthetic meaning of a painting, architecture, calligraphy, or ornament?

The artistic career of Aguéli, who moved from Theosophy to Sufism without fundamentally changing his pictorial style, can inspire similar questions.[44] With no knowledge of their author, do Aguéli's paintings evoke a mysticism by virtue of their proper aesthetics? Or is it only through the knowledge of the painter's ideas (implying a preliminary and even subjective selection of them) that we can become aware of a Swedenborgian color symbolism in a Gotland landscape painting, or that we may see in an Egyptian landscape painting the Sufi metaphor of a fragile world suspended in the divine light? And if we explore the potential meanings of Aguéli's works in the mirror of his life and texts, can we obtain any confirmation that these meanings were intended, foreseen, imagined by Aguéli? If not, to what extent are these interpretations adventurous extrapolations, which feed a continuing, living relationship to the work of Aguéli, but hardly allow us to recover its historical significance and the personal approach of Aguéli himself? If we can have a Sufi interpretation of Aguéli's pictorial styles and motifs, although there is nothing in his paintings that can be identified strictly speaking as "Sufi" (and representing an Egyptian mausoleum or mosque is hardly enough to make a painting a "mystical work"), we could also propose a Sufi hermeneutic of other postimpressionist painters—even the ones that we know were very far from expressing any mystical vision—following the principle that for a mystic, everything can be interpreted in a mystical way. But then, where does the "truth" of art lie, the relevance of interpretation, the limits of hermeneutic?

To avoid the fluctuation and vagueness of interpretations and judgments on art, Traditionalists have tried to define precisely what traditional art is, or should be, in the perspective of a holistic doctrine that links a metaphysical foundation of symbolism to a spiritual perception activated by a methodical initiation process: a totalizing vision, impressive in many ways, but whose efforts could not embrace the complexity of past civilizations and modern times. Traditionalists in fact brought a new hermeneutic,[45] appealing because of its apparent clarity and universalist ambition, but whose selectivity and shortcomings raise more questions than they provide answers, and whose scholastic tendencies tend to dry out a creativity and to widen the classical rift between theory and reality.

The confrontation between Aguéli (a "traditional" Sufi, but a "nontraditional" painter) and Traditionalist authors (failing to inspire an aesthetics satisfactory from their "traditional" point of view) shows that questions of creativity and hermeneutics in art (from the artists' and audiences' points of view) remain immense and essential. The debate is still wide open and proves that art is not dead, that the history of art is not over, and that hermeneutic is one of the keys to the very life of the arts.

Part Four

Writings by Ivan Aguéli

Letter from Paris

Ivan Aguéli
Translated from Swedish by Annika Öhrner and Mark Sedgwick

This letter was written by Aguéli, then aged twenty-four, at the start of his second and longest period in Paris. It is addressed to the Swedish painter and art theorist Richard Bergh (1858–1919), a former teacher and patron of Aguéli. It shows Aguéli at a personal level during his early years in Paris.

Paris, October 10, 1893

Honored brother,[1]

It is already a long time since I decided to bother you. As you know, I have such great difficulty in converting my ideas into action. A very clear external impulse is required to get me going.

My good friend and neighbor Luce[2] suggested to me this morning, during a somber conversation on the bad state of my finances, a rather useful idea. To his question of whether I could write in Swedish, I answered that I probably would if I really had to, and then he said I should try to get a commission from some Swedish paper that pays its employees in Paris to write correspondent articles. Not the least, as one does not paint successfully during winter.

The season looks threatening.

I have followed political developments rather intensively since the student unrest.[3] I participated, of course. Contributed with heart and soul some material to the barricades, and enjoyed the scenery as the Guards prepared to charge. I have never in my life had such a good time. I did not have to part my hair over my forehead. But I will talk about this on another occasion.

Our Lord initiated that revolution just in order for me to learn how a *real* revolution should be staged. Have had revolutionary fever since then. Have visited old anarchist friends, they wondered where I have been all this time. They live in the neighborhood, and we meet almost every day. Politics are heavily discussed.

One is rather *au courant* with the politics of today, and as the anarchists generally tend not to use clichés, I believe that I can see the circumstances in a rather impartial light. *L'en dehors*[4] [the outsider] is the only label one can apply to an anarchist. It is a beautiful phenomenon, anarchism. It is for certain the most beautiful in our filthy time. Imagine a sunrise and a sunset at the same time. The dynamiters' superb, mindful, calm heroism; the revenge of the culture victims; the dreams of utopists, intuition, and artists—this may be a pale light, but it embodies the first rays of the new sun. But I will talk about anarchism another time, if you like. Does the subject interest you?

I believe that I am capable of writing rather decent articles from here on domestic politics, and about art and literature. Not the least since I am intimately positioned within a good journalistic milieu. Could you imagine, one of my comrades sat down and wrote an almost anarchist article in ... *Figaro*. It was obviously directed against socialism, in between the lines against all parliamentarianism; basically anarchist. It wasn't visible, but I felt it. This is just one example out of many of finesse.

Speaking of all this about milieu, etc., to make you believe that it could happen that he (that is to say, I) could be capable of other than folly in this regard.

If you could do me the invaluable favor of recommending me to one of your friends from the press so that he accepts me as Paris correspondent and *pays*, then I would be most grateful. I am ashamed of exploiting you in this way. Don't believe that I don't realize the cynicism in demanding practical help from you, as you have already encouraged me so much through, as a good friend, sharing matters of artists' reflections, in order (if possible) to teach me something. I have a deuced respect for you and your ability to express authority without being in the least authoritative.

This is what follows, in case you would think of taking on my case. My intention is to start with several articles on the political parties in France, their importance and influence, and their history. This to create points of departure. Additionally, parliamentarianism and socialism as decently treated as possible. The Paris press (foreign policy does not interest me. Just occasionally, English conditions as judged in Paris. Ditto, *l'alliance franco-russe* [the Franco-Russian alliance]). I would like to touch upon French patriotism as little as possible. One rejects it in theory, of course, but one cannot bay at it. It may have a certain raison d'être. But patriotism in general, militarism, the scandals of barracks, police, court, and culture, will be discussed mercilessly.

This year appears to be rather rich with events to talk about. That is, one knows in advance that on December 31, 1894, we will be at exactly the same place as now, viewed in general, unless some bigger commotion happens, because it is really just commotion that changes things, and it is only the anarchists that make the world move forward. That is, if it is man who leads the world. But the socialists are preparing for the chamber, and since I have good relations among ex-socialists, so-called possibilists, I will have plenty to write about. In the art world we will soon have Gauguin's exhibition, he returned from Tahiti with about ninety canvases. Another exhibition with Constantin Guys's "Le peintre de la vie moderne" [Painter of Modern Life],[5] "Exposition d'art musulman" [Exhibition of Muslim Art].[6] I want to make representative portraits of artists and literary men, etc. I think I could write two to three articles each week, without changing my way of life.

Did I tell you that I was engaged in a symbolistic aesthetic? It is progressing. I am quite content. The framework is splendid. Here and there good in color. The synthesis is very simple, enlightens a rather large space, and sharp. Now and then I put in a rather peripheric thing, pretty direct under a large principle, which gives a lot of nerve to the rhythm in the light. I do see, however, that it is all too austere and I will change this as much as possible, through keeping the tone somewhat female. And through exclusively using the most common words, as intending, *in this case*, to be read *within* the words, rather than *behind* them. Architecture, by the way, is so much about composition and idea that it gains by being constructed in rough material.

Don't you think it is beautiful to regard a synthesis as a sun with several atmospheres within each other, the extent and nature of these, as well as their worlds, dependent on the sun's generative force?

You can imagine that we have a beautiful circle of friends. Rendez-vous at Félix [Fénéon],[7] an art critic who played a brilliant part in the campaign for the impressionists a couple of years ago. Much listened to and respected in the school Pissaro-Signac-Monet-Degas-Geffroy, Lecomte, etc. That is, the French-Parisian *pure impressionistic* naturalists, lyrics, portraitists, *narrateurs de la vie moderne et des actualités* [narrators of modern life and news]—aagh, what a dull phrase, forgive me. I really like him, not the least as he is so representative. I will make a dozen portraits of him. He finds himself very well put in some of my sketches, as do relations and friends. I cannot resist the temptation to talk about a new-French type in formation, a type that is decent, simple, sober, completely free from snobbery and pose. Emancipated as a social creature, international to the limit of being antipatriotic ... "Yes, it's proved now, we disclaim the national sentiment. All our spiritual patrons, all those I just mentioned (Tolstoy, Wagner, Ibsen) and Carlyle and Fichte and all the music from Bach to Wagner, from Schumann to Borodin, all foreigners; and Rosetti, and Swinburne and finally Nietzsche, and everybody," a hopeful twenty-year old (Mauclair)[8] wrote the other day in *Mercure de France*, September, in a very moderate and very solid article. Mauclair is a highly talented and interesting fellow. Naturalist *en attendant* [in waiting], for lack of something better, to avoid rascals in mysticism, which he reveres, he takes a stand for art as a form of intuition. Respect for synthesis, but unfit for it. As *esthétie* [aesthetic] rather dematerialized, however focused on personal experience. Completely lost or dreadfully dry, except as regards what is seen or dramatic. But conscious of it and therefore, leaving the great synthesizes aside as well as *l'abstrait substantiel* [the substantial abstract], without Germanizing those who occupy themselves with it. Far from godless, because among them a great, though *bien vague* [very vague] belief in "le sens caché des choses" [the hidden meaning of things], a belief which is one of the Prophet's *first* commandments (the second or the third verse in the Qur'an if I remember properly).[9] I am convinced that his type is of the New Mankind, in its first state. I am positive that they have the future ahead of them. Because they are (1) nice lads (2) sensible lads that just believe in what is substantial. And that they have no clue of the abstract substantial is not that bad; to that from the concrete substantial is just a matter of degree. The question of time, the question of evolution, within *idé-généalogie* [the genealogy of ideas], of course. And Our Lord still leads them, for the two things just mentioned. They admire the gray shadows, winter things, twilights, they want nature veiled, and find mists mystical. I find them interesting and rather playful. Can you imagine, many of them are walking around believing that the light will come from the north? There is some sense to it, since the neophyte entered the pyramid through a little hole in the northern wall. And the northern man nowadays has *some little* of the qualities that were required to present oneself in the sacred house asking to be prepared for the first and lowest degree of initiation. By all account they are a beautiful contrast to Satanists, spiritists, German socialist-materialists. You could imagine that the socialists are bright birds. One of them says, completely naively in the light of the day, and at election meetings, "Messieurs, le socialisme n'est qu'une question de ventre et de sous-ventre" [Gentlemen, socialism is just a matter of the stomach and belly]. Damn it all. A social question that is just a food question. Damned nonsense. But let us get back to Félix. He is one of the best of this type I have seen. Superb and great critical intelligence. All ask for his advice, and it is so nice to see the unquestionable esteem everybody has for him. As intelligence active, *un sceptique rôdant* [a skeptical wanderer, literally wandering skeptic]. Very ironical humor. Reading verse and drama extremely well. I stand very high in his esteem, something which encourages me greatly.

And then there is a Dutch guy who can be rude in every possible language. French, Dutch, German, English, Frisian, Flemish, Spanish, and Malay. He has been in the land of my dreams, Java and Sumatra, for many years. He is the funniest bastard you could imagine. A lively little devil. You cannot look at him without laughing, especially if he by accident happens to adopt a sincere face for a minute, and so forth.

And so many beautiful girls on top of that. And so kind as well. I paint all of them. But unfortunately they have work and studios to attend to. One of them is extravagant. I dare not start talking about her because then I will never stop. Every single part of her is like a cleverly written thesis on symbolism. I see visions as I paint her. I and a couple of good friends follow her home and if it is in the small hours, we can forget ourselves until dawn. Then we are positioned on the floor like reverential heathens. In silent worship. And she is on a *canapé* [couch] between us, happy to be a goddess, if only for a moment, Goddess, source of light. And she shows us once her arm, her leg, her shoulders, her neck, her breasts, naked, radiating beauty.

The sinful litterateur touches her very respectfully, and then licks his fingers. But I think he is stupid in doing that. He would do better to hold his breath.

I need to add that none of us even touches spirits.

Read Aurier, *Oeuvres posthumes* [Posthumous Works], ed. Mercure de France, 15 Rue de l'Echandé, St. Germain, Paris.[10] The most solid symbolist critic I have met. Damned good criticism about Van Gogh, Gauguin, etc. It is a male brain that criticizes, which is unusual. J.-K. Huysmans,[11] you know him. He has developed in a funny way. Have read [Huysmans's] *Là bas* [The Damned], which I like a lot as a document, less as a work of art. As I have heard, [*À*] *rebours* [Against the Grain] is something like that as well. It is rather peculiar that the author of *L'Art moderne* [Modern Art][12] has come to better thoughts. Remy de Gourmont,[13] *Le Latin mystique* [Mystical Latin] (ed. Le Mercure)[14] is valuable, a real revelation as a book on mysticism in poetry. Huysmans's introduction to that volume is among the best pages I have read on *l'histoire actuelle* [contemporary history], among the soundest and most sensible after Baudelaire. Huysmans has taken on, it seems, a grand job to fight Satanism in favor of sound mysticism and real spirituality. Because there is some truth in Nordau's *Entartung* [Degeneration].[15] Unfortunately, his mob-like nature cannot distinguish between Satanism and religion. He calls all supranaturalism *perversité sexuelle* [sexual perversion], bad stomach, hallucination just because one has not eaten enough good steak, etc.[16] Bloody idiot. Does the bastard not realize that the philosophy of chemistry is phallicism, as clear as can be. One realized that already in school. And one of Europe's most clever poets, August Strindberg, agrees on that in many places. He must be married to a real cow, that Nordau.

I quote the following words by Aurier in order for you to get an idea of him, words chosen almost randomly, because I have not read him entirely, just here and there; because that is enough, a couple of pages, to get an idea of a likable author. With some *pénétration* [perspicacity]:

A work of art is a new being that has not only a soul, but a double soul (the soul of the artist and the soul of nature, father and mother).[17]

The only way to penetrate a thing is love. To understand God you have to love him. Understanding stands in proportion to love.[18]

The only way to understand a work of art is to be its lover, which is possible since the work is a being that has a soul and reveals it through a language that you can learn. It is even easier to love a work of art than a woman, since in the case of the work of art matter barely exists, and almost never makes love degenerate into sensuality.

One might ridicule this method. If so, I will not respond.

Our soul's most noble faculties are atrophying (through positivism).[19] One has to react. We must again nurture the highest properties [of the soul]. We must again become mystics. We must again learn that love is the source of all understanding. But oh, it is too late to reconquer love in all its primitive, unspoiled nature. The sensualism of our century has made us look at woman as a piece of meat, served to extinguish our material lust. Love of woman is not allowed anymore. The skepticism of our century has made us see in God just a nominal abstraction that may not exist. Love of God is no longer allowed.

One single love is still allowed, that for works of art. Let us throw ourselves into this rescue. Let us be the mystics of art.

And if we cannot succeed in this, let us sadly return to our troughs while sighing a last *Finis Galliae*—Gaul is finished.

Beautiful pages—aren't they?

His perspective on contemporary art is damned good. And I do not dare to talk more about him, so as to end this longwinded letter.

Excellent publications: *Mercure de France*, primus inter pares, *La jeune Belgique*, *l'Ermitage*, *Les essais d'art libre*. If you could trouble yourself with returning them to me, I will let you borrow some issues of certain publications with interesting essays. But as I need to return them in my turn ... *Pardon* [sorry].

I want to make Strindberg known here. I have translated some parts of *Röda rummet* [The Red Room] as bits to taste, even though they were fragments. It hurts me to see how much admiration Ibsen gets. He does not deserve it, damn it. Strindberg is rather European, whether his every-day is Swedish or not. And he has a certain European value, because he has created a new temperament, something which is the social duty of an artist, a temperament that some of the human beings of our day need for their higher and inner life. While Ibsen, in his turn, just tries to convince doltish Norwegian small-town dwellers to do what in France and Spain goes without saying, at least among the non-bourgeois. Can no one really see that he only pulls very gently at the farthest edge of our damned civilization and its connected society, which only remains standing with great effort and is otherwise undermined internally in every possible way? I do not give one single Ravachol[20] for one dozen Ibsens. His method as drama writer is rather solid. But do you know *Les flaireurs* [The trackers] by van Lerberghe?[21] There you have *le théâtre symboliste* [symbolist theater]. A friend read it for me, and damn it, did I not see ghosts! I felt it in each part of my body. And yet, it was so simple. Just an old poor woman dying, so content, and the staging was as if a young shepherd boy had done it.

How does one become an authorized translator of Strindberg? Could you give me his address and if possible, a recommendation? Then I can write to him and send a piece of translation and so forth. I would just discuss about the most necessary, the work, etc. Because I do not like him at all as a personality. And Nietzsche, and Nordau, and German gentlemen, I am wary of. It is the Strindberg-impressionist, the *paysagiste* [landscaper] in particular that I will emphasize. And the critic of society, no, the anarchist rather. And possibly one or another of his monumental work. *Röda rummet* or the archipelago novels. Other than that, my opinion on details is quite changeable, especially negotiable. Are there any economic *fla-flas* [hooplas] or other formalities to attend to, other that writing to the author? Could you be so kind and help me with this promptly, as *La Révolte* and *La Revue anarchiste* are waiting for essays that are almost finished, that is, translations of Strindberg.

And *painting*. You paint the men of the coming century and the eternal female. Carefully rendered portraits are always good exercise. That is by the way the most sensible I can do at the moment. It has "humanized" me somewhat. And then a contrivance. I will paint Paris horizons from Montmartre and from the windows of friends with a good view. I have made six good sketches and finally found the key to the oscillations of the line in this sea of roofs, marked by lines (streets), towers, monuments, parks, etc. My friends like them a lot, Félix keeps two of them with him. I have found him many times in contemplation in front of them. But the first thing I do if I see them is turn them around and place them in a corner. But I am so undecided with the color, in this case. I have painted them gray-blue, ultramarine, and a foul brown, just to get to draw with the brush. I have found that in order to paint I must have either bright light or a wide horizon, or best, both. I cannot stand anyone but kids watching me. From this summer I have a stack of sketches in color and lines as usual, that no one understands except for me, five to six uncompleted works. I have wasted more than twenty sessions on a motif that I am crazy about. I have not been able to finish it. How in hell could one paint with a bunch of people around oneself, saying one is *fin-de-siècle*? However, I will finish them indoors. They are some streets in sunshine. One of my friends who has been in the tropics recognizes "le grand silence de la chaleur" [the great silence of heat] in some of them. Shall I send you photographs of some of the portraits? And then there are some *natures mortes* [still lives] here and there. *C'est tout* [That's all]. Madame B's portrait, Félix's as well, a park at Moulin de la Galette [on Montmartre], and a couple of "Paris-marins" [marine-style scenes of Paris] I might send to *les indépendants* [the exhibition of the Salon des indépendants] next year. We will see what the park looks like as it is ready. Madame B's portrait is damned suggestive as a female portrait. She is very content herself, thinks that I have made her so beautiful. And that is a damn lie, because she is a thousand time more beautiful in reality. It is very much alike, and her paramour, a young poet, very nice boy, is damned content as well, and thinks there is something *imprévue* [unplanned, unexpected] in it. Now everyone is happy except me. But she will pose for me with "sa frimousse" [face] (a very beautiful word for a young, beautiful woman's head, isn't it) in the near future, and then I will make something really damned good. Have you noticed how joyful it is to paint women that remind you of girlfriends from the time when you were so much in love that were blue flashes before your eyes as you kissed them?

You might think that it is strange to see me so *épris* [taken] with zeal for my work, a positive sense eagerness to throw myself into *la vie moderne* [modern life]. Now I can do it without being harmed. Now it is a rest for me. Before, that was impossible for me. I am skeptic enough to study it without living it. Maybe that is the best way to avoid being overwhelmed by it, to control it.

I long more than ever to get away from this damned Europe, for some primitive land where it is very beautiful and very clear, and where polemics, dialectics, rhetoric, politics, and socialism are unknown diseases. Where people don't argue with one another just for the sake of taking joy in arguing, and don't prefer to consume each other's cadavers than each another's vitality and joy in living.

How can you explain this phenomenon? I am *un flaneur enragé* [a passionate loafer]. To thrive in crowded streets or in quite desolate, barely planned quarters, is like eating good, healthy food when one is hungry. It is like having ears and eyes over the whole body. And everything around me is as one mouth that speaks, and *gente* [unknown meaning]. But I always get the impression that all these houses, these trees, these human beings are hardly real. And that a certain noise within the street noise is the only reality. The houses seem to me to be mostly *en attendant* [in waiting]. I often surprise myself asking myself, quite seriously: "But will they not tear this barracks down soon? It seems so thin in its colors. They are ready to dissolve in a colorless, invisible gas at any minute." The trees seem to me least fugitive and improvised. The heavens and perspective are deep and motionless. This sensation is a rule for me. It reappears in any street interior that I see and sense. That is, I have it almost every time I walk down the street, in certain quarters I like, and in an intelligent, awakened, observing state of mind. Very intensely if the street appears quickly. I can talk about the Paris atmosphere the next time if you like. I don't care for painting it. If I was a musician or poet, I would make art of this sensation. Except we will see if I can represent the strange sound, which is the base for all detailed sensation, in some color, possibly copper muting a most strange, intense blue-white, sharp but completely silent.

I want to make portraits in iron, forged not cast. The tension in the face of the townsman seems hammered in iron. Nervousness in copper, in granite, in marble exist as well, but are rarer. I know a smith who is an artist. He makes only flowers. But of iron and so artistic that you can feel the fragrance and the color, sometimes even the symbolism of the flower, as you weigh it in your hand. The form is the most naturalistic and *vêtu* [dressed], but a naturalism à la Corot that this smith carries with him as a *conception* [an idea] of nature. The man is a genius of nature, *au point de vue de métier* [from a craft perspective], *seulement* [only], the drawing is most correct (and a damn good intelligence and feel. Artists wouldn't even be able to copy this delicacy in a drawing after his iron flowers). But ask the gentleman to make a drawing with paper and pen, or with any damn anything except a rather heavy hammer and a piece of iron, and you will see how anxious he gets. It is not his flowers that have inspired me to make portrait in iron, but a friend connected me to him as result of my inclination to forge. Some horse heads, I would also like to forge.

Could you please *donner un coup d'épaule* [give a push] to my friends Lindberg or Sjögren,[22] one of them, they really need to get out? And that would not be that difficult, they are both productive as rabbits. If I am right, Mr. Zorn[23] had a high esteem for something called decorative arts. As had Mr. Hasselberg after his return from Copenhagen.[24] They have now a marvelous opportunity to show if their love for decorative arts is something more than Platonism, which as we know they are not much accustomed to, except in the case of the Holy Ghost, by giving travel money and if possible something more to the young men in question. As being probably the most promising decorators in Sweden. Of course, a bit after you, and Nordström, and Josephson, and Count Rosen.[25] I have not heard from Åkerberg.[26] He has gone to hell, it appears. Another large spirit has gone overboard. But it is true, we have such damn talented men in Sweden. Just look at the art academy, the artists association, etc. *Merde* [shit]. As you can see, I cannot stand being ironic anymore.

I will now finish this up, begging your forgiveness for having taken your attention for such a long time. I will never do that again. In my case, bad manners or disheveled expressions do not mean a lack of respect for the addressee. On the contrary: I am in *négligé* [undress] to give the opportunity to judge whether I am an idiot or crazy. If I am, you need to find out as quickly as possible "pour ne pas perdre son temps" [so as not to waste your time].

With highest respect and affection

　　Ivan Aguéli

　　16 rue Cortot

　　(Butte Montmartre)

[Postscript omitted.]

Letter from Ceylon

Ivan Aguéli
Translated from French by Nadine Miller

This letter (Figure 16.1) was written by Aguéli, then aged twenty-nine, at the start
of his second journey outside Europe, shortly after his conversion to Islam. It is
addressed to his French friend and sponsor, Marie Huot (1846–1930). It shows us
Aguéli at a personal level during his earliest years as a Muslim.

Colombo, March 21 (Tuesday), 1899

Dear Marie,

Received your letter of March 1 yesterday at the French Consulate, after having been
alerted to it by the postcard of March 3. I can't possibly tell you how much I enjoyed it.
I have had no news from you since Port Said. Nothing at Aden. We need to keep track
of the letters we write, in order to be sure that none have gone missing. I am still at
the hotel, for another week, as I had committed myself to nineteen days. But in a few
days I shall have lodgings, a very small apartment consisting of two very large rooms,
sufficiently out of the way, for four rupees a month. It couldn't be better. I owe this to
my Javanese [servant] who is devoted to me to an extent I shall never forget. Should
the man turn out to be a rascal it would prove my complete ignorance of physiognomy.
Still, as is my habit, I have arranged everything in such a way so that he could not
possibly harm me, if that were his intention. I have also seen his younger brother, who
is very nice, very gentle. He lives near me with his family. Will tell you later about the
native dwellings.

But how did I get to know these people here? I have told you already that in a
Muslim country, the very best recommendation is a knowledge of the Arabic language.
One day I was strolling through the Cinnamon Garden, an immense untended park in
the middle of the town. I stopped in front of a building which I took to be a mosque.
There actually was an Arabic inscription on it, which I was interested in deciphering. A
man showed up, wearing a red sarong, a European jacket, and a Malay turban of white,
black, blue, snakeskin-patterned, and asked me if I was able to read it. I told him no, I

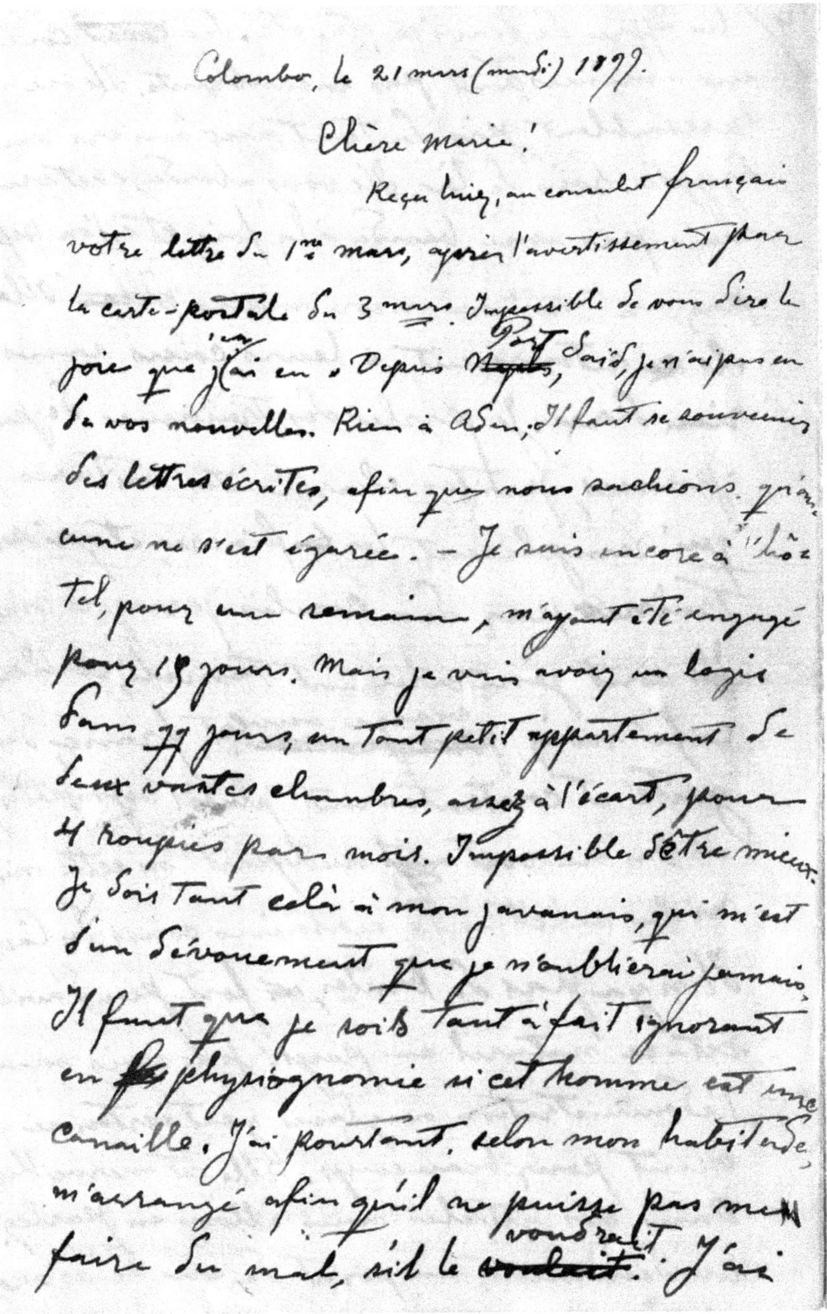

Colombo, le 21 mars (mardi) 1899.

Chère Marie!

Reçu hier, au consulat français votre lettre du 1er mars, après l'avertissement par la carte-postale du 3 mars. Impossible de vous dire la joie que j'en ai eu. Depuis Port Saïd, je n'ai pas eu de vos nouvelles. Rien à Aden, il faut se souvenir des lettres écrites, afin que nous sachions qu'aucune ne s'est égarée. – Je suis encore à l'hôtel, pour une semaine, m'ayant été engagé pour 15 jours. Mais je viens avoir un logis dans 77 jours, un tout petit appartement de deux vastes chambres, assez à l'écart, pour 4 roupies par mois. Impossible d'être mieux. Je dois tout cela à mon javanais, qui m'est d'un dévouement que je n'oublierai jamais. Il faut que je sois tout à fait ignorant en physiognomie si cet homme est une canaille. J'ai pourtant, selon mon habitude, m'arrangé afin qu'il ne puisse pas me faire du mal, s'il le voudrait. J'ai

Figure 16.1 Letter from Ivan Aguéli to Marie Huot, 1899. Original in the Ivan Aguéli Archive of the National Museum, Stockholm.

couldn't, at that distance. He led me to a nearby shop and showed me a piece of Qur'an, which I did read, to the astonishment of the onlookers. I told them that I was a Muslim, that I wanted to go to school, to the *madrasa*, as it is called, and they sent me to the director of that institution who received me well, albeit with some embarrassment. I realize that the English are not overly pleased for the Muslims to accept converts into their fold. On the other hand, their religion obliges them to accept them etc. etc. In the end we went our ways, and I am *very happy* with the attitude of the Muslims here.

After all, in this country Islam makes its presence felt by lending a bit of taste and spirit to their mentality. I find it a bit difficult to describe land and people to you. Imagine a country where you encounter not a single fierce face. They are all very calm, very gentle, very tranquil. No shouting, screeching, or jostling. There are no beggars, none of that insistence in offering services to foreigners. Even the coolies are not troublesome. They in no way resemble the donkey-drivers of Egypt, far from it. They do approach you, it is true, but not all at once as a mob, and if you refuse them by saying "no," or preferably "illè," they go back to their places without another word. I'm talking of the pullers of rickshaws, charming little vehicles that take the place of fiacres and which are drawn by nearly naked coolies. They are generally Tamils, coffee-colored, open-faced, honest, and of a rather pleasant gaiety and contentment. Nowhere is the filth and misery of certain corners of Cairo to be seen. There are no ruffians, very few low-lifes. Is this the natural state of the country? I believe so; but the English administration certainly has a lot to do with it. It is marvelous. We will speak about it in our articles.[1] Obviously, as far as their get-up is concerned, that leaves a lot to be desired, obliging scores of people to adopt European dress styles, which is ridiculous in all respects. You see women who would be as charming and pretty as anything wearing horrible outfits. But I'm not going to tell you about that now, and the Christians are not in the majority.

I have already spoken to you about the beauty of the men here. There are real beauties among them, with long, gorgeous, dark, jet-black hair, falling upon bare shoulders, half way down their backs. Moreover, they are very proud of this. You see them in their corners, combing their hair, rubbing it with coconut oil, or preening their hair which falls about them like a veil or coat with graceful, coquettish gestures. It is a charming sight. I assure you, these people are incapable of any malice, least of all savagery. In terms of humanity, it is perfect.

I also feel completely changed. First of all, to get worked up about things, to get angry or to lose your temper is very dangerous, on account of the temperature. Yet it is exquisite, beyond all description, when you are calm and half naked. No, you can be wearing clothes, but it is *absolutely* essential to wear loose and flowing garments. It is a dreadful torment to be squeezed tightly into your clothes. I refuse to do that. At the hotel, I potter about draped in a sarong, my bedspread around my shoulders, my feet in Arab shoes from Aden.

I can give you no better illustration of this country than by telling you that it is full of flowers, not of architecture. There are no flowers in Arabia/Egypt, there is only architecture. Ceylon and Egypt are complementary contrasts. I love them both, each in its own way. In Egypt, all is power, splendor, mysticism, unreal, even infernal, passion. Here, everything is sweetness, elegance. It is like Italy with mysticism, but it is much more elegant than Italy. No, I give up trying to describe to you the delicacy, the lightness of touch of everything to be seen here.

I went out with a gentleman who wished to learn French by instructing me in Sinhalese. He had offered me a room in his house for 2½ rupees. He is a professor at the Theosophical College. At first he offered me a room for free. I did not want to accept that, jealously guarding my independence. Finally we parted. So I went to find my Javanese, and we chatted. This is the result of our conversation. There are three worlds here. The English administration, the Buddhists, and the Muslims. I leave out the different Christian sects which I don't trust at all. The Buddhists and the Muslims are rivals and they hardly associate with each other. Jalal, my Javanese, told me that the Muslims here will have less trust in me if I live among the Buddhists with whose customs, incidentally, I am not at all familiar, and whose faces inspire much less confidence. He told me that later I could pursue all those studies there, but that I had to begin with and give preference to Muslim studies. I found his words very sensible. So I have made my choice, and for several reasons. The Buddhists lack style and vision; they do not strike me as being quite honest. They have neither the politeness nor the (at least apparent) kindness of the Muslims. I haven't any serious recommendations regarding them. Who is Mr. Bambery, how will he receive me? I will know in a few days. I do not want to depend on him, even if I happen to find him agreeable. If I end up not liking him, then that would be the last straw. Finally, Buddhism has never been my favorite field of study. And then, an Indian who had converted to Buddhism was subjected to their religious "patriotism" in that they alleged that he was not a born Buddhist. Yet he belonged to the Brahmin caste. All this shows me that they are petty-minded clerics, people I do not like. The attitude of their children was one of curiosity and sneers. So I have no hesitation. I feel that I have no business among them, while the Muslims may need me, they have already made that clear to me. There are some well-heeled Muslims who do a lot for education. [Marginal notation: At Vellore, near Madras, there is a Muslim college where you are schooled and fed for two years. But I want to do my painting. I could still go and study there, but, you see, I want to paint.] But the main reason is that among them I would have my freedom, without the control of the clerics. At the madrasa or at their college, I will gain their respect, don't you worry. Even if my Javanese were a rascal—one must always assume the worst—I have seen enough to know that it is among the Muslims that I must spend my days. I have often given them the opportunity to rob me, even of rupees, as a bait, but they have always been honest. So, if they are scoundrels, they are scoundrels possessing modesty and good judgment, and I prefer having to deal with them.

Whatever the case, whatever happens, I have made my decision. Among them I can study ten languages, while the Buddhists can teach me only two. Muslim studies are my introduction to the countries I love, Arabia, Africa. They can study everything. They are not prejudiced. They have their pride, perhaps even arrogance; if they do something bad, I can assume they are just as likely to do some good, given their freedom. Above all, they never exhibit contempt for the poor. When I told them that I had to subsist on nineteen rupees a month, they did not wince, but replied right away, "So you need a house for 4 rupees a month," and a few hours later they had found me one. I continue to take my precautions, as a matter of principle. I carry my money on me, in my belt, until I can safely deposit it. [Marginal notation: Burglaries with forced entry are to be feared.] I will deposit my valuables with Mr. Freudenberg[2] etc. etc. and then we'll see. No one in this country is capable of any act of violence or robbery. Some are prone to crimes of passion. And I rely only on myself, and the English police. Then I take refuge in Allah. Once I have taken all my precautions. A disaster will be terrible in its consequences, but I cannot worry all the time, twenty-four hours a day; that is extremely detrimental to one's health.

I sense that I am also becoming mellow, calm, and determined at the same time. My agitation, my overexcitement, my "bad character," all of it fading away like the darkness before the sun. When the other day I whipped these two fellows, it was slowly, deliberately, without the slightest trace of emotion on my part. I was laughing deep down in my heart. The effect was also overwhelming. They rolled in the dust, and I did not see them again.[3]

I have discovered something that I ask you to pass on to the doctors. Health is the feeling of transparency of the body. When diseased, the body is opaque, clogged, out of touch with its inner feeling. The other day, I was walking by the sea, a delightful thing to do. It is like being in a globe of crystal and of precious stones. Impossible to paint any of that. Then I saw a Tamil in the distance, stark naked, who was splashing around on the beach, the foam of the breakers caressing his backside. I thought that must be a delightful sensation. I went down, took off my shoes, and walked for a few miles, sometimes in the water, sometimes on the blazing sand. I'm telling you, the beach was burning hot. But I felt rays of heat rising from the soles of my feet to my chest and spreading out all over from there. It is a shame that I am no consumptive; I claim that this is the cure. But it is necessary that it be the beach here, under this sun, in this sand. I checked from time to time to see if I had burns on my feet. None at all. I will develop this treatment. Please believe that this is indeed a good experience. I found out later that the natives make their sick amble about the beach like this to strengthen their legs.

Nothing bad must be said about the Buddhists in the *Encyclopédie*.[4] I will attempt to make use of the situation and the exhibition next year. Best to be on good terms with everybody.

Do not board a German ship without making sure you hold a second-class ticket; try to get one that doesn't include meals, and live on canned food. That works very well. You can resupply anywhere en route. The longest stretch is seven days, from Aden to Colombo. The cats can certainly be on board. They can have meat on board, alas, tears come to my eyes at the mere thought of that hell. In Aden everything is good except for the oranges. One is not fleeced there, at least not very much. And the Somalis are so beautiful that you do not mind losing money. My notes are still at customs; next week I will send them to you.

[Several postscripts omitted.]
Until later,
    Ivan

The Enemies of Islam

Abdul-Hadi El Maghrabi
[Ivan Aguéli]
Translated from Italian by Alessandra Marchi

This article was written in 1904 by Aguéli, then aged thirty-five, under his Muslim name (Abdul Hadi El Maghrabi), early in his second and longest period in Egypt. It was published in Il Convito/Al-Nadi, *in several installments, and shows us Aguéli's political and religious positions during this period. It discusses Islamophobia (islamofobia), and may well be the first ever use of a term that has since become widely used.*[1]

Introduction

In this column we will publish a series of articles in which we will make every effort to be as impartial and fair as possible.[2] We gave this task to our editor Abdul-Hadi El Maghrabi, who lived for a long period of time in Europe and is an expert on the subject, and judges people mainly on the basis of their position regarding Islam. We will begin by dealing with a question raised by *Arafate*[3] in its penultimate number, a question as interesting as it is delicate, being the disdain of Europeans for Muslims.[4]

Our editor says that those educated Europeans, who are not fanatics of Protestantism or of Roman or Slavic Catholicism, nor of socialism or of any barracks or bag philosophy, never despise Orientals save when they themselves *despise their own religion and the Shari'a.* As a matter of principle, the management shares this opinion, and we will later demonstrate that the only true friends of the Orient are those who want Muslims to observe their own religion. Even those who use violent methods love Muslims more sincerely than those who do not [but] want Islam to be abandoned little by little, using sweet means and caressing the evil instincts with which the human heart is filled in all countries.

The Management

Why Muslims Are Detested: Islam Should Not
Be Confused with Muslims

The June 23 [1904] issue of *Arafate* includes a very interesting and striking article on the bad opinion that a large number of Europeans have of Muslims in general. I find that the author does not make a clear difference between those who are forcibly the enemies of Islam and those who are not, yet blaming more or less rightly or wrongly a large number of Muslims.

I do not claim that the *Arafate* columnist is not saying the truth, but he does not give the whole truth that he could have given, and for this reason I want to respond to the amiable journal, of which we all appreciate the efforts and capability. Our article is not a refutation, but a kind of complement, because I only want to put things properly and give the facts their right value, which, it seems to me, is a principle of elementary wisdom. At the same time, this article will serve as a response to *Arte*,[5] from which we have accepted remarks with much regard, as they have been made very sincerely. An adversary in good faith can never be an enemy.

I have myself been convinced up to the limit that has been called fanaticism, so I know what it means to have convictions, and I find that the emotion of faith is infinitely superior to the dogma for which it exists, and I have often seen a man who fought me with rage until just the day before become a supporter. All I can do is to be happy to respond to *Arafate* and *Arte*, which are antipodes.

On Islamophobia

In Europe there are people who hate both Islam and Muslims at the same time; there are others who do not want Islam, yet sympathize with Orientals; and there are people who love both Islam and Orientals, like the director of this journal. A last category includes those who deeply admire Islam, the Prophet, the first Muslims and Arab civilization, but who make a great distinction between them and the Muslims in our days, as they do not consider them Muslims. They believe that true Islam has disappeared from the earth and is without protagonists, having left an immense legacy of artistic and literary beauty, an admirable monument founded on a prodigious leap of humanity; in short, they believe that Islam no longer exists save in some precious artistic masterpiece or in a few hundred beautiful books of mysticism, science and poetry, but never in the hearts of the men of today.

The first category includes mainly Catholic clerics, who, by dogma, must consider Muslims, as well as all non-Catholic Christians, damned in this world and in the next. Indeed, there are many ignorant people who believe this damnation as evident due to outward signs, such as the small fact that *Arafate* has mentioned: educated Parisians of the bourgeois class believe that when a Muslim washes himself, the water fills with worms. We cite this detail on the authority of *Arafate* because such abuse is insulting even to those who use it; now, when such a thing happens in the middle of Paris, "ville lumière," what cannot happen in the midst of rural populations! There are thousands of Oriental Christians who have always lived among Muslims, who seriously believe that Muslims are obliged to wash four or five times a day (ablutions) in order not to rot! And they tell this to the Europeans, among whom there are enough fools to believe it. Do not good Catholics believe that Jews cannot celebrate Easter according to the rite of their religion without slaughtering a Christian child? Does there not exist a whole literature based on these absurdities? But a Muslim who believed that this is the opinion of the majority of Europeans would do better not to say so, because he would risk being considered as stupid as the Catholic obscurantists.

Arafate also quotes the book of [Daniel] Kimon.[6] I can say that this is not the way Europeans are persuaded. Once the book is read, the author's exasperation is very amusing, and the reading ends by concluding only one thing: "Here is a gentleman who does not like Muslims." Enough. Such attacks always go in favor of the one who is their target. May it please God that Muslims never have enemies!

Added to this rather grotesque category, there is a certain number of Protestant clerics and materialists who are as fanatical as any inquisitor.[7] This "English-style" and "socialist-style" Islamophobia (*islamofobia*) [is] like the Islamophobia which we discussed [above][8] that takes root in Latin countries and can be classified as "Hispanic-Franco-Levantine type" Islamophobia, a baroque formula for a baroque thing.

There are two more types of Islamophobia: the German type and the Russian type.

The German type is confused with the theory of inferior races: it has its origin in a philosophical school commonly called "the philosophy of the barracks," which aims to prove logically and philosophically that the Aryans alone are those who have human rights, and not all of them, but only the Germans, who are Aryans par excellence: for this, one is German or is a Negro. It is extremely dangerous to laugh at such a theory, since this school—systematically, logically, philosophically—establishes that Germany has not only the right, but the sacrosanct duty to subject all the other people of the earth, to forbid them to think, to live, to speak otherwise than in German. Luminaries of this lovable school do not yet preach a crusade against Islam, since the emperor, who sometimes has excellent ideas, has discovered that it is not yet a good time. It will be for later.

However, we should not believe that all Germans belong to this ridiculous school. There are Germans who really have common sense and wide erudition; we can just remember that half of the best European works on Islam are in German, and that [Hans] Barth, the German author of *Droit du Croissant* [The Right of the Crescent],[9] wrote the best work on the Armenian and Bulgarian issues,[10] which is a real treasure trove of precious information, of which even the smallest sheds new light on those mysterious events and their causes.

We will discuss Russian Islamophobia in detail on another occasion. It is a Byzantine Islamophobia and simply consists in telling the Turks: "Do not believe in the Qur'an," it is a book that spoils your soul and body. Be Russian, that is, be like us; then you will have everything you want. Now, everyone knows that Russians want no more than three things: icons, vodka, and the [Cossack] *nagaika* [whip].

All these people are more or less clerical: the doctrines vary a little, but all these "believers" resemble each other in deceiving themselves.

Every cleric is Islamophobic, that is obvious! About a century and a half ago all of Europe was clerical, ergo Islamophobic, and then all possible evil was thought about Muslims: but now times have changed a lot, especially in the so-called liberal countries, like Italy, France, and England among the great powers, and Switzerland, the Netherlands, and the Scandinavian countries among the second-order powers. In all these countries discussion is perfectly free and everyone has the right to expand their ideas and theories, provided they don't attack the honor, life, or property of citizens.

Furthermore, there are still in these countries, especially before the Armenian turmoil, considerable elements of real Islamophilia. Now, it must be confessed that Muslims have not taken any advantage of free institutions or Islamophile tendencies to end once and for all the ridiculous legends which have been spread about Islam and Muslims from a century before the crusades to the present day, legends unceasingly revived through the biased and fabulous stories of the missionaries, the Christian priests of the Orient.

On European Regard for Islam

As is known, however, there is a large number of people in Europe who know Islam very well and who recognize its value; but it must be made clear that the cause of this phenomenon is due in large part not to Muslims, whose sacred duty would be to make Islam loved and respected, but to a select group of artists and scholars, among whom, and above all among the scholars, there is a large number of Israelites.

[Above][11] I spoke about the causes of European disdain for Muslims; I spoke about those who act by *parti pris*, and about whom nothing can be done. First of all, they are clerics, whether they are believers in Christ, materialists, or Germans. I discussed people who hate Muslims through ignorance of what Islam is. Those are at the same time excusable and correctable; excusable above all because Muslims did not do anything to spread the knowledge of Islam in Europe.

Now I will discuss the Orientals who make themselves hated.

Europeans designate the inhabitants of the East with three terms: Levantine, Oriental, and Muslim. The first term designates a very special population, spread throughout the Levant; their religion is very vague, but they have many priests, many superstitions, a good dose of Byzantinism, but rarely of theology and devotion. They speak all languages without knowing any one, in the sense that they know how to express their ignominy in all the spoken idioms, but they are absolutely incapable of reading and understanding a single line of any literary work. They have an instinctive and ferocious hatred for all that is beauty, generosity, or mysticism. They know only one thing in life: money and nothing else, and all means are good to succeed in getting it. They cannot conceive another form of consciousness outside the fear of the *gendarme*. It is precisely these scoundrels who inspired in that fine psychologist the Count de Gobineau so much anxiety for the future of Europe in the Orient.[12] As regards nationality, they are above all Armenians, then Syrians, Lebanese, Coptic, Greeks, and rarely Jews, whatever the anti-Semites say. It is useless to add that a sense of disdain is always associated with the term "Levantine"; the term "Muslim" in Europe does not have this meaning, except in those circles whose members are progressively diminishing. We have already spoken enough of them, so it is not worth to come back to this.

There are so many good memories attached to the term "Muslim": first of all the whole of medieval Spain—Seville, Cordoba, Toledo, Granada, the Alhambra—and then Baghdad, Damascus, Samarkand, Delhi, Agra, Lahore, Golconda [Fort], and the whole of flowered, artistic, poetic, and spiritual Persia. I can guarantee that outside clerical and colonial [circles], which are two monstrosities, there is not a young man susceptible to fantasies and to the taste of the marvelous who does not feel his heart beating stronger at the very term "Orient," which for him is a kind of magic formula, which makes one see, as in a flash, a whole universe of glory and splendor.

We must not forget that the Italian [Renaissance] and Romanticism are the two poles of modern civilization in Europe, and that outside of them there only remains the hysterical Puritan, the German pedant, the socialist, the colonial, and the clerical, all very ugly things. Now, Romanticism is two-thirds Oriental.

The Arabs are known in Europe above all through the Maghrebis, meaning the Muslims of the Berber countries: Algerians, Tunisians, and Moroccans. Now, despite the conquest and the strict laws against the natives, the Algerians have been able to inspire sympathy and at the same time respect among the intellectual flower of French society, and it seems to me that Muslims do not realize enough of the gratitude due to them because of the good attitude taken before the winner. But the truth will come to light one day or another.

On the Modernized European Egyptian

It is clear then that the term "Levantine" evokes great disdain, while "Muslim" does quite the opposite, and that these two terms refer to two essentially different worlds. However, the sad mission of Egypt has been to have merged these two incompatible elements into one body. They wanted to combine what was essentially bitter with what was healthy, and this has produced nothing but total corruption, since the Egyptians themselves wanted to confuse things, and it would be in bad taste to get angry with those who have only confused the names. Once all the symbols used to distinguish them from Levantines have been abolished, Muslims, disturbed when they are taken for Levantines, receive nothing but what is due to them. They would deserve something more—that is, the disdain of other Muslims—since they put the entire Muslim world in a bad light in front of educated Europeans, who can be very clever even without being Orientalists. Semi-European official Egypt is by no means a line of connection between intellectual Europe and the Muslim world, but just the opposite.

When you see a traveler who has good taste admiring the vestiges of the past but obliged to hold his nose in front of the present, let it be known by all that the one who makes him sick is not the good Sunni Muslim, whose behavior is always very much correct, nor the *fellah* [farmer] who has many good qualities (although negative if you wish), but the ignoble Levantine, the embodiment of all ancient and modern baseness, together with his emulator, the modernized European Egyptian. You must also know that when you are inspired by a great collecting cloaca, where all the rubbish of the three parts of the ancient world meets, and when you can do nothing but despise yourself, you must not complain.

To be continued.
[In fact, no further articles on this topic were actually published.]

Pure Art

Abdul-Hâdi
[Ivan Aguéli]
Translated from French by Nadine Miller

*This article was written in 1911 by Aguéli, then aged forty-one, under his Muslim
name (Abdul-Hâdi), during his final period in Paris. It was published in La Gnose
in two installments as one of a number of articles by Aguéli gathered under the
title "Pages Dedicated to Mercury (Sahaif Ataridiyah)." This article is Aguéli's key
text when it comes to art, and is discussed by Patrick Ringgenberg in Chapter 14.
The footnotes are those given in the original, mostly added anonymously by René
Guénon, but some probably by Aguéli.*

The title of this series of articles ["Pages Dedicated to Mercury, *Saha'if Ataridiya*"] is
in itself a commentary on the diversity of subjects we are dealing with here.[1] In any
case, in no way do we wish to expound on contemporary aesthetics, but only want
to delineate the question, demonstrate the importance of pure art in esoteric studies,
outline the principles of this art, and illustrate our theory by a few brief reviews serving
as examples.

The visual arts are, as it were, the graphology of the human soul in that they are a
spontaneous if abstract disclosure of personal and superior longing. The study of these
arts is an excellent way of learning how to see, as well as of providing training in solar
logic, knowledge of which is practically indispensable for being able to devote oneself
to the metaphysics of form. In many cases this is situated between theory and practice.
Those who have read Tolstoy—who I would by no means describe as an initiate—will
perhaps remember one of the heroes in his novel *War and Peace*, who, when struck by
a bullet, looks up at the blue sky in utter astonishment, as if he were seeing it for the
very first time. The sensation of the luminous void, comforting and rich in thought that
ordinary words cannot convey, is in a sense the raw material from which one might
fashion an esoteric mentality. With great regret I confess my ignorance of ancient
Greek civilization, but I suppose that the philosophers of Hellenic antiquity used the
word "music" in a much wider sense than only that of signifying harmonious sounds.
By this term they may have wished to express the emotive cypher, which evokes a new
world, approximately what nowadays we might call *esthesis*, sense experience or the
process of perceiving. One can say that art is the passion that practices mathematics;

mind playing with matter. However, one must bear in mind that passion here stands for mind, and that mathematics relates to matter, of which it is the perfect science. Moreover, matter itself is a science, and science is matter. Now, whatever the preachers have to say about it, matter as the "Great Innocent" is absolutely sacred. Above all it is so thanks to the Holy Virgin and the Immaculate Conception, the fundamental and indispensable dogma, without which esotericism would be nothing but an idle quietist daydream or some form of warped addiction.[a]

More specifically, art offers a glimpse of "motionless time" or "the permanent presence of the extra-temporal and undying self," which in turn leads to the knowledge of the fourth dimension, the esoteric importance of which it is unnecessary to dwell upon.

Besides, in publications devoted to esoteric studies numerous people have written about modern music. Thus I am only following a precedent, though in a more generalized sense.

I can speak only of pure art, the only one that is of interest here. That is why I distinguish between cerebral and sentimental art.[2] The latter, which is most widespread, produces its effect primarily by means of the viewer's memory, by the association of ideas, by stirring more or less confused recollections. By contrast, the former impresses itself directly, without any intermediary, through an internal *material sensing* of the beating pulse of life itself. Please note that it is the great range of its scope that accounts for its superiority, distinguishing the abstract from the concrete, even quality from quantity—as well as the concentration of everything between these two extremes. It is useless trying to make people of a secular bent understand the primordial grandeur of a realistic work of art, in which material accuracy increases in direct proportion to the abstraction the designer of the piece achieves from his own person, and his self-effacement in life universal.[b] Understanding this transcendent simplicity is a line of demarcation separating the vulgar from the elite.

When one speaks of pulsation, one means rhythms, that is to say, an effect of numbers.[c] Pure art brings to bear its astounding authority over the spirit solely by the fact that it takes from matter only its subtleties and its immutable laws, leaving all the rest. Actually, in the final analysis, matter is limited by time and space, both of which are directly ruled by numbers. An English aesthete whose name escapes me once said, "In art everything is sequence, contrast and repetition." In this more than anything lies the knowledge of aesthetic perception.

---

[a] The author has shown us Arabic texts that support his claims. These texts are not manuscripts of dubious provenance, but rather books printed in Muslim countries under the auspices of the religious authorities which are often hostile to esoteric ideas. It is strange that the Catholic Church has for so many centuries been able to ignore a dogma of such importance; and what was the remarkable event that has finally caused that neglect to be redressed?

[b] When overcome by bitterness, Cezanne used to say, "I am off to the country." Gauguin went to Tahiti primarily to re-immerse himself in the primitive world of simple feelings. In a way, this return to the origins was a bath of innocence. Parisian critics could not comprehend that his journey was more of a displacement in time than in space.

[c] It is through the *dhikr* that the dervishes assimilate certain rhythms. The *dhikr* is thus a type of *Hatha Yoga*.

When, for instance, according to the principles of the purity of art, we refuse to see anything in a picture but color upon canvas, the esoteric cast of mind concurs with common sense—as it always does, I might add. By this we mean to say that picture painting must be pictorial and sculpture sculptural, etc. All feeling aroused by the subject falls without the artistic ambit and is therefore detrimental because inappropriate, even if it is morally correct. Anything that art expresses by means other than eloquent proportion, i.e., numerical harmony possessing individual and impassioned significance, is from the Devil. That is why a still life by Chardin (vegetables, kitchen utensils) has greater artistic value than the pompous religious and historical tableaux of our academic painters.

Whoever scorns the art of still life is not a painter. He may be a man of letters, a poet, or whatever you like, but not a painter, for what is called "still life" on canvas corresponds to mime in the dramatic arts.

Every act of the visual arts consists of imposing one's impassioned or enamored will upon three-dimensional Euclidean space with well-considered emphasis, in other words, through drawing. In its widest and most artistic sense, this term signifies the form, which always implies light, hence color, expressly or implicitly. The perfect identity of drawing and coloring, as it is commonly called, is the touchstone of the artistic or non-artistic nature of a piece, for the antithesis of line and color finds its immediate resolution in light. One need only consider a drawing of the old masters: despite the monochrome or the black and white it always gives us the impression of color.

Their paintings, though blackened or faded by the passage of time, always appear lit by a sun created by God specifically for each one of them.

To summarize, pure visual art is not so much the creation of objects as it is the establishing of personal and deliberate proportions in all directions of Euclidean space. We shall represent each dimension of this space by its typical axis. We therefore have three axes: the vertical, the horizontal, and the optical or visual, as I choose to call the front to back direction, which passes from the eye to the horizon. I wish to avoid the term "perspective," because in current use it has only a very narrow meaning, that of linear perspective, to the exclusion of all else. Now in art, the solar perspective, and above all the perspective corresponding to the mental state of the affected viewer, to mention only two, are far more important than the engineer's perspective.

The element of mystery in art manifests above all in drawing along that axis. Its harmony with drawing along the two other axes (the vertical and the horizontal) is what causes line and color to melt together to form an impression of luminosity that gives a work of art its life and magic. Its accuracy can never become the object of any calculation, no matter how ingenious, while the drawing upon the two other planes bears calculation and discussion up to a certain point. The profundity of a painting, that is to say, its luminous, mental or other perspectives, arises exclusively from spontaneity and inspiration. Either you have got it or you have not. If you have not got it, you cannot have it, save through an unexpected act of deliverance, whereas anyone can be taught to draw in the other two directions. Such a drawing might even possess a certain interest beyond the pictorial. It might be literary, dramatic, psychological, whatever you like. But from the point of view of pure art, it will never be more than a platitude, a banality.

The drawing of some of the modern masters is a mental one. The figure is not what the material lines represent, but another, implicit one, ever so precise, which is formed by the tendencies of these lines. It is drawing by obliquely marked out movement. A dynamic parallelogram [Figure 18.1] will help us grasp this idea.

A and B are the lines that are expressed. They are the components of the parallelogram; C is their resultant. It is implicit, and its direction and intensity determine the mental figure that was the object of the artistic activity. An average drawing has an incalculable number of components and resultants; I am just formulating the theory.

The fundamental antithesis, the solution of which is the artist's task, is feeling (individual love, personality, nature) versus style (collectivity, external arrangement, tradition). Exclusive perfection of style produces a flawless but meritless work of art. Without feeling, there is no merit, but a personal work of art lacking style is a confusion of merits and defects which is hardly any better than an impersonal work in cold style. Paris wields its absolute power over all modern art only on account of the correct balance it strikes between tradition and nature. Nowhere but in Paris does one see supposedly romantic painters appreciating and studying the ancient masters in an intelligent way. The most ostensibly modernist painters are at the same time the most enthusiastic visitors to the Louvre. Tradition without initiative produces nothing but trickery and illusion in art, mind you; whereas the secret of equaling the grand masters of epochs more fortunate from the point of view of beauty consists of combining initiative with method, of joining the enamored and personal study of nature with the understanding and sense of taste engendered by age-old tradition. It is thus that masterworks of royal allure are born, for although they are of *personal style*, they give us the impression of a collective subservient to the benevolent and hieratic mandate of a single personal and luminous will. The purest and most cerebral painters of the nineteenth century are Daumier and Cézanne. Among our youthful contemporaries are Picasso, Le Fauconnier, and Léger. We will return to this topic in the next issue of *La Gnose*.

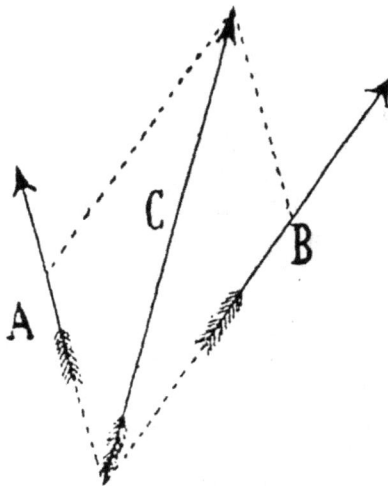

Figure 18.1 Abdul-Hâdi [Ivan Aguéli], Dynamic parallelogram, 1911.

Pure Art—continued[3]
(For the understanding of the following, we will first summarize the first part of this article, published in the previous issue.)

We have found a profound difference between cerebral and sentimental art. From an esoteric point of view, only the former is of interest to us. It teaches us *solar logic* and helps us develop a sense of *motionless time* or the *permanent presence of the extra-temporal and undying self*, without which the fourth dimension is not possible.

This art, based on the *emotive cypher*, corresponds, in part, to classical Western music. There are several Muslim esoteric treatises in the guise of an explanation of the principles of Arabic grammar. The *esthesis*, sense experience or process of perceiving, of sentimental art is *indirect*. It operates primarily in the viewer's memory by associations of ideas, through stirring of confused memories, atavistic or quotidian. Cerebral art deserves to be called pure art, because the process of its perception is direct (*direct esthesis*), through its ability to impress without the intervention of any alien self or external object, solely by an inner apprehension, an internal sensing of the beating pulse of life itself, in other words by its rhythm. Now, in any psycho-physiological activity, rhythm is nothing but the number, the count. This is why the "dhikr" of the dervishes [Sufis] is an essential assimilation of certain initiate rhythms. Therefore, the first condition for a sacred or even a sacerdotal language is that it can pace itself without much difficulty, that is to say, that its consonants and vowels find an easy balance of their own accord. From a gnostic point of view, the importance of pure art is to link the concrete with the abstract, quantity with quality, space with time, only through the ultimate limit of matter, meaning, through numbers. This is what I call pure art, for it uses only the sheer principles of matter, that which is most profound, most general and most subtle about it. Therefore, we say that all feeling stemming from the subject falls without the artistic ambit, hence it is harmful, on account of its irrelevance. Anything that art tries to express by means other than eloquent proportion, in other words through numerical harmony having an individual and impassioned meaning, is from the Devil.

Every act of visual art consists in imposing one's passionate or enamored will upon three-dimensional Euclidean space by means of well-considered emphasis, in other words through drawing, through form-giving, in the widest sense of the word. Now, form indicates light, and light indicates colors, whether expressed or implicit. It is thus conceivable that, given a certain elevation of the spirit, the antithesis of line versus color may vanish into luminous perfection.

The identity of line and color is the criterion of accuracy of the *solar* or *mental perspective*. It is the perspective of the affected viewer, and it is formed by a novel arrangement of the three planes. Only the dominant one is what is called subjective; the rest follow known laws.

This article addresses itself only to those who know what the mental perspective is. Those who do not know what this means would do better to read something else. But whoever really wants to learn about it need only study the world of Muhyiddin ibn 'Arabi. If lacking the language skills, one may simply study Arab art. You need only consider why ancient monuments of purely Arab architecture, even the most modest, always appear to be larger than life. They seem to grow and expand as you gaze at them, a kind of spreading of wings or a fan being opened. However, in the absence of Arabic scholarship, one may just as well study the transformation that space always undergoes at the approach of death. One need only treat with artistic attention a moment of real and conscious mortal danger. There are many sailors and soldiers who engage in the study of the Kabbalah; they most frequently are products of this school.

The human antithesis that the artist is called upon to resolve is that of *feeling* versus *style*. There are various approaches to this problem, depending on the different forms of universal opposition. To name only a few of these: there is individual love, personality, nature, the innate gift (on the side of feeling), versus community, external order, tradition, acquired skill (on the side of style). Without feeling, one produces work of a banal style, impeccable, perhaps, but equally without merit. A work lacking style results in a confusion of flaws and strengths, which is hardly better than a cold work of style, soulless, and vaguely degraded and dishonorable.

The aim of the scrupulous artist is a personalized style, a combination of the loving and personal study of nature and the intelligence and taste developed by the study of the artistic past. Art is the balance between nature and tradition, not only in alchemy, but also in aesthetics.

* * *

We can say that all depicted feeling oscillates between two poles, China and Spain. China represents that element of inner feeling termed *formal sequence*, whereas Spanish art transports you all at once into the novel world of the artist, the fullness of its perspective erasing all preoccupation with the past and the future. Chinese art is to be savored one morsel at a time. By contrast, Spanish art encloses you in a mental atmosphere of simultaneous bursts of light. In art, China signifies time, while Spain stands for space. I must add, however, that without the joining of both these elements there is never any art at all, that is, no progress towards God through the union of complementary contrasts in formal reality. Both China and Spain each provide this union, but not in the same way: what in one is the beginning, in the other is the end. The personality of the Chinese artist becomes evident through a sequence of tones against an expanding and authoritative background of tradition, whereas the Spanish artist manifests his self by simultaneously accentuating the three traditional planes of space. Hence the emotional intensity of his art against which the shapes stand out. In art, Italy is closer to China than to Spain, while France is closer to Spain, and Tintoretto is the most Spanish of the great Italian artists. Many people may object to my classification of French aesthetic perception, but here I am only speaking of principles. One need only consider the French primitive painters to note the enormous difference existing between them and the old Flemish, German, or Italian masters. Only a Spanish connection can be attributed to them.

Nowhere is the union between sequence and simultaneity more complete, more profound than in Arabian, African, and Malayo-Polynesian art. By African art I mean not only the sculptures of Egyptian antiquity, but also that of the Berbers of the Sudan [now known as Mali] and of the Abyssinians. Certain elements of Khmer art must be linked to Malay art as well. I would like to use a single name for all these forms of beauty: *equatorial art*, although Egypt and Arabia are not, strictly speaking, tropical countries. Singhalese art, antique Javanese art, and even Dravidian art must be excluded, because a Nordic element has deflected their primitive trend.

Equatorial art is distinguished among all other art forms by a high degree of what I can only call *living immobility*, which lends extraordinary significance to all its productions—even to the most modest. It possesses a character of eternity and infinity, which exerts the fascination of great calm upon the mind, and has much greater mind-blowing power than the most sophisticated narcotics.

The contradictory and countermanding antithesis of this art is (modern) German art. Despite its ecstasy, equatorial art is never sentimental; the other is always so and cannot be otherwise. The former is always cerebral, despite the intensity of its emotion; the other is never so. The artist of the tropics, even a savage, instinctively knows that the balance of aesthetic perception is based on trinitarian accord, the very foundation of the eurythmic tradition. All Chinese, Spanish, Italian, and French artists are agreed on this matter, whereas the German artist, even though he may be a first-class scholar, never sees more than two spatial planes. This is the only reason for their lack of success in Paris; chauvinism has nothing to do with it, no matter what they say about it. Have we not seen the French unduly exaggerate even the slightest musical quality of Wagner at the expense of Berlioz?

The Purists, though quite numerous, form a homogeneous group. In spite of this, they are by no means dogmatic, far less are they plagiarists. They may be quite distinct from each other, but they differ to a much greater extent from other painters, as they pursue the same end by the same path. I believe all their theories can be summed up by saying that they seek the truth in the accuracy of light, by way of the greatest simplicity of means. The result of this double condensation is an intense and personal theory, and an art of frankness and lucidity. In the face of a Purist work of art, we know at first glance who we are dealing with. The bias of its extreme clarity alone makes it worthy of respect, if not necessarily likable, since it is never a waste of time.

In every school, there is a doctrine (theory) which points to the goal, and a discipline (practice) which leads to the goal proposed by the theory. Let us examine both these terms in the given case. Is pictorial truth found exclusively in the accuracy of light? I would say that this is the case, and all French painting asserts that the most important thing in a painting are the values, meaning the exact, and intelligent distribution of light. Moreover, this is the architecture of space and the balance of masses in the void. There are unformed rough shapes that convey a striking impression of reality. This is due to the superb accuracy of certain principal values which serve as the contours giving the objects their forms.

You may object that establishing the gradation between a white spot and a black spot is not an occupation that engages man's higher faculties, but here you are deeply mistaken. Wisdom (*ḥikma*) is nothing but the art of setting everything in its proper place, of giving it its correct value, of presenting it in its true light. The unconscious (or subconscious) esoteric proclivities of the Purist painters—some of whom have realized the admirable type of transcendental beast—have grasped the fact that this humble manual labor, this tiny detail of nothing at all, is in fact the Great Arcanum, the core of orthodoxy, the crown of sacred and primitive tradition. Therefore they offer up everything to the correctness of tone. This alone proves that the first principle of this school is absolute honesty and common sense. It is deplorable to see them treated as jokers who are just making fun of people. People whose sole discipline consists in turning away from anything that might muddle their predominant idea cannot be liars. The only reproach a staunch opponent might level against them could be their desire for too much clarity, for pushing the evidence as far as brutal nakedness. To this attack one might respond by saying that there is paradisiacal nudity versus profane nakedness, and that the Lady of the Well [the Virgin] can be no better clad than in a ray of sunlight. It is good to have intelligent opponents, for they teach you in spite of themselves.

You might also say, perhaps we do not understand well enough the relations between the self and a conscious gradation from white to black. I maintain that the light of the same Sun is not the same for everyone. We have (in the previous issue of this Review) posited in principle that the artist is one for whom God seemingly has created a special Sun. It is by bringing into evidence the light of this Sun, of his very own personal Sun, through the efforts of a simple diligent laborer, that the artist reaches the heights of wisdom and character. I see nothing wrong in it if he likes to imagine that his *personal Sun* is really the only one existing in the Universe. It is more a matter of his inner awareness; perhaps his quirky preoccupation with this harmless obsession forms a part of his occupational hygiene. There are few things in modern life that are a solace to the artist; a bit of alcoholism—figuratively speaking, of course—is therefore a venial sin.

Simplism is the principle not only of all art but also of all activity of the spirit. It is the seal of mastery. Cézanne with his bias towards parallel strokes, from the upper right of the canvas to the lower left, uses it as a means for controlling a material element of his work, this being an element that distracts searching artists from the highest problems of painting. Neither able nor willing to remove this essential and often rebellious material, he regulated it by confining it into conventional shapes, from which he fashioned eloquent rhythms. By thus controlling it, he was able to easily guide it into his technical speculations, from which were born the superb visions that became his magnificent works of high cerebrality. The Purists of our day have taken up and expanded on this idea, and compared to other painters, their drawing is what algebra is to ordinary arithmetic. The reduction of all forms to geometrical figures gives an unfamiliar appearance to their works which shocks the uninitiated. It is, however, an ingenious system for determining with precision, not only the masses, planes, and distances, but also the values and the chiaroscuro. Thus an indissoluble link between line and color is obtained, which produces a rhythmic progression directed towards the visual axis. It builds up luminous and psychic perspectives, by which all the occult content of a work of art is made manifest. We have already said[d] that the drawing along the visual or optical axis cannot be arrived at through any sort of apprenticeship, being the result of inspiration alone. The same is true of drawing by

---

[d] Cf. the previous issue of *La Gnose*, 37.

geometric abstraction and of mental drawing.[e] The latter, formed by implicit resultants of which only the components are visually expressed, is in painting with regard to color what in literature is "only the nuance," to quote Verlaine's famous aphorism. Obviously, this system is not suitable for everyone; one needs to be very inspired and self-assured to draw in this way.

Purist discipline makes all sentimentality impossible. But this loss on the one hand is redoubled by the gain of cerebrality. I have seen works by Picasso wherein rays of light have crystallized into a mosaic of precious cut stones and enormous diamonds of extraordinary transparency. But I have also seen drawings by the same master which are well able to stand up to those of the greatest Italians. It is through Purism that we will eventually discover the secret of the ancient arts, Greek, Arab, Gothic, and Renaissance. Picasso has advanced all the aesthetic sensibilities of ancient Iberia by bending them towards the tenderness and virginity of Polynesia. Le Fauconnier possesses all the magnificent qualities of the old primitives of France, in addition to his modernity. Léger has taken up the aesthetic problem that haunted Ingres, who sought the secret of Raphael. Raphael, in his turn, pursued the ideal of the Greeks. And yet Léger has expressed all the beauty that Ingres sought, while remaining true to himself. It goes without saying that the Purist of our day and age has taken any sort of guitar out of the picture.

When we say that art is the union of contrasts, we mean in particular the union of complimentary contrasts, above all that of time and space, of sequence and simultaneity. The union of mutually exclusive contrasts is not our topic here, for it falls not under the influence of Mercury. We can sum it up neatly and succinctly by saying that rhythm is a sequence that unifies linear and dynamic contrasts; that values, the contrasts between light and dark, are only rhythms towards depth of the visual axis. That is why the perfect gradation of values immediately evokes the other rhythms, those that advance along the other two axes, the horizontal and the vertical, constituting form in the ordinary sense of the word. The Purists neglect the contrast of complimentary colors for a reason, because the famous theory relating to these has poisoned a whole generation of painters, yet it is no more than an experimental theory. On the contrary, they pay more careful attention to the contrasts of dull and dark colors, far more important contrasts than those of greens and reds for instance, because they sometimes resemble a conflict between the active and the inert, or even between life and death.

The Purist movement is the modern manifestation of the eternal principle of art for art. Cézanne can be considered as its founder, while he himself carried on the tradition of Chardin.

[e] Ibid.

19

Universality in Islam

Abdul-Hâdi
[Ivan Aguéli]
Translated from French by Nadine Miller

This article was written in 1911 by Aguéli, then aged forty-one, under his Muslim name (Abdul-Hâdi), during his final period in Paris. It was published in La Gnose, *and is one of Aguéli's key texts when it comes to Islam and Sufism, and is discussed by Anthony T. Fiscella in Chapter 7 and, especially, by Meir Hatina in Chapter 11. The footnotes are those given in the original.*

We have attempted, under the form of a solar transfiguration of an exotic landscape, to elaborate the doctrine of the real as "Ultimate Identity."[1] We have shown that despite absolute unity, there are actually two realities, as seen from a disjointed, individuated, human perspective: a collective and a personal reality. The former is acquired (imposed or chosen), it is historical, hereditary, temporal, and pertaining to mankind. The latter is original, innate, extra-temporal, pertaining to the sphere of the Lord. It may be more or less obscured or obstructed, but it always exists. You cannot renounce it, it is indestructible and inevitable, since it is the basis of everyone's existence, that is to say, the destiny to which any kind of spiritual and cosmic work is but a return.[a] The first is

---

[a]   See the I Ching, interpreted by [Paul Louis Felix] Philastre [*Le Yi: King; ou, Livre des changements de la dynastie des Tsheou*, Paris: E. Leroux, 1885], vol 1, p. 138; the 6th hexagram [*gua*], Song, § 150. "The word destiny refers to the true reason for the existence of all things; failure to arrive at the precise reason for the existence of *all things constitutes what is called 'to oppose destiny;' wherefore submission to destiny is considered as a return. To oppose it means not to conform in submission*" (*Traditional commentary by Cheng [Yi]*). "*Destiny, or the Will of Heaven, is the true* and correct reason for the existence of all things" (Commentary entitled *Original Meaning* [*Zhouyi benyi* by Zhu Xi]). I would like to add that in Chinese Muslims call themselves *Huihui*, which means "those who return obediently to their destiny." Muslim tradition maintains that Allah calls to Himself all things so that they come to Him, willingly or unwillingly. Nothing can resist that call. That is why in a general sense everything is Muslim. The human beings who come to Him willingly are called Muslims in a more restricted sense. People who do not come to Him willingly, that is to say, those who follow their destiny only by constraint, in spite of themselves, these are the unbelievers.

reality as it appears to ordinary people, meaning people in possession of their five senses and their combinations according to the laws of mathematics and elementary logic. The second reality is an *awareness of eternity*.[b] In the tangible world, the one corresponds to quantity, the other to quality. Collective reality is often termed the Universal Will, but I prefer to call it *Necessity*, reserving the term *Will* to signify personal reality. *Will* and *Necessity* can be compared to *Knowledge* and *Being*. These terms are familiar, not only to European thought since Wronski (as in Warrain: *La Synthèse concrète*, p. 169),[2] but also to an important school of esoteric Islam, followed especially in India. Knowledge and Being literally correspond to *al-ʿilm wa-l-wujūd* [knowledge and presence], the two primary aspects of the Divinity. There is little need to recall that only Will exists in an absolute sense and that Necessity has only relative or illusory existence. All religions and philosophies agree on this point. That is why a spiritual aristocracy can be found everywhere. Muslims say: *al-tawḥīd wāhid* [unity is singular], which literally and properly interpreted means, "The doctrine of Ultimate Identity is basically the same everywhere," or put another way, "The theory of Ultimate Identity is always the same." But I wish to point out a distinct feature of Islamic teaching, the crucial importance of the idea of Muhammad the Prophet. Will can attain to its fullness only through Necessity; on the one hand through heavenly necessity, and on the other through the effort of responding to the just demands of collective reality. This beneficial effort is therefore indispensable, as a means for developing all the latent faculties of Will. The negative inertia of the one is just as essential as the positive energy of the other. One has as much need to receive as the other has a need to give. They therefore have a mutual need of one another. In the rare cases when they actually operate as they should, there will be no opportunity for them to ask which of them is better off.

In the order of romantic, humanist psychology, personal reality corresponds somewhat to the element of Don Quixote, whereas collective reality corresponds to Sancho Panza. Cervantes's immortal masterpiece must be understood as an admission of the impotence of Christianity (at least in the forms in which it is presently known to us). Has this religion ever really been Catholic (meaning esoteric, Oriental) and Roman (exoteric, Occidental) at one and the same time? It has never been able to be one without detriment to the other. As for the Christians who are not beholden to Rome, are they truly Christians? I do not know. When a religion seriously declares that its ritual and dogma have no hidden or inner meaning, it has publicly admitted to being a superstition, and is only worthy of being housed in a museum of antiquities.

Europe has made various attempts at merging Don Quixote and Sancho Panza into a single person. All these attempts have failed, as the successful ones departed from Christianity and blended into free thinking. I will mention only two of these failed attempts, two extremes, the satanical and the grotesque: the Jesuit, and Tartarin of Tarascon.[3] I see only one Westerner capable of resolving the problem: Saint Rabelais. But he was an initiate, and he probably knew that the solution has existed for centuries, in the Malamatiyya. In order to illustrate our analysis, we shall compare the Malamati with Tartarin. The former manifests Sancho Panza while hiding Don Quixote within himself as a kind of ulterior motive that constantly haunts him, but which he never declares openly. By contrast, Daudet's hero externalizes the Don Quixote in the

[b]   See *La Gnose*, year 2, no. 2: 65 [Abdul-Hadi, "Pages dediees a Mercure (Sahaif Ataridiyah)"].

Tartarin with his expeditions to distant lands, while their Sancho Panza, Tartarin in flannel pajamas, remains well-hidden from everyone, except from the servant girl.

The personal and collective realities, Will and Necessity, exterior and interior, unity and plurality, One-and-All merge in a third reality which only the religion of Islam acknowledges, recognizes, and professes. This reality is the Muhammadan or prophetic reality. Our Prophet was not only *nabi* [prophet], the eloquent recipient of inspiration, but also *rasūl* [prophetic messenger], the law-giving messenger. Through *al-nubūwwa* [prophesy], by his inspired eloquence, he affected the (intellectual) aristocracy, while by *al-risāla* [the message], the Divine Law, he forestalled the complete decadence of the people and their shortcomings. The fusion of the elite with the common, the aristo-democracy of Islam, can be effected without violence and without chaotic disorder, thanks to the particular Islamic institution of a type of conventional humanity, which for lack of a better expression, I shall term the "average man," or human normalcy. Some Anglo-Saxon philosophers speak of "the average man" [in English in the original], or the man of mediocrity, but I am not familiar enough with their theories to venture an opinion. This type is always fictitious, never real. It acts as a neutral and impersonal insulation that facilitates certain relations, foreseen and regulated in advance, and makes impossible irregular contacts and overly personal relations among people who do not wish to know each other socially. Being no one and being everyone, with no tangible reality, always the rule, never the exception, it is only a universal measuring device for all possible social, moral, and religious rights and obligations. This formalism, this perfect equilibrium between various interests (material, spiritual-material, and religious-ritual), this complete encasing of all exterior circumstances of social and religious life, is the best promoter of Islamic propaganda. Thanks to this, the social status of the Semitic Arab tribe, which is an ideal of justice, inclusion, cooperation, and solidarity, was able to stretch across the entire universe.

Several sociologists, ethnographers, and poets have remarked on the perfection of some truly primitive societies. But the virtues of the "savage" never extend beyond the narrow boundaries of the tribe. That is why he is an ideal only in poetry. His antithesis, present-day civilized man, hardly does any better regarding human inclusivity. In the one, quality is developed to the detriment of quantity. In the other we have quantity, which admittedly is something, but his quality is far from being praiseworthy. Formalism, the introduction of the concept of the average man, allows primitive man to reach universality without the loss of any of those precious characteristics associated with his primeval and quasi-paradisal humanness.

It is precisely the "average man" who is the object of the Shari'a or the sacred law of Islam. It is very simple as long as there is no great external difference between the elite and common folk. The basic wording is good enough. But with social progress, the complications of life and the change in external conditions, the direct application of the letter of the law would come to contradict the spirit of the law. The average man has undergone a series of variations, the texts have acquired their commentaries, and the science of jurisprudence has progressed with the demands of life. However, the difference between the text and the commentaries is only apparent. Evolution is natural and logical, whatever Orientalists of different walks of life have to say.

Certain prescriptions of Shari'a law might appear absurd to European eyes. Yet they do have their purpose. A universal religion needs to take into account all intellectual and moral levels. Up to a certain point, the simplicity, the weaknesses, and the peculiarities of others have a right to be accommodated. But intellectual culture also has its rights and its requirements. Average man establishes a kind of neutrality around each individual which guarantees all the individualities, though it also requires everyone to work for humanity as a whole. History knows no other practical form of development of the whole human. Experience bears irrefutable witness in favor of Islamic universality. Thanks to Arab formulas, there exists an instrument for perfect understanding among all possible races living between the Atlantic and the Pacific Oceans. One can hardly conceive of greater ethnic distances than those existing, for example, between a Sudanese and a Persian, a Turk and an Arab, a Chinese and an Albanian, an Indo-Aryan and a Berber. Never has any religion or civilization accomplished so much. Therefore, we can say that there is no better agent of spiritual communication than Islam. Europe can only furnish a material international. That is something, but it is not everything. Moreover, this achievement is not accomplished by Christianity, but rather by the school of Western positivistic thought, if not by free-thinking.

That is why we consider the prophetic chain of transmission to have come to an end, to be *sealed* with the Prophet Muhammad, the Prophet of Arabs and non-Arabs alike, because he is its peak, its culmination. The prophetic spirit is the doctrine of "Ultimate Identity," the One-and-All of metaphysics, the Universal Man of psychology, and full humanity in social structure. This process began with Adam and reached completion with Muhammad.

* * *

The word *Islam* is an infinitive of the causative verb *aslama*, to give, deliver, hand over.[4] There is an ellipsis: *li-llāhi* (to God) is understood; *al-Islāmu li-llāhi* therefore means: to hand oneself over to Allah, that is to say, to obediently and consciously follow one's destiny. So, since man is a microcosm, composed of all the elements of the universe, it follows that his destiny is to be universal. If his superior faculties are dominated by inertia, he is not following his destiny. As a religion, Islam is the path of unity and totality. Its fundamental dogma is what is called *al-tawhīd*, that is unity, or the action of unification. As a universal religion it comprises degrees, but each of these degrees is truly Islam, which is to say that any aspect of Islam reveals the same principles. Its formulas are exceedingly simple, but the number of its forms is incalculable. The more numerous its forms, the more perfect the law. A person is a Muslim when he follows his destiny, that is, his basic reason for existence. Since everyone carries his destiny within himself, it is evident that all discussions about determinism or free will are pointless. Islam, even in its exoteric form, is beyond this question. That is why the great scholars never wanted to make any statement on this subject. It is impossible to explain to an ordinary man how God does everything, how He is omnipresent, and how every man carries Him within himself. All this is clear to the man "who knows himself" (*man ya'raf nafsahu*), that is to say, his ego, his own self, and who knows that all is vain but "the perception of eternity." The *ex cathedra* pronouncements of the mufti [jurisconsult] must be clear and comprehensible to all, even to an illiterate negro. He has no right to give his opinion on anything but on a commonplace of everyday life. Besides, he will never do so, all the more so as he can avoid questions that exceed his area of competence. It is this clear, well-known limitation between Sufi questions and problems of Shariʿa which allows Islam to be esoteric and exoteric at one and the same time without ever contradicting itself. That is why Muslims who understand their religion never have any serious conflicts between knowledge and faith.

Now, the formula of *al-tawhīd*, or of monotheism, is the commonplace of Shariʿa. It is entirely up to you personally what range you assign to this formula, for this depends upon your Sufism. All you are able to deduce from this formula is more or less good, provided, however, that your conclusion does not abrogate its literal meaning. For then you would be destroying the unity of Islam, meaning its universality, its ability to adapt and conform to all mentalities, circumstances, and times. Its formalism is essential; it is not superstition, but a universal language. As universality is its principle, and the purpose of Islam, and as on the other hand language is the means of communication between beings endowed with reason, it follows that the exoteric formulas are as important to the religious organism as are blood vessels to the animal body. I have embarked on this subject mainly in order to demonstrate that "intelligence" (*inter* + *legere*, *al-ʿaql*), I mean universal intelligence, resides in the heart, the center of the circulation of the blood.

Sentimentality has nothing to do with this location, since it has its own place in the mucous membranes of the intestines, when it occupies its correct place within the physiological organization.

Intelligence and discernment are the two principal aspects of human reason. The one forms the concept of unity, the other that of plurality. Sound reason possessing both these faculties, perfected to their highest degree, can thus conceive of the idea of a Being which is One-and-All: but that Being is not the Absolute, which lies beyond all intellectual processes. When you know that you can proceed no further, you have arrived at the limits not only of knowledge but also of all that is knowable, *scibile*. The admission of unknowability is cognizance of the Infinite (*al-ʿajz ʿan* [*darak*] *al-idrāk idrākun*[5] [The failure to attain perception is itself perception]). It is the only kind there is, granted, but you will arrive at a disclosure of mysteries in affirming that this is no paradox or merely a figure of speech, but a form of real knowledge, fertile, and ultimately sufficient. Anything that is only exoteric inevitably leads to skepticism. Now, skepticism is the point of departure for the elect. Beyond the limits of the knowable, there is still scientific progress, but its insights turn entirely into negatives. They are all the more productive, since they expose our poverty (*al-faqr*), that is to say, our need of heaven. Aware of our needs, we will know how to formulate our requests. I speak of requests, not of prayers, because one has to avoid at all costs anything that resembles any sort of clergy. All that matters is to know how to ask, for in that case heaven is like nature, which always responds with the truth when it is asked properly, but only then. A chemical or physical experiment produces a revelation. If badly executed, it will lead to error. Heaven will always grant a gift when it is asked as it ought to be asked. It gives nothing or even harm when the request is badly made. This is an effect of divine mutuality, or of the law of universal catadioptrics.ᶜ

ᶜ According to one *hadith*, life is organized according to *lex talionis*, the principle of retaliation.

Sentimental moralists, Christians, Buddhists, and others have glorified humility. Very well, but being humble or not is of no significance, since we are all nothings. They have made a virtue of humility, a goal, whereas it is only a means, an exercise, a sort of training. It is nothing but a small station along the way, where one may stop according to the requirements of the voyage. Vanity is a stupidity. Humility at the wrong moment can be just as stupid.

We have already seen[d] that the Muslim *credo* [No *ilaha* (god) save Allah] begins with a negation, followed by an affirmation. Both what I deny and what I affirm bear the same name, A-L-H; however, in the first case, it is indeterminate (36) and in the second case it is determined (66). I mean that the vague, indefinite is nonexistent, but that the definite is what is real. Considering only the shape of the letters, it is a transformation of the infinite, represented by the straight (vertical) line [of the letter *alif* ١] (A), into the indefinite, represented here by the circle [of the letter *ha* ه] (H), passing through the angle [of the letter *lam* ل] (L). In the case of the affirmation of the definite, the angle (L) is repeated twice.

The greatest part of practical esotericism concerns destiny, the identity of self and non-self, and the art of giving, based on the teachings of the *faqir*s [lit. "the impoverished" or "the poor" also a common epithet for Sufis]. The order consists of following one's destiny *obediently and consciously*, which means to live, to live one's entire life, which is that of all lives, that is to say, to live the lives of all beings.[e]

Life is indivisible; what makes it appear to be divisible is that it is susceptible to gradation. The more the life of self identifies with the life of non-self, the more intense living becomes. The fusion of self into non-self takes place through the more or less ritual, conscious, or voluntary gift. It is easy to understand that the *art of giving* is the principal arcanum of the Great Work. The secret of this art consists in absolute disinterestedness, in the perfect purity of the spirit in the act, i.e., of the intention; in the complete absence of all hope of return, of any sort of recompense, even in the world to come. The action must in no way resemble an exchange of goods. Consequently, it is more perfect, more pure, to give to one who appears weak or inferior than to one who is on an equal footing, or more powerful. From an esoteric point of view, to give to a species far removed from one's own is better than giving to one's fellow men. That is why the attraction of the opposite, the taste for the exotic, a love of animals, and a passion for the study of nature are such indications of an esoteric disposition. The celebrated poet Abu'l-'Ala' al-Ma'arri,[6] whom some consider a heretic, materialist, or freethinker, in reality holds a very high rank in the spiritual hierarchy of esoteric Islam. To focus on humanitarianism is therefore a social-sentimental error. A basic reduction of one's psychic and nutritional egoism is enough to be perfect in a social context, for all civic virtues are only more or less successful policies, that is to say, advantageous. It is actually impossible to do good to humanity without some ulterior utilitarian motive. Charity

---

[d] *La Gnose*, year 2, no. 2: 64, and no. 3: 111 (errata in no. 2) [Abdul-Hadi, "Pages dediees a Mercure"].
[e] I am not referring to the theory of Ibsen: to live one's life. Those who have not the courage, who haggle over their pleasure, are ill prepared to receive esoteric ideas. Ibsen, Tolstoy, Nietzsche etc. are all very respectable people, I in no way deny this, but they have no traditional value. Moralists of local influence, they can interest us only as minor provincial prophets.

towards one's own kind is an obligation, an act of precaution, or of lofty foresight. It can hardly contain anything enacted "only for God." Sentimentality always leaves a stain of egoism on anything undertaken in its name, be it only adorning oneself in attractive motivations for simple actions. The Malamatiyya always find a set of bad reasons before carrying out any acts of goodness they are called upon to perform.

Good done to an animal draws us even closer to God because our egoism is less invested in this, at least in ordinary situations. The mental shift is greater, achievement in the universal soul is further removed. You attach yourself to human beings, they become attached to you for all sorts of practical reasons. The attachment of a human being to an animal is of a higher order. In addition to this, it is very instructive, for according to the formula: x is in relation to you as you are in relation to your cat, you can discover a great many secrets of destiny. It is true that the action of the animal-lover is of great usefulness from a sidereal point of view; but even to merely understand this usefulness, your egoism must already have evolved considerably in the realm of the transcendental. A man who perceives that the powerful judge him just as he himself judges the weak, such a man is no longer in need of a spiritual guide. He is definitely on a good path, in the process of becoming the Universal Law himself by beginning to incarnate inevitability. He may be in need of technical instruction in order to evolve more quickly, but since he knows how to give without conducting some kind of business transaction, he already has his own private heaven. It would therefore be quite inappropriate to accuse of selfishness those who cultivate a love of animals for an astral purpose, for instance in order to ward off what in the internal order is called "misfortune," or to restore as much as possible the paradisiacal state of primordial humanity.[f] These are the people who know something, and who employ their knowledge in order to obtain an earthly happiness which the tradition regards as lawful.

I cannot emphasize strongly enough that the Grand Arcanum is the art of giving. The absolutely pure and disinterested gift is the perception of nothingness in its practical implementation. This crystallized perception is the touchstone—the best—for verifying Existence in the Absolute. This precious instrument of investigation from beyond can be very simple in its appearance, it may be rustic, even coarse, but it is instantly spoiled when touched by a single atom of sentimentality. One may quote Saint Rabelais, but one can never be cautious enough regarding Christian (in the ordinary sense) or Buddhist theories.

The reader who has been kind enough to follow me thus far without fatigue or irritation can easily comprehend that the humanitarian gift is the proper assessment of our material advantages and disadvantages. In fact, anyone can see that it is helpful for all if everyone possesses what is essential for a life worthy of a human being. True charity begins at the level of the beast; it continues on to that of plants, but beyond that initiatory knowledge is required. This knowledge leads to alchemy, which is human charity towards stones and metals, i.e., towards inorganic nature. The climax of such charity is to donate one's Self to simple numbers, for the Universe is thereby maintained

---

[f] Muslim tradition speaks of a time when wild animals did not flee from man; they began to flee him only after the fratricide of Cain. Prior to this event they sought his nearness for reassurance and protection in the great peace that emanated from him.

through one's rhythmical breathing. I venture so far as to indicate that cosmic charity progresses in a reverse order to that of material evolution, as it is commonly called.

Thanks to the perfect harmony between the esoteric and the exoteric established by Islam, we can speak of it any which way, that is to say, Islam bears being propagandized, even its esoteric aspects—at least to a certain extent. Propaganda strengthens it, enriching it from a purely intellectual point of view. Admittedly, several branches of the Islamic sciences did not develop until several non-Arab peoples had joined the fold of Islam. Observing this phenomenon, a number of Orientalists have attributed it to a juxtaposition of the Aryan or Turanian spirit to the Semitic Arab mentality.[7] This, however, is erroneous.

The seeds of these sciences were already contained in Islam in its early form. As Islam allowed for rationalism and freedom of thought, it sustained the obligation of making itself comprehensible to newcomers, to assume a form that suited their mentality. This process was accomplished through a collaboration of students and teachers. Questions provoked answers. The rational sciences and scholastics of Islam were born from the external need to formulate the subconscious. The Arabs brought nothing new to the foreigners. All they did was to transform a bit of their gold into silver, so to speak, with the unique aim of simplifying relations among peoples.

I urge students of Kabbalah to kindly note that through teaching others one teaches oneself, from a purely scientific point of view; the internal is enhanced through the external work; heaven gives to you just as you distribute among creatures the little you already possess. But one needs to know how to do this.

Let it be said right at the outset that the term altruism is an empty word; it should be banned from metaphysical discourse, because that "other" [*alter*] does not exist. There is not the slightest difference between you and the others. You are the others, all others, all things. All things and all the others are you. We are only mutual reflections of one another. There is but one life, and all individualities are only inferences of the destiny that radiates in the crystal of creation. The identity of self and non-self is the Great Truth, just as the realization of this identity is the Great Work. If, in the case of a robbery, you cannot understand that you are the robber at the same time as you are the robbed; that, in case of murder, you are simultaneously the murderer and the victim; if you do not blush from shame or guilt at the account of a monstrous, novel, and inconceivable crime that you have never in your life been tempted to commit; if you do not even minimally feel that you had something to do with the earthquake in Turkestan or the plague in Manchuria, then you had better give up your esoteric studies, because you are wasting your time.

More than anything else it is the criminal collectivity which demonstrates that isolated action hardly exists at all, and that it is difficult to distinguish between one person and another. I am not saying that all men are the same, but I am saying that they are all "the same." Let us consider a sequence of events. Have you ever noticed that a general suspicion, albeit unjustified, gives rise to sufficient evidence of guilt around an alleged perpetrator? It happens all the more quickly in the event that he is innocent or has absolutely no knowledge of the crime committed. If he is guilty, but intelligent, he can create a negative aura around his person, a negative and determined aura, which repels the collective aura that threatens to overwhelm it. It is easy to see how the moral aura of a group slowly gathers around the nerve center of society, condenses and assumes human form, most often that of the perpetrator of a crime. But this criminal is only the striking hand. The true origin of the action is found in the group. Arguably, the group has not engaged in any action, but it has caused something to happen, which amounts to the same thing. That is why there are no innocents.[g]

When I state that everyone is guilty, I am not pleading for the acquittal of the criminal. Even less am I advocating generalized punishment. Esotericism has nothing to do with a code of law, which, no matter how bad, is a natural product of history and of society. Man can only exercise human justice. Divine justice will always remain a mystery for him. Wishing to handle this justice is, in our view, one of the most serious crimes which man can commit. I would like to quote a few examples. Robbery and murder are crimes, at least in principle; therefore, the robber or murderer must be punished according to the current conventions of the society, but that is all. Once he has undergone his punishment you are free to shun him or to consort with him. You can refuse to give him your daughter in marriage, etc., but if you say that this man is evil, that he deserves hellfire, etc., then you are worse than he is, because you wish to set yourself up on the throne of God. You want to judge him in an area into which no one has any insight.

Another example: you condemn prostitution, and you are not at all wrong in doing so. Still, you cannot condemn the prostitute, unless there is a public breach of decency. Her crime is nothing but a crime of reaction. In terms of current society, the man is the interior, the cause, and the woman is the exterior, the effect. Woman sells her body, because man sells his soul. You can apprehend the one, but the other, the truly guilty one, escapes all pursuit, since he is anonymous and legion. We must limit ourselves to judging the facts alone. It is impossible to judge conscience.

One last example: the outrageous acquittals of crimes of passion. Some people want to see in this a sign of amorality. It is nothing of the sort. They are only statements of the court's incompetence. The scrupulous judge avoids pronouncing on cases of which only God can have knowledge.

Universal consciousness is becoming more and more fatalistic. A long time ago people used to say, "People get only the governments they deserve." A good government cannot rule a villainous people; it would have to be corrupted if it wished to hang on to power. Day by day, the great truth of the logic of events is better understood: that man is always judged after his own laws, that is to say, according to the laws which he imposes on beings that fall under his vital influence. There are subtle links between the executioner and the victim, as they are both two aspects of the same actuality. Everyone can understand that poor people exist on account of the rich; that there are ignorant people because of the learned; that there are depraved people because the virtuous leave much to be desired. Many Islamic saints have repined at having received the gift of second sight. They have perceived too many extraordinary things in the minor events of everyday life. Those who seek superhuman faculties outside the order are naive. When sorcerers' apprentices incur no more than intellectual or moral derangement, it is because God has shown them kindness.

---

[g] All impersonal or anonymous crime is, *a priori*, collective crime.

* * *

The law of universal poverty (*al-faqr*) is therefore a principle of Islam. Each one of us is poor (*faqīr*), we are all poor (*fuqarā'*), because we are all in need of the Creator or of creation, most often of both. As one needs to give in order to receive, it follows that the great curse consists in no longer being able to do good, to have lost one's right of exercising charity. When you give, you need to give more humbly, so that the beggar does not receive the alms from your hand.[8]

Above all, Islam is clearly distinguished from all religions, civilizations, or philosophies by its concept of collective reality. All enlightened beings know that collective reality is a fiction, and enlightened Muslims know this just as well, if not better. Consequently, in order to follow the Prophet, he does not withdraw into the desert, but pretends to take the world seriously. There is a *hadīth* [report of a saying of the Prophet] which enjoins working for this world as if we thought to live for a thousand years, while also working for the other world as if we expected to die tomorrow. In Islam, the doctrine of identity and unity is better developed than in other systems of thought. Its precious esoteric-exoteric quality derives mainly from its concept of collective reality as an indispensable agent for the transformation of personal reality into human universality or prophetic reality. Christianity and Buddhism reject collective reality with suspicion and horror, and attempt to develop Universal Man in devout stillness. Thus they differ qualitatively from Islam, as well as in their psychological aspect. Quantitatively, Islam differs from esoteric Brahmanism in that it is more expansive. Brahmanism is only local, at least from a practical point of view, whereas Islam is universal. It differs from anti-doctrinarian positivism in its formal and metaphysical aspect. It is in direct opposition to German philosophy, which has completely distorted the idea of government by confusing the feudal system with the aristocracy. Everywhere else but in Germany responsibility is the measure of nobility: the nobler you are, the more responsible you are, and vice versa. According to Shari'a, the crime of the free and the nobleman is judged more severely than that of the slave or the ignorant. Unfortunately, the feudal system everywhere has managed to arrange things in such a way as to ensure its impunity, but even so it can be distinguished from nobility, whereas in Germany, feudality is the only precondition to aristocracy. The strong man in power is held in no way accountable for one to whom an inauspicious fate has allotted an inferior position.

On the other hand, Islam has many points of comparison and contact with most other systems of belief or of social organization. It is neither a mixed nor a new religion. The Prophet expressly states that he has invented nothing whatsoever as far as dogma or religious law is concerned. He has only restored the ancient and primeval faith. That is why there are so many similarities between Taoism and Islam. This assertion is not mine, but one that has been made by famous Muslim and Chinese authors. Taoism differs in no way from Islam except in that it is exclusively esoteric, whereas Islam is both esoteric and exoteric. That is why its doctrines can be propagandized, while those of Taoism cannot. Islam embraces both neophytism and adepthood, whereas Taoism acknowledges only the latter of these two forms of expansion.

Notes

Chapter 1

1   Following French orthography, the hard *g* of Agelii in Swedish would be transformed into a soft *g* or *j* in French; inserting a *u* after the *g* keeps it hard, and adding an acute accent to the *e* places the stress in the right place.

2   In Egypt, it referred to the Arab west, i.e. Morocco.

3   For a succinct summary of Swedenborg's theology, see Emanuel Swedenborg, *De Nova Hierosolyma et Ejus Doctrina Coelesti* (1758), translated as *New Jerusalem* (West Chester, PA: Swedenborg Foundation, 2016).

4   There is a very extensive literature on Neoplatonism. My own contribution is Mark Sedgwick, *Western Sufism, From the Abbasids to the New Age* (New York: Oxford University Press, 2017), 15–29.

5   Michel de Certeau, *The Mystic Fable* (Chicago, IL: University of Chicago Press, 1992). See also Leigh Eric Schmidt, "The Making of Modern 'Mysticism,'" *Journal of the American Academy of Religion* 71, no. 2 (2003): 273–302, and Annette Wilke, ed., *Constructions of Mysticism as a Universal: Roots and Interactions across Borders* (Wiesbaden: Otto Harrassowitz, forthcoming).

6   Simon Sorgenfrei, "The Great Aesthetic Inspiration: On Ivan Aguéli's Reading of Swedenborg," *Religion and the Arts* 23, no. 1 (2019): 1–25.

7   A good summary, which places Blavatsky in her wider context, is in Nicholas Goodrick-Clarke, *The Western Esoteric Traditions: A Historical Introduction* (New York: Oxford University Press, 2008).

8   Olav Hammer and Mikael Rothstein, eds., *Handbook of the Theosophical Current* (Leiden: Brill, 2013).

9   Sedgwick, *Western Sufism*, 95–6.

10   Ibid., 109–10.

11   There may, of course, have been some Sufis among Western Europe's (very small) population of Muslim origin. For this, see Bernard Vincent and Jocelyne Dakhlia, eds., *Les Musulmans dans l'histoire de l'Europe* (Paris: Albin Michel, 2011).

12   Sedgwick, *Western Sufism*, 146.

13   Mark Sedgwick, *Against the Modern World: Traditionalism and the Secret Intellectual History of the Twentieth Century* (Oxford: Oxford University Press, 2004), 65–7. Sebottendorf established the Thule-Gesellschaft, which played an accidental role in the origins of the Nazi Party.

14   Sedgwick, *Western Sufism*, 159–60, 162.

15   Ibid., 86–9.

16   Aldous Huxley, *The Perennial Philosophy* (New York: Harper & Brothers, 1945).

17   For a study of the Traditionalist movement, see Sedgwick, *Against the Modern World*.

18   Abdul-Hâdi [Ivan Aguéli], "Pages dédiées à Mercure (Sahaif Ataridiyah)," *La Gnose* 2, no. 1 (January 2011): 33–4.

19   Werner von Hausen, "Minnen från samvaron med Gustaf Ageli i Paris och Cairo 1894–1895," *Ord och Bild* 35 (1926): 605–15.
20   As "Den Rena Konsten," *Flamman: tidskrift för modern konst*, 1919, 5 pp. Pagination is not clear. The translation omits the introductory and middle sections of the original, and is thus 2/3 of the original in length.
21   Marita Lindgren, "Ivan Gustave Aguéli: Ett sällsamt svenskt konstnärsöde," *Ord och Bild* 43 (1934): 513–23.
22   Axel Gauffin, *Ivan Aguéli: människan, mystikern, målaren*, 2 vols. (Stockholm: Sveriges allmänna konstförening, 1940–1).
23   Paul Chacornac, *La Vie Simple de René Guénon* (Paris: Éditions Traditionnelles, 1958).
24   Artistic circles in Sweden had already begun to take notice of Aguéli's work shortly before his death, and at an exhibition in Stockholm three years after his death, in 1920, the first sales of his paintings took place. His reputation as an artist continued to grow, and further exhibitions were held in 1939, 1947, and 1948. In 1961, an Aguéli museum was opened in his native Sala. The most recent major exhibitions devoted to Aguéli in Stockholm were in 2016 and 2018–19.
25   Centre culturel suédois, Paris, March 11 to April 24, 1983.
26   Torbjörn Säfve, *Ivan Aguéli: en roman om frihet* (Stockholm: Prisma, 1981). Translated into Turkish as *Ivan Agueli: Özgürlüğün Romanı* (Istanbul: İz Yayıncılık, 2010).
27   Mohamed Omar, "Hammaren och månskäran," *Nya Il Convito*, August 1, 2012. https://nyailconvito.wordpress.com/2012/08/01/hammaren-och-manskaran/, Accessed January 24, 2020.
28   Torbjörn Säfve, *De sanna och de falska* (Stockholm: Ruin, 2007).
29   Susanne Olsson and Simon Sorgenfrei, "Den fiktive Aguéli: Identifikationsobjekt och projektionsyta för unga manliga konvertiter till islam," *Aura: Tidskrift för akademiska studier av nyreligiositet* 9 (2017): 80–106.
30   *Nya Il Convito*, https://nyailconvito.wordpress.com/
31   Viveca Wessel, *Ivan Aguéli: porträtt av en rymd* (Stockholm: Författarförlaget, 1988).

Chapter 2

1   Letter from Ivan Aguéli to Carl Wilhelmson Etlidem, Egypt, January 19, 1915. In the Aguéli archive, Konstbiblioteket, Nationalmuseum Stockholm.
2   Anton Ehrenzweig, *The Hidden Order of Art* (Berkeley: University of California Press, 1971), preface, xii.
3   Axel Gauffin, *Ivan Aguéli: Människan, Mystikern, Målaren* (Stockholm: Sveriges allmänna konstförening, 1940–1), vol. 1, 22.
4   Letter to Marie Huot, March 18, 1908. In the Aguéli archive. Printed in Gauffin, *Ivan Aguéli*, vol. 2, 142.
5   Letter to Anna Agelii, April 15, 1890. In the Aguéli archive. Printed in Gauffin, *Ivan Aguéli*, vol. 1, 45.
6   Letter to Anna Agelii in the Aguéli archive. Printed in Gauffin, *Ivan Aguéli*, vol. 1, 54–5.
7   Salme Sarajas-Korte, *Vid symbolismens källor: den tidiga symbolismen i Finland* (Jakobstad: Jakobstads tryckeri och tidnings AB, 1981), 53–4.

8   See discussion on the difference between French and German symbolism by
     Margaretha Rossholmin, "Bilden som mikrokosmos eller bilden som själsspegel,"
     Konsthistorisk Tidskrift 41 (1972): 95–112.
9   Sarajas-Korte, *Vid symbolismens*, 29–35.
10   Letter to Richard Bergh Malakoff, March 16, 1893. In the Aguéli archive.
11   Gabriel-Albert Aurier, "Le Symbolisme en peinture: Paul Gauguin," *Mercure de
     France* 2 (1891): 159–64, reprinted in G. Albert Aurier, *Oeuvres Posthumes* (Paris:
     Mercure de France, 1893), 211–18.
12   Sarajas-Korte, *Vid symbolismens* 42.
13   Ibid., 40.
14   Letter to artist Richard Bergh, October 10, 1893. In the Aguéli archive. Printed in
     Gauffin, *Ivan Aguéli*, vol. 1, 104.
15   Émile Bernard and Van Gogh painted his portrait.
16   Gauffin, *Ivan Aguéli*, vol. 1, 56.
17   Owen Jones, *The Grammar of Ornament* (London: Day & Son, 1856). The book
     contained 112 plates in chromolithography. Owen Jones's purpose was not that
     artists and designers should copy the ornaments but be inspired by their "grammar,"
     their principles of composition. See also Wessel, *Ivan Aguéli. Porträtt av en rymd*
     (Stockholm: Författarförlaget, 1988), 37–41.
18   The sculptor Knut Åkerberg later wrote to Gauffin that he had received copies of this,
     and of parts of Eugène Delacroix's periodical, in the Fall of 1892. Gauffin, *Ivan Aguéli*,
     vol. 1, 82–4.
19   Wessel, *Ivan Aguéli*, 42–3.
20   Sarajas-Korte, *Vid symbolismens*, 44.
21   Gauffin, *Ivan Aguéli*, vol. 1, 61–2.
22   Ibid., 74.
23   In the Kungliga biblioteket's list of visitors. Gauffin, *Ivan Aguéli*, vol. 1, 73.
24   Fragment of manuscript in Aguéli's handwriting in the Aguéli archive. The text is
     published in the essay "Aguéli och Ljuset," *Moderna Museets tidning* no. 2 (1982) and
     in Wessel, *Ivan Aguéli*, 90. In a letter to the author, Kurt Almqvist connects the "Eye
     of the Horizon" with Qur'an 41:53. Wessel, *Ivan Aguéli*, 183, n. 42.
25   Gauffin, *Ivan Aguéli*, vol. 1, 67 mentions that Aguéli on his way back to Sweden
     passed through London, visited the Anarchist Club, and probably met with Prince
     Kropotkin.
26   Letter to Richard Bergh, October 10, 1893. In the Aguéli archive. Printed in Gauffin,
     Ivan Aguéli, vol. 1, 101–8.
27   "Le procès des anarchistes," *Journal des débats*, August 6, 1894, morning edition, p. 3;
     "Le procès des anarchistes," *Journal des débats*, August 6, 1894, evening edition, 2–3,
     p. 3.
28   Letter to Werner von Hausen, May 6, 1894. In the Aguéli archive. Printed in Gauffin,
     Ivan Aguéli, vol. 1, 159–61.
29   Letter to Werner von Hausen, October 27, 1894. In the Aguéli archive. Printed in
     Gauffin, *Ivan Aguéli*, vol. 1, 196–8.
30   Letter to Werner von Hausen, May 6, 1894. In the Aguéli archive. Printed in Gauffin,
     Ivan Aguéli, vol. 1, 159–62.
31   In Colombo he was offered a room for free at a mosque, already at his arrival in
     March 1899, but rejected and rented a room elsewhere. He later accepted the offer, as
     he wrote to Marie Huot, August 2, 1899.

32 Letter from Marie Huot to Aguéli, December 21, 1909. In the Aguéli archive. Printed in Gauffin, *Ivan Aguéli*, vol. 2, 116 and Wessel, *Ivan Aguéli*, 20.

33 Among other places, copies are available in the Konstbibliotek, Nationalmuseum, Stockholm.

34 All numbers with Aguéli's contributions starting May 1904 and ending with issue 7–8 November-December 1907 in the Konstbibliotek, Nationalmuseum, Stockholm.

35 Including Aguéli, "I Grandi Initiati Musulmani," *Il Convito* 4, no. 1 (May 1907): 19–20; and "Dio Il Bello—la Maesta della Bellezza" (a translation of chapter 558 of Ibn ʿArabi's *The Meccan Revelations*), *Il Convito* 4, no. 1 (May 1907).

36 Aguéli, "El Akbariya," *Il Convito* 4, no. 2 (June 1907): 48–55; "El Akbariya— continua," *Il Convito* 4, no. 3–4 (July 1907): 90–103; "El Akbariya—continua," *Il Convito* 4, no. 5–6 (September 1907): 154–7; and "El Akbariya—continua," *Il Convito* 4, no. 7–8 (November 1907): 194–5.

37 "Miscellanea/Notizie," *Il Convito* 4, no. 3–4 (July1907), 130–1.

38 "Projet d'explication des termes techniques des différentes doctrines traditionnelles," *La Gnose* 1, no. 12 (December 1910): 268–9.

39 *La Gnose* 1, no. 12 (December 1910): 270–5. Notes to this essay in *La Gnose* 2, no. 1 (January 1911): 20–2.

40 Aguéli, "Pages dédiées à Mercure," *La Gnose* 2, no. 1 (January 1911): 28–38, and no. 2 (February 1911): 66–72.

41 Aguéli, "Pages dédiées au Soleil," *La Gnose* 2, no. 2 (February 1911): 59–66.

42 Aguéli, "El-Malâmatiyah," *La Gnose* 2, no. 3 (March 1911): 100–7.

43 Aguéli, "L'Universalité en l'Islam," *La Gnose* 2, no. 4 (April 1911): 121–31.

44 Aguéli, "L'Islam et les religions anthropomorphiques," *La Gnose* 2, no. 5 (May 1911): 152–3.

45 Aguéli, "L'Identité suprème dans L'ésotérisme musulman," *La Gnose* 2, no. 6 (June 1911): 168–74, and no. 7 (July 1911): 199–202.

46 Aguéli, "Les catégories de l'initiation," *La Gnose* 2, no. 12 (December 1911): 323–8.

47 Henry Corbin, *Creative Imagination in the Sufism of Ibn ʿArabi* (Princeton, NJ: Princeton University Press, 1969), 200–7.

48 Aguéli, "L'art pur," *La Gnose* 1911, 67, trans. Nadine Miller.

49 Aguéli, "L'art pur," 67, trans. Nadine Miller.

50 Aguéli, "L'art pur," 71–2, trans. Nadine Miller.

51 Aguéli, "Le Salon des Indépendants," *L'Encyclopédie contemporaine illustrée*, April 15, 1910, 118–20. Translated from the Swedish translation by Kurt Almqvist and the author in Wessel, *Ivan Aguéli*, 105.

52 Aguéli, "Expositions d'Art à Paris: celle de la Section d'or," *L'Encyclopédie contemporaine illustrée*, November 15, 1912, 175. Translated from the Swedish translation by Kurt Almqvist in Wessel, *Ivan Aguéli*, 109–13.

53 Aguéli, "L'art pur," 71–2.

54 Aguéli, "Expositions d'Art à Paris," 175.

55 Aguéli, "Chronique d'art: La 29ᵉ Exposition du Salon des Indépendants," *L'Encyclopédie contemporaine illustrée*, May 25, 1913, 32.

56 Apollinaire's undated note with proposal of collaboration, in the Aguéli archive.

57 Letter to Ernfried Nyberg, June 17, 1913. In the Aguéli archive.

58 Aguéli, "L'art pur," 70, trans. Nadine Miller.

59 Aguéli, "L'art pur," 66–8.

60 Aguéli, "Pages dédiées au Soleil," *La Gnose*, year 2, no. 2 (February 1911), 60.

61 The document is in the Aguéli archive. Translation in Wessel, *Ivan Aguéli*, 129–32.

62   Letter in the Aguéli archive.
63   Letter to Richard Bergh from Barcelona, June 27, 1916. In the Aguéli archive.
64   Hans Henrik Brummer, ed., *Ivan Aguéli* (Stockholm: Atlantis, 2006), 69. Wessel, *Ivan Aguéli*, 32.
65   An Nawwawî: *Quarante Hadiths* (Beirut: Dar al-Koran al-Kareem, 1980), trans. A. Khaldoun Kinany and A. Vâlsan. English translation by Wessel.

Chapter 3

1   Béatrice Joyeux-Prunel, "'L'art mobilier' La circulation de la peinture avant-gardiste et son rôle dans la géopolitique cultuelle de l'Europe," in *Le temps des capitales culturelles. XVIII-XX siécles*, edited by Christophe Charle (Seysell: Epoques Champ Vallon, 2009).
2   Anna Brzyski, "Introduction; Canons and Art History," in *Partisan Canons*, edited by Anna Brzyski (Durham, NC: Duke University Press, 2007), 7.
3   A passage from the back cover of the exhibition catalog of the 2006 retrospective at Waldemarsudde, summons the image of the artist within Swedish art history: "The painter Ivan Aguéli stood obstinately and free from the career demands of the institutions and the art market. Within the limits of Swedish art history, he fills a unique position as an outsider with experiences that reached far beyond the domestic." Hans Henrik Brummer, "'Friheten gratis är ingen lycka'. Ivan Aguéli, en resenär," in *Ivan Aguéli*, edited by Hans Henrik Brummer (Stockholm: Atlantis & Prins Eugens Waldemarsudde, 2006), 8. The exhibition *Klee/Aguéli*, Moderna Museet (2019) represented somewhat an exception to the rule, in taking as one of its departure points the artist's "dialogue with the modern."
4   Viveca Wessel, *Ivan Aguéli: Porträtt av en rymd* (Stockholm: Författarförlaget, 1988), and Simon Sorgenfrei, *Det monoteistiska landskapet. Ivan Aguéli och Emanuel Swedenborg* (Stockholm: Eureka/Ellerströmss akademiska, 2018).
5   For Augéli's biographical details, I have referred to Axel Gauffin, *Ivan Aguéli: människan, mystikern, målaren* (Stockholm: Sveriges Allmänna Konstföreningen, 1940–1).
6   See, for example, Piotr Piotrowski, "Towards a Horizontal History of Art," in *Writing Central European Art History*, PATTERNS travelling Lecture Set 2008/2009 (Vienna: Erste Foundation, 2008); Béatrice Joyeux-Prunel, *Nul n'est prophète en son pays? L'internationalisme de le peinture des avant-gardes parisiennes, 1855–1914* (Paris: Musée d'Orsay and Éditions Nicolas Chaudun, 2009); Béatrice Joyeux-Prunel, *Les avant-gardes artistiques 1848–1918. Une historie transnationale* (Paris: Galleimard, 2015); Thomas DaCosta Kaufmann, Catherine Dossin and Béatrice Joyeux-Prunel, *Circulation in the Global History of Art* (Farnham & Burlington: Ashgate, 2018).
7   David Cottington, "The Formation of the Avant-Garde in Paris and London, c. 1880–1915," *Art History* 35 (June 2012): 596–621.
8   David Cottington, "The Transnational Hierarchies and Networks of the Artistic Avant-garde ca. 1885–1915," in *Decentering European Intellectual Space*, edited by Marja Javala, Stefan Nygård, and Johan Strang (Leiden: Brill, 2019), 72.
9   Christophe Charle, "Introduction," in *Le temps des capitales culturelles. XVIII–XX siécles*, edited by Christophe Charle (Seysell: Epoques Champ Vallon, 2009), 21.

10 This theory is developed in Pierre Bourdieu, *The Rules of Art* (1993).

11 "Paris n'exerce son pouvoir absolu sur l'art moderne tout entier que par la juste mesure qu'il tient entre la tradition et de la nature." Ivan Aguéli, "Pages dédiés à Mercure," *La Gnose* 1 (1911), in *La Gnose. Édition intégrale 1909–1912* (Paris: Edition de l'homme libre, 2009), 38.

12 Annika Öhrner, "Hilma af Klint och Ivan Aguéli. Andlighetens och konstens rum," *AURA. Tidskriften av akademiska studier i nyreligiositet* 9 (2017): 41–59.

13 Konstnärsförbundets utställning 1912. Aguéli exhibited, according to the catalog, two *Landscapes outside Visby, Young girl,* and *Tenement House in Stockholm*.

14 Christophe Charle, "Introduction," in *Le Temps des Capitales Culturelles XVIIIe–XXe siècles* (Seysel: Champ Vallon, 2009), 22. Michel Espagne, *Les Transferts culturels franco-allemands* (Paris: PUF, 1999).

15 In a letter to his wife of May 24, 2013, Richard Bergh writes: "Aguéli is there [at van Dongen's] as a fish in the sea. He is a strange figure, much sought for by the women—he lives nowhere and everywhere—refuse to give any address, turns up and disappears, dressed in a tight black velvet coat, and trousers as wide as sacks, half shabby all in all. But the Parisian women love the apache more than anyone else." Gauffin, *Ivan Aguéli*, vol. 2, 220.

16 The artist Ture Holm in an undated letter to Axel Gauffin, *Ivan Aguéli*, vol. 2, 200.

17 Christina G. Wistman, "Prins Eugen and Ivan Aguéli i källor och litteratur," in *Ivan Aguéli*, edited by Wistman (Stockholm: Prins Eugens Waldemarsudde, 2006), 53–76.

18 Ivan Aguéli, "Den rena konsten," *Flamman* 1919 (no pages).

19 Vibeke Röstorp, *Le Mythe du Retour. Les artistes scandinaves en France de 1889–1908* (Stockholm: Stockholm universitets förlag, 2013).

20 Letter from Ivan Aguéli from Paris to his mother in Sweden dated April 24, 1890, cited in Gauffin, *Ivan Aguéli*, vol. 1, 47–9.

21 Gauffin, *Ivan Aguéli*, vol. 1, 53–5.

22 See Alexandra Herlitz, *Grez-sur-Loing Revisited. The International Artists' Colony in a Different Light* (Gothenburg: Makadam, 2013).

23 Gauffin, *Ivan Aguéli*, vol. 1, 145.

24 Béatrice Joyeux-Prunel, *Les avant-gardes artistiques 1848–1918. Une histoire transnationale* (Paris: Gallimard, 2017), 160–4.

25 Letter from Aguéli to his mother, May 1, 1890, Gauffin, *Ivan Aguéli*, vol. 1, 48.

26 Ivan Aguèli, to Werner von Hausen, November 1, 1895, cited in Gauffin, *Ivan Aguéli*, vol. 2, 21.

27 Cottington, "Translational Hierarchies," 68.

28 Jouyeux-Prunel, *Les avant-gardes artistiques*, 180.

29 Gauffin, *Ivan Aguéli*, vol. 1, 123.

30 "Les Indépendants nous offrent toujours du nouveau et de l'imprévu. C'est tout un champ d'observation pour qui pense. C'est parmi les isolés, les libertaires, les inquiets et les tâtonnants, que l'on aperçoit les indices de l'art de demain. C'est l'acheminement d'un art naturiste vers le décoratif et le style." G. Ivan [Ivan Aguéli], "Le Salon des Indépendants," *L'Encyclopédie contemporaine illustrée* April 18, 1897, 63.

31 Wessel, *Ivan Aguéli*, 115.

32 Ivan Aguéli to Werner von Hausen, October 27, 1893, in Gauffin, *Ivan Aguéli*, vol. 1, 196.

33 In Aguéli archive, Nationalmuseum.

34 Hans Henrik Brummer, "Richard Bergh—ett konstnärskall," in *Richard Bergh: ett konstnärskall*, edited by Hans Henrik Brummer (Stockholm: Atlantis/Prins Eugens Waldemarsudde, 2002), 12.

35 Thomas Millroth, "Molards salong," *Forum* 1993, 114–23.
36 Gauffin, *Ivan Aguéli*, vol. 1, 56. Gauffin does not establish who made the recommendation.
37 Èmile Bernard in letter to Axel Gauffin, undated, cited in Gauffin, *Ivan Aguéli*, vol. 1, 58. Sorgenfrei *Det monoteistiska landskapet.*
38 Gauffin, *Ivan Aguéli*, vol. 1, 59.
39 Ivan Aguéli, "L'art pur," *La Gnose* 1, no. 1–2 (1911): n. 1, 36.
40 Letter from Ivan Aguéli to Richard Bergh, Nationalmuseum. In Gauffin, *Ivan Aguéli*, vol. 1, 101–8.
41 See *Félix Fénéon: The Modern Times, from Seurat to Matisse* (Paris: Musée de l'Orangerie, 2019).
42 Abdul Hadi, "Le Salon des Indépendants. 27me Exposition," *L'Encyclopédie contemporaine illustrée* no. 641 (April 30, 1911): 32.
43 Henri Le Fauconnier to Ivan Aguéli, correspondance Nationalmuseum. In Gauffin, *Ivan Aguéli*, vol. 1, the card is dated to June 1913, which I take as an indication that the date was found on an envelope that has since been lost.
44 See, for example, David Cottington, *Cubism in the Shadow of War: The Avant-Garde and Politics in Paris 1905–1914* (New Haven, CT: Yale University Press, 1998), 88–108.
45 Abdul Hadi [Ivan Aguéli], "Les Indépendants, 29eme," *L'Encyclopédie contemporaine illustrée*, May 25 and June 30, 1913.
46 Ivan Aguéli, "L'art Pur."
47 Cottington, *Cubism in the Shadow of War*, 104.
48 Gauffin, *Ivan Aguèli*, vol. 2, 19.
49 He does this, for example, in the letter to Richard Berg of October 1893, published in this book.
50 This work is thoroughly documented in Gunhild Osterman, *Richard Bergh och Nationalmuseum. Några document* (Stockholm: Nationalmuseum, 1958).
51 Gunhild Osterman, Richard Bergh, and Nationalmuseum, Nationalmusei Skriftserie 4, Lund 1958.
52 Gauffin, *Ivan Aguéli*, vol. 1, 32–5.
53 Ibid., 36.
54 Ibid., 43.

Chapter 4

1 Faivre conceived of esotericism as "a form of thought," distinguished by a set of four primary and two secondary characteristics. Antoine Faivre, *Access to Western Esotericism* (Albany: State University of New York Press, 1994), 10–15.
2 Wouter Hanegraaff, *Esotericism and the Academy: Rejected Knowledge in Western Culture* (Cambridge: Cambridge University Press, 2012).
3 See, for example, Marco Pasi, "The Problems of Rejected Knowledge: Thoughts on Wouter Hanegraaff's *Esotericism and the Academy*," *Religion* 43, no. 2 (April 2013): 201–12.
4 Kahn-Harris discusses "transgressive subcultural capital" in his study of the Black Metal scene. Keith Kahn-Harris, *Extreme Metal: Music and Culture on the Edge* (Oxford: Berg, 2007).

5 Inga Sanner, *Att älska sin nästa såsom sig själv: Om moraliska utopier under 1800-talet* (Stockholm: Carlssons, 1995), 274–330.

6 On Müller's debates with Theosophists, see Joy Dixon, *Divine Feminine: Theosophy and Feminism in England* (Baltimore, MD: The Johns Hopkins University Press, 2001), 4–5, 43.

7 On Strindberg and Theosophy, see Eszter Szalczer, *Strindberg's Cosmic Theatre: Theosophical Impact and the Theatrical Metaphor* (Diss., New York: City University of New York, 1997). An excellent unpublished overview of some of the debates concerning Theosophy in Swedish newspapers is Åsa Stark, *Madame Blavatsky och teosofin: En kvalitativ diskursanalys av svensk dagspress på sent 1800-tal* (BA thesis, Dept. of the History of Religions, Stockholm University, 2015).

8 Robert Carleson and Caroline Levander, "Spiritualism in Sweden," in *Western Esotericism in Scandinavia*, edited by Henrik Bogdan and Olav Hammer (Leiden: Brill, 2016), 522.

9 The most up-to-date discussion of af Klint's mediumistic practice is Hedvig Martin, *Hilma af Klint och De Fem: Förberedelsetiden 1896–1907* (MA thesis, Dept. of History, Södertörn University, 2018).

10 Carleson and Levander, "Spiritualism," 522.

11 Martin, *Hilma af Klint*, 36–41.

12 On Carl Larsson and Western esotericism, see Mats David Ranaxe, *Carl Larsson & evigheten* (Borlänge: Golden Section Publishing, 2011), 15–20, 126–31, 147–52, 156, 183–5. Ranaxe points out several important things, but his work must be used with some caution due to its at times speculative nature and the partially questionable secondary sources employed.

13 Niclas Franzén, "Tyra Kleen som symbolist," in Niclas Franzén et al. (no editor), *Tyra Kleen* (Björkvik: Kerstin Gullstrand Hermelin, 2016), 68–71, 76, 83–6. The fact that Kleen exhibited at the Theosophical Society's premises in Stockholm was highlighted in the label for the watercolor painting "Hjärnans spektrum" (1915) in the recent (2018) exhibition of her work at the Thiel Gallery in Stockholm.

14 Hans-Olof Boström, "Tanke och struktur i Gustaf Fjaestads måleri," in *Det skapande jaget: konsthistoriska texter tillägnade Maj-Brit Wadell*, edited by Irja Bergström and Maj-Brit Wadell (Gothenburg: Konstvetenskapliga institutionen Göteborgs universitet, 1996), 69–80.

15 Original: "Kung Oskar lär vara teosof." Quoted in Axel Gauffin, *Ivan Aguéli: Människan, Mystikern, Målaren,* (Stockholm: Sveriges Allmänna Konstförening, 1940), vol. 1, 118.

16 See the interview with Aguéli's mentor and friend Carl Wilhelmsson, "Två konstiga konstnärer," *Dagens Nyheter*, November 19, 1922.

17 David Thurfjell, *Det gudlösa folket: De postkristna svenskarna och religionen* (Stockholm: Molin & Sorgenfrei, 2015), 140–1.

18 Josephine Selander, *Mellan öst och väst, profetior och entreprenörskap, vetenskap och tro: Meningsproduktion om alternativa andligheter i svensk press och offentlighet 1899–1926* (MA thesis, Dept. of the History of Ideas, Stockholm University, 2018), 21, 32, 40–3.

19 On Dalström and Theosophy, see Fredrik Ström, *Kata Dalströms liv, öden och äventyr i kampen mot herremakten* (Stockholm: Tidens förlag, 1931), 312f.

20 On Theosophy and progressive politics see Dixon, *Divine Feminine*; Siv-Ellen Kraft, *The Sex Problem: Political Aspects of Gender Discourse in the Theosophical Society, 1875–1930* (diss., Department of the History of Religions, University of Bergen, 1999). On this topic in a Swedish context, see Inga Sanner, *Att älska sin nästa*

såsom sig själv: Om moraliska utopier under 1800-talet (Stockholm: Carlssons, 1995), 296–330.

21   Original: "en öfverklass-sekt." Anon., "Annie Besant," *Svenska dagbladet*, May 24, 1894, 2.

22   Mark Sedgwick, *Western Sufism: From the Abbasids to the New Age* (New York: Oxford University Press, 2017), 155.

23   For an introduction to Swedish Freemasonry, see Henrik Bogdan, "Freemasonry in Sweden," in *Western Esotericism in Scandinavia*, edited by Henrik Bogdan and Olav Hammer (Leiden: Brill, 2016), 168–81. It should, however, be borne in mind that Swedish freemasonry increasingly emphasized a Christian moral interpretation of its rituals and symbols, rather than an esoteric understanding of them, during the course of the nineteenth century. Ibid., 179–80.

24   Sedgwick, *Western Sufism*, 155.

25   Einar Petander, "Theosophy in Sweden," in *Western Esotericism in Scandinavia*, edited by Henrik Bogdan and Olav Hammer (Leiden: Brill, 2016), 578–9.

26   Original: "une certaine connaissance des sciences occultes devient nécessaire à l'intelligence d'un grand nombre d'œuvres littéraires de ce temps." Anatole France, "Papus," *Revue illustrée*, February 1890, 185.

27   Sedgwick, *Western Sufism*, 150.

28   Ibid., 154.

29   In a letter to his mother from 1906, he writes: "I'm working on a work about the secret doctrines in the Orient and then (=*when* it is finished) people will see how great similarities there are between Swedenborg and the holy group of great souls … " Original: "Jag arbetar på ett arbete om de hemliga lärorna i Orienten o. då (= *när* det blir färdigt) skall man få se huru stora likheter det är mellan Swedenborg o. den heliga skara av stora själar (…)." Further, he says, "this spiritual lineage goes from the secret doctrines in the temples of Egypt, Assyria and India to shine at its brightest in the so-called fakirs and dervishes and is concluded by the Swedenborgian light." Quoted in Axel Gauffin, *Ivan Aguéli: Människan, Mystikern, Målaren* (Stockholm: Sveriges Allmänna Konstförening, 1941), vol. 2, 142.

30   Sedgwick, *Western Sufism*, 152–4.

31   See, for example, Aguéli's comment regarding "mysticism" (which can here be read as denoting esotericism) that it "on closer inspection is found to be non-mysticism, rather the Chemistry and Mathematics of Thought and Will or rather Chemistry and Physiology." Letter of 1893 to his friend the Swedish painter Artur Bianchini, quoted in Gauffin, *Ivan Aguéli*, vol. 1, 91. On occultism as a response to secularization, see Wouter Hanegraaff, *New Age Religion and Western Culture: Esotericism in the Mirror of Secular Thought* (Leiden: Brill, 1996), 422–3.

32   Sedgwick, *Western Sufism*, 144; Olav Hammer, *Claiming Knowledge: Strategies of Epistemology from Theosophy to the New Age* (Leiden: Brill, 2004), 221–330.

33   Gauffin, *Ivan Aguéli*, vol. 1, 105.

34   Original: "en Leonardo i filosofiens form." Quoted in Gauffin, *Ivan Aguéli*, vol. 2, 142.

35   On the reception of Leonardo among turn-of-the-century esotericists, see Per Faxneld, "Mona Lisa's Mysterious Smile: The Artist Initiate in Esoteric New Religions," *Nova Religio: The Journal of Alternative and Emergent Religions* 19, no. 4 (May, 2016): 14–32.

36   The list of books is reproduced in Simon Sorgenfrei, *Det monoteistiska landskapet: Ivan Aguéli och Emanuel Swedenborg* (Lund: Ellerströms, 2018), 94–8. Mather's name is given as "Matter (?)," ibid., 98.

37 Gauffin, *Ivan Aguéli*, vol. 1, 155.

38 Sorgenfrei, *Det monoteistiska landskapet*, 33; Viveca Wessel, *Ivan Aguéli: Porträtt av en rymd* (Stockholm: Författarförlaget, 1988), 33.

39 John Senior, *The Way Down and Out: The Occult in Symbolist Literature* (Ithaca, NY: Cornell University Press, 1959), 88.

40 Original: "Huysmans har tagit sig före, synes det, ett grannt arbete genom att bekämpa satanismen till förmån för sund mysticism o. verklig spiritualitet." Letter to Rickard Bergh: Paris, October 10, 1893. In Gauffin, *Ivan Aguéli*, vol. 1, 104.

41 Original: "Konstnären i kontakt med sitt autentiska själv, och därmed en av de initierade, utvalda." Quoted in Sorgenfrei, *Det monoteistiska landskapet*, 49.

42 On Przybyszewski's art theories, see Per Faxneld, "Witches, Anarchism, and Evolutionism: Stanislaw Przybyszewski's fin-de-siècle Satanism and the Demonic Feminine," in *The Devil's Party: Satanism in Modernity*, edited by Per Faxneld and Jesper Aa. Petersen (New York: Oxford University Press, 2013), 53–77.

43 Original: "Kristus ingiver mig också idén om den antropomorfa förmågan d.v.s. att skänka mänsklig form åt idéerna och åt känslorna, en förmåga som troligen är resultatet av en intensiv och harmonisk kärlek och känd med själens innersta djup, konstnärens och skaparens förmåga, som står i förhållande till det estetiska sinnet" (1894 letter to Werner von Hausen), Gauffin, *Ivan Aguéli*, vol. 1, 154–5.

44 Gauffin, *Ivan Aguéli*, vol. 2, 292.

45 Gösta Adrian-Nilsson, *Den gudomliga geometrien: En uppsats om konst* (Stockholm: Thure Wahledow, 1922).

46 Gísli Magnússon, "Visionary Mimesis and Occult Modernism in Literature and Art Around 1900," in *The Occult in Modernist Art, Literature, and Cinema*, edited by Tessel M. Bauduin and Henrik Johnsson (Cham: Palgrave Macmillan, 2018), 51–2.

47 On these factors in Swedish culture, see Thurfjell, *Det gudlösa folket*.

48 An important early Swedish work on esotericism and art, that still did not manage to sway the biases of art historians, was Peter Cornell's *Den hemliga källan* (Hedemora: Gidlunds, 1981), which begins with a discussion of Aguéli (13–19).

49 Original: "någon slags anarko-stalinist i unga år." Quoted in KN [Kurt Nilsson], "Sufisten Säfve känner sig befryndad med Ivan Aguéli," *Aguélimuseets vänners årsskrift*, vol. 8, 1995, 33.

50 Ibid.

51 Torbjörn Säfve, *Ivan Aguéli: En roman om frihet* (Stockholm: Prisma, 1981), 90–3.

52 Original: "står utanför karusellen." Säfve, *Ivan Aguéli*, 92.

53 Ibid.

54 Original: "tack och lov genomskådat Sar Peladans sjukligt mystiska symbolism." Ibid., 112. He later calls Peladan's "ideal art" "humbug." Ibid., 130.

55 Original: "Paris har feber och kvacksalvarna gör pengar." Ibid., 93.

56 Iris Müller-Westermann, "Paintings for the Future: Hilma af Klint—A Pioneer of Abstraction in Seclusion," in *Hilma af Klint—A Pioneer of Abstraction*, edited by Iris Müller-Westermann and Jo Widoff (Stockholm: Moderna Museet, 2013), 33.

57 Original: "Aguéli och Säfve forsar fram i tidens idéström av teosofi, anarki, begynnande krig, kubism, futurism och koloniala händelser i Egypten." Thomas Millroth, "Ivan Aguéli som romanfigur," *Aftonbladet*, November 27, 1981.

58 Original: "Där sätter hon in Aguélis ofta publicerade essä om den Rena Konsten i sitt esoteriska sammanhang." Torbjörn Säfve, "Ivan Aguéli—En dold skatt," *Aftonbladet*, September 28, 1988.

59   https://www.modernamuseet.se/stockholm/sv/2016/02/05/verk-av-hilma-af-klint-visas/
60   One good example is Bo Gustavsson, "Ivan Aguéli sökte efter det lysande tomrummet," *Svenska dagbladet*, October 1, 2017.

Chapter 5

1   Axel Gauffin, *Ivan Aguéli människan, mystikern, målaren* (Stockholm: Sveriges Allmänna Konstföreningen, 1940–1), 49.
2   Ibid., 80.
3   Joscelyn Godwin, Christian Chanel, and John P. Deveney, *The Hermetic Brotherhood of Luxor: Initiatic and Historical Documents of an Order of Practical Occultism* (York Beach, ME: S. Weiser, 1995), 381; Marie-José Delalande, "Le mouvement théosophique en France 1876–1921" (PhD thesis, Université du Maine, 2007), 469.
4   Gauffin, *Ivan Aguéli*, vol. 1, 61–2.
5   For in-depth studies of Aguéli's time in Paris and Swedenborg's influence see Simon Sorgenfrei, "The Great Aesthetic Inspiration: On Ivan Aguéli's Reading of Swedenborg," *Religion and the Arts* 23 (2019): 1–25; Simon Sorgenfrei. *Det monoteistiska landskapet. Ivan Aguéli och Emanuel Swedenborg* (Lund: Ellerströms, 2018).
6   Quoted from Gauffin, *Ivan Aguéli*, vol. 1, 101.
7   Gauffin, *Ivan Aguéli*, vol. 1, 142.
8   Aguéli to Hausen, April 6, 1894, quoted from Gauffin, *Ivan Aguéli*, vol. 1, 147.
9   Aguéli to Hausen, April 24, 1894, quoted from Gauffin, *Ivan Aguéli*, vol. 1, 145.
10   Quoted from Gauffin, *Ivan Aguéli*, vol. 1, 142.
11   Letter to Werner von Hausen, April 19, 1889, quoted from Gauffin, *Ivan Aguéli*, vol. 1, 142.
12   Emanuel Swedenborg, *True Christian Religion: Containing the Universal Theology of the New Church Foretold by the Lord in Daniel 7:13–14 and Revelation 21:1–2* (West Chester, PA: Swedenborg Foundation, 1996), § 5.
13   Aguéli to Hausen, May 6, 1894, quoted from Gauffin, vol. 1, 154.
14   Jane Williams-Hogan, "Emanuel Swedenborg's Aesthetic Philosophy and Its Impact on Nineteenth-Century American Art," *Toronto Journal of Theology* 28, no. 105–24 (2012): 109.
15   Emanuel Swedenborg, *Angelic Wisdom about Divine Providence*, trans. William Frederic Wunsch (New York: Citadel Press, 1963), § 24.
16   Aguéli to Bianchini, December 25, 1888, in Gauffin, *Ivan Aguéli*, vol. 1, 91–2.
17   Hans Henrik Brummer, *Ivan Aguéli på klassiska*. Available online: http://auktionsverket.se/aktuellt/ivan-agueli-pa-klassiska/, Accessed March 25, 2017.
18   Emanuel Swedenborg, *Heaven and Its Wonders and Hell: From Things Heard and Seen* (West Chester, PA: Swedenborg Foundation, 1995), § 29.
19   Gauffin, *Ivan Aguéli*, vol. 1, 84.
20   Ibid.
21   Aguéli to Hausen, May 6, 1894, quoted from Gauffin, *Ivan Aguéli*, vol. 1, 154.
22   Gauffin, *Ivan Aguéli*, vol. 1, 84–5.
23   Ibid., 86.
24   Ibid., 88.
25   He borrowed them at the National Library the same day as he borrowed the Qur'an.

26 Ivan Aguéli to Richard Bergh, March 16, 1893, in Gauffin, *Ivan Aguéli*, vol. 1, 94–5.

27 Gauffin, *Ivan Aguéli*, vol. 1, 96.

28 Ibid.

29 Viveca Wessel, *Ivan Aguéli: porträtt av en rymd* (Stockholm: Författarförlaget, 1988), 41.

30 Wessel, *Porträtt av en rymd*, 42, writes that Portal never names Swedenborg, "but the connection must be pointed out and was well known and was well known by Aguéli."

31 Pierre Paul Frédéric Portal, *Des couleurs symboliques dans l'antiquité, le moyen-âge et les temps modernes* (Paris: Treuttel et Würtz, 1837), 96.

32 Emanuel Swedenborg, *Arcana coelestia* (Loschberg, Austria: Jazzybee Verlag, 2013), vol. 11, § 9467, § 9462, and § 9467.

33 Wessel, *Porträtt av en rymd*, 45.

34 In her study of Aguéli "the Symbolist," Wessel briefly mentions Swedenborg, while highlighting the influence of Bernard and Baudelaire, Owen Jones and Portel. Wessel, *Porträtt av en rymd*, 33–48.

35 As discussed in Chapters 10 and 11, ʿIllaysh was of importance for Aguéli's Sufi orientation. I however argue that Aguéli's experience of living Sufi traditions was weak. ʿIllaysh had inherited the leadership of the ʿArabiyya branch of the Shadhiliyya *ṭarīqa* (Frederick De Jong, *Ṭuruq and Ṭuruq-linked Institutions in Nineteenth Century Egypt: A Historical Study in Organizational Dimensions of Islamic Mysticism* [Leiden: Brill, 1978], 23–4). ʿIllaysh is also said to have initiated Aguéli into the *ṭarīqa* and to have given him an *ijāza* (authorization) as a *muqaddam*, a representative of the *ṭarīqa* with the authority to initiate others (Paul Chacornac, *The Simple Life of René Guénon* [Ghent, NY: Sophia Perennis, 2001], 33–4, 45.). No documentation, however, has however been produced to substantiate this, and as De Jong has stated, ʿIllaysh gave *ijāzas* "to anyone applying for them" and "he does not seem to have taken the requirements of [this] position seriously" (*Ṭuruq and Ṭuruq-linked Institutions*, pp. 173–4). De Jong further shows how the ʿArabiyya branch of the Shadhiliyya *ṭarīqa* had been inactive for almost a hundred years when Aguéli met with ʿIllaysh (pp. 113–14). This suggests that even if Aguéli did get an initiation into the *ṭarīqa*, he was most probably not part of an active and practicing Sufi environment. Rather his interest in Sufism (as in other religions) was primarily intellectual.

36 For further discussion see Sorgenfrei, "The Great Aesthetic Inspiration."

37 For Aguéli in Egypt see Mark Sedgwick, *Western Sufism: From the Abbasids to the New Age* (New York: Oxford University Press, 2017), 148–56.

38 Quoted from Gauffin, *Ivan Aguéli*, vol. 2, 126.

39 *The Meaning of the Glorious Koran: An Explanatory Translation by Marmaduke Pickthall* (London: A.A. Knopf, 1930), 24, 35.

40 Gerhard Böwering, "The Light Verse: Qurʾanic Text and Sufi Interpretation," *Oriens* 36 (2001): 113.

41 In *Le Traité de l'Unité*, which is discussed below, a different understanding is however argued for.

42 Mohammed ibn Fazlallah El-Hindi, "Le Cadeau. Sur la manifestation du Prophète par le Shaikh initié et inspire," *La Gnose* 1, no. 12 (1910): 270. Aguéli's translation was published in *La Gnose* 2, no. 12 (1911): 270–5, and 2, no. 13 (1911): 20–2.

43 Awhad al-Din Balyānī, *Epître sur l'unicité absolute. Présentation et traduction de l'arabe par Michael Chodkiewicz* (Paris: Deux Océans, 1982).

44 Mohyiddin Ibn ʿArabi, "Le Traité de l'Unité," *La Gnose* 2, no. 6 (1911): 170, 173.

45   For a similar discussion, see Wessel, *Porträtt av en rymd*, 91.

46   Yngve Berg, "*Ett huvud för sig.*" *Bohemer och akademister* (Stockholm: Norstedt, 1931).

47   The essay was partially translated to Swedish and published by the Swedish artist
     Yngve Berg, in an issue of the journal *Flamman*, in 1919. It has later been translated
     in full and published by Viveca Wessel together with an analysis in Wessel, *Porträtt
     av en rymd*, 99–105. It is translated into English in this book.

48   Abdul-Hâdî, "L'Art Pur." *La Gnose* 2, no. 1 (1911): 34–8; no 2 (1911): 66–72.

49   Abdul-Hâdî, "Pages dédiées au soleil," *La Gnose* 2, no. 2 (1911): 59–66, 60.

50   This theme has also been discussed by Wessel, *Porträtt av en rymd*, 87–90.

51   Wessel, *Porträtt av en rymd*, 77.

Chapter 6

1   "Bref, l'aventure cubiste offrait tous les traits d'un réveil religieux. D'un réveil
     religieux, avec ses adeptes et ses prosélytes enthousiastes qui savent enfin ce qu'est
     Dieu, ce que signifie le monde, qui vivent désormais dans la Vérité." Jean Paulhan, *La
     Peinture cubiste* (1970; Paris: Gallimard, 1990), 41.

2   Paulhan, *La Peinture cubiste*, 85.

3   Sylvie Patry, "Cézanne, Paul," in *Dictionnaire du Cubisme*, edited by Brigitte Lean
     (Paris: Robert Laffont, 2018), 147; Paulhan, *La Peinture cubiste*, 51.

4   Ariane Coulondre, "Géométrie," in *Dictionnaire du Cubisme*, 308.

5   Guillaume Apollinaire, "Aesthetic meditations on painting: The Cubist painters," in
     Cubism, edited by Dorothea Eimert and Anatolu Podoksik (New York: Parkstone,
     2014), 12–17. On this subject see Linda Henderson, *The Fourth Dimension and
     Non-Euclidean Geometry in Modern Art*, revised edition (Harvard, MA: MIT Press,
     2013).

6   Quoted by Gladys C. Fabre, "Occultisme et cubisme," in *Dictionnaire du Cubisme*,
     543.

7   Margareta Tillberg, *Coloured Universe and the Russian Avant-Garde. Matiushin on
     Coloured Vision in Stalin's Russia, 1932* (PhD thesis Stockholm University, 2003),
     227–32.

8   "Car cet art pur, que ne voile aucun sentimentalisme à la mode, qui ne fait aucune
     concession aux habitudes esthétiques de la multitude," Abdul-Hâdî, "Les Expositions
     d'art à Paris. Celle de la 'Section d'Or' à la galerie Boetie," *Encyclopédie contemporaine
     illustrée* 659 (November 15, 1912): 175–6.

9   Fabre, "Occultisme et cubisme," 535–43. See also Flaurette Gautier, "Stupéfiant
     Cubisme: de la peinture de 'vision' à la peinture de conception," in *Images mentales.
     L'Hallucination dans les arts du XIXe et du XXe siècles* (Paris: Institut national
     d'histoire de l'art, 2016), 14–15; Gautier "'L'Art Pur:' Aguéli and Apollinaire towards
     Cubism," unpublished paper given at the conference on "Esoteric Modernism: The
     Influence of Esotericism on Modernist Culture," Aarhus University, 2015.

10   "Et il est exact que le Sacré s'oppose en tout point à un monde profane, fait d'intérêts
     et d'habitudes, de réflexions et de simples idées claires … Le plus simple que l'on
     puisse dire des cérémonies du cubisme est qu'elles donnent l'impression d'une sorte
     de hiérophanie," Paulhan, *La Peinture cubiste*, 140–1.

11   Nella Arambasin, *La Conception du sacré dans la critique d'art en Europe entre 1880 et
     1914* (Geneva: Droz, 1996), 410.

12 "Toute spiritualité est une esthétique de l'âme. L'esthétique des marabouts intimide parce qu'elle est dépouillée, leur simplicité nous émeut et nous renvoie à la métaphysique de nos questionnements," Tahar Ben Jelloun, *Marabouts, Maroc* (Paris: Gallimard, 2009), 10.

13 Mark Antliff, *Inventing Bergson: Cultural Politics and the Parisian Avant-Garde* (Princeton, NJ: Princeton University Press, 1993). On the Parisian Bergsonian milieu see François Azouvi, *La Gloire de Bergson. Essai sur le magistère philosophique* (Paris: Gallimard, 2007).

14 In his *Le Règne de la quantité et les signes des temps* (Paris: Gallimard, 1945), chapter 34.

15 Xavier Accart, *Guénon et le renversement des clartés: influence d'un métaphysicien sur la vie littéraire et intellectuelle française (1920–1970)* (Milan: Archè, 2005), 322–32.

16 "Le cubisme conçu comme discipline est, en effet, la voie qui mène infailliblement à la simple vérité, c'est-à-dire au maximum d'exactitude rendu par le minimum de moyens," Abdul-Hâdî, "Les Expositions d'art à Paris."

17 "La matière n'est qu'un reflet et un aspect de l'énergie universelle. Des rapports de ce reflet à sa cause, qui est l'énergie lumineuse, naissent ce qu'on appelle improprement les objets, et s'établit ce non-sens: la forme," Anonymous, "L'évolution de l'art vers l'amorphisme," *Les Hommes du jour* (May 3, 1913), 10.

18 "C'est par le purisme que nous finirons par découvrir le secret des arts anciens, grec, arabe, gothique et renaissance," Abdul-Hâdî, "Pages dédiées à Mercure (Sahaif Ataridiyah). L'art pur," *La Gnose* (February 1911), reprinted in Abdul-Hâdî, *Écrits pour la Gnose* (Milan: Archè, 1988), 46, 48.

19 "Plus spécialement, l'art fait entrevoir ce que c'est que le 'temps immobile' ou 'l'actualité permanente du moi extra-temporel et immarcescible', qui, à son tour, mène à l'intelligence de la quatrième dimension, sur l'importance ésotérique de laquelle il est superflu d'insister," Abdul-Hâdî, "Pages dédiées à Mercure," 35.

20 "Rien ne relève plus des sciences occultes, en effet, que la transmutation complète de la forme naturelle en les formes rationnelles de la géométrie euclidienne. N'est-ce pas une opération de haute sorcellerie que d'exprimer la vie la plus concrète par des formes aussi abstraites que possible," Abdul-Hâdî, "Les Expositions d'art à Paris."

21 "Qui dit pulsations dit rythme, c'est-à-dire une action de nombres," Abdul-Hâdî, "Pages dédiées à Mercure," 36.

22 "L'art pur, au point de vue de la Gnose, est de relier le concret à l'abstrait, la quantité à la qualité, l'espace au temps, rien que par l'extrême limite de la matière, c'est-à-dire les nombres," Abdul-Hâdî, "Pages dédiées à Mercure," 41.

23 "Akbariya," *Il Convito*, no. 3–4 (1907): fn. 1, 96.

24 Abdul-Hâdî, "Les Expositions d'art à Paris."

25 Accart, *Guénon ou le renversement des clartés*, 329.

26 "C'est par le '*dikr*' que les Dervishes assimilent certains rythmes. Le '*dikr*' est donc une sorte de 'Hatha-Yoga," Abdul-Hâdî, "Pages dédiées à Mercure," 36.

27 "Or, le rythme n'est que le nombre en activité psycho-physiologique. C'est pourquoi le *dikr* des Dervishes est une assimilation vitale de certains rythmes d'initiés," Abdul-Hâdî, "Pages dédiées à Mercure," 41.

28 "Le rite, comme l'art, met, sur le plan du symbole, en contact avec la réalité," Emile Dermenghem, *Le Culte des saints dans l'islam maghrébin* (Paris: Gallimard, 1954), 331.

29 "La maîtrise dans l'art, comme l'état de grâce dans le dervichisme, portent tous les deux le même signe caractéristique: le ciel qui s'ouvre," Abdul-Hâdî, "Chronique d'art (suite). La 29ᵉ exposition du Salon des Indépendants," *Encyclopédie contemporaine illustrée* 665 (June 30, 1913): 40.

30   Robert Pouyaut, "Art sacré et Tradition," *L'Atelier de la Rose* 3 (June 1951), reprinted in *L'Atelier de la Rose* (Busloup: Le Moulin de l'Etoile, 2008), 78–9. On Gleizes's school of painting see Bruce Adams, *Rustic Cubism: Anne Danger and the Art Colony at Moly-Sabata* (Chicago, IL: University of Chicago Press, 2004).

31   Accart, *Guénon ou le renversement des clartés*, 327.

32   Albert Gleizes, "Réflexions sur l'art dit abstrait et du caractère de l'image dans la non-figuration," *L'Atelier de la Rose* 4 (October 1951), reprinted in *L'Atelier de la Rose*, 81; Robert Pouyaut, "Le Principe directeur dans la peinture," *L'Atelier de la Rose* 6 (March 1952), reprinted in *L'Atelier de la Rose*, 130–3.

33   Abdul-Hâdî, "Sur les principes du monument et de la sculpture," *Encyclopédie contemporaine illustrée* 661 (January 31, 1913): 7–8, 7.

34   See Kajsa Grip, *Ivan Aguéli, Drömmen om österlandet* (B Essay, Uppsala Universitet, 2004).

35   Yassine Karamti, *Le Maraboutisme de chambre noire en Tunisie. Récit visuel d'un corpus de cartes postales photographiques anciennes* (Tunis: Editions Latrash et Centre des études islamiques de Kairouan, 2015).

36   James Thompson and Barbara Wright, *Eugène Fromentin, 1820–1876, visions d'Algérie et d'Egypte* (Paris: ACR Editions, 2008), 123; Denise Brahimi, *La Vie et l'œuvre de Etienne Dinet* (Paris: ACR Edition, 1984), 137.

37   Jade Cowart, "Matisse's Moroccan Sketchbooks and Drawings: Self-Discovery through Various Motifs," in *Matisse in Morocco. The Paintings and Drawings, 1912–1913* (New York: National Gallery of Art, 1990), 124.

38   See Thierry Zarcone, "Le Croisement des regards ou le peintre des deux rives," in *Auguste Chabaud, Fascination et nostalgie entre Provence et Tunisie*, Catalogue of exhibition (February 9–June 2, 2013, Graveson: Musée de région Auguste Chabaud, 2013), 56.

39   Reproduced in Serge Fauchereau, *Le Cubisme. Une revolution esthétique, sa naissance et son rayonnement* (Paris: Flammarion, 2012). There are many examples in Northern Africa and in Anatolia, in Seljuk architecture, of "marabout" edifices with a conical dome.

40   "Mon but est de construire un univers de formes architecturales qui répondent à une recherche d'harmonie." See the following footnote.

41   "Car son géométrisme vacille entre les formes en courbe et les formes angulaires (…) l'apparition dans ses dernières toiles d'une forme en dôme. Un symbole ascétique que la vie dans la ville de Moulay Bouchaib semble imprimer sur ses toiles"; quoted by Abdellah Cheikh, "Mohamed Hamidi à la Galerie Bab Rouah: Miroirs et architecture du vide," *Libération Maroc* [Casablanca], March 2009, https://www.libe.ma/Mohamed-Hamidi-a-la-Galerie-Bab-Rouah-Miroirs-et-architecture-du-vide_a1326.html, Accessed June 2019.

42   Stephen Hirtenstein, "The Cubic Wisdom of the Heart according to Ibn 'Arabî," *Journal of the Muhyiddin Ibn 'Arabi Society* 48 (2010): 39–42.

43   Robert Pouyaud has developed similar ideas about the square, the circle, and esoterism in art and architecture in his article "Le Principe directeur dans la peinture," in *L'Atelier de la Rose* 6 (March 1952), reprinted in *L'Atelier de la Rose*.

44   "L'uomo è il legame tra il mondo celeste e la natura. Il cuore è il centro della vita. La spiritual corrispondenza del cuore tiene il mezzo tra le facoltà superiori dell'uomo e la di lui animalità," in "Akbariya," *Il Convito*, no. 3–4 (1907): 95.

45   Translated from the Arabic by S. Hirtenstein in *The Unlimited Mercifer. The Spiritual Life and Thought of Ibn 'Arabî* (Oxford: Anqa, 1999), 115.

46 E. Baillon, "La Lente Procession du cubisme vers l'art traditionnel," in Robert Pouyaud, ed., "Albert Gleizes," special issue of *L'Atelier de la Rose* (Lyon: Académie Minotaure 1954) 46.

Chapter 7

1 Simon Sorgenfrei, "The Great Aesthetic Inspiration: On Ivan Aguéli's Reading of Swedenborg," *Religion and the Arts* 23 (2019): 1–22.
2 Ibid.
3 Adolph Boyesen, *Hvarför är det Plikt att Behandla Djuren med Godhet* (Stockholm: Svanbäcks Boktryckeri, 1889), 6. Translations from Swedish by author.
4 Ibid., 10–11.
5 Ibid., 11.
6 Ibid., 8.
7 Ibid., 12.
8 Perhaps as significant as his teachings, Swedenborg managed to visit heaven and speak with angels without having his head chopped off, marked a significant milestone in European history and undoubtedly inspired others toward grassroots prophecy.
9 Sorgenfrei, "Great Aesthetic Inspiration," 5.
10 Axel Gauffin, *Ivan Aguéli: Människan, Mystikern, Målaren*, 2 vols. (Stockholm: Sveriges allmänna konstförening, 1940–1), vol. 1, 146.
11 Friedrich Wilhelm Nietzsche, "Schopenhauer as Educator," [1874] in *Thoughts out of Seasons*, trans. Adrian Collins (Edinburgh: T.N. Foulis, 1909), part 2, 149–55, quoted in *Animal Rights: A Historical Anthology*, edited by Andrew Linzey and Paul Barry Clarke (New York: Columbia University Press, 2004), 148–52.
12 D. T. Suzuki, *Swedenborg: Buddha of the North*, trans. Andrew Bernstein (Wester Chester, PA: Swedenborg Foundation, 1996), 95.
13 Helen Keller, *Light in My Darkness* (1927), revised and edited by Ray Silverman (West Chester, PA: Chrysalis Books, 1994), 90, 108.
14 Viveca Wessel, *Ivan Aguéli: Porträtt av en rymd* (Stockholm: Författarbolaget, 1988), 97.
15 Gauffin, *Ivan Aguéli*, vol. 1, 154.
16 See ibid., 124.
17 Ibid., 102.
18 Ivan Aguéli to Richard Bergh, October 10, 1893, printed in ibid., 101.
19 Ibid., 146.
20 Ibid., vol. 2, 188. The Qur'anic verses here repeat the phrase that "in hardship comes ease."
21 Ivan Aguéli, "Individualism och solidaritet: En lifsfråga," unpublished letter, National Archive, Sweden. *Brand* started in 1898 and has run continually up until today, making it one of the longest running anarchist periodicals in the world (*Freedom* started in 1886).
22 Rob Sparrow wrote, "Direct Action aims to achieve our goals though our own activity rather than through the actions of others. It is about people taking power for themselves. In this, it is distinguished from most other forms of political action such as voting, lobbying, attempting to exert political pressure through industrial action or through the media." Cited in David Graeber, *Direct Action: An Ethnography* (Oakland, CA: AK Press, 2009), 202.

23 Rudolf Rocker, *Anarcho-Syndicalism: Theory and Practice* (1938; London: Secker and Warburg, 2009), 76.

24 For Malatesta in Egypt see Anthony Gorman, "'Diverse in Race, Religion and Nationality ... but United in Aspirations of Civil Progress': The Anarchist Movement in Egypt 1860–1940," in *Anarchism and Syndicalism in the Colonial and Postcolonial World, 1870–1940*, edited by Steven Hirsch and Lucien van der Walt (Leiden: Brill, 2010), 28. For Edward Joris, see Maarten Van Ginderachter, "Edward Joris: Caught between Continents and Ideologies?" in *To Kill a Sultan: A Transnational History of the Attempt on Abdülhamid II (1905)*, ed. Houssine Alloul, Edhem Eldem, and Henk de Smaele (London: Palgrave Macmillan, 2018), 67–97.

25 Ilham Khuri-Makdisi, *The Eastern Mediterranean and the Making of Global Radicalism, 1860–1914* (Berkeley: University of California Press, 2010), 133.

26 Gorman, "Diverse in Race, Religion and Nationality," 29. For more on this period in the Mediterranean region, see Khuri-Makdisi, *The Eastern Mediterranean*, 180.

27 For union organizing by anarchist-syndicalists in Egypt during this period, see Anthony Gorman, "Foreign Workers in Egypt 1882–1914," in *Subalterns and Social Protest: History from Below in the Middle East and North Africa*, edited by Stephanie Cronin (London and New York: Routledge, 2008), 237–59.

28 See Anthony Gorman, "Anarchists in Education: The Free Popular University in Egypt (1901)," *Middle Eastern Studies* 41, no. 3 (2005): 303–20.

29 Abdul Hadi, "L'Universalité en l'Islam," originally published in *La Gnose* (1911), quoted here from "Universality in Islam," trans. Farid Nur ad-Din, in *Universal Dimensions of Islam*, ed. Patrick Laude (Bloomington, IN: World Wisdom, 2011), 139.

30 Gauffin, *Ivan Aguéli*, vol. 1, 65, 97.

31 The ʿArabiyya-Shadhiliyya had, by then, died out. See Mark Sedgwick, *Against the Modern World: Traditionalism and the Secret Intellectual History of the Twentieth Century* (New York: Oxford University Press, 2004), 62. According to Sedgwick, "*bayʿa* (the oath of allegiance that marks initiation in Sufism) may be given or taken 'for guidance' or 'for *baraka* (blessings).' Given that the ʿArabiyya-Shadhiliyya had by then died out, the initiation was probably not for guidance, but for *baraka*" (private correspondence with Sedgwick). Regardless of the intent of ʿIllaysh, it seems that in joining an empty order and receiving ʿIllaysh's *ijāza* (permission to initiate others), Aguéli could "re-start" and re-fashion the order without restrictions as he did when he acted as a gatekeeper and initiated fellow Europeans René Guénon and Léon Champrenaud into the ʿArabiyya-Shadhiliyya (Ibid., 63).

32 Abdul Hadi, "El-Malâmatiyah," *La Gnose* 2, no. 3 (March 1911). Posted online March 23, 2013, by Abdoullatif: http://esprit-universel.over-blog.com/article-abdul-hadi-ivan-agueli-el-malamatiyah-suivi-de-la-traduction-des-principes-des-malamatiyah-116442900.html, Accessed March 19, 2019. Translated by author.

33 Abdul Hadi, "Universality in Islam," 142.

34 Ibid., 143.

35 Ibid., 145.

36 Ibid., 143.

37 Ibid.

38 Ibid., 144.

39 Farid Nur ad-Din, Introduction to Abdul Hadi, "Universality in Islam," 144, no. 45.

40 Gustaf Aguéli [Ivan Aguéli], "Djurens bok." Unpublished partial translation of Ramon Llul's *Llibre de les bèsties* (The Book of Beasts) from M. Obrador Bennassar's Spanish translation of the original Catalan text. National Archive, Sweden. Undated.

41   Al-Hafiz Basheer Ahmad Masri, *Animal Welfare in Islam* (Markfield, Leicestershire: The Islamic Foundation, 2007), 24.

42   Peter Kropotkin, "Nature Teaches Mutual Aid," [1902], in *Animal Rights: A Historical Anthology*, edited by Andrew Linzey and Paul B. Clarke (New York: Columbia University Press, 2004), 90.

43   Robert E. Zegger, "Protecting Animals in Paris: 1815–1870," *History Today* 28, no. 2 (1978): 105–12.

44   Gauffin, *Ivan Aguéli*, vol. 2, 93.

45   Ibid., 96.

46   Ibid.

47   Ibid. One might contrast this apparent support for mass violence with his support for nonviolent action: "Tolstoy and his passive resistance is perhaps the most beautiful of what we can claim in Christianity." Ibid., vol. 1, 155.

48   Ibid., 104.

49   Ibid., 105.

50   Ibid., 112.

51   Ibid., 115.

52   This does not mean, however, that his act led to the ban. Popular opposition to Spanish bullfighting made it unlikely to take root in France (which permitted French bullfighting that, in contrast to the Spanish, did not entail killing the bulls). In 1896 alone, animal rights activists in France brought 376 legal suits against bullfighters. See Adrian Shubert, *Death and Money in the Afternoon: A History of the Spanish Bullfight* (Oxford: Oxford University Press, 1999), 12. As for French-style bullfighting in southern France, it continues to this day.

53   Aguéli/Abdul Hadi did not, however, take a purely anti-colonialist stance but seemed to support a sort of pro-Islamic European colonialism: "We have created a large colonial empire not just with the national (immediate) welfare in mind but also in the interest of civilization." Gauffin, *Ivan Aguéli*, vol. 2, 181. This topic deserves far more coverage than possible here.

54   Hans Henrik Brummer, "Friheten gratis är ingen lycka," in *Ivan Aguéli*, ed. Hans Henrik Brummer et al. (Stockholm: Prins Eugens Waldemarsudde, 2006), 13.

55   Ibid. For more on Aguéli and Insabato's relationship, see Eileen Ryan, *Religion as Resistance: Negotiating Authority in Italian Libya* (New York: Oxford University Press, 2018), 37–43.

56   Wessel, *Ivan Aguéli*, 28.

57   For some context to these questions see Ralph Grillo, "Islam and Transnationalism," *Journal of Ethnic and Migration Studies* 30, no. 5 (2004): 861–78 and Davide Turcato, "Nations without Borders: Anarchists and National Identity," in *Reassessing the Transnational Turn*, edited by Constance Bantman and Bert Altena (Oakland, CA: PM Press, 2017), 25–42.

58   Lori Gruen, *Entangled Empathy: An Alternative Ethic for Our Relationships with Animals* (New York: Lantern Books, 2015), 63–4, 69.

59   Sedgwick, *Against the Modern World*, 2004; Robert Carleson, "Traditionalism in Sweden," in *Western Esotericism in Scandinavia*, edited by Henrik Bogdan and Olav Hammer (Leiden: Brill, 2016), 624–9.

60   See, for example, Annette Kobak. *Isabelle: The Life of Isabelle Eberhardt* (New York: Alfred A. Knopf, 1989). We see other early examples of European anarchist converts in two Italians: Cesare Camilieri aka Hasan bin Abdullah (*c.* 1882–?) and Leda Rafenelli. See, respectively, Axel Çorlu, "Anarchists and Anarchism in the Ottoman Empire, 1850–1917," in *History from Below*, edited by Selim Karahasanoglu (Istanbul:

Istanbul Bilgi University Press, 2016), 553–83 and Andrea Pakieser, *I Belong Only to Myself: The Life and Writings of Leda Rafanelli* (Oakland, CA: AK Press, 2014).

61   Affiliated with people such as Robert Anton Wilson, Toshihiko Izutsu, and Henry Corbin, Peter Lamborn Wilson (born *c.* 1945) has written numerous books related to Islamic heretical movements, anarchism, and ecology, most notably, under his pseudonym "Hakim Bey," *T. A. Z.: The Temporary Autonomous Zone, Ontological Anarchy, Poetic Terrorism* (1985). Versluis described him as "among the most influential anarchist authors of the late twentieth and early twenty-first centuries." Arthur Versluis, "A Conversation with Peter Lamborn Wilson," *Journal for the Study of Radicalism* 4, no. 2 (2010): 139.

62   From an interview published in 2010:
     "Arthur Versluis: What I was going to suggest is that Traditionalism and anarchism …
     Peter Lamborn Wilson: They absolutely have an interface.
     AV: They have a point of interface.
     PLW: I can't remember his name now, but the person who converted René Guénon to
        Islam was actually an anarchist. This is also published.
     AV: Ivan Aguéli.
     PLW: Yes, him. And Ananda Coomaraswamy was an anarchist; I don't think he ever
        actually gave up being some sort of anarchist. These ideas can easily interface."
     Ibid., 142.

63   See "Ivan Aguéli," *Wikipedia*, https://en.wikipedia.org/wiki/Ivan_Aguéli, Accessed July 5, 2019.

64   See, for example, Torbjörn Säfve, *Ivan Aguéli: En roman om frihet* (1981; Stockholm: Man 1994) and Susanne Olsson and Simon Sorgenfrei, "Den Fiktive Aguéli: Identifikationsobjekt och Projektionsyta för Unga Manliga Konvertiter till Islam," *Aura* 9 (2017): 81–106. In 2006, Omar claimed that "Ivan Aguéli … made me who I am … [and] shaped not only my spirituality and my way of thinking but also my daily life," Mohamed Omar, "Om muslimen 'Abdalhâdî'," in *Ivan Aguéli*, edited by Hans Henrik Brummer et al. (Stockholm: Prins Eugens Waldemarsudde, 2006), 89; *Agueli Against Civlization—Free Jonatan*, http://agueliagainstcivilisation.blogg.se, Accessed May 11, 2009.

65   Abdul Hadi, "Universality in Islam," 144; Peter Lamborn Wilson, *Sacred Drift: Essays on the Margins of Islam* (San Francisco, CA: City Lights, 1993), 64–5.

66   In 1909 Tolstoy wrote: "To me, Jesus' teachings are merely one of the beautiful and great religious teachings we have received from antiquity be it Egyptian, Jewish, Hindu, Chinese or Greek. … Religious and moral truth is everywhere and always the same, and I try to make it my own wherever I find it, without any preference for Christianity," Luigi Stendardo, *Leo Tolstoy and the Bahá'í Faith*, trans. Jeremy Fox (Oxford: George Ronald, 1985), 41–2.

67   Paul Cudenec, *The Anarchist Revelation* (Sussex: Winter Oaks Press, 2013).

68   Gregory A. Lipton, *Rethinking Ibn 'Arabi* (New York: Oxford University Press, 2018), 18, 23.

69   Olsson and Sorgenfrei, "Den Fiktive Aguéli," 103–4.

Chapter 8

1   Henrik Samuel Nyberg, "Aguéli och Islam," in Axel Gauffin, *Ivan Aguéli. Människan, mystikern, målaren* (Stockholm: Sveriges Allmänna Konstförening, 1940–1), vol. 2, 302.

2 Letter by Ivan Aguéli to his mother, undated, conserved in the Aguéli collection of the Swedish national archives (*Riksarkivet*). The letter also appears in Gauffin, *Ivan Aguéli*, vol. 2, 133.

3 The definitive reference on the subject remains the article by Angelo Scarabel, "Una rivista italo-araba di inizio secolo: *an-Nâdî* (*Il Convito*)," *Oriente Moderno* 58 (1978): 51–67.

4 To our knowledge, there are only two nearly complete series that have survived the passage of time. The first is in Rome, in the Biblioteca Nazionale Centrale, in the collection donated by the Istituto Italiano per l'Africa e l'Oriente. The second is in Stockholm, in the Ivan Aguéli collection of the Swedish national archives.

5 The exact number of articles truly written by Ivan Aguéli is difficult to pin down: many texts appear in Italian (30 texts), in Arabic (5 texts), or Turkish (1 text) under the signature Abdul Hadi, Abdul Hadi al Maghrabi, Habdu Hadi, Abdul-Hadi-Al-Maghrabi, Abdel Hadi El Maghrabi, Abdul Hadi Agueli, or in Arabic, 'Abd al-Hādī, 'Abd al-Hādī al-Maghrabi, 'Abd al-Hādī 'Aqīlī. But to this already large body of works should be added an approximately equivalent number of unsigned texts, or texts attributed to the pseudonyms "Dante," "Il Convito," "I Musulmani di redazione," in both Italian and Arabic. To be exhaustive, let us note that periodicals from the year 1907 also include the publication of two translations—texts by al-Qāsim b. Salāh al-Din al-Khāni and Ibn 'Arabi—which are no doubt attributable to Aguéli.

6 As indicated by its Italian subtitle as of the second issue: *Periodico ebdomadario italo-islamico.*

7 Dante, *Il Convivio*, I, i, 7: "Oh beati quelli pochi che seggiono a quella mensa dove lo pane delli angeli si manuca!" ("Oh joyous are the chosen few seated at this table who eat the bread of angels!").

8 This *sura* contains the 120 verses of the story of the table spread given by God to 'Isā (Jesus).

9 While the first twenty-nine issues were regularly numbered (from no. 1 to no. 29), the numbering of these three issues is different (year 3, from no. 1 to no. 3).

10 The numbering changes again: the four issues are marked "year 4," and carry the indication no. 1, no. 2, no. 3–4 and no. 5–8.

11 The 1910 issue (year 6, no. 9, April 1910) seems to have been an isolated attempt to bring back the journal. Aguéli's signature had disappeared and the issue is almost an entire reprint, in the Arabic, of the final issue of 1907. The 1912 issue, presented as a supplement ("Supplemento al numero del Gennaio—Febbraio 1912"), only contains texts in Arabic related to the war in Libya, occupying a separate place in the periodical's history.

12 This is the expression found on the first page, near the title, on each copy of *Il Convito/Al-Nadi*.

13 Giolitti was prime minister from November 3, 1903–March 12, 1905, then from May 29, 1906–December 11, 1909, and May 30, 1911–March 21, 1914, in addition to also serving as interior minister.

14 Daniel J. Grange, *L'Italie et la Méditerranée (1896–1911). Les fondements d'une politique étrangère* (Rome: École Française de Rome, 1994), 1473.

15 Foreign Affairs Ministry Archives (ASMAE), 179/4-3: for a presentation of the document, see Anna Baldinetti, *Orientalismo e colonialismo. La ricerca di consenso in Egitto per l'impresa di Libia* (Rome: Pubblicazioni dell'Istituto per l'Oriente Carlo Alfonso Nallino, 1997), 35–7.

16   ASMAE, AE 120/4.

17   Issue 10, Editorial, "Cose nuove," August 14, 1904, also lambasts the "fanatical consuls who do not content themselves with rejecting our journal, but who try to destroy its effects." An article in Arabic in issue 13 (September 4, 1904), relaunches the debate on the lack of support by the Libyan consulate.

18   Eileen Ryan, *Religion as Resistance: Negotiating Authority in Italian Libya* (New York: Oxford University Press, 2018), 38–48.

19   Grange, *L'Italie et la Méditerranée*, 1476.

20   Ibid., 1481–5.

21   Anne K. Bang, *The Idrisi State in Asir: Politics, Religion and Prestige in Arabia* (Bergen: Bergen Studies on the Middle East & Africa, 1997).

22   In the photograph, Sharif Sharaf is simply identified as a representative of the Sharif Husayn. However, Sharif Sharaf ʿAbd al-Muhsin al-Barakati was later appointed Husayn's agent in Cairo, and there can hardly have been two Sharif Sharaf's in Husayn's service. Eliezer Tauber, *The Arab Movements in World War I* (London: Frank Cass, 1993), 163–4.

23   The provenance of this other photograph is unknown.

24   Ryan, *Religion as Resistance*, 39–40.

25   Undated letter, cited in Carlo Gotti Porcinari, *Rapporti italo-arabi (1902–1930): dai documenti di Enrico Insabato* (Rome: E.S.P., 1965), 17–18.

26   Technically, ʿAlawi became honorary dragoman, but in practice his functions were taken over by an Italian diplomat. Grange, *L'Italie et la Méditerranée*, 1497.

27   Ryan, *Religion as Resistance*, 43.

28   Ibid., 51.

29   *Il Convito/al-Nadi*, respectively no. 9 (August 7, 1904), 4; no. 19 (November 20, 1904), 3; no. 26 (April 15, 1905), 3.

30   *Il Convito,* no. 17 (October 16, 1904), 4, and no. 18 (October 30, 1904), 4.

31   *Il Convito*, no. 20 (December 11, 1904), 1.

32   *Il Convito*, no. 15 (September 25, 1904), 1; no. 17 (October 16, 1904), 1; no. 24 (February 26, 1905), 1.

33   *Il Convito*, no. 17 (October 16, 1904), 1.

34   *Il Convito*, no. 18 (October 30, 1904), 1.

35   *Il Convito*, no. 24 (February 26, 1905), 1.

36   On this subject, see namely Romolo Garbati, *Mon Aventure dans l'Afrique civilisée* (Alexandria: Éditions du Commerce, 1933), 198, which refers to a "panoramic dictionary" inspired by "the new theories of Alfredo Trombetti on the monogenesis of languages."

37   Abdul Hadi el-Maghrabi, "Orientalismo," *Il Convito*, no. 25 (March 26, 1905): 2.

38   See for example, *Il Convito*, no. 9 (August 7, 1904), 4; no 11 (August 21, 1904), 4; no. 15 (September 25, 1905), 4.

39   *Il Convito*, no. 7 (July 17, 1904), 1; no. 8 (July 31, 1904), 1; no. 10 (August 14, 1904), 1; no. 11 (August 21, 1904), 1.

40   *Il Convito*, year 3, no. 1 (May 20, 1906), 3, and no. 29 (June 25, 1905), 1.

41   Abdul Hadi El Maghrabi, "Il sacrificio nell'umanità. Sua evoluzione nelle diverse religioni," *Il Convito*, no. 21 (January 1, 1905): 1.

42   "Letteratura straniera," *Il Convito*, year 4, no. 2 (June 1907): 65.

43   "Fra libri e riviste," *Il Convito*, no. 23 (February 5, 1905), 3. See C. Grolleau, *Reliquiae* (Paris: Carrington, 1904).

44   Gauffin, *Ivan Aguéli*, vol. 1, 156–78.

45 Dupré frequented neo-spiritualist circles in France and spent time in Egypt during the same years as Aguéli; they were quite close in Cairo, even living together. Dupré never contributed to *Il Convito*, but in an interview at the end of his life, he confided about Aguéli: "I knew him very well for twelve years—of which the first three were intimate. During that period, we even lived together in Gizeh." Account collected by Patrice Genty, cited in Mahdî Brecq, "Nouveaux éclairages sur Ivan Aguéli," *Cahiers de l'Unité* 8, October 2017.

46 *Il Convito*, year 4, no. 2 (June 1907): 62–4. The article signed "Il Convito" is almost certainly by Aguéli.

47 "Gli italiani all'estero e il congresso di Roma," *Il Convito*, year 4, no. 5–8 (September–December 1907): 158–66.

48 Garbati, *Mon Aventure dans l'Afrique civilisée*. We have recently republished this work, the title of which must of course be read ironically (Alexandria: CEAlex, 2019). There are some clues about the tumultuous life of the author in the biographical note accompanying the text. All page numbers of the quotes which follow, refer first to the original and then to the new edition.

49 Garbati, *Mon Aventure*, 153–5 (ed. 1933), 144–5 (ed. 2019).

50 Ibid., 192 and 197–9 (ed. 1933), 174 and 178–9 (ed. 2019).

51 Ibid., 199 (ed. 1933), 179 (ed. 2019).

52 Michel Vâlsan (*L'Islam et la fonction de René Guénon*, Paris: Éditions de l'Œuvre, 1984) quotes a letter addressed to him by René Guénon, in which the French intellectual pays homage to ʿAbd al-Rahman ʿIllaysh and clarifies his role: "Shaykh Elîsh was the Shaykh of a Shâdhilite branch, and at the same time in the exoteric order he was chief of the Maliki *madhhab* at al-Azhar." In 1931, René Guénon dedicates to the memory of ʿAbd al-Rahman ʿIllaysh his *Symbolisme de la Croix* in these terms: "To the venerated memory of Shaykh Abder-Rahman Elîsh El-Kebir, El-Alim, El-Malki El-Maghribi to whom is due the first idea of this book."

53 See Abdul Hadi Aguéli, "La moschea 'Umberto,'" in *Il Convito*, year 4, no. 3–4 (July–August 1907), 103–11. Abd al-Rahman ʿIllaysh is presented by Aguéli as "one of the most famous men of Islam, son of the restorer of the Maliki rite and himself profound scholar, respected by all, from the humblest to princes and sultans." See also the synthesis on the matter presented by Anna Baldinetti (*Orientalismo e colonialismo. La ricerca di consenso in Egitto per l'impresa di Libia*, 42–3).

54 *Il Convito*, year 4, no. 2 (June 1907): 59–60.

55 *Il Convito*, year 4, no. 5–6 (September–December 1907): 154–7.

56 See "La schiavitù e l'Islam," *Il Convito*, no. 23 (February 5, 1905): 1 (Italian text) and no. 24 (February 26, 1905), 6 (Arabic text).

57 See the comments on "l'ottimo *Arafate*" (the excellent *Arafate*) in *Il Convito*, no. 7 (July 17, 1904): 4, and no. 18 (October 30, 1904): 4. Rashid Rida, who was close to Mahmud Salim, also mentioned *Arafate* in favorable terms in *al-Manar*, year 6, no. 21 (June 19, 1904): 840.

58 Presented in no. 4 (June 19, 1904) as "one of the most important reformist reviews of the Muslim world," the journal *al-Manâr* is then called into question for its dogmatism and narrow views. See, for example, the attacks on Rashid Rida, "I calvinisti dell'Islam," in *Il Convito*, year 4, no. 3–4 (July–August 1907): 110, and *Il Convito*, year 4, no. 5–8 (September–December 1907): 208.

59 *Il Convito*, year 4, no. 5–8 (September–December 1907), 196.

60 See Michael Ezekiel Gasper, *The Power of Representation. Publics, Peasants, and Islam in Egypt* (Stanford, CA: Stanford University Press, 2009), 181.

61 Muhamad Farid Wagdy, "L'Islam religione universale," *Il Convito*, year 4, no. 2 (June 1907): 40–8.

62 Enrico Insabato exposes his ideas in two articles published in 1905, under the title "Gli Snussia:" this presents the Sanusis of the Sahara, praises their spirituality, their moral rigor, their devotion. He stresses that their influence is spread over the entire Saharan zone—and even beyond—and that their very centralized religious organization is comparable to a true "nation." See E. Insabato, "Gli Snussia," *Il Convito/Al-Nadi*, no. 26 (April 15, 1905): 1, and no. 27 (May 7, 1905): 2.

63 See the three articles entitled "Panislamismo" published during the summer of 1904: *Il Convito/Al-Nadi*, no. 6 (July 10, 1904): 4, no. 7 (July 17, 1904): 4, no. 8 (July 31, 1904): 4.

64 Abdul Hadi, "La moschea 'Umberto,'" *Il Convito/Al-Nadi*, year 4, no. 3–4 (July–August 1907): 103–11. As we have said, the newspaper's position on *al-Manar* became increasingly skeptical.

65 For a historical analysis of this ideal (from the French campaign in Egypt and Syria to the Saint-Simonians), see Henry Laurens, *Le Royaume impossible. La France et la genèse du monde arabe* (Paris: Armand Colin, 1990).

66 Some sentences sound like political slogans: "To be progressive in the East, you have to start by being intelligently reactionary," "we see progress as a huge trick" (*Il Convito*, no. 1), "we are against the Europeanization of Muslim countries" (*Il Convito*, no. 19), "a truly Islamophilic policy will therefore be a reactionary policy" (*Il Convito*, no. 27).

67 Garbati, *Mon Aventure*, 174 (ed. 1933), 149–50 (ed. 2019).

68 To illustrate the very different political positioning of the two newspapers, we can cite the comments on the situation of the Muslim minorities in Russia, who occupied the news during the winter of 1904–5: while *Il Convito/Al-Nadi* defended these Russian Muslims considered as oppressed, *Ictihad* invited them to take their destiny in their own hands and to take advantage of the relative freedom which the Russian regime allowed them. See Enrico Insabato, "Nuove infamie russe," *Il Convito*, no. 16 (October 9, 1904): 1, and Abdullah Cevdet, "Rusya müsülmanları," *Ictihad*, no. 4 (March 1905): 9.

69 From terms used by Insabato in the letter cited in Porcinari, *Rapporti italo-arabi*, 17–18.

Chapter 9

1 For a comparison of the two women's conversions see Alessandra Marchi, "La conversion à la spiritualité musulmane de Leda Rafanelli et Valentine de Saint-Point," in *Valentine de Saint-Point. Des feux de l'avant-garde à l'appel de l'Orient*, edited by Paul-André Claudel and Elodie Gaden (Rennes: Presses Universitaires de Rennes, 2019), 253–64. On Leda Rafanelli's religiosity see notably Enrico Ferri, "Leda Rafanelli: un anarchismo islamico?" in *Leda Rafanelli tra letteratura e anarchia*, edited by Fiamma Chessa (Reggio Emilia: Archivio Berneri-Chessa, 2008), 151–81; Chessa, "Leda Rafanelli: un anarchismo islamico?" *Tigor: rivista di scienze della comunicazione* 4, no. 2 (July 2012): 69–87; Andrea Pakieser, *I Belong Only to Myself: The Life and Writings of Leda Rafanelli* (Oakland, CA: AK Press, 2014).

2 Mark Sedgwick updated the new research on Aguéli in his blog: *New articles on Ivan Aguéli*, https://traditionalistblog.blogspot.com/2018/01/new-articles-on-ivan-

agueli.html, Accessed January 5, 2019. See also Sorgenfrei, "The Great Aesthetic Inspiration. On Ivan Aguéli's Reading of Swedenborg," *Religion and the Arts* 23 (2019): 1–25.

3   I had access to the original collection of *Il Convito* in Rome at the library of the Istituto Italiano per l'Africa e l'Oriente (IsIAO), which was unfortunately closed in 2012. The collection has been transferred to the National Library, where it is finally available to the public since 2019 with the collection of African and Oriental documents of the Biblioteca IsIAO.

4   In his book, Garbati described Aguéli while reading the drafts for *Il Convito* and wrote that Aguéli met Insabato for the first time in Bologna, then later in Paris and finally in Egypt, where they all met through Insabato. Romolo Garbati's book has been recently re-published by Paul-André Claudel, see *Mon aventure dans l'Afriquecivilisée* (Alexandria: Editions du Centre d'Etudes Alexandrines, 2018), 145, 179. Also Insabato has been sometimes described as a "fellow-convert" (as in the Agueli's Museum website, http://aguelimuseet.se/om-agueli/?lang=en), but there is no information available about his conversion.

5   Cited by Ivan Aguéli, "Il sacrificio dell'umanità," *Il Convito*, no. 21 (January 1, 1905).

6   There is some other minor information on the artistic, anarchist, cultural and esoteric milieu in which Aguéli immersed himself. The Alexandrian magazine *L'Atelier* dedicated an article to Emile Bernard, whom Aguéli met in Paris and later again in Cairo, where he and his Finnish friend, the painter Werner von Hausen, moved to a house in front of Bernard's, joining the group of painters close to him. Bernard's description of Cairo is quoted in the article: "Paris is good for analytic studies, but here you can find the synthesis!" See Jean Jacques Luthi, "Sur les pas d'Emile Bernard en Egypte (1893–1904)," *Bulletin de l'Atelier d'Alexandrie. Le Cinquatenaire (1934–1984)*, 6 (1985): 85–8.

7   Mark Sedgwick, *Western Sufism. From the Abbasids to the New Age* (New York: Oxford University Press, 2017), 150.

8   Sedgwick, *Western Sufism*; Jamal Malik and John Hinnels, eds., *Sufism in the West* (New York: Routledge, 2006).

9   Ilham Khuri-Makdisi, *The Eastern Mediterranean and the Making of Global Radicalism, 1860–1914* (Berkeley: University of California Press, 2010), 1.

10   Anthony Fiscella, *Varieties of Islamic Anarchism: A Brief Introduction* (NP: Alpine Anarchist Production, 2014), 6. See also Laura Galián Hernández, and Costantino Paonessa, "Caught between Internationalism, Transnationalism and Immigration: A Brief Account of the History of Anarchism in Egypt until 1945," *Anarchist Studies* 26, no. 1 (2017): 29–54.

11   Fiscella, *Varieties of Islamic Anarchism*, 3. The example of Isabelle Eberhardt is also relevant.

12   There is no evidence about Leda Rafanelli's conversion to Sufism specifically. See Marchi, "La conversion à la spiritualità musulmane"; Andrea Pakieser, *I Belong Only to Myself: The Life and Writings of Leda Rafanelli* (Oakland, CA: AK Press, 2014); Ferri, *Leda Rafanelli: un anarchismo islamico?*

13   In his introduction to Leda Rafanelli's book *Una donna e Mussolini* (Milan: Rizzoli, 1946), the historian Pier Carlo Masini interpreted her indifference to economic and practical daily problems and to her future, and her non-dogmatic religiosity, as signs of the relation between her anarchism and Muslim faith. See Masini, "Introduction," in *Una donna e Mussolini*, by Leda Rafanelli (Milan: Rizzoli, 1975), 9.

14   Fiscella, *Varieties of Islamic Anarchism*, 5.

15 See Barbara Ballardin, *Valentine de Saint-Point* (Milan: Selene 2007); Marchi, "La conversion à la spiritualité musulmane," *Le Phoenix. Revue de la Renaissance orientale*, no. 1, 1926.

16 See Henri Viltard, "Saggio storico sulla caricatura. Henri Viltard, Abdul-'l-Karim Jossot: polemiche di un rinnegato in Tunisia," *Institut des belles lettres arabes 71*, no. 201 (2008), reproduced at http://letteraturagrafica.over-blog.com/article-saggio-storico-sulla-caricatura-henri-viltard-abdul-l-karim-jossot-polemiques-d-un-renegat-en-tunisi-52456431.html, Accessed January 10, 2019. See also Henri Viltard, "Gustave Henri Jossot. 1866–1951. Biography," http://gustave.jossot.free.fr/bioanglais1.html, Accessed January 10, 2019.

17 Marchi, "La conversion à la spiritualité musulmane," 262.

18 Among her publications: *Abbasso la guerra!* (Milan: Società Editrice Sociale, 1915); *L'Oasi. Romanzo arabo*, published under the name of Etienne Gamalier in 1929 (Milan: Casa Editrice Monanni) and recently re-published by Milva Maria Capellini (Reggio Emilia: Corsiero Editore, 2017); *Una donna e Mussolini*; *Memorie di una chiromante* (Cuneo: Nerosubianco, 2010), ed. Milva Maria Capellini (Reggio Emilia: Corsiero Editore, 2017).

19 Alessandra Marchi, "La presse italophone d'Egypte. Un long siècle d'histoire," in *Presses allophones de Méditerranée*, edited by Jean-Yves Empereur and Marie Delphine Martellière (Alexandria: Etudes Alexandrines, 2017), 179–88.

20 Alessandra Marchi, "Italian Pro-Islamic Politics in the Writings of Enrico Insabato: Between Libya and Egypt," in *Images of Colonialism and Decolonisation in the Italian Media*, edited by Paolo Farnetti Bertella and Cecilia Dau Novelli (Newcastle upon Tyne: Cambridge Scholars Publishing, 2017), 132–48.

21 Habdul Hadi El Maghrabi, "Perché sono disprezzati i mussulmani. Non bisogna confondere l'Islam con i Mussulmani," *Il Convito*, no. 7 (July 17, 1904).

22 Sedgwick, *Western Sufism*, 154.

23 Abdul Hadi el-Maghrabi, "Perché sono disprezzati i mussulmani," *Il Convito*, no. 7 (July 17, 1905): 1.

24 Ibid.

25 Ibid.

26 *Il Convito* declared its opposition to forced assimilation, because it did not recognize the existence of "inferior races," but nonetheless did not want a policy of isolation. This is what they called pro-Islamic politics: "simple, not adventurous, morally helpful for Easterners and materially helpful for Italy." This article is signed by the pseudonym Dante, "Ai socialisti," in *Il Convito*, no. 12 (1904).

27 Enrico Insabato's presentation of the periodical to the readers, "Ai lettori," *Il Convito*, no. 1 (May 22, 1904).

28 Abdul Hadi El Maghrabi, "I nemici dell'Islam," *Il Convito*, no. 9 (July 31, 1904): 1.

29 "Miscellanea," *Il Convito*, II series, no. 1 (May 1907): 28–9. Exclamation marks are in the original text, where the verb "imagined" is in bold. In the same issue, in the article "Necessità e base di una politica filo islamica," Insabato wrote that "it is necessary to create a group of men: politicians, intellectuals, artists and scientists, who study the issue in its multiple aspects [the spread of Italy's good image among Muslim people] and serve as a spur for the government," 27.

30 Enrico Insabato and Abdul Hadi El Maghrabi, "Ai lettori," *Il Convito*, no. 19 (November 20, 1904): 1.

31 The word "alliance" is mentioned in several articles, like: Dante, "Il dovere del governo," in *Il Convito*, no. 6 (July 10, 1904): 1; Enrico Insabato and Abdul Hadi El Maghrabi, "Ai lettori," in *Il Convito*, no. 19 (November 20, 1904).

32   Aguéli wrote about "the great aesthetic inspiration," i.e., the spirit and soul of all religions. Sorgenfrei, "Great Aesthetic Inspiration," 14.

33   Enrico Insabato and Abdel Hadi El Maghrabi, "Ai lettori," in *Il Convito*, no. 19 (1904): 2.

34   Ibid.

35   Ibid.

36   Ibid.

37   Enrico Insabato, "Ai lettori," *Il Convito*, no. 1 (May 22, 1904).

38   "I grandi iniziati musulmani" (followed by Aguéli's translation of some pages of the *Futuhhat* on the concept of beauty and a letter addressed to the *Convito*'s director), in *Il Convito*, no. 1 (May 1907, II series), 19–25.

39   It is said about four parts divided into eight volumes for about 3,000 pages. The original transliteration in *Il Convito* is *Futuhat al Mecchiya*.

40   In the article "Civiltà araba o civiltà mussulmana?" Aguéli discussed the right definition of and distinction between the Muslim/Islamic civilization and the Arab civilization (which needs the plural form because of the existence of different Arab cultures, he said) and insisted on the exotic character of each civilization in addition to its metaphysics. He also discussed the way in which a civilization is a product of alchemy, a complementary and harmonious reunion of hostile and irreconcilable opposites. In *Il Convito*, no. 19 (1904): 2.

41   In his letter to Insabato, Aguéli specified that Ibn 'Arabi never fell into the Persians' "intellectualism and preciousness," as he was totally Arab in this sense, as his "beauty consisted in the art of limiting himself and the sudden silence." See *Il Convito*, no. 1 (1907): 25.

42   "Miscellanea," *Il Convito*, no. 2 (May1907): 130–1.

43   Ibid. The editors added that the board of directors of this Akbarian society had promised them more details about the program and the organization that they would publish in a future issue of the periodical. To my knowledge, no other information about it yet exists, so we can only make hypotheses about its creation and existence.

44   Abdul Hadi El Maghrabi, "I nemici dell'Islam."

45   Abdul Hadi, "La moschea 'Umberto,'" *Il Convito*, no. 3–4 (July–August 1907): 110. In this issue again, Italy is described as the most religious, hospitable and universal, and the least fanatic and exclusivist among the other nations visited by the Sanusi shaykh. Due to the very warm relations with the king and his "spiritual son," Muhammad 'Ali 'Alawi, venerated by Muslims, he could confirm the Italian engagement in "favor of Islam and Muslims" (in Banaadir, Somalia, and in Eritrea too). Since Italians were supposed to build mosques for Muslims, Shaykh 'Illaysh decided to build one in their name, it is said. See Abudl Hadi Aguéli, "La moschea 'Umberto,'" in *Il Convito*, no. 3–4 (July–August 1907) [Binding 1907–10, IV], 103–11. The article continued in *Il Convito*, no. 7–8 (1907), as a synthesis of the Arabic article written by Shaykh Muhammad al-Sharbatli in response to those Muslims who contested the legitimacy of that mosque. The mosque was built and then funded by the Italian government for several years, probably until 1917. Anna Baldinetti, *Orientalismo e colonialismo. La ricerca di consenso in Egitto per l'impresa di Libia* (Rome: Ist. per l'Oriente "C. A. Nallino," 1997), 43–4.

46   Aguéli, "La moschea 'Umberto.'"

47   Enrico Insabato, "Gli Snussia", *Il Convito*, no. 26 (15 April 1905).

48   Abdul Hadi el Maghrabi, "Le crociate moderne," *Il Convito*, no. 2 (June 10, 1906): 1–2. The Italian colonization of Eastern Africa started in Ethiopia, ancient Abyssinia,

and led to the Italo-Abyssinian war between 1895 and 1896. In this article, Aguéli surprisingly spoke about the "recognition" of natives' rights "since the war in Abyssinia and before the defeats"; he was maybe convinced of the myth of Italians' good colonizing mission.

49   Abdul Hadi el Maghrabi, "Le crociate moderne," *Il Convito*, no. 2 (1906): 1. It is not clear which periodicals were referred to.

50   Ibid.

51   Ibid.

52   Abdul Hadi el Maghrabi, "Le crociate moderne," *Il Convito*, no. 2 (1906): 2.They proposed in the same article to organize a big "Euro-Islamic" or "Italian-Islamic" conference to promote and build a future of mutual peace, progress, and civilization.

53   Aguéli wrote about the Islamic reformist and modernist movement, spread during the nineteenth century by shaykhs such as Muhammad ʿAbduh, Al Afghani and Rida, already mentioned, in response to the question of the compatibility between Islam and Modernity.

54   Abdul Hadi el Maghrabi, "Il sacrificio dell'umanità," *Il Convito*, no. 21 (January 1, 1905): 1.

55   Abdul Hadi el Maghrabi, "Note sull'islam" (section *VIII. L'accordo sociale con i musulmani*), *Il Convito*, no. 2 (June 1907): 39–40.

56   Abdul Hadi el Maghrabi, "Note sull'islam," *Il Convito*, no. 1 (May 1907): 3.

57   See Marcel Gauchet, *Le désenchantement du monde. Une histoire politique de la religion* (Paris: Gallimard, 1985); Mark Sedgwick, *Against the Modern World. Traditionalism and the Secret Intellectual History of the Twentieth Century* (New York: Oxford University Press, 2004); Mercedes Garcìa-Arenal, ed., *Islamic Conversions. Religious Identities in Mediterranean Islam* (Paris: Maisonneuve & Larose, 2001).

58   P. Laude, *Pathways to an Inner Islam. Massignon, Corbin, Guenon, and Schuon* (Albany: SUNY Press, 2010), 3.

59   Thierry Zarcone, "Rereadings and Transformations of Sufism in the West," *Diogènes* 47, no. 187 (1999): 117.

60   Laude, *Pathways to an Inner Islam*, 5, 8.

61   Antonio Gramsci mainly referred to the consciousness of being part of a social class as a fundamental step to change the hegemonic relationship with power, but his ideas continue to stimulate new thought on various subjects. See the *Selections from the Prison Notebooks*, ed. and trans. Quintin Hoare and Geoffrey Nowell Smith (London: Lawrence and Wishart, 1971).

62   "Miscellanea," *Il Convito*, no. 1 (May 1907): 30. Readers could be varied due to the two languages used, as the articles in Italian and in Arabic did not always coincide. The comparison between the two versions would certainly add new insights to our research.

63   The anarchist Enrico Pea described Alexandria in his autobiography with many examples of the worker and poor people. In "Prefazione," in, *Vita in Egitto* edited by Enrico Pea (Florence Ponte alle Grazie, 1995), xiv.

64   Abdul Hadi el Maghrabi, "Civiltà araba o mussulmana?" *Il Convito*, no. 19 (1904): 2.

65   There is another issue of *Il Convito*, published on January–February 1912, now "Rivista Italo-Araba," with an article by Insabato addressed to the people of Tripolitania, Cyrenaica, Fezzan, and nearby regions, about the "agreement with Italy," and two letters by Shaykh Muhammad al-Idrisi from Asir and by Imam Yahia from Yemen. Except for the summary, the entire issue is written in Arabic.

66   The articles concern mainly Italian politics (Italian Somalia and Benadir; Italian expansion through the East; Catholics' defeat in the East and the separation of schools from the State, notably in France).

67 In reality, rough Italian attempts at colonial occupation were usually called "ragged imperialism" (*imperialism straccione*). See Patrizio di Massimo, "Orientalismo italiano," April 25, 2017, http://www.flashartonline.it/article/orientalismo-italiano/, Accessed January 10, 2019. On Italian colonialism, see also *Le guerre coloniali del fascismo*, edited by Angelo Del Boca (Rome: Laterza, 1991).

68 Marchi, "*Italian Pro-Islamic* Politics in the Writings of Enrico Insabato," 145–7; Enrico Insabato, *Gli Abaditi del Gebel Nefusa e la politica islamica in Tripolitania* (Rome: Tipografia dell'Unione Editrice, 1918).

69 He then published *L'islâm vivente nel nuovo ordine mondiale* (Rome: L'Espansione imperiale, 1941) and *La collaborazione italo-araba e il Sudan. Indipendenza per la Libia, lavoro per l'Italia, ricchezza per la comunità mediterranea* (Rome: Danesi-Centro Mediterraneo, 1950). See also http://www.bfscollezionidigitali.org/entita/13221-insabato-enrico/, Accessed July 20, 2019.

70 Carlo Gotti Porcinari, *Rapporti italo-arabi (1902–1930). Dai documenti di Enrico Insabato* (Rome: E.S.P., 1965); Baldinetti. *Orientalismo e colonialismo*; Eileen Ryan, *Religion as Resistance: Negotiating Authority in Italian Libya* (Oxford: Oxford University Press, 2018). See also Vittorio Ianari, *La politica islamica dell'Italia durante la Triplice Alleanza. L'attività di Enrico Insabato*, ed. Stefano Trinchese. *Mare Nostrum. Percezione ottomana e mito mediterraneo in Italia all'alba del '900* (Milan: Guerini, 2005), 199–246.

Chapter 10

1 Ivan Aguéli to Werner von Hausen, May 5, 1894, 777:1, Series IA3, Box 4:1, Archives of the National Museum, Stockholm.
2 Aguéli to von Hausen, May 13, 1894.
3 Ibid.
4 Aguéli to von Hausen, April 24, 1894.
5 Ibid.
6 Ibid.
7 Ivan Aguéli to Marie Huot, 1903, 777:1, Series IA4, Box 3:4, Archives of the National Museum, Stockholm.
8 Ibn ʿArabi was also known as *al-shaykh al-akbar* (the greatest master). The school developed later by his followers was therefore known as al-akbariyya.
9 Many biographies and studies were dedicated to the life of ʿAbd al-Qadir, I will name here some of those written by people who personally knew the emir: *Tuhfat al-zāir fī akhbār al-amīr ʿAbd al-Qādir* (Alexandria: Gharzūzi wa Jawīsh, 1903) by his son Ahmad Pasha al-Jazāiri; the biography of the emir written by his student Abd al-Razzāq al-Bītār in his *Holiat al-bashar fī tārīkh al-qarn al-thālath ʿashar* (Beirut: Dar al-Sāder, 1993); the biography of ʿAbd al-Qadir given by Abd al-Majīd al-Khānī in his *al-Hadāiq al-wardiyya fī haqāiq Ajella al-naqshabandiyya* (Arbil: Dar Āras, 2002); *The Life of Abdel Kader* (London: Chapman and Hall, 1867) of Charles Henry Churchill. In recent scholarship, the most detailed biographies and studies of Emir ʿAbd al-Qadir are: Ahmed Bouyerdene, *Emir Abd el-Kader, Hero and Saint of islam* (Bloomington: World Wisdom Books, 2013); Bruno Etienne, *Abdel kader, isthme des isthmes* (Paris: Hachette, 1994). John W. Kiser, *Commander*

of the Faithful: The Life and Times of Emir Abd el-Kader (New York: Monkfish Book Publishing, 2008); Elsa Marston, *The Compassionate Warrior: Abd el-Kader of Algeria* (Bloomington: World Wisdom Books, 2013); Ahmed Bouyerdene, Éric Geoffroy, and Setty G. Simon-Khedis, *Abd el-Kader, Un spirituel dans la modernité* (Paris: Presses de l'Ifpo, 2010).

10 Jacques Suchet was born in 1795 in Villefranche-sur-Saône where he lived before volunteering as a missionary in a newly conquered Algeria. Suchet stayed in Constantine until his death and most of the chronicles that mention him describe him as a man with a mission who had a deep interest in getting in contact with local populations. For more details about the life of abbé Suchet see the biography prepared by Paul Fournier in the special issue of the journal *Rencontres, Semaine religieuse d'Alger,* July–August 2002.

11 Jacques Suchet, *Lettres édifiantes et curieuses sur l'Algérie* (Tours: Ad Mame et Cie, 1840), 405–9.

12 Suchet, *Lettres édifiantes,* 410.

13 Ibid.

14 Among of the most telling texts in that regard we can mention Suchet, *Lettres édifiantes,* Antoine-Adolphe Dupuch, *Abd el-Kader au château d'Amboise* (Bordeaux: H. Faye, 1849), and the testimonies of French prisoners released by 'Abd el-Qadir during the war and collected in *Les Prisonniers d'Abd el-Kader ou Cinq mois de captivité chez les Arabes* (Paris: Desesart, 1837).

15 Gustave Dugat, trans., *Rappel à l'intelligent, Avis à l'indifférent* (Paris: Benjamin Duprat, Librairie de l'institut, 1858), 104.

16 Ibid., 29.

17 Ibid., 105.

18 Ibid., 106.

19 Ibid., 138.

20 Reynold A. Nicholson, *Tarjuman al-ashwaq* (London: Royal Asiatic Society, 1911), 67.

21 *Meccan Revelations*, vol. 3, 132. Cited in Itzchak Weismann, *Taste of Modernity: Sufism, Salafiyya, and Arabism in Late Ottoman Damascus* (Leiden: Brill, 2001).

22 In his letter to the Freemasonic lodge Henri IV of February 1864 the emir states: "What excellency could surpass that of the Love for mankind? If this love did not find a place in me, would I still have a sincere religion? God forbid! Indeed, love is the foundation of religion, God is the lord of all and loves us all."

23 Al-Nabulusi elaborated scholarly responses against the Ulama who attacked Ibn 'Arabi's belief that non-Muslims could go to heaven. Shaykh al-Nabulusi used classical texts of Hanafi jurisprudence to support his defense of Ibn 'Arabi. He argued that even Sunni orthodoxy made a difference between *wa'd* (promise of heaven made by God to Muslims) and *wa'id* (threat of hell addressed to non-Muslims) and that while God has to honor his *wa'd*, he does not necessarily have to put his threat into execution. God, in a paternal way. will withdraw his threat out of divine generosity. In 1692, the Damascene scholar wrote a book he entitled *al-Radd 'ala man takallam 'an Ibn al-'Arabi* twenty years after writing a shorter treatise with the evocative title *Hadha kitab al-radd al-matin 'ala muntaqis al-'arif Muhyi al-Din.*

24 'Abd al-Majīd al-Khānī, *Al-Hadāiq al-wardiyya fī haqāiq ajeilla' al-naqshabandiyya* ([Kurdistan, Iraq]: Dar Tarras, 2002), 378.

25 Michel Chodkiewicz, "The Diffusion of Ibn ʿArabi's Doctrine," *The Journal of the Muhyiddin Ibn ʿArabi Society* 9 (1991). In his article, Chodkiewicz reports having examined numerous Near Eastern and Maghribi *silsila* and found that the name of ʿAbd al-Qadir appeared in most of them. For him, this was a proof of the "wholly central importance in the propagation of the akbarian heritage since the end of the nineteenth century."

26 Michel Chodkiewicz, *The Spiritual Writings of Amir ʿAbd al-Kader* (New York: State University of New York Press, 1995), 24.

27 ʿAbd al-Qadir al-Jazaʾiri, *Kitab al-mawaqif fi al-waʿdh wa al-irshād* (Cairo, 1911). *Mawqif* 246. vol. 1, 496.

28 Chodkiewicz, *Spiritual Writings of Amir ʿAbd al-Kader*, 128.

29 ʿAbd al-Qadir, *Kitab al-mawaqif. Mawqif* 364, 68–9.

30 Marie D'Aire: born Boissonnet, niece of Baron Laurent Estève Boissonnet (1811–1901) who was the commander of the army detachment that was responsible for the protection of the emir during his detention in Pau and Amboise. He later became a close friend of the emir. Marie gathered and edited a collection of letters, testimonials, notes, and other documents about Emir ʿAbd al-Qadir.

31 Marie D'Aire, *ʿAbd al-Qadir, Quelques documents nouveaux lus et approuvés par l'officier en mission auprés de l'émir* (Amiens: Imprimerie Yvert & Tellier, 1900), 247.

32 Muhammad al-Hafnāwi, *Taʾrif al-khalaf bi rijāl al-salaf* (Algiers: Imprimerie Pierre Fontana, 1906), 312.

33 In a letter to Marie Huot from 1907 (Series IA4, Box 3:4, Archives of the National Museum, Stockholm) Ivan Aguéli mentions that 'Illaysh was sentenced to death along with his father who died before the execution. In his article "L'Islam et la fonction de René Guénon" (*Etudes Traditionnelles* 305, January–February 1953), Michel Vâlsan quotes an article from *Al Convito* where Aguéli states that "the two shaykhs 'Illaysh, father and son, were thrown in prison and condemned to death. The father died in prison, the son was pardoned and exiled." In her richly documented book *Islamic Reform and Conservatism: Al-Azhar and the Evolution of Modern Sunni Islam* (London: I.B. Tauris, 2014), Indira Falk Gesink does not mention the possible imprisonment of Abd-al-Rahman with his father. The nationalist uprising that was led by the Colonel Ahmed Urabi aimed at ending Western interference in Egyptian affairs and deposing the Khedive Tewfik Pasha. It lasted between 1879 and 1882 and ended with the British invasion of the country. In the aftermath of the invasion, a large wave of reprisals against the supporters of Urabi took place. Many scholars and shaykhs were imprisoned, killed, or exiled.

34 In the 1844 treaty of Tangiers, the Moroccan kingdom officially recognized French sovereignty over Algeria. After fighting along the troops of Emir ʿAbd al-Qadir, the Moroccan cavalry endured several serious defeats. The French army also bombarded the ports of Tangiers and Mogador. Sultan Abd al-Rahman decided to outlaw Emir ʿAbd al-Qadir and his men, expelled them and settled with the French a final agreement on the Moroccan-Algerian borders.

35 "Praise be to Allah, Lord of the worlds and may prayers and peace be upon our prophet Muhammad and his guided companions, yes the mentioned Sultan—may God repair his state—is forbidden (*harām*) to do the things you mentioned he did. Its prohibition is a known fact, and no one will doubt it among those who have a grain of faith in their hearts. And we never expected that our master Sultan Abd al-Rahman—may God guide him to success—will commit such acts with someone like you, especially that you are now a bridge between him and his enemies."

36 "Husām Al-Dīn Li-Qat' Shubah al-Murtaddīn," n.d., https://www.alukah.net/manu/
    files/manuscript_6208/makhtotah.pdf. This is the document that was mentioned
    by Michel Chodkiewicz in *Spiritual Writings of Amir Abd al-Kader*, 196. The writer
    mentioned that this manuscript was then not available to him to read, and that it
    comprised an exchange between ʿAbd al-Qadir and ʿAbd al-Rahman. The truth is
    that it was his father to whom ʿAbd al-Qadir was answering.

37 In his *Emir Abd el-Kader, Hero and Saint of Islam* (Bloomington, IN: World Wisdom
    Books, 2012), Ahmed Bouyerdene wrote: "A small nucleus would increasingly form
    around the Emir and would meet regularly in one of his residencies in the center of
    the city. The existing documents enable one to have a rather precise idea regarding
    the participants at these sessions: Let us mention those who are present most often:
    Al-Khani, Al-Baytar, At-Tantawi, At-Tayyib, ʿIllaysh." 157.

38 In the introduction to *'Abdul-Hādī, Écrits pour La Gnose* (Milan: Arché, 1988) it is
    stated that ʿIllaysh died on May 11, 1922, and that this date was found in an "Arab
    manuscript," xiv.

39 Aguéli to Huot.

40 The question of Aguéli's attachment to Shariʿa's basic premises remains debatable.
    His letters and texts suggest an obvious respect for Islamic law while at the same time
    his contemporaries such as Romolo Garbati in his book *Mon Aventure dans l'Afrique
    Civilisée* (1933; Alexandria: Editions du Centre d'Etudes Alexandrines, 2018)
    described him as a man who spent his money, whenever he had any, on ham, beer,
    and his mistress (179). In that regard, it is difficult to clearly depict the religious life
    of Aguéli in Cairo or to assess the degree of its orthodoxy.

41 Both Abd al-Rahman ʿIlaysh and Emir ʿAbd al-Qadir belonged to the Madani branch
    of the Shadhili *ṭarīqa*. ʿAbd al-Qadir was the disciple of Shaykh Muhammad Ibn
    Masʿud al-Fasi (1798–1872) who was the student of Shaykh Muhammad Hasan Ibn
    Hamza Dhafer al-Madani (died 1847). Daniel J. Grange, *L'Italie et la Méditerranée
    (1896–1911). Les fondements d'une politique étrangère* (Rome: École Française de
    Rome, 1994), 1478. ʿAbd al-Rahman ʿIlaysh received the Madani Shadhili *ṭarīqa* from
    his father who was the disciple of Muhammd Dhafer al-Madani (1829–1903).

42 'Abd al-Majīd al-Khānī, *al-Hadāiq al-wardiyya fī haqāiq ajella' al-naqshabandiyya*,
    369.

43 Aguéli to Huot.

44 Ibid.

45 Ibid.

46 Ibid.

47 Ibid.

Chapter 11

1 Aguéli's writings in *La Gnose* were later compiled and published as book collections:
   Abdul-Hâdi (John Gustav Aguéli), *Écrits pour La Gnose, comprenant la traduction
   de l'arabe du Traité de l'Unité* (Milano: Archè, 1988); *Abdul-Hâdi dans* La Gnose—
   Recueil posthume (Paris: Éditions Kalki, 2016).

2 This chapter, while relying mainly on the Arabic edition *Al-Nadi*, also refers to the
   Italian one, *Il Convito*, for two main reasons: first, some relevant essays in Italian did
   not appear in Arabic, or only in a partial way; and second, *Il Convito* served Aguéli as
   a platform for reaching out to European audiences.

3   On public intellectuals' definitions and features see Edward Shils, "The Intellectual
      and the Powers: Some Perspectives for Comparative Analysis," *Society and History* 1,
      no. 1 (October 1958): 5–22.

4   These developments were closely linked to the *Nahda* (renaissance) movement of the
      nineteenth and early twentieth centuries, in which Sufi circles were also involved,
      and sought to rejuvenate Arab-Muslim legacies by linking them to progress, and
      humanism. On the emerging of printed culture in the Middle East, see Ami Ayalon,
      The Arabic Print Revolution: Cultural Production and Mass Readership (Cambridge:
      Cambridge University Press, 2016); James L. Gelvin and Nile Green, eds., *Global
      Muslims in the Age of Steam and Print* (Berkeley: University of California Press,
      2014); Anthony Gorman and Didier Monclaud, eds., *The Press in the Middle East
      and North Africa, 1850–1950* (Edinburgh: Edinburgh University Press, 2017). On
      the *Nahda* enterprise, see, for example, Albert Hourani, *Arabic Thought in the Liberal
      Age 1798–1939*, 3rd ed. (Cambridge: Cambridge University Press, 1983 [1962]);
      Fruma Zachs and Sharon Halevi, *Gendering Culture in Greater Syria: Intellectual
      and Ideology in the Late Ottoman Empire* (London: I.B. Tauris, 2015); Tarek El-Ariss,
      ed., *The Arab Renaissance: A Bilingual Anthology of the Nahda* (New York: Modern
      Language Association, 2018).

5   On Ibn ʿArabi and his mystical thinking see Michel Chodkiewicz, *An Ocean without
      Shore: Ibn ʿArabi, The Book and the Law* (Albany: State University of New York,
      1993); and his *Seal of the Saints: Prophethood and Sainthood in the Doctrine of Ibn
      ʿArabi* (Cambridge: Cambridge University Press, 1993).

6   Most of Aguéli's essays in *Il Convito/Al-Nadi* were on religious and cultural issues.
      Only few dealt with politics and the situation in the Ottoman Empire. Thus, for
      example, he fiercely denounced the Armenian revolts against Istanbul, which he
      attributed to greed and lust. *Al-Nadi* (August 7, 1904): 2.

7   As an indication of his delicate relations with Insabato, Aguéli resented the 1911
      Italian invasion to Libya.

8   *Al-Nadi* (August 19, 1904): 1–2; also ibid., 3–4 (July–August 1907): 98.

9   Guy Stroumsa, *A New Science: The Discovery of Religion in the Age of Reason*
      (Cambridge, MA: Harvard University Press, 2010), 124–44.

10   W. Montgomery Watt, *Muhammad: Prophet and Statesman* (Oxford: Oxford
      University Press, 1961), 231–6; Bernard Lewis, *Islam in History*, new ed. (Chicago, IL:
      Open Court, 1993), 1–23; Albert Hourani, *Islam in European Thought* (Cambridge:
      Cambridge University Press, 1991), mainly 1–25; Ursula Wokoeck, *German
      Orientalism: The Study of the Middle East and Islam from 1800 to 1945* (Abingdon:
      Routledge, 2009).

11   "Jaridat al-Nadi," *Al-Nadi* (May 22, 1904): 2.

12   *Al-Majmuʿa al-ula li-jaridat al-Nadi, 1904–1905* (Cairo: n.p., 1905), 10. Also 11–14.

13   Aguéli, "L'Universalité en l'Islam," in his *Écrits pour La Gnose*, 95–6; and in *Al-Nadi*
      (November 20, 1904): 1–3 (with Enrico Insabato).

14   See, for example, the catalogue exhibition held in Stockholm, October 6, 2018–
      February 10, 2019 (https://www.thielskagalleriet.se). On the visual expressive
      dimension of literature in the East, see Edward Said, *Orientalism* (London: Penguin,
      2003), mainly chapter 5.

15   Quoted in Axel Gauffin, *Ivan Aguéli: Människan, Mystikern, Målaren* (Stockholm:
      Sveriges Allmänna Konstförening, 1940–1), vol. 2, 282.

16   Apparently, this ecumenical endeavor was also inspired by the reformist circle of
      Amir ʿAbd al-Qadir al-Jazaʾiri in Damascus, with whom ʿIllaysh, Aguéli's patron,

was in close contact following his exile to Syria by the British authorities for his role in the ʿUrabi revolt. ʿAbd al-Qadir, who adhered to Ibn ʿArabi's teachings, called for an Islamic renaissance based on rapprochement between reason and revelation and advocated the premise that all human beings are God's creatures and should be treated as equals. See Meir Hatina, *Ulama, Politics and the Public Sphere: An Egyptian Perspective* (Salt Lake City: The University of Utah Press, 2010), 80–1; David Commins, *Islamic Reform: Politics and Social Change in Late Ottoman Syria* (New York: Oxford University Press, 1990), 26–30; Itzchak Weismann, *A Taste of Modernity: Sufism, Salafiyya and Arabism in Late Ottoman Damascus* (Leiden: Brill, 2001), 193–224; and Iheb Gumermazi's chapter in this book.

17 Notably, Aguéli had no personal experience of Shiʿi Islam and did not address it in his writings.

18 *Al-Nadi* (August 2, 1904): 2; (August 14, 1904): 1–2; *Al-Majmuʿa*, 17–19, 30–2. See also Aguéli, "L'Islam et les religions anthropomorphiques," in his *Écrits pour La Gnose*, 91, 106.

19 *Al-Nadi* (July 17, 1904): 1–2; (August 28, 1904): 2; (September 3, 1904): 2; *Al-Majmuʿa*, 28, 55–7, 78–89.

20 *Al-Majmuʿa*, 81–90.

21 Aguéli, "L'Universalité en l'Islam," 86–8.

22 Ibid., 92–4, 99–101. See also Frithjof Schuon, "Outline of the Islamic Message," in *Universal Dimensions of Islam: Studies in Comparative Religion,* edited by Patrick Laude (Bloomington, IN: World Wisdom, 2011), 3–4.

23 Aguéli, "L'Universalité en l'Islam," 87–90.

24 Ibid.; *Il Convito* 4, no. 5–8 (September–December 1907): 133–5.

25 Aguéli, "L'Universalité en l'Islam," 99–101.

26 Ibid., 100. See also *Al-Nadi* (August 19, 1904): 1, where ʿAbd al-Hadi (Aguéli) accused the Buddhist monks as being sworn enemies of Islam.

27 Aguéli, "L'Universalité en l'Islam," 85.

28 Gauffin, *Ivan Aguéli*, vol. 1, 151.

29 Still, Olcott's and Balvatsky's work was quite bold and sweeping. They explicitly attacked the Buddhist practice of veneration, which Aguéli refrained from in the case of Sufism. Moreover, in reshaping traditional Buddhism they also had a clear liberal Protestant model, which in the case of Aguéli and given his anarchist lineage, cannot be verified. In fact, in a letter to a colleague in Egypt after his expulsion in 1916, he cursed Protestantism and its founder Martin Luther for their religious zealots pointing at the Sweden government's harassment of Mormons and of those who spoke in favor for freedom of religion. Peter J. Leithart, "When East Is West," *First Things* 153 (May 2005): 11–12; also René Guénon, *The Reign of Quantity and the Reign of the Times*, new ed. (New York: Sophia Perennis, 2004), 74–8.

30 ʿAbd al-Hadi (Aguéli), "Al-ittihad al-milli aw al-mujtamaʿ al-Islami," *Al-Nadi* (August 14, 1904): 1–2.

31 Ibid., 2. For a similar approach which highlighted the theme of "poverty" in Sufi-Islamic teaching (*faqr*), transcending oneself and trusting God's mercy was adopted by Frithjof Schuon in his "Outline of the Islamic Message," 4.

32 Aguéli's letter to an Egyptian colleague, National Art Museum, Stockholm; also Romolo Garbati, *Mon Aventure dans l'Afrique Civilisée*, edited by Paul-André Claudel (Alexandria: Centre d'Études Alexandrines, 2018), 178.

33 *Al-Majmuʿa*, 17.

34 *Al-Nadi* 3-4 (July–August 1907): 85–91, 93–5; Aguéli, "L'Identité suprême dans l'ésotérisme musulman (Le Traité de l'unité)," in *Écrits pour La Gnose*, 107–33; also *Al-Nadi* (June 15, 1907): 59–60.

35 *Al-Nadi* (June 15, 1907): 59–60; ibid., 9 (April 1910): 170–204.

36 *Ibn Taymiyyah Expounds on Islam*, compiled and translated by Muhammad ʿAbdul-Haqq Ansari (Riyadh: Imam Muhammad Ibn Saud University, 2000), 167–73. Indeed, *waḥdat al-wujūd* became associated with a pantheistic or monist trend in Islam. However, Annemarie Schimmel has argued that this understanding should be revised since the concept does not involve a substantial continuity between God and creation, but rather that in their actual existence the creatures are only reflections of God's attributes. Schimmel, *Mystical Dimensions of Islam* (Chapel Hill: University of North Carolina Press, 1975), 267–72; also William C. Chittick, "Waḥdat al-Wujūd in Islamic Thought," *Bulletin of the Henry Martyn Institute of Islamic Studies* 10 (1991): 7–27.

37 *Al-Nadi* (June 15, 1907): 97, 99; *Il Convito* 4, no. 3–4 (July–August 1907): 100–3; Aguéli, "L'Identité suprême dans l'ésotérisme musulman."

38 *Al-Nadi* 3-4 (July–August 1907): 93.

39 Ibid., 89–90, 93–5.

40 Ibid., 85.

41 Ibid., 86, 92. On the *dahriyya* see I. Goldziher and A. M. Goichon, "Dahriyya," *Encyclopaedia of Islam*, 2nd edition, (1991): 95–7, which also cites al-Ghazali's polemic.

42 *Il Convito* 4, no. 3–4 (July–August 1907): 48–55, 194–5.

43 Khuri-Makdisi, *The Eastern Mediterranean*; Anthony Gorman, "The Anarchist Press in Egypt before World War I," in *The Press in the Middle East*, edited by Gorman, 237–62.

44 Garbati, *Mon Aventure*, 144–5, 178–9, 249–50, 292, 303.

45 Aguéli, "L'Universalité en l'Islam," 98–9.

46 Alexandre Christoyannopoulos and Matthew S. Adams, eds., *Essays in Anarchism and Religion* (Stockholm: Stockholm University Press, 2018), vol. 2 (and introduction, 1–19).

47 Aguéli, "L'Universalité en l'Islam," 90; also Simon Sorgenfrei, "The Great Aesthetic Inspiration: On Ivan Aguéli's Reading of Swedenborg," *Religion and the Arts* 23 (2019): 4–13.

48 *Al-Nadi* (August 14, 1904): 1–2.

49 Aguéli, "L'Universalité en l'Islam," 91.

50 *Al-Nadi* (August 2, 1904): 2.

51 Aguéli, "L'Universalité en l'Islam," 99.

52 See also Guénon's own observation about the Sufi system as no different in substance from the caste system in Hindu culture. Meir Hatina, "Where East Meets West: Sufism, Cultural Rapprochement and Politics," *International Journal of Middle East Studies* 39 (August 2007): 400–1.

53 Aguéli, "El-Malâmatiyah," in his *Écrits pour La Gnose*, 65–79.

54 Seyyed Hossein Nasr, *The Heart of Islam: Enduring Values for Humanity* (New York: HarperCollins, 2002), mainly 203–36, 313–15.

55 However, as also argued by Frédéric Brusi, it is unclear if Aguéli actually participated in the Shadhili Sufi tradition, more so in Egyptian Sufism in general. Brusi, "De äro allesammans muhammedaner, men jag gör allt hvad jag kan för att följa deras seder!;

Tankar kring ett fotografiskt porträtt av Ivan Aguéli," *Aura. Tidskrift för akademiska studier av nyreligiositet* 9 (2017): 61–80.

56   Mark Sedgwick, *Against the Modern World: Traditionalism and the Secret Intellectual History of the Twentieth Century* (New York: Oxford University Press, 2004), 63–7.
57   *Al-Nadi* (August 2, 1904): 2.
58   Ibid., 2; *Al-Nadi* (August 19, 1904): 1–2; (November 20, 1904): 1–3 (with Enrico Insabato); also *Al-Majmu 'a*, 28–9.
59   Garbati, *Mon Aventure*, 179.
60   *Al-Majmu 'a*, 29–30.
61   Sorgenfrei, "The Great Aesthetic Inspiration," 11.
62   Aguéli, "L'Universalité en l'Islam," 85–7; and his "L'Islam et les religions anthropomorphiques," 106.
63   Sufism and universalism, mainly based on Ibn 'Arabi's teaching, were recurring themes in Guénon's and other adherents of the Perennial or Traditional philosophy, as discussed also in Laude, ed., *Universal Dimensions of Islam*; Isobel Jeffery-Street, *Ibn 'Arabi and Contemporary West: Beshara and the Ibn 'Arabi Society* (London: Equinox Publishing, 2012).

Chapter 12

1   Ivan Aguéli, "Femminismo," *Il Convito* 1, no. 2 (May 1904): 4. Axel Gauffin, *Ivan Aguéli: Manniska, Mystikern, Malaren* (Stockholm: Sveriges allmänna konstförening, 1940–1), vol. 2, 131.
2   In-depth study of female figures in Aguéli's life and in his paintings would form an important complement to the material treated here and remains a topic for further research.
3   Viveca Wessel, "Ivan Aguéli Malare och Sufi," in *Aguélimuseets Vanner* (Sala: Aguélimuseets Vanner, 2002), 20.
4   Aguéli himself wrote an introduction to a treatise on this topic which he translated: "El-Malāmatiyah" in *La Gnose* (1911), 100–7, reprinted in *Écrits pour La Gnose, comprenant la traduction de l'arabe du Traité de l'Unité*, ed. G. Rocca (Milan: Archè, 1988), 65–79. This selection also mentions the category of the *afrād* (unique ones), 67.
5   Sorgenfrei, "Great Aesthetic Inspiration," 3.
6   Wessel, "Ivan Aguéli," 17–24.
7   One source on Egyptian feminist writing states the following: "The term 'feminism' was first used in its official capacity in 1923 with the establishment of the Egyptian Feminist Union. With French as the dominant language of the union's members, given its upper-class affiliations, there was a dear understanding *of* the words *féministe* and *féminisme* The Arabic translation, however was and remains ambiguous. The word *nisa'i* (women) is the Arabic equivalent which must always be clarified in its 'feminist' context to be properly understood." See Margot Badran and miriam cooke, eds., *Opening the Gates* (Bloomington: Indiana University Press, 1990), xiv.
8   On the disagreement between Rashid Rida and the Manar group and the Sufi-influenced Ilsabato see Hatina, "Where East Meets West," 392–3.

9   Ivan Aguéli, "Femminismo," as a section of "Note sull'Islam," *Il Convito* 4, no. 5–8 (1907): 139.

10   Ibid., 139.

11   Ibid., 142.

12   Hatina, "Where East Meets West," Angelo Scarabel, "Una Rivista Italo-Araba D'inizio Secolo: An-Nādī (Il Convito)," *Oriente Moderno* 58, no. 1/3 (1978): 51–67.

13   Kathryn Gleadle and Zoë Thomas, "Global feminisms, *c.* 1870–1930: Vocabularies and Concepts—A Comparative Approach," *Women's History Review* 27, no. 7 (2018): 1209–24, 1210 citing Karen Offen, *European Feminisms, 1700–1950: A Political History* (Stanford, CA: Stanford University Press, 2000), 19.

14   Ibid., 394.

15   Ibid., 394.

16   Aguéli, "Femminismo" (1907): 134–42.

17   Syed Ameer Ali, *The Spirit of Islam* (London: W.H. Allen, 1891).

18   Marilyn Booth, *Classes of Ladies of Cloistered Spaces: Writing Feminist History through Biography in Fin-de-Siècle Egypt.* (Edinburgh: Edinburgh University Press, 2015), 18.

19   Guglielmo Marconi (1874–1937) achieved his most dramatic success in the late 1890s through the early 1900s and received the Nobel Prize in 1909.

20   Marie Curie (1867–1934) won the Nobel Prize for physics in 1903 jointly with her husband. She later won the prize for chemistry on her own in 1911.

21   Aguéli, "Femminismo" (1904), 4.

22   Aguéli apparently had a theory of four types of liberty, the most important being "lordly" or divine which subsumes the political, intellectual, and emotional. *La Gnose*, "Pages dédiées au Soleil (Sahaif Shamsiyah)," 63 note #32.

23   Aguéli, "Femminismo" (1904), 4.

24   Ibid.

25   Ibid.

26   Ibid.

27   Mark Sedgwick, *Against the Modern World: Traditionalism and the Secret Intellectual History of the Twentieth Century* (New York: Oxford University Press, 2004).

28   The original Italian version is *Rivolta contro il Mondo Moderno* (Milan: Hoepli, 1934).

29   Jung therefore appreciated the Catholic doctrine of the assumption of Mary (1950) as responding to a contemporary need to integrate the female principle in Christianity, but was concerned about a lack of such in Protestant Europe. C. G. Jung, *The Collected Works of C. G. Jung* 18 (Princeton, NJ: Princeton University Press, 1976), 714.

30   Joan Chamberlain Engelsman, *The Feminine Dimension of the Divine: The Study of Sophia and Feminine Images in Religion* (Wilmette, IL: Chiron, 1994), 40.

31   Chamberlain Engelsman, *Feminine Dimension of the Divine*, 41.

32   Seyyed Hossein Nasr, "The Male and Female in the Islamic Perspective," *Studies in Comparative Religion* 14, no. 1 & 2 (Winter–Spring, 1980): 7. http://www.studiesincomparativereligion.com/uploads/ArticlePDFs/351.pdf, Accessed August 16, 2019.

33   Aguéli presents "Marian initiation" as the most direct form of "ta'līm rabbānī." *La Gnose*, 30. Aguéli believes that this is now more common in Europe than in the East.

34   Aguéli, "Femminismo" (1904), 4.

35 Time, and the rhythms of succession and simultaneity were a topic of some fascination for Aguéli, rather this is hinted at here is speculative. See *La Gnose*, 32–3.

36 Aguéli, "Femminismo" (1904), 4.

37 For example Schuon and Coomaraswamy have written extensively on *maya*, including its association with the feminine principle including both creative and inspirational aspects as well as maleficent and deceptive elements. See James S. Cutsinger, "Femininity, Hierarchy, and God," in *Religion of the Heart: Essays Presented to Frithjof Schuon on His Eightieth Birthday*, edited by Seyyed Hossein Nasr and William Stoddart (Chicago, IL: ABC International Group, 2000).

38 Aguéli, "Femminismo" (1904), 4.

39 *La Gnose*, 61–3 where he speaks of the "Tyranny of the collective," 61.

40 Aguéli, "Femminismo" (1904), 4.

41 The figure of Valentine de Saint-Point who authored a feminine futurist manifesto and later was associated with Guénonian Traditionalism is intriguing here. See *Valentine de Saint-Point: Des feux de l'avant-garde à l'appel de l'Orient*, ed. Paul-André Claudel and Elodie Gaden (Rennes: Presses Universitaires de Rennes, 2019), and *Feminine Futures—Valentine de Saint-Point—Performance, Dance, War, Politics and Eroticism* edited by Adrien Sina that interestingly has a chapter by the Traditionalist, Martin Lings, that includes a discussion of René Guénon and the Egyptian milieu, thus connecting, art, Traditionalism, and feminism. "Valentine de Saint-Point's Initiation into Sufism (as told by Martin Lings to Nancy G. Moore)" and "Concerning my friendship with Valentine de Saint-Point—1940–1953" in *Feminine Futures* ed. Adrien Sina (Dijon: Les presses du réel, 2011).

42 Beth Baron, *The Women's Awakening in Egypt: Culture, Society, and the Press* (New Haven, CT: Yale University Press, 1994), 135.

43 For example, this argument was used by Qasim Amin in *Tahrir al-Mar'a* (Emancipation of Women). *The Liberation of Women and the New Woman: Two Documents in the History of Egyptian Feminism* (Cairo: American University in Cairo Press, 2005).

44 Aguéli. "Femminismo" (1907), 142.

45 Aguéli, "Femminismo" (1904), 4.

46 Ibid., 4.

47 Aguéli, "Femminismo" (1907), 140.

48 Ibid., 141.

49 Ralph Austin, "The Feminine Dimensions in Ibn 'Arabi's Thought," *Muhyiddin ibn 'Arabi Society Journal* 2 (1984): 5–14; Huda Lutfi, "The Feminine Element in Ibn 'Arabi's Mystical Philosophy," *Alif: Journal of Comparative Poetics* 5 (Spring, 1985): 7–19; Souad Hakim, "Ibn 'Arabi's Twofold Perception of Woman as Human Being and Cosmic Principle," *Journal of the Muhyiddin Ibn 'Arabi Society* 39 (2006): 1–29.

50 Sachiko Murata, *The Tao of Islam: A Sourcebook on Gender Relationships in Islamic Thought* (Albany: State University of New York Press, 1992), 79.

51 Sa'diyya Shaikh, "In Search of al-Insān: Sufism, Islamic Law and Gender," *Journal of the American Academy of Religion* 77 (2009): 781–822, 790.

52 Ibid.

53 Cutsinger, "Femininity, Hierarchy, and God," 117.

54 Nasr, "Male and Female in the Islamic Perspective," 9.

55 Julius Evola, "Man and Women," in *Revolt against the Modern World* (Rochester, VT: Inner Traditions International, 1995), 157–66.

56 This characterization was part of the title of a mini-symposium: "Ivan Aguéli's 150th Anniversary. Artist, Anarchist, Swedish Sufi" related to the conference that was the basis for the present volume. https://www.thielskagalleriet.se/en/kalender/mini-symphosia-ivan-agueli-150-year-artist-vagabond-sufi/ (accessed June 20, 2020).

57 Rocca, *Écrits pour La Gnose*, ix.

Chapter 13

1 The meeting is reported in a letter of Aguéli to unknown recipient, translated in Axel Gauffin, *Ivan Aguéli: Människan, Mystikern, Målaren* (Stockholm: Sveriges allmänna konstförening, 1940–1), vol. 2, 188–90.

2 Michel Vâlsan, "L'islam et la fonction de René Guénon," *Études traditionnelles* 305 (January 1953): 44–6.

3 By Patrick Laude, "Universality in Islam: Abd humain ul Hadi," in *Universal Dimensions of Islam: Studies in Comparative Religion*, edited by Laude (Bloomington, IN: World Wisdom, 2011), 134–48.

4 I would like to thank Marcia Hermansen for her comments on a draft of this chapter.

5 Aguéli to unknown recipient, in Gauffin, 189. It is assumed that the 'Abd al-Wahid mentioned in this letter is Guénon, as that was the Muslim name that Guénon later used, and no other French Muslim of the period using that name has been identified. Only one other name is given in Aguéli's letter, 'Abd al-Halim, who has not been identified. As Aguéli refers to "many of our friends," however, there were presumably others, and these probably included Léon Champrenaud. There is no rival account of how Champrenaud became 'Abd al-Haqq.

6 La Direction, "Projet d'explication des termes techniques des différentes doctrines traditionnelles," *La Gnose* 1, no. 12 (December 1910): 268.

7 René Guénon, *Le Symbolisme de la Croix* (Paris: Éditions Véga, 1931).

8 Palingénius [René Guénon], "Le Symbolisme de la Croix," *La Gnose* 2, no. 2 (February 1911): 55–9, refers to Palingénius [René Guénon], "La prière et l'incantation," *La Gnose* 2, no. 1 (January 1911): 23–8.

9 This must have happened after 1932, when Abdul-Hâdi was presented to readers of *Le voile d'Isis* in much the same terms as he had been introduced to readers of *La Gnose* in 1910. La Rédaction [René Guénon], "Abdul-Hâdi," *Le voile d'Isis* 1932, 714.

10 Guénon to Marcel Clavelle, March 26, 1938, partially reproduced in A. Balestrieri, "Nuove tecniche di attacco all'opera di René Guénon," in *René Guénon e l'Occidente*, edited by P. Nutrizio (Milan: Luni Editrice, 1999), 74.

11 As Geneviève Dubois has pointed out, "Palingénius" is a play on "René," which echoes *re-nait*, reborn. Dubois, *Fulcanelli and the Alchemical Revival: The Man behind the Mystery of the Cathedrals* (NP: Destiny Books, 2005), unpaginated Kindle.

12 As many articles were published in multiple parts, the names of other authors appeared on the tables of contents of these last issues, but only in the context of continuations of earlier articles, not as authors of new articles. Even F.-Ch. Bartlet's regular series on astrology ended with the final issue of 1911.

13 "Le Symbolisme de la Croix" (1911) became *Le Symbolisme de la Croix* (1931); Palingénius [René Guénon], "Les Néo-Spiritualistes," *La Gnose* 2, no. 8 (August 1911): 223–7 et seq. became René Guénon, *L'Erreur spirite* (Paris: Marcel Rivière, 1923); Palingénius [René Guénon], "La Constitution de l'être humain et son

évolution posthume selon le Vedanta," *La Gnose* 2, no. 9 (September 1911): 236–45 *et seq.* became René Guénon, *L'Homme et son devenir selon le Vêdânta* (Paris, Bossard, 1925).

14 Palingénius [René Guénon], "La Gnose et les Écoles spiritualistes," *La Gnose* 1, no. 2 (December 1909): 21.

15 Palingénius [René Guénon], "La Religion et les religions," *La Gnose* 1, no. 10 (September 1910): 219–20.

16 Ibid., 221.

17 Ibid., 219.

18 Guénon "La Constitution de l'être humain."

19 Abdul-Hâdi [Ivan Aguéli], "Pages dédiées à Mercure (Sahaif Ataridiyah)," *La Gnose* 2, no. 1 (January 2011): 28–30. "Pages dédiées à Mercure" was in fact a collection of shorter and longer pieces on a variety of topics, cited below according to their individual sub-headings. The first piece, cited here, had no individual sub-heading.

20 Aguéli, "Pages dédiées à Mercure," 32.

21 Aguéli, "Les deux chaines initiatiques," in "Pages dédiées à Mercure," 32.

22 Mark Sedgwick, *Against the Modern World: Traditionalism and the Secret Intellectual History of the Twentieth Century* (New York: Oxford University Press, 2004), 151–2.

23 As "Épître intitulée *Le Cadeau* sur la manifestation du prophète par le Sheikh initié et inspiré Mohammed ibn Fazlallah Al-Hindi (traduction)," *La Gnose* 1, no. 12 (December 1910): 270–5.

24 With an introductory discussion, "El-Malamatiyah," *La Gnose* 2, no. 3 (March 1911): 100–7.

25 As "L'Identité Suprême dans l'ésotérisme musulman: Le Traité de l'Unité (Risalatul-Ahadiyah), par le plus grand des Maitres spirituels, Mohyiddin ibn ʿArabi (traduction)," *La Gnose* 2, no. 6 (June 1911): 168–74, 2, no. 7 (July 1911): 199–202, and 2, no. 8 (August 1911): 217–23; and "Les Catégories de l'initiation (Tartibut-Taçawwuf), par le plus grand des Maitres spirituels, Seyidi Mohyiddin ibn ʿArabi (traduction)," *La Gnose* 2, no. 12 (December 1911): 323–8 and 3, no. 1 (January 1912): 16–21.

26 Abdul-Hâdi [Ivan Aguéli], "Pages dédiées au Soleil (Sahaif Shamsiyah)," *La Gnose* 2, no. 2 (February 1911): 59–66.

27 Abdul-Hâdi [Ivan Aguéli], "L'Islam et les religions anthropomorphiques," *La Gnose* 2, no. 5 (May 1911): 152 and 153.

28 "L'identité suprême" (1911), republished in *Le Voile d'Isis* 157 (January 1933): 13–17, and 158 (February 1933): 52–72, and "El-Malâmatiyyah" (1911), republished in *Le Voile d'Isis* 166 (October 1933): 404–16.

29 "L'universalité en l'Islam" (1911), republished in *Le Voile d'Isis* 169 (January 1934), 17–33.

30 "Épître intitulée *Le Cadeau*" (1910), republished in *Le Voile d'Isis* 187 (July 1935), 293–303; "Pages dédiées au Soleil" (1911), republished in *Le Voile d'Isis* 191 (November 1935), 452–61; and "Les catégories de l'initiation" (1911), republished in *Le Voile d'Isis* 194 (February 1936), 51–65.

31 "Pages dédiées à Mercure" (1911), republished in *Etudes traditionnelles* 253 (August 1946): 312–30, and 254 (September 1946): 366–72.

32 "L'Islam et les religions anthropomorphiques," 152 and 153.

33 Guénon was not writing for the scholarly market, and so did not follow scholarly conventions. Perhaps more importantly, his purpose was not to explain and discuss

the views of other writers, but to explain the truth, and the origin of the truth was not a particular book or writer but, ultimately, God Himself.

34 Abdul-Hâdi (John Gustav Agelii, dit Ivan Aguéli), *Écrits pour La Gnose, comprenant la traduction de l'arabe du Traité de l'Unité*, ed. G. Rocca (Milan: Archè, 1988).

35 *La Gnose 1909–1912* (Paris: Les éditions de l'Homme Libre, 2009).

36 L'Homme Libre, https://editions-hommelibre.fr, visited June 3, 2019.

37 Awhad al-Din Balyani, *Epître sur l'unicité absolu*, trans. Michel Chodkiewicz (Paris: Deux Oceans, 1982).

38 Sedgwick, *Against the Modern World*, 135.

39 Jean Robin, *René Guénon, témoin de la Tradition* (Paris: Guy Trédaniel, 1978), 17–18.

40 Published in the Indian journal *Jayakarnataka*, and quoted in Paul Chacornac, *La vie simple de René Guénon* (Paris: Editions Traditionelles, 1958), 41–2.

41 Paul Chacornac, "La vie simple de René Guénon," *Études traditionnelles* 293 (1951): 323, n. 1.

42 Ibid., 323–4.

43 Ibid., "Vie simple," 324.

44 Vâlsan, "L'islam et la fonction de René Guénon," 35–7.

45 Ibid., 40.

46 Ibid., 44, 46.

47 Ibid., 44, 45–6.

48 In Paul Sérant, *René Guénon* (1953; 2nd edition Paris: Courrier du Livre, 1977), 10.

49 Quoted in Chacornac, *Vie simple*, 66. I have been unable to identify or locate the original.

50 Jean Reyor [Marcel Clavelle], "A propos des 'Maîtres' de René Guénon," *Etudes traditionnelles*, January 1955, cited by Robin, *René Guénon*, 67–8.

51 Chacornac, *Vie simple*, 83.

52 Gauffin, *Ivan Aguéli*.

53 Chacornac, *Vie simple*, 43–50.

54 Ibid., 46.

55 Ibid., 49–50.

56 Ibid.

57 Jean-Pierre Laurant, *Le sens caché dans l'œuvre de René Guénon* (Lausanne: L'Age d'homme, 1975), 9.

58 Ibid., 18–20, 21–2, 29–33, 37–40.

59 Aguéli's conversion to Islam moved from before his trip to Ceylon to Egypt, his date of death moved to 1915, and his initiation was moved to the London mosque, on the basis that the Paris mosque had then not yet been built, Laurant, *Sens caché*, 51. Laurant evidently supposed that a mosque was necessary for Sufi initiation.

60 Robin, *René Guénon*, 17–18.

61 Ibid., 66–9, 207–12.

62 Marie-France James, *Ésotérisme et christianisme: Autour de René Guénon* (Paris: Nouvelles Éditons Latines, 1981), 69–101.

63 Ibid., 83–93.

64 Robin Waterfield, *René Guénon and the Future of the West: The Life and Writings of a 20th-Century Metaphysician* (1987; NP: Sophia Perennis, 2017), 28–31.

65 G. Rocca, Introduction to *Écrits pour La Gnose*, xix.

66 Harry Oldmeadow, "René Guénon," in *The Reign of Quantity*, edited by René Guénon (New York: Sophia Perrenis et Universalis, 1995), manuscript available https://www.academia.edu/18006106/René_Guénon

67 Harry Oldmeadow, *Journeys East: 20th Century Western Encounters with Eastern Religious Traditions* (Bloomington, IN: World Wisdom, 2004), 185.

68 Ibid., 208–9.

69 Harry Oldmeadow, "Biography of René Guénon," World Wisdom ND, available http://www.worldwisdom.com/public/authors/Rene-Guenon.aspx

70 Harry Oldmeadow, "Biography of René Guénon," Counter-Currents Publishing November 15, 2010, https://www.counter-currents.com/2010/11/biography-of-rene-guenon/

71 Review of Wikipedia.org, June 3, 2019.

72 Jean Foucauld, "Le Musulman, Cheykh 'Abdu-l-Hedi al-Maghribi 'Uqayli," *Vers La Tradition* 72 (June 1998), republished in *Esprit-universel* December 25, 2012, available http://esprit-universel.over-blog.com/article-une-rehabilitation-d-ivan-agueli-abdul-hadi-113790002.html

73 Ibid.

74 Patrick Laude, *Pathways to an Inner Islam: Massignon, Corbin, Guenon, and Schuon* (Albany, NY: SUNY Press, 2010), 8–9.

75 Laude, "Universality in Islam: Abdul Hadi," 135–6.

Chapter 14

1 This section is largely based on my book *Les théories de l'art dans la pensée traditionnelle* (Paris: L'Harmattan, 2011).

2 Reprinted in Guénon, *Mélanges* (Paris: Gallimard, 1976), 71–7.

3 See Guénon, *Aperçus sur l'initiation* (Paris: Éditions Traditionnelles, 1946), which gathers articles published in the 1930s. It should be noted that it is in his texts devoted to initiation that Guénon made a few references to Aguéli/Abdul-Hâdi, and to his articles originally published in *La Gnose* ("Pages dédiées à Mercure," "El-Malâmatiyah"), but republished in the *Voile d'Isis*, renamed *Études traditionnelles* in 1936. Guénon, *Initiation et Réalisation spirituelle* (Paris: Éditions Traditionnelles, 1967), 55, 218.

4 Guénon wrote many articles on symbols, later gathered in posthumous collections, in particular *Symboles fondamentaux de la science sacrée* (Paris: Gallimard, 1962).

5 Ringgenberg, *Les théories de l'art dans la pensée traditionnelle*, 61–2, 83, 85–6.

6 Mainly in *Mediaeval Sinhalese Art* (Broad Campden: Essex House Press, 1908); *Essays in National Idealism* (Colombo: Colombo Apothecaries Co., 1909); *Rajput Painting* (London: Oxford University Press, 1916); *The Dance of Śiva: Fourteen Indian Essays* (New York: The Sunwise Turn, 1918).

7 He developed the concept of "traditional art" mainly in three books: *The Transformation of Nature in Art* (Cambridge, MA: Harvard University Press, 1934); *Why Exhibit Works of Art?* (London: Luzac & Co., 1943; reprinted in 1956 under the title *Christian and Oriental Philosophy of Art*, New York: Dover); *Figures of Speech or Figures of Thought: Collected Essays in the Traditional or "Normal" View of Art* (London: Luzac & Co., 1946). For a presentation of his ideas see Ringgenberg, *Les théories de l'art dans la pensée traditionnelle*, 273–335.

8   Ringgenberg, *Les théories de l'art dans la pensée traditionnelle*, 95–129.

9   Already in his first book published in French (*De l'unité transcendante des religions*,
     Paris: Gallimard, 1948), Schuon included a chapter devoted to "La question des
     formes d'art." He frequently mentioned the question of the arts in his subsequent
     books, mainly in *Perspectives spirituelles et faits humains* (Paris: Les Cahiers du Sud,
     1953), *Principes et critères de l'art universel* (Lyon: Derain, 1957), *L'ésotérisme comme
     principe et comme voie* (Paris: Dervy-Livres, 1978), and *Avoir un centre* (Paris: G.-P.
     Maisonneuve & Larose, 1988). Burckhardt summarized his doctrine of art in a major
     book, first published in German (*Vom Wesen heiliger Kunst in den Weltreligionen*,
     Zürich: Origo-Verlag, 1955), then in French (*Principes et méthodes de l'art sacré*,
     Lyon: Derain, 1958), and which gathered articles published in *Études Traditionnelles*
     between 1953 and 1955.

10   See, for instance, Nader Ardalan and Laleh Bakhtiar, *The Sense of Unity: The Sufi
     Tradition in Persian Architecture* (Chicago: The University of Chicago Press, 1973);
     Issam El-Said and Ayşe Parman, *Geometric Concepts in Islamic Art* (London: World
     of Islam Festival Publishing Company, 1976); Keith Critchlow, *Islamic Patterns:
     An Analytical and Cosmological Approach* (London: Thames and Hudson, 1976);
     Seyyed Hossein Nasr, *Islamic Art and Spirituality* (Ipswich: Golgonooza Press, 1987);
     Martin Lings, *The Quranic Art of Calligraphy and Illumination* (London: Scorpion,
     1987); Jean-Louis Michon, *Lumières d'Islam. Institutions, art et spiritualité dans
     la cité musulmane* (Milan: Archè, 1994). For a general survey of these authors see
     Ringgenberg, *Les théories de l'art dans la pensée traditionnelle*, 631–61.

11   See, for instance, Jean Hani, *Le symbolisme du Temple chrétien* (Paris: Guy Trédaniel,
     1962); abbé Henri Stéphane, *Introduction à l'ésotérisme chrétien* (Paris: Dervy-Livres,
     1979), vol. 1, 145–88; Jean Biès, *Athos. Voyage à la Sainte Montagne* (Paris: Dervy-
     Livres, 1980) and *Art, gnose et alchimie. Trois sources de régénérescence* (Paris: Le
     Courrier du Livre, 1987).

12   For a general survey of Guénon and Schuon's universalist concepts, see Patrick
     Ringgenberg, *Diversité et unité des religions chez René Guénon et Frithjof Schuon*
     (Paris: L'Harmattan, 2010).

13   *Orient et Occident* (Paris, 1924), *La crise du monde moderne* (Paris, 1927), *Le règne de
     la quantité et les signes des temps* (Paris, 1945).

14   Ringgenberg, *Les théories de l'art dans la pensée traditionnelle*, 447–56.

15   *Principes et critères de l'art universel*, Lyon, 1954, reprinted in *Castes et races* (Milano:
     Archè, 1979), 89.

16   In 'Abdul-Hâdî (John Gustav Agelii, dit Ivan Aguéli), *Écrits pour* La Gnose (Milan:
     Archè, 1988), 35.

17   "L'art pur," in *Écrits pour* La Gnose, 35.

18   "L'art pur," 34.

19   Ibid., 42.

20   Ibid., 43.

21   Ibid., 37.

22   Ibid., 46–7, 49.

23   Ibid., 48.

24   Ibid., 45.

25   Ibid., 44.

26   He published a very critical book in Paris in 1921 (*Le théosophisme. Histoire d'une
     pseudo-religion*, Paris: Nouvelle librairie nationale).

27   See Guénon, *Le théosophisme* (Paris: Éditions Traditionnelles, 1986 [1921]), 389–90, 424–5. Other references can be found on https://www.index-rene-guenon.org/ (accessed May 31, 2019).

28   "Pages dédiées au soleil," published in *La Gnose*, 1911 (in *Écrits pour* La Gnose, 62).

29   "L'universalité en l'Islam," 85.

30   "L'art pur," 48.

31   Ibid., 43.

32   Aguéli wrote: "la peinture doit être picturale, la sculpture sculpturale, etc." ("L'art pur," 36–7). A quite similar idea—although with different aesthetic references and intellectual purposes—was frequently expressed by Traditionalists (Ringgenberg, *Les théories de l'art dans la pensée traditionnelle*, 314, 377, 572).

33   "L'art pur," 46–7.

34   Ringgenberg, *Les théories de l'art dans la pensée traditionnelle*, 453.

35   Some of his pre-Guénonian books, such as *The Dance of Śiva* (1918), are typical of an "East and West" eclecticism.

36   He published a few drawings along with his photographs in his first book on Morocco: *Land am Rande der Zeit. Eine Beschreibung der marokkanischer Kultur* (Basel: Urs Graf-Verlag, 1941).

37   A selection of his paintings was published in *Images of Primordial and Mystic Beauty: Paintings by Frithjof Schuon* (Bloomington, IN: Abodes, 1992).

38   Ardalan and Bakhtiar, *The Sense of Unity*.

39   Nader Ardalan, "The Paradise Garden Paradigm," in *Consciousness and Reality. Studies in Memory of Toshihiko Izutsu*, edited by Sayyid Jalâl al-Dîn Ashtiyânî, Hideichi Matsubara, Takashi Iwami, Akiro Matsumoto (Leiden: Brill, 2000), 97–127.

40   One interesting point—and this issue would require further studies and reflections— is that Aguéli traveled a lot and even lived in Egypt (in 1894–5, and between 1902 and 1909), where he could have had access to some local and "traditional" conceptions of arts and crafts, but nothing appears in his French texts on art, published in 1910–11. A quite similar remark can be made about Burckhardt, who spent a few years in Morocco, but his books inspired by the Guénonian metaphysics show no significant influence from the contacts he must have had with the craftsmen perpetuating their artistic traditions. The question that arises is in particular this: What is this theory of "traditional art," supposedly universal, but developed without taking into account the conceptions of artists or craftsmen perceived as being still "traditional," and by means of concepts or even preconceptions that are essentially Western?.

41   "Pages dédiées à Mercure," published in *La Gnose*, 1911, in *Écrits pour* La Gnose, 33.

42   For the early twentieth century, see among other references: Roger Lipsey, *The Spiritual in Twentieth-Century Art* (Mineola, NY: Dover, 2004), and Maurice Tuchman and others, *The Spiritual in Art. Abstract Painting, 1890-1985* (Los Angeles, CA: Los Angeles County Museum of Art, 1986). These past decades, numerous books have been published about the relationship between arts and spirituality. See, for instance, Earle J. Coleman, *Creativity and Spirituality. Bonds between Art and Religion* (Albany: SUNY Press, 1998); Dawn Perlmutter and Debra Koppman, ed., *Reclaiming the Spiritual in Art. Contemporary Cross-Cultural Perspectives* (Albany, NY: SUNY Press, 1999); James Elkins, *On the Strange Place of Religion in Contemporary Art* (New York: Routledge, 2004); Rina Arya, ed., *Contemplations*

of the Spiritual in Art (Bern: Peter Lang, 2013); Janis Lander, *Spiritual Art and Art Education* (New York: Routledge, 2014).

43 Some of the works created by the students are to be seen on the School's website (www.psta.org.uk; Accessed June 18, 2019). One will also read there the ideals of the School, directly inspired by the Traditionalists, and whose aim is—in the words of Prince Charles—"to continue the living traditions of the world's sacred and traditional art forms" (https://www.psta.org.uk/about/hrh-the-prince-of-wales; Accessed June 18, 2019).

44 Sorgenfrei, "The Great Aesthetic Inspiration," 1–25.

45 This is particularly striking in the field of premodern Islamic arts, as mentioned by Burckhardt, Nasr, Ardalan, Michon, Critchlow and Lings. On a sometimes undifferentiated vision of Islamic cultures, inherited from nineteenth-century Orientalism, Traditionalists have projected a generalizing metaphysical interpretation, which occasionally ignores ancient sources that shed light on the meaning of certain arts. See Ringgenberg, *Les théories de l'art dans la pensée traditionnelle*, 645–61, and, Ringgenberg, *L'ornement dans les arts d'Islam* (Tehran/London: Candle & Fog, 2013), 147–66, 225–60.

Chapter 15

1 Richard Bergh (1858–1919), Swedish painter and art theorist, friend, teacher, and patron of Aguéli. Bergh had lived in France, in Paris and Grez-sur-Loing, was a leading member of the Swedish Opponents and a co-founder of Konstnärsförbundet (the Artist's Union) in 1886. The original of this letter is in the Richard Bergh archive at the Thiel Gallery in Stockholm. The letter was published in Swedish in Axel Gauffin, *Ivan Aguéli: Människan—Mystikern—Målaren*, (Stockholm: Sveriges Allmänna Konstförening, 1940), vol. 1, 101–8. This publication is the basis of this translation.

2 Maximilien Luce (1858–1941), French impressionist painter and anarchist.

3 In early July 1893, a student demonstration against the conviction of one student escalated into conflict with the police and one death, after which the students occupied the Quartier latin for several days, building barricades and attacking properties.

4 Artistic and anarchist weekly published between 1891 and 1893.

5 *Le peintre de la vie moderne* was a collection of essays devoted to the work of Constantin Guys (1802–92), a French painter, by Charles Baudelaire in 1863. Aguéli may be referring to a posthumous exhibition of the work of Guys.

6 An "Exposition d'art musulman" was held at the Palais de l'Industrie in Paris in 1893. It focused on the decorative arts, drawing on a number of private collections.

7 Félix Fénéon (1861–1944), French art critic, journalist, and anarchist.

8 Camille Mauclair (1872–1945), French poet, novelist, art historian, and literary critic.

9 Aguéli is referring to the third verse of the second chapter of the Qur'an, which is there described as a guidance for "those who believe in the unseen [*ghayb*]."

10 Albert Aurier (1865–92), French art critic and publisher, a selection of whose writings were collected and published after his death. The importance of Aurier for Aguéli is discussed elsewhere in this book.

11 Joris-Karl Huysmans (1848–1907), French novelist, writer, and art critic.

12 A collection by Huysmans published in 1883.

13 Remy de Gourmont (1858–1915), French novelist, art critic, and symbolist. A friend of Huysmans.

14   *Le Latin mystique. Les poètes de l'antiphonaire et la symbolique au Moyen Âge*
      [Mystical Latin: The Poets of the Antiphonary and Symbolism in the Middle Ages].
      Preface by J.-K. Huysmans. Paris: Mercure de France, 1892.
15   Max Nordau (1849–1923), Austrian-French journalist and writer. His *Entartung*
      attacked the decadence he found in contemporary culture, especially French culture,
      especially in art and in spiritism.
16   Nordau had trained as a physician.
17   This and following excerpts are taken from Aurier, *Oeuvres posthumes* (Paris:
      Mercure de France, 1893).
18   Aguéli has lightly edited the original, which reads: "The only way to penetrate a thing
      is love. To understand God you have to love him; to understand woman, you must
      love her; understanding stands in proportion to love." *Oeuvres posthumes*, 201.
19   "Through positivism" is Aguéli's summary of a part of the original that has been
      omitted. The original reads: "Our soul's most noble faculties are atrophying, In one
      hundred years we will be beasts whose only ideal is the easy satisfaction of our bodily
      needs; we will have reverted, through positive science, to pure and simple animality."
      Oeuvres posthumes, 202.
20   Misspelled as "Ravachal." Ravachol was François Claudius Koenigstein (1859–92), a
      French anarchist bomber, executed in 1892.
21   Charles van Lerberghe (1861–1907), Belgian symbolist poet.
22   Frans Lindberg (1857–1944), Swedish artist who studied decorative arts in Berlin,
      and C. Arthur Sjögren (1874–1951), illustrator and book designer.
23   Anders Zorn (1860–1920), Swedish painter and sculptor, a former teacher of Aguéli
      in Stockholm.
24   Per Hasselberg (1850–94), Swedish sculptor.
25   Karl Nordström (1855–1923), Ernst Josephson (1851–1906), and Georg von Rosen
      (1843–1923) were all well-known Swedish artists. Nordström was Aguéli's first
      teacher and promoter.
26   Knut Åkerberg (1868–1955), Swedish artist and friend of Aguéli, who studied in
      Paris 1890–2. In fact he had not gone to hell, and enjoyed a long career as an artist in
      Sweden and elsewhere in Europe.

Chapter 16

1   Proposed articles for the *Encyclopédie contemporaine illustrée*, a journal edited by
     Huot's husband, for which Aguéli wrote at various points in his life.
2   Probably Philipp Freudenberg (1843–1911), a successful merchant who was the
     German consul in Colombo.
3   Aguéli is evidently referring to defending himself against a attack by robbers.
4   This is the *Encyclopédie contemporaine illustrée*.

Chapter 17

1   The first known use of the term in French was in 1910, and the first known use in
     English was in 1923. For early uses see Fernando Bravo López, "Towards a Definition
     of Islamophobia: Approximations of the Early Twentieth Century," *Ethnic and Racial
     Studies* 34, no. 4 (2011): 556–73.
2   Published in *Il Convito*, July 17, 1904: 1; July 31, 1904: 1; and August 14, 1904: 1.

3   *Arafate. Revue islamite mensuelle* (Arafat: Islamist Monthly Review) was a French-language journal published in Cairo.
4   The original uses the short paragraphs typical of popular journalism. These have sometimes been amalgamated into longer paragraphs in this translation. Subtitles have been added.
5   An Italian periodical published, in Italian and French, in Alexandria and later in Cairo at the end of the nineteenth century.
6   Daniel Kimon, *La Pathologie de l'Islam et les moyens de le détruire, étude psychologique* (The Pathology of Islam and the Means to Destroy It: A Psychological Study) (Paris, NP: 1897).
7   The following section was published in *Il Convito*, July 31, 1904.
8   The original reads not "above" but "in the previous issue."
9   Hans Barth (1862–1928), German journalist. *Le droit du croissant* (The Right of the Crescent) (Paris, H.C. Wolf, 1898).
10   Aguéli is referring to what the European press generally saw as massacres of Bulgarian and Armenian separatists. These are discussed in Hans Barth, *Türke, wehre dich!* (Turk, Defend Yourself) (Leipzig: Rengersche Buchhandlung, 1898).
11   The following section was published in *Il Convito*, August 14, 1904. The original begins not "Above" but "In the previous issue."
12   Arthur de Gobineau (1816–82), French diplomat and writer, remembered for his *Essai sur l'inégalité des races humaines* (Essay on the Inequality of the Human Races) (Paris, Firmin-Didot frères, 1853–5).

Chapter 18

1   Published as "L'Art Pur" in *La Gnose* 2, no. 1 (January 1911): 34–8.
2   In effect, abstract and concrete art.
3   Published as "L'Art Pur (suite)," in *La Gnose* 2, no. 2 (February 1911): 66–72.

Chapter 19

1   Originally published as "L'universalité en l'Islam," *La Gnose* 2, no. 4 (April 1911): 121–31. The reference here is to an earlier article of Aguéli's, "Pages dédiées au Soleil (Sahaif Shamsiyah)" (Pages Dedicated to the Sun), published in *La Gnose* 2, no. 2 (February 1911): 59–66.
2   Francis Warrain, *La synthèse concrète. Étude métaphysique de la vie* (Paris: Société d'éditions contemporaines, 1906; reprinted Paris: Chacornac, 1910). Warrain (1867–1940) was a sculptor who drew on the work of the Polish neo-Pythagorean philosopher and mathematician Josef Hoëné-Wronski (1776–1853) who was much appreciated by Éliphas Lévi.
3   Tartarin of Tarascon was the anti-hero of a novel of the same name by Alphonse Daudet.
4   In fact, it is a verbal noun of Form IV, which is indeed often causative.
5   Aguéli misses one word from this famous *hadith*, though the meaning remains intact.

6   Abu'l-ʿAlaʾ al-Maʿarri (973–1057) was a controversial Arab poet who appeared to criticize exoteric Islam while himself following extremely ascetic practice.

7   Aguéli is here referring to the theory, once popular, that distinguished Aryan spirituality from Semitic legalism, and thus assigned a Persian, Aryan origin to the spirituality of Sufism, contrasted with the legalism of Arab, Semitic Islam.

8   This is widely understood to be *sunna*, proper behavior, in Islam.

Select Bibliography

By Ivan Aguéli

In Il Convito, *writing as Abdul Hadi El Maghrabi*

"Akbariya." *Il Convito*, no. 3–4 (1907): 90–103.

"Civiltà araba o mussulmana?" *Il Convito*, no. 19 (1904): 2.

"Femminismo." *Il Convito*, no. 2 (May 1904): 4.

"Femminismo." In "Note sull'Islam." *Il Convito* 4, no. 5–8 (1907): 134–42.

"I nemici dell'Islam." *Il Convito*, no. 7 (July 1904): 1, and subsequent issues. Translated in this book.

"Il sacrificio dell'umanità." *Il Convito*, no. 21 (January 1, 1905): 1.

"Note sull'islam." *Il Convito* 4, no. 1 (1907): 2–11 and 4, no. 2 (1907): 33–40.

Note that the early years of Il Convito *(to 1905) had sequential issue numbers and no volume numbers, and that from 1906 onwards the volumes were numbered by year (1906 was year 3) and had non-sequential issue numbers.*

In La Gnose, *writing as Abdul-Hâdi*

"Épître intitulée «*Le Cadeau*» sur la manifestation du prophète par le Sheikh initié et inspiré Mohammed ibn Fazlallah Al-Hindi (traduction)." *La Gnose* 1, no. 12 (December 1910): 270–5.

"L'Art Pur." *La Gnose* 2, no. 1 (January 1911): 34–8 and no. 2 (February 1911): 66–72. Translated in this book.

"Les Catégories de l'initiation (Tartibut-Taçawwuf), par le plus grand des Maitres spirituels, Seyidi Mohyiddin ibn 'Arabi (traduction)." *La Gnose* 2, no. 12 (December 1911): 323–8 *et seq.*

"L'Identité Suprême dans l'ésotérisme musulman: Le Traité de I 'Unité (Risalatul-Ahadiyah), par le plus grand des Maitres spirituels, Mohyiddin ibn 'Arabi (traduction)." *La Gnose* 2, no. 6 (June 1911): 168–74, *et seq.*

"L'Islam et les religions anthropomorphiques." *La Gnose* 2, no. 5 (May 1911): 152–3.

"Le Traité de l'Unité" [of Muhyiddin ibn 'Arabi]. *La Gnose* 2, no. 6 (1911): 168–74, no. 7 (1911): 199–202, and no. 8 (1911): 217–22.

"L'universalité en l'Islam," *La Gnose* 2, no. 4 (April 1911): 121–31. Translated as "Universality in Islam." In *Universal Dimensions of Islam*, ed. Patrick Laude, 134–47. Bloomington, IN: World Wisdom, 2011. Also translated in this book.

"Pages dédiées à Mercure (Sahaif Ataridiyah)," *La Gnose* 2, no. 1 (January 2011): 28–38 and no. 2 (February 1911): 66–72.

"Pages dédiées au Soleil (Sahaif Shamsiyah)." *La Gnose* 2, no. 2 (February 1911): 59–66.

These articles are all reprinted in 'Abdul–Hâdî (John Gustav Agelii, dit Ivan Aguéli). *Écrits pour La Gnose, comprenant la traduction de l'arabe du Traité de l'Unité*, ed. G. Rocca (Milan: Archè, 1988) and in *La Gnose. Èdition intégrale 1909–1912* (Paris: Edition de l'homme libre, 2009).

In L'Encyclopédie contemporaine illustrée, *writing as Abdul-Hâdi*

"Le Salon des Indépendants." *Encyclopédie contemporaine illustrée* 355 (April 18, 1897): 63.
"Le Salon des Indépendants. 27me exposition." *Encyclopédie contemporaine illustrée* 641 (April 30, 1911): 32.
"Les Expositions d'art à Paris. Celle de la 'Section d'Or' à la galerie Boetie." *Encyclopédie contemporaine illustrée* 659 (November 15, 1912): 175–6.
"Les Indépendants, 29eme." *Encyclopédie contemporaine illustrée*, May 25 (1913), continued as "Chronique d'art (suite). La 29ᵉ exposition du Salon des Indépendants." *Encyclopédie contemporaine illustrée* 665 (June 30, 1913): 40.
"Sur les principes du monument et de la sculpture." *Encyclopédie contemporaine illustrée* 661 (January 31, 1913): 7–8.

Other works

Accart, Xavier. *Guénon ou le renversement des clartés: Influence d'un métaphysicien sur la vie littéraire et intellectuelle française (1920–1970)*. Milan: Archè, 2005.
Acciai, Enrico. "Esilio e anarchismo: i cavalieri erranti del Mediterraneo." In *L'Anarchismo italiano. Storia e storiografia*, ed. Giampietro Berti and Carlo De Maria, 301–19. Milan: Biblion, 2016.
Ådahl, Karin and Unge Sörling, Susanne, Wessel, Viveca (eds.). *Sverige och den islamiska världen—ett svenskt kulturarv*. Stockholm: Wahlström & Widstrand, 2002.
Adrian-Nilsson, Gösta. *Den gudomliga geometrien: En uppsats om konst*. Stockholm: Thure Wahledow, 1922.
al-Bītār, Abd al-Razzāq. *Huliat al-bashar fī tārīkh al-qarn al-thāleth 'ashar*. Beirut: Dār al-Sāder, 1993.
al-Jazāiri, Ahmad Pasha. *Tuhfat al-zāir fī akhbār al-amīr 'Abd al-Qādir*. Alexandria: Gharzūzi wa Jawīsh, 1903.
al-Jazāiri, 'Abd al-Qadir. *Al Miqrādh al-Hād*. Beirut: Dār maktabat al-Hayāt, 1966a.
al-Jazāiri, 'Abd al-Qadir. *Al-Mawāqif al-rūhiyya wa al-fuyūdhāt al-sabūhiyya*. Beirut: Dār al-kutub al-'ilmiyya, 2004.
al-Jazāiri, 'Abd al-Qadir. *Dhikra al-'āqil wa tanbih al-ghāfil*. Damascus: Dār al-yaqdha al-'arabiyya, 1966b.
al-Khānī, Abd al-Majīd. *Al-Hadāiq al-wardiyya fī haqāiq Ajella' al-naqshabandiyya*. Arbil: Dar Āras, 2002.
Al-Majmu 'a al-ula li-jaridat al-Nadi 1904–1905. Cairo: n.p., 1905.
Alloul, Houssine, Edhem Eldem and Henk de Smaele (eds.). *To Kill a Sultan: A Transnational History of the Attempt on Abdülhamid II*. London: Palgrave Macmillan, 2018.
Aneer, Gudmar. "Konstnären Ivan Aguéli och drömmen om en enad värld." In *Religionsvetenskap i Göteborg 25 år*, ed. Martin Berntson and Henrik Bogdan. Göteborg, 2002.

Apollinaire, Guillaume. "Aesthetic Meditations on Painting: The Cubist Painters." In *Cubism*, ed. Dorothea Eimert and Anatolu Podoksik, 7–28. New York: Parkstone, 2010.

Arambasin, Nella. *La Conception du sacré dans la critique d'art en Europe entre 1880 et 1914*. Geneva: Droz, 1996.

Ardalan, Nader. "The Paradise Garden Paradigm." In *Consciousness and Reality: Studies in Memory of Toshihiko Izutsu*, ed. Sayyid Jalâl al-Dîn Ashtiyânî, Hideichi Matsubara, Takashi Iwami and Akiro Matsumoto, 97–127. Leiden: Brill, 2000.

Ardalan, Nader and Laleh Bakhtiar. *The Sense of Unity: The Sufi Tradition in Persian Architecture*. Chicago, IL: University of Chicago Press, 1973.

Aurier, Gabriel-Albert. "Le Symbolisme en peinture: Paul Gauguin." *Le Mercure de France* 2 (1891): 155–65.

Aurier, Gabriel-Albert. *Oeuvres Posthumes*. Paris: Mercure de France, 1893.

Ayalon, Ami. *The Arabic Print Revolution: Cultural Production and Mass Readership*. Cambridge: Cambridge University Press, 2016.

Baldinetti, Anna. *Orientalismo e colonialismo. La ricerca di consenso in Egitto per l'impresa di Libia*. Rome: Edizioni Istituto per l'Oriente C. A. Nallino, 1997.

Balestrieri, A. "Nuove tecniche di attacco all'opera di René Guénon." In *René Guénon e l'Occidente*, ed. P. Nutrizio, 67–164. Milan: Luni Editrice, 1999.

Balyani, Awhad al-Din. *Epître sur l'unicité absolu*. trans. Michel Chodkiewicz. Paris: Deux Oceans, 1982.

Ben Jelloun, Tahar. *Marabouts, Maroc*. Paris: Gallimard, 2009.

Berg, Yngve. "Ett huvud för sig." In *Bohemer och akademister*. Stockholm: Norstedt, 1931.

Bogdan, Henrik. "Freemasonry in Sweden." In *Western Esotericism in Scandinavia*, ed. Henrik Bogdan and Olav Hammer, 168–81. Leiden: Brill, 2016.

Booth, Marilyn. *Classes of Ladies of Cloistered Spaces: Writing Feminist History through Biography in Fin-de-Siècle Egypt*. Edinburgh: Edinburgh University Press, 2015.

Boström, Hans-Olof. "Tanke och struktur i Gustaf Fjaestads måleri." In *Det skapande jaget*, ed. Irja Bergström and Maj-Brit Wadell. Gothenburg: Konstvetenskapliga institutionen, Göteborgs universitet, 1996.

Bourdieu, Pierre. *Rules of Art*. Stanford, CA: Stanford University Press, 1996.

Bouyerdene, Ahmed. *Abd el-Kader par ses contemporains*. Paris: Ibis Press, 2008.

Bouyerdene, Ahmed. *Emir Abd el-Kader, Hero and Saint of Islam*. Bloomington, IN: World Wisdom, 2013.

Bouyerdene, Ahmed, Éric Geoffroy and Setty G. Simon-Khedis. *Abd el-Kader, Un spirituel dans la modernité*. Paris: Presses de l'Ifpo, 2010.

Böwering, Gerhard. "The Light Verse: Qur'anic Text and Sufi Interpretation." *Oriens* 36 (2001): 113–44.

Boyesen, Adolph. *Hvarför är det Plikt att Behandla Djuren med Godhet*. Stockholm: Svanbäcks Boktryckeri, 1889.

Brahimi, Denise. *La Vie et l'œuvre de Etienne Dinet*. Paris: ACR Edition, 1984.

Briani, Vittorio. *La Stampa Italiana all'estero dalle origini ai nostri giorni*. Rome: Istituto Poligrafico dello Stato, 1977.

Brummer, Hans Henrik. "'Friheten gratis är ingen lycka.' Ivan Aguéli, en resenär." In *Ivan Aguéli*, ed. Hans Henrik Brummer, 7–16. Stockholm: Atlantis & Prins Eugens Waldemarsudde, 2006a.

Brummer, Hans Henrik (ed.). *Ivan Aguéli*. Waldemarsudde exhibition catalog. Stockholm: Atlantis, 2006.

Brummer, Hans Henrik. "Richard Bergh—ett konstnärskall." In *Richard Bergh: ett konstnärskall*, ed. Hans Henrik Brummer. Stockholm: Atlantis & Prins Eugens Waldemarsudde, 2002.

Brummer, Hans Henrik, Anna Meister and Pontus Reimers (eds.). *Ivan Aguéli*. Stockholm: Atlantis, 2006b.

Brusi, Frédéric. "'De äro allesammans muhammedaner, men jag gör allt hvad jag kan för att följa deras seder!': Tankar kring ett fotografiskt porträtt av Ivan Aguéli." *Aura: Tidskrift för akademiska studier av nyreligiositet* 9 (2017): 61–80.

Brzyski, Anna. "Introduction; Canons and Art History." In *Partisan Canons*, ed. Anna Brzyski. Durham, NC: Duke University Press, 2007.

Burckhardt, Titus. *Art of Islam: Language and Meaning*. Translated by J. Peter Hobson. London: World of Islam Festival, 1976.

Burckhardt, Titus. *Principes et méthodes de l'art sacré*. 1958. Paris: Dervy-Livres, 1976.

Burén, Jan af. *Ivan Aguéli*. Stockholm: Moderna Museet, 1986.

Carleson, Robert and Caroline Levander. "Spiritualism in Sweden." In *Western Esotericism in Scandinavia*, ed. Henrik Bogdan and Olav Hammer. Leiden: Brill, 2016.

Chacornac, Paul. "La vie simple de René Guénon." *Études traditionelles* 293 (1951): 317–33.

Chacornac, Paul. *La vie simple de René Guénon*. Paris: Editions Traditionnelles, 1958.

Chacornac, Paul. *The simple Life of René Guénon*. Ghent, NY: Sophia Perennis, 2001.

Charle, Christophe (ed.). *Le temps des capitales culturelles. XVIII–XX Siécles*. Seysell: Epoques Champ Vallon, 2009.

Cheikh, Abdellah. "Mohamed Hamidi à la Galerie Bab Rouah: Miroirs et architecture du vide." *Libération Maroc*. Casablanca, March 2009. https://www.libe.ma/Mohamed-Hamidi-a-la-Galerie-Bab-Rouah-Miroirs-et-architecture-du-vide_a1326.html

Chodkiewicz, Michel. "The Diffusion of Ibn ʿArabi's Doctrine." *The Journal of the Muhyiddin Ibn ʿArabi Society* 9 (1991), available https://ibnarabisociety.org/the-diffusion-of-ibn-arabis-doctrine-michel-chodkiewicz/

Chodkiewicz, Michel. *An Ocean without Shore: Ibn ʿArabi, The Book and the Law*. Albany: State University of New York Press, 1993.

Chodkiewicz, Michel. *Le sceau des saints, Prophétie et sainteté dans la doctrine d'Ibn Arabî*. Paris: Gallimard, 1986.

Chodkiewicz, Michel. *Seal of the Saints: Prophethood and Sainthood in the Doctrine of Ibn ʿArabi*. Cambridge: Cambridge University Press, 1993b.

Chodkiewicz, Michel. *The Spiritual Writings of Amir ʿAbd al-Kader*. Albany: State University of New York Press, 1995.

Christoyannopoulos, Alexandre and Matthew S. Adams (eds.). *Essays in Anarchism and Religion*. Stockholm: Stockholm University Press, 2018. 2 vols.

Churchill, Charles Henry. *The Life of Abd-el-Qader*. London: Chapman and Hall, 1867.

Commins, David Dean. *Islamic Reform: Politics and Social Change in Late Ottoman Syria*. New York: Oxford University Press, 1990.

Coomaraswamy, Ananda K. *Christian and Oriental Philosophy of Art*. New York: Dover Publications, 1956 [originally published in 1943 under the title: *Why Exhibit Works of Art?*].

Coomaraswamy, Ananda K. *Figures of Speech or Figures of Thought. Collected Essays in the Traditional or "Normal" View of Art*. 1946. New Delhi: Munshiram Manoharlal, 1981.

Coomaraswamy, Ananda K. *The Transformation of Nature in Art*. New York: Dover Publications, 1934.

Corbin, Henry. *Creative Imagination in the Sufism of Ibn ʿArabi*. Princeton, NJ: Princeton University Press, 1969.

Çorlu, Axel. "Anarchists and Anarchism in the Ottoman Empire, 1850–1917." In *History from Below: A Tribute in Memory of Donald Quataert*, ed. Selim Karahasanoglu, 553–83. Istanbul: Istanbul Bilgi University Press, 2016.

Cornell, Peter. *Den hemliga källan*. Hedemora: Gidlunds, 1981.

Cottington, David. *Cubism in the Shadow of War: The Avant-Garde and Politics in Paris 1905–1914*. New Haven, CT: Yale University Press, 1998.

Cottington, David. "The Formation of the Avant-Garde in Paris and London, c. 1880–1915." *Art History* (June 2012).

Cottington, David. "The Transnational Hierarchies and Networks of the Artistic Avant-Garde ca. 1885–1915." In *Decentering European Intellectual Space*, ed. Marja Javala, Stefan Nygård and Johan Strang. Leiden: Brill, 2019.

Coulondre, Ariane. "Géométrie." In *Dictionnaire du Cubisme*, ed. Gladys C. Fabre. Paris: Lafont, 2018.

Cowart, Jade. "Matisse's Moroccan Sketchbooks and Drawings: Self-Discovery through Various Motifs." In *Matisse in Morocco. The Paintings and Drawings, 1912–1913*, 113–53. New York: National Gallery of Art, 1990.

Cudenec, Paul. *The Anarchist Revelation*. [Sussex]: Winter Oak Press, 2013.

Cutsinger, James. S. "Femininity, Hierarchy, and God." In *Religion of the Heart: Essays Presented to Frithjof Schuon on His Eightieth Birthday*, ed. Seyyed Hossein Nasr and William Stoddart, 110–31. Chicago, IL: ABC International Group, 2000.

Kaufmann, DaCosta, Dossin Catherine Thomas, and Béatrice Joyeux-Prunel. *Circulation in the Global History of Art*. Farnham & Burlington: Ashgate, 2018.

Danell, Å.C. and Johnny Ekman (eds.). *Boken om Aguélimuseet*. Sala: Sala Konstförening, 2017.

Danziger, Raphael. *Abd Al-Qadir and the Algerians: Resistance to the French and Internal Consolidation*. Teaneck, NJ: Homes & Meier, 1977.

De Jong, Frederick. *Ṭuruq and Ṭuruq-linked Institutions in Nineteenth-Century Egypt: A Historical Study in Organizational Dimensions of Islamic Mysticism*. Leiden: Brill, 1978.

Delalande, Marie-José. "Le mouvement théosophique en France 1876–1921." PhD thesis, Université du Maine, 2007.

Dermenghem, Émile. *Le Culte des saints dans l'islam maghrébin*. Paris: Gallimard, 1954.

Dixon, Joy. *Divine Feminine: Theosophy and Feminism in England*. Baltimore, MD: The Johns Hopkins University Press, 2001.

Dubois, Geneviève. *Fulcanelli and the Alchemical Revival: The Man behind the Mystery of the Cathedrals*. NP: Destiny Books, 2005.

Ehrenzweig, Anton. *The Hidden Order of Art*. Berkeley: University of California Press, 1971.

Ekelöf, Gunnar. *Ivan Aguéli*. Göteborg: Bokkonst, 1944.

El-Ariss, Tarek (ed.). *The Arab Renaissance: A Bilingual Anthology of the Nahda*. New York: Modern Language Association, 2018.

Engelsman, Joan Chamberlain. *The Feminine Dimension of the Divine: The Study of Sophia and Feminine Images in Religion*. Wilmette, IL: Chiron, 1994.

Espagne, Michel. *Les transferts culturels franco-allemands*. Paris: PUF, 1999.

Étienne, Bruno. *Abd el-Kader et la franc-maçonnerie*. Paris: Dervy, 2008.

Étienne, Bruno. *Abdelkader, isthme des isthmus*. Paris: Hachette, 1994.

Fauchereau, Serge. *Le Cubisme. Une revolution esthétique, sa naissance et son rayonnement*. Paris: Flammarion, 2012.

Faxneld, Per. "Mona Lisa's Mysterious Smile: The Artist Initiate in Esoteric New Religions." *Nova Religio: The Journal of Alternative and Emergent Religions* 19, no. 4 (May 2016): 14–32.

Faxneld, Per. "Witches, Anarchism, and Evolutionism: Stanislaw Przybyszewski's
fin-de-siècle Satanism and the Demonic Feminine." In *The Devil's Party: Satanism
in Modernity*, ed. Per Faxneld and Jesper Aa. Petersen, 53–77. New York: Oxford
University Press, 2013.

Félix Fénéon. The Modern Times, from Seurat to Matisse. Paris: Musée de l'Orangerie, 2019.

Ferri, Enrico. "Leda Rafanelli: un anarchismo islamico?" In *Leda Rafanelli tra letteratura
e anarchia*, ed. Fiamma Chessa, 151–81. Reggio Emilia: Archivio Berneri-Chessa, 2008.

Fiscella, Anthony. *Varieties of Islamic Anarchism. A Brief Introduction*. NP: Alpine
Anarchist Production, 2014, 1–20.

Foucauld, Jean. "Le Musulman, Cheykh 'Abdu-l-Hedi al-Maghribi 'Uqayli." *Vers La
Tradition* 72 (June 1998). Republished in *Esprit-universel*, December 25, 2012, available
http://esprit-universel.over-blog.com/article-une-rehabilitation-d-ivan-agueli-abdul-
hadi-113790002.html

Franzén, Niclas. "Målaren Ivan Aguéli: dödsbegreppet hos en swedenborgiansk anarkist."
In *Föreställningar om döden: forskares aspekter på vår existens och dess begränsning*, ed.
Kjell O. Lejon, 120–37. Stockholm: Carlsson Bokförlag, 2017.

Franzén, Niclas. "Tyra Kleen som symbolist." In *Tyra Kleen*, ed. Niclas Franzén et al.
Björkvik: Kerstin Gullstrand Hermelin, 2016.

Furlong, Paul. *Social and Political Thought of Julius Evola*. London: Routledge, 2011.

Galián Hernández, Laura and Costantino Paonessa. "Caught between Internationalism,
Transnationalism and Immigration: A Brief Account of the History of Anarchism in
Egypt until 1945." *Anarchist Studies* 26, no. 1 (2017): 29–54.

Garbati, Romolo. *Mon Avennture dans L'Afrique Civilisée*, ed. Paul-André Claudel.
Alexandria: Centre d'Etudes Alexandrines, 2018.

Garcìa-Arenal, Mercedes (ed.). *Islamic Conversions: Religious Identities in Mediterranean
Islam*. Paris: Maisonneuve & Larose, 2001.

Gauchet, Marcel. *Le désenchantement du monde. Une histoire politique de la religion*. Paris:
Gallimard, 1985.

Gauffin, Axel. *Ivan Aguéli: människan, mystikern, målaren*. Stockholm: Sveriges Allmänna
Konstföreningen, 1940–1. 2 vols.

Gauffin, Axel. *John Gustaf Agelii, med konstnärsnamnet Ivan Aguéli*. Stockholm:
Nationalmuseum, 1939.

Gay, Peter. *The Enlightenment: A Comprehensive Anthology*. New York: Simon and
Schuster, 1985.

Gelvin, James L. and Nile Green (eds.). *Global Muslims in the Age of Steam and Print*.
Berkeley: University of California Press, 2014.

Gesink, Indira Falk. *Islamic Reform and Conservatism: Al-Azhar and the Evolution of
Modern Sunni Islam*. London: I.B. Tauris, 2014.

Giordani, Demetrio. "La confraternita al-akbariyya. Indizi e supposizioni." *Islam. Storia e
civiltà* 31-IX, no. 2 (April 1990): 101–7.

Gleadle, Kathryn and Zoë Thomas. "Global Feminisms, c. 1870–1930: Vocabularies and
Concepts—A Comparative Approach." *Women's History Review* 27, no. 7 (2018):
1209–24.

Gleizes, Albert. "Réflexions sur l'art dit abstrait et du caractère de l'image dans la non-
figuration." *L'Atelier de la Rose* 4 (October 1951). Reprinted in *L'Atelier de la Rose*.
Busloup: Le Moulin de l'Etoile, 2008, 80–7.

Godwin, Joscelyn, Christian Chanel and John P. Deveney. *The Hermetic Brotherhood of
Luxor: Initiatic and Historical Documents of an Order of Practical Occultism*. York
Beach, ME: S. Weiser, 1995.

Gorman, Anthony. "'Diverse in Race, Religion and Nationality ... but United in Aspirations of Civil Progress': The Anarchist Movement in Egypt 1860–1940." In *Anarchism and Syndicalism in the Colonial and Postcolonial World, 1870–1940*, ed. Steven Hirsch and Lucien van der Walt, 3–31. Leiden: Brill, 2010.

Gorman, Anthony. "Foreign Workers in Egypt 1882–1914." In *Subalterns and Social Protest: History from below in the Middle East and North Africa*, ed. Stephanie Cronin, 237–59. London: Routledge, 2008.

Gorman, Anthony and Didier Monciaud. *The Press in the Middle East and North Africa, 1850–1950: Politics, Social History and Culture*. Edinburgh: Edinburgh University Press, 2018.

Gotti Porcinari, Carlo. *Rapporti italo-arabi (1902–1930): dai documenti di Enrico Insabato*. Rome: ESP, 1965.

Grange, Daniel J. *L'Italie et la Méditerranée (1896–1911). Les fondements d'une politique étrangère*. Rome: École Française de Rome, 1994.

Grillo, Ralph. "Islam and Transnationalism." *Journal of Ethnic and Migration Studies* 30, no. 5 (2004): 861–78.

Grip, Kajsa, *Ivan Aguéli, Drömmen om Österlandet*. Uppsala: Uppsala University, 2004.

Gruen, Lori. *Entangled Empathy: An Alternative Ethic for Our Relationships with Animals*. New York: Lantern Books, 2015.

Guénon, René [as La Direction]. "Projet d'explication des termes techniques des différentes doctrines traditionnelles." *La Gnose* 1, no. 12 (December 1910): 268–69.

Guénon, René [as La Rédaction]. "Abdul-Hâdi," *Le Voile d'Isis* 1932, 714.

Guénon, René [as Palingénius]. "La Constitution de l'être humain et son évolution posthume selon le Vedanta." *La Gnose* 2, no. 9 (September 1911): 236–45 *et seq.*

Guénon, René [as Palingénius]. "La Gnose et les Écoles spiritualistes." *La Gnose* 1, no. 2 (December 1909): 20–1.

Guénon, René [as Palingénius]. "La prière et l'incantation." *La Gnose* 2, no. 1 (January 1911): 23–8.

Guénon, René [as Palingénius]. "La Religion et les religions." *La Gnose* 1, no. 10 (September 1910): 219–22.

Guénon, René [as Palingénius]. "Le Symbolisme de la Croix." *La Gnose* 2, no. 2 (February 1911): 55–9.

Guénon, René [as Palingénius]. "Les Néo–Spiritualistes." *La Gnose* 2, no. 8 (August 1911): 223–7.

Guénon, René. *Aperçus sur l'initiation*. 1946. Paris: Éditions Traditionnelles, 1977.

Guénon, René. *L'Erreur spirite*. Marcel Rivière: Paris, 1923.

Guénon, René. *L'Homme et son devenir selon le Vêdânta*. Bossard: Paris, 1925.

Guénon, René. *Le Symbolisme de la Croix*. Paris: Éditions Véga, 1931.

Guénon, René. *The Reign of Quantity and the Reign of the Times*. New York: Sophia Perennis, 2004.

Guénon, René. *Symboles fondamentaux de la science sacrée*. Paris: Gallimard, 1962.

Hanegraaff, Wouter. *Esotericism and the Academy: Rejected Knowledge in Western Culture*. Cambridge: Cambridge University Press, 2012.

Hanegraaff, Wouter. *New Age Religion and Western Culture: Esotericism in the Mirror of Secular Thought*. Leiden: Brill, 1996.

Hanley, Will. "Grieving Cosmopolitanism in Middle East Studies." *History Compass* 6, no. 5 (2008): 1346–67.

Hatina, Meir. "Where East Meets West: Sufism, Cultural Rapprochement, and Politics." *International Journal of Middle East Studies* 39, no. 3 (2007): 389–409.

Hatina, Meir and Chen Bram. "Cultural Exchange and Cosmopolitan Vision: Murat Yagan and the Teaching of Kebzeh." *Journal of Sufi Studies* 3 (2014): 67–92.

Hausen, Werner von. "Minnen från samvaron med Gustaf Ageli i Paris och Cairo 1894–1895." *Ord och Bild* 35 (1926): 605–15.

Hermansen, Marcia. "Women in Sufism: North America." In *Encyclopedia of Women in Islamic Cultures*, ed. Suad Joseph, 770–2. Leiden: Brill, 2005.

Hirtenstein, Stephen. "The Cubic Wisdom of the Heart according to Ibn 'Arabî." *Journal of the Muhyiddin Ibn 'Arabi Society* 48 (2010): 19–43.

Hirtenstein, Stephen. *The Unlimited Mercifer: The Spiritual Life and Thought of Ibn 'Arabî*. Oxford: Anqa, 1999.

Hogeman, Anders. *Med Strindberg, Hill och Aguéli i Paris: på promenad i Parissvenskarnas fotspår*. Hedemora: Gidlund, 2012.

Ianari, Vittorio. "La politica islamica dell'Italia durante la Triplice Alleanza. L'attività di Enrico Insabato." In *Mare nostrum: percezione ottomana e mito mediterraneo in Italia all'alba del '900*, ed. Stefano Trinchese, 199–246. Milano: Guerini Studio, 2005.

Ibn 'Arabi. *Al-Futuhat al-Makkiyya*, trans. Michel Chodkiewicz as *The Meccan Revelations*. New York: Pir Press, 2002.

Ibn Taymiyyah Expounds on Islam: Selected Writings of Shaykh Al Islam Taqi Ad Din Ibn Taymiyyah on Islamic Faith, Life and Society ed. and trans. Muhammad 'Abdul-Haqq Ansari. Riyadh: Imam Muhammad Ibn Saud University, 2000.

Insabato, Enrico. *Gli Abaditi del Gebel Nefusa e la politica islamica in Tripolitania*. Rome: Istituto Coloniale Italiano, 1918.

Insabato, Enrico. "Necessità e base di una politica filo islamica." *Il Convito*, year 4 second series, no. 1 (1907): 26–8.

Insabato, Enrico. *L'islâm vivente nel nuovo ordine mondiale*. Rome: L'Espansione imperiale, 1941.

Insabato, Enrico. *La collaborazione italo-araba e il Sudan. Indipendenza per la Libia, lavoro per l'Italia, ricchezza per la comunità mediterranea*. Rome: Danesi-Centro mediterraneo, 1950.

Iversen, Gunilla. "En bok om Ivan Aguéli?" In *Årsbok för kristen humanism*, 140–1. Stockholm: Förbundet Kristen Humanism, 1982.

James, Marie-France. *Esotérisme et christianisme: Autour de René Guénon*. Paris: Nouvelles Éditons Latines, 1981.

Jeffery-Street, Isobel. *Ibn 'Arabi and Contemporary West: Beshara and the Ibn 'Arabi Society*. London: Equinox Publishing, 2012.

Jones, Owen. *The Grammar of Ornament*. London: Day and Son, 1856.

Jong, Frederick De. *Turuq and Turuq-linked Institutions in Nineteenth-Century Egypt: A Historical Study in Organizational Dimensions of Islamic Mysticism*. Leiden: Brill, 1978.

Joyeux-Prunel, Béatrice. "'L'art mobilier' La circulation de la peinture avant-gardiste et son role dans la géopolitique cultuelle de l'Europe." In *Le temps des capitales culturelles. XVIII–XX Siécles*, ed. Christophe Charle. Seysell: Epoques Champ Vallon, 2009, 172–210.

Joyeux-Prunel, Béatrice. *Les avant-gardes artistiques 1848–1918. Une historie transnationale*. Paris: Galleimard, 2015.

Joyeux-Prunel, Béatrice. *Nul n'est prophète en son pays? L'internationalism de le peinture des avant-gardes parisiennes, 1855–1914*. Paris: Musée d'Orsay and Éditions Nicolas Chaudun, 2009.

Kahn-Harris, Keith. *Extreme Metal: Music and Culture on the Edge*. Oxford: Berg, 2007.

Karamti, Yassine. *Le Maraboutisme de chambre noire en Tunisie. Récit visuel d'un corpus de cartes postales photographiques anciennes.* Tunis: Editions Latrash et Centre des études islamiques de Kairouan, 2015.

Khuri-Makdisi, Ilham. *The Eastern Mediterranean and the Making of Global Radicalism, 1860–1914.* Berkeley: University of California Press, 2010.

Kiser, John. *Commander of the Faithful: The Life and Times of Emir Abd el-Kader.* New York: Monkfish Book Publishing, 2008.

Kraft, Siv-Ellen. *The Sex Problem: Political Aspects of Gender Discourse in the Theosophical Society, 1875–1930.* Dissertation, Department of the History of Religions, University of Bergen, 1999.

Kropotkin, Peter. *Mutual Aid.* 1902. London: Freedom Press, 1987.

Laude, Patrick. "Introduction to Abdul Hadi's 'Universality in Islam.'" In *Universal Dimensions of Islam: Studies in Comparative Religion*, ed. Laude, 134–7. Bloomington, IN: World Wisdom, 2011.

Laude, Patrick. *Pathways to an Inner Islam: Massignon, Corbin, Guenon, and Schuon.* Albany: State University of New York Press, 2010.

Laude, Patrick (ed.). *Universal Dimensions of Islam: Studies in Comparative Religion.* Bloomington, IN: World Wisdom, 2011.

Laurant, Jean-Pierre. *Le sens caché dans l'œuvre de René Guénon.* Lausanne: L'Age d'homme, 1975.

Leithart, Peter J. "When East Is West." *First Things* 153 (May 2005): 11–12.

"L'évolution de l'art vers l'amorphisme." *Les Hommes du jour*, May 3, 1913, 10.

Lindgren, Marita. "Ivan Gustave Aguéli: Ett sällsamt svenskt konstnärsöde." *Ord och Bild* 43 (1934): 513–23.

Lipsey, Roger. *The Spiritual in Twentieth-Century Art.* Mineola: Dover, 2004.

Lipton, Gregory A. *Rethinking Ibn 'Arabi.* New York: Oxford University Press, 2018.

Luthi, Jean Jacques. "Sur les pas d'Emile Bernard en Egypte (1893–1904)." *Bulletin de l'Atelier d'Alexandrie. Le Cinquatenaire (1934–1984)* 6 (1985): 85–8.

Magnússon, Gísli. "Visionary Mimesis and Occult Modernism in Literature and Art around 1900." In *The Occult in Modernist Art, Literature, and Cinema*, ed. Tessel M. Bauduin and Henrik Johnsson. Cham: Palgrave Macmillan, 2018.

Mahmud, 'Abd al-Halim. *Al-Madrasa al-Shadhiliyya al-haditha wa-imamuha Abu al-Hasan al-Shadhili.* Cairo: Dar al-Kutub al-Haditha, 1968.

Malik, Jamal and John Hinnels (eds.). *Sufism in the West.* New York: Routledge, 2006.

Marchi, Alessandra. "Italian Pro-Islamic Politics in the Writings of Enrico Insabato: Between Libya and Egypt." In *Images of Colonialism and Decolonisation in the Italian Media*, ed. Paolo Bertella Farnetti and Cecilia Dau Novelli, 132–48. Cambridge: Cambridge Scholars Publishing, 2017.

Marchi, Alessandra. "La conversion à la spiritualité musulmane de Leda Rafanelli et Valentine de Saint-Point." In *Valentine de Saint-Point. Des feux de l'avant-garde à l'appel de l'Orient*, ed. P.-A. Claudel and E. Gaden, 253–64. Rennes: Presses Universitaires de Rennes, 2019.

Marchi, Alessandra. "La presse d'expression italienne en Égypte. De 1845 à 1950." *Rivista dell'Istituto di Storia dell'Europa Mediterranea* 5 (2010): 91–125.

Marchi, Alessandra. "La presse italophone d'Egypte. Un long siècle d'histoire." In *Presses allophones de Méditerranée*, ed. Jean-Yves Empereur and Marie Delphine Martellière, 179–88. Alexandria: Etudes Alexandrines, 2017.

Marston, Elsa. *The Compassionate Warrior: Abd el-Kader of Algeria.* Bloomington, IN: World Wisdom Books, 2013.

Marzullo, Claudio. "Leggere Ibn ʿArabi in italiano. Quando il sufismo diventa affare di stato." *El Azufre Rojo* 3 (2016): 189–99.

Masri, Al-Hafiz Basheer Ahmad. *Animal Welfare in Islam*. Markfield, Leicestershire: The Islamic Foundation, 2007.

Millroth, Thomas. *Molards salong*. Stockholm: Forum, 1993.

Moses, Claire Goldberg. *French Feminism in the Nineteenth Century*. Albany: State University of New York Press, 1984.

Müller-Westermann, Iris. "Paintings for the Future: Hilma af Klint—A Pioneer of Abstraction in Seclusion." In *Hilma af Klint—A Pioneer of Abstraction*, ed. Iris Müller-Westermann and Jo Widoff. Stockholm: Moderna Museet, 2013.

Murata, Sachiko. *The Tao of Islam: A Sourcebook on Gender Relationships in Islamic Thought*. Albany: State University of New York Press, 1992.

Nasr, Seyyed Hossein. *The Heart of Islam: Enduring Values for Humanity*. New York: HarperCollins, 2002.

Nasr, Seyyed Hossein. *Islamic Art and Spirituality*. Ipswich: Golgonooza Press, 1987.

Nasr, Seyyed Hossein. "The Male and Female in the Islamic Perspective." *Studies in Comparative Religion* 14, nos. 1 and 2 (Winter–Spring 1980), republished at http://www.studiesincomparativereligion.com/Public/articles/The_Male_and_Female_in_the_Islamic_Perspective-by_Seyyed_Hossein_Nasr.aspx.

Nasr, Seyyed Hossein. *Three Muslim Sages: Avicenna, Suhrawardi, Ibn ʿArabi*. Cambridge, MA: Harvard University Press, 1964.

Nyberg, H. S. "Aguéli och islam." In *Ivan Aguéli, människan, mystikern, målaren*, vol. 2, ed. Axel Gauffin, 299–304. Stockholm: Sveriges Allmänna Konstförening, 1941.

Öhrner, Annika. "Hilma af Klint och Ivan Aguéli. Andlighet och konstens rum." *Aura: Tidskrift för akademiska studier av nyreligiositet* 9 (2017): 42–60.

Oldmeadow, Harry. *Journeys East: 20th Century Western Encounters with Eastern Religious Traditions*. Bloomington, IN: World Wisdom, 2004.

Oldmeadow, Harry. "René Guénon." In *The Reign of Quantity* by René Guénon. New York: Sophia Perrenis et Universalis, 1995.

Olsson, Susanne and Simon Sorgenfrei. "Den fiktive Aguéli: Identifikationsobjekt och projektionsyta för unga manliga konvertiter till islam." *Aura: Tidskrift för akademiska studier av nyreligiositet* 9 (2017): 80–106.

Pakieser, Andrea. *I Belong Only to Myself: The Life and Writings of Leda Rafanelli*. Oakland, CA: AK Press, 2014.

Pasi, Marco. "The Problems of Rejected Knowledge: Thoughts on Wouter Hanegraaff's *Esotericism and the Academy*." *Religion* 43, no. 2 (April 2013): 201–12.

Patry, Sylvie. 2017. "Cézanne, Paul." In *Dictionnaire du Cubisme*, ed. Gladys C. Fabre, 143–8. Paris: Robert Laffont, 2018.

Paulhan, Jean. *La Peinture cubiste*. 1970. Paris: Gallimard, 1990.

Pea, Enrico. *Vita in Egitto*. Florence: Ponte alle Grazie, 1995.

Petander, Einar. "Theosophy in Sweden." In *Western Esotericism in Scandinavia*, ed. Henrik Bogdan and Olav Hammer, 578–9. Leiden: Brill, 2016.

Piotrowski, Piotr. "Towards A Horizontal History of Art." In *Writing Central European Art History*, PATTERNS travelling Lecture Set 2008/2009. Vienna: Erste Foundation, 2008.

Portal, Pierre and Paul Frédéric. *Des couleurs symboliques dans l'antiquité, le moyen-âge et les temps modernes*. Paris: Treuttel et Würtz, Libraires, 1837.

Robert, Pouyaut. "Art sacré et Tradition." *L'Atelier de la Rose* 3 (June 1951). Reprinted in *L'Atelier de la Rose*, Busloup: Le Moulin de l'Etoile, 2008, 78–9.

Robert, Pouyaut. "Le Principe directeur dans la peinture." *L'Atelier de la Rose* 6 (March 1952). Reprinted in *L'Atelier de la Rose*, Busloup: Le Moulin de l'Etoile, 2008, 130–3.

Rafanelli, Leda. *L'Oasi. Romanzo arabo*, ed. Milva Maria Capellini. Reggio Emilia: Corsiero Editore, 2017.

Rafanelli, Leda. *Una donna e Mussolini*. Milan: Rizzoli, 1975.

Ranaxe, Mats David. *Carl Larsson & evigheten*. NP: Golden Section Publishing, 2011.

Rasmussen, P. "Ivan Aguéli: 'One Day My Art Will Explain the Eccentricities of My Life.'" *Lakartidningen* 100, no. 34 (August 2003): 2614–16.

Ringgenberg, Patrick. *Diversité et unité des religions chez René Guénon et Frithjof Schuon.* Paris: L'Harmattan, 2010.

Ringgenberg, Patrick. *Les théories de l'art dans la pensée traditionnelle.* Paris: L'Harmattan, 2011.

Robin, Jean. *René Guénon, témoin de la Tradition.* Paris: Guy Trédaniel, 1978.

Rocker, Rudolf. *Anarcho-Syndicalism: Theory and Practice.* London: Secker and Warburg, 1938.

Röstorp, Vibeke. *Le Mythe du Retour. Les artistes scandinaves en France de 1889–1908.* Stockholm: Stockholm universitets förlag, 2013.

Ryan, Eileen. *Religion as Resistance: Negotiating Authority in Italian Libya.* Oxford: Oxford University Press, 2018.

Säfve, Torbjörn. *Ivan Aguéli: en roman om frihet.* Stockholm: Prisma, 1981.

Said, Edward. *Orientalism.* London: Penguin, 2003.

Sanfilippo, Matteo. "Araldi d'Italia? Un quadro degli studi sulla stampa italiana d'emigrazione." *Studi Emigrazione/Migration Studies* 46, no. 175 (2009): 678–95.

Sanner, Inga. *Att älska sin nästa såsom sig själv: Om moraliska utopier under 1800-talet.* Stockholm: Carlssons, 1995.

Sarajas-Korte, Salme. *Vid symbolismens källor: den tidiga symbolismen i Finland.* Jakobstad: Jakobstads tryckeri och tidnings AB, 1981.

Scarabel, Angelo. "Una Rivista Italo-Araba d'inizio Secolo: An-Nādī (Il Convito)." *Oriente Moderno* 58, nos. 1/3 (1978): 51–67.

Schuon, Frithjof. *Avoir un centre.* 1988. Paris: L'Harmattan, 2010.

Schuon, Frithjof. *Castes et races* suivi de *Principes et critères de l'art universel.* 1957. Milan: Archè, 1979.

Schuon, Frithjof. *De l'unité transcendante des religions.* 1948. Paris: L'Harmattan, 2014.

Schuon, Frithjof. *Images of Primordial and Mystic Beauty: Paintings by Frithjof Schuon.* Bloomington, IN: Abodes, 1992.

Schuon, Frithjof. *In the Face of the Absolute: A New Translation with Selected Letters.* Bloomington, IN: World Wisdom, 2014.

Schuon, Frithjof. *L'ésotérisme comme principe et comme voie.* 1978. Paris: Dervy, 1997.

Schuon, Frithjof. *Perspectives spirituelles et faits humains.* 1953. Paris: Maisonneuve et Larose, 1989.

Schuon, Frithjof. *The Transcendent Unity of Religions.* London: Harper and Row, 1975.

Sedgwick, Mark. *Against the Modern World: Traditionalism and the Secret Intellectual History of the Twentieth Century.* Oxford: Oxford University Press, 2004.

Sedgwick, Mark. "The 'Traditionalist' Shâdhiliyya in the West: Guenonians and Schuonians." In *Une Voie soufie dans le monde. La Shâdhiliyya*, ed. Eric Geoffroy, 453–71. Paris: Maisonneuve & Larose, 2005.

Sedgwick, Mark. "Traditionalist Sufism." *Aries* 22 (1999): 3–24. Available online: http://www.traditionalists.org/write/tradsuf.htm#N_13_, Accessed June 25, 2019.

Sedgwick, Mark. *Western Sufism, From the Abbasids to the New Age.* New York: Oxford University Press, 2017.

Selander, Josephine. *Mellan öst och väst, profetior och entreprenörskap, vetenskap och tro: Meningsproduktion om alternativa andligheter i svensk press och offentlighet 1899–1926.* MA thesis, Dept. of the History of Ideas, Stockholm University, 2018.

Senior, John. *The Way Down and Out: The Occult in Symbolist Literature.* Ithaca, NY: Cornell University Press, 1959.

Sérant, Paul. *René Guénon.* 1953. Paris: Courrier du Livre, 1977.

Shaikh, Sa'diyya. "In Search of Al-Insān: Sufism, Islamic Law and Gender." *Journal of the American Academy of Religion* 77, no. 4 (2009): 781–822.

Shaikh, Sa'diyya. *Sufi Narratives of Intimacy: Ibn 'Arabi, Gender and Sexuality.* Chapel Hill: University of North Carolina Press, 2012.

Shils, Edward. "The Intellectual and the Powers: Some Perspectives for Comparative Analysis." *Society and History* 1, no. 1 (October 1958): 5–22.

Sirriyeh, Elizabeth. *Sufis and Anti-Sufis.* Richmond: Curzon Press, 1999.

Soldi, Émile. *Les arts méconnus: les nouveaux musées du Trocadéro.* Paris: Ernest Leroux, 1881.

Sörbom, Per. "Ivan Aguéli: The Significance and Importance of His Life and Opus for the Understanding of the Plurality of the World." *Forum Bosnae* 48 (2009): 155–70.

Sorgenfrei, Simon. *Det monoteistiska landskapet. Ivan Aguéli och Emanuel Swedenborg.* Stockholm: Eureka/Ellerströms akademiska, 2018.

Sorgenfrei, Simon. "The Great Aesthetic Inspiration on Ivan Aguéli's Reading of Swedenborg." *Religion and the Arts* 23 (2019): 1–25.

Sorgenfrei, Simon. "Målare, mystiker, muslim—Ivan Aguéli 1869–1917." *Aura: Tidskrift för akademiska studier av nyreligiositet* 9 (2017): 5–8.

Ström, Fredrik. *Kata Dalströms liv, öden och äventyr i kampen mot herremakten.* Stockholm: Tidens förlag, 1931.

Stroumsa, Guy. *A New Science: The Discovery of Religion in the Age of Reason.* Cambridge, MA: Harvard University Press, 2010.

Stuckrad, Kocku von. *Locations of Knowledge in Medieval and Early Modern Europe: Esoteric Discourse and Western Identities.* Leiden: Brill, 2010.

Swedenborg, Emanuel. *Angelic Wisdom about Divine Providence.* New York: Citadel Press, 1963.

Swedenborg, Emanuel. *Arcana coelestia*, vol. 11. Loschberg, Austria: Jazzybee Verlag, 2013.

Swedenborg, Emanuel. *Heaven and Its Wonders and Hell: From Things Heard and Seen.* West Chester PA: Swedenborg Foundation, 1995.

Swedenborg, Emanuel. *True Christian Religion: Containing the Universal Theology of the New Church Foretold by the Lord in Daniel 7: 13–14and Revelation 21: 1–2.* West Chester PA: Swedenborg Foundation, 1996.

Taymiyya, Ibn. *Expounds on Islam.* trans Muhammad 'Abdul-Haqq Ansari. Riyad: Imam Muhammad Ibn Saud University, 2000.

Temimi, Abdeljelil. "Lettres inédites de l'Émir Abd el-Kader." *Revue d'histoire maghrébine* 10–11 (1978): 159–202.

Thompson, James and Wright Barbara. *Eugène Fromentin, 1820–1876, visions d'Algérie et d'Egypte.* Paris: ACR Editions, 2008.

Thurfjell, David. *Det gudlösa folket: De postkristna svenskarna och religionen.* Stockholm: Molin & Sorgenfrei, 2015.

Tuchman, Maurice *et al. The Spiritual in Art. Abstract Painting, 1890–1985.* Los Angeles, CA: Los Angeles County Museum of Art, 1986.

Turcato, Davide. "Nations without Borders: Anarchists and National Identity." In *Reassessing the Transnational Turn*, ed. Constance Bantman and Bert Altena, 25–42. Oakland, CA: PM Press, 2017.

Vâlsan, Michel. "L'islam et la fonction de René Guénon." *Études traditionnelles* 305 (January 1953): 14–47.

Versluis, Arthur. "A Conversation with Peter Lamborn Wilson." *Journal for the Study of Radicalism* 4, no. 2 (2010): 139–65.

Waterfield, Robin. *René Guénon and the Future of the West: The Life and Writings of a 20th-Century Metaphysician.* 2017. NP: Sophia Perennis, 1987.

Weismann, Itzchak. "The Shâdhiliyya-Darqâwiyya in the Arab East xixth/xxth Centuries." In *Une voie soufie dans le monde*, ed. Éric Geoffroy, 255–67. Paris: Maisonneuve & Larose, 2005.

Weismann, Itzchak. *Taste of Modernity: Sufism, Salafiyya, & Arabism in Late Ottoman Damascus.* Leiden: Brill, 2001.

Wessel, Viveca. "Aguéli och ljuset." In *Moderna Museets tidning N: o2.* Stockholm: Moderna Museet, 1982. Reprinted Sala: Aguélimuseet, 2013.

Wessel, Viveca. "Ivan Aguéli." Exhibition catalog, Millesgården Stockholm, 1991.

Wessel, Viveca. "Ivan Aguéli Malare och Sufi." In *Sverige och den islamiska världen— ett svenskt kulturarv.* Stockholm: Wahlström & Widstrand, 2002. Reprinted in *Aguélimuseets Vanner* (2002): 17–24.

Wessel, Viveca. "Ivan Aguéli—Abdul-Hâdi." In *Ivan Aguéli*, 16–51. Stockholm: Atlantis, 2006.

Wessel, Viveca. *Att skåda igenom tecknens värld: några drag i Ivan Aguélis symbolistiska estetik, med tyngdpunkt i några verk han studerade under 90-talet.* Stockholm: Stockholms universitet, 1983.

Wessel, Viveca. *Ivan Aguéli. Porträtt av en rymd.* Stockholm: Författarförlaget, 1988. 2nd edn. Stockholm: Bokförlaget T. Fischer & Co, 1990.

Wessel, Viveca. "Solnedgång och gryning—Orienten i Heidenstams Endymion och hos Ivan Aguéli." *Allt om böcker n.o 5/6* (1993).

Westerlund, Marianne. *Ivan Aguéli: landskapet, ordet och den ljusaste av öar.* Visby: Länsmuseet på Gotland, 2003.

Williams-Hogan, Jane. "Emanuel Swedenborg's Aesthetic Philosophy and Its Impact on Nineteenth-Century American Art." *Toronto Journal of Theology* 28 (2012): 105–24.

Wistman, Christina G. "Prins Eugen and Ivan Aguéli i källor och litteratur." In *Ivan Aguéli*, ed. Hans Henrik Brummer, 5. Stockholm: Atlantis & Prins Eugens Waldemarsudde, 2006.

Zarcone, Thierry. "Le Croisement des regards ou le peintre des deux rives." In *Auguste Chabaud, Fascination et nostalgie entre Provence et Tunisie.* Catalog of exhibition, *9 February–2 June 2013*, 46–57. Graveson: Musée de région Auguste Chabaud, 2013.

Zarcone, Thierry. *Le Mystère Abd-el-Kader, la franc-maçonnerie, la France et l'Islam.* Paris: Les Éditions du Cerf, 2019.

Zarcone, Thierry. "Rereadings and Transformations of Sufism in the West." *Diogènes* 47, no. 187 (1999): 110–21.

Zegger, Robert E. "Protecting Animals in Paris: 1815–1870." *History Today* 28, no. 2 (1978): 105–12.

Contributors

Alessandra Marchi is a researcher at GramsciLab, University of Cagliari, Italy. Her PhD (2009) is from the EHESS, Paris. As well as publishing on Gramsci, she has several articles on the Franco-Italian press and community in turn-of-the-century Egypt, mostly published in French.

Annika Öhrner is Associate Professor in Art History at Södertörn University, Sweden, a member of the board of the Thielska Gallery, and a former vice-chair of the Public Art Agency in Sweden. Her research interests include the early artistic avant-garde, and the art and the art field during the decades after the Second World War, with focus on transnational cultural transfer.

Anthony T. Fiscella has a PhD from Lund University, Sweden, where he worked at the Centre for Theology and Religious Studies before returning to the United States. He is best known for his "From Muslim Punks to Taqwacore: An Incomplete History of Punk Islam" (2012) but has also published on the Symbionese Liberation Army and the Religious Anarcho-Primitivist Message of Lynyrd Skynyrd.

Iheb Guermazi is a PhD student in the History, Theory and Criticism of Architecture and Art at MIT. His research interests include the place of postmodern architectural theory in postcolonial contexts, modern and contemporary narratives of regionalism, and questions of identity and representation in architecture. He recently published "An Archeology of Postmodern Architecture: A Reading of Charles Jencks' work."

Ivan Aguéli was a Swedish anarchist, artist, and Sufi. His work on art and Sufism has been published in French, Italian, Arabic, Swedish, and (now) in English translation. Much of his extensive correspondence has also been published in Swedish. Aguéli is also known for painting and for his political and religious activism.

Marcia Hermansen is Director of the Islamic World Studies Program and Professor in the Theology Department at Loyola University Chicago. She received her PhD from the University of Chicago in Arabic and Islamic Studies. She is best known for her *Muslima Theology: The Voices of Muslim Women Theologians* (2013) and for her work on American Sufism.

Mark Sedgwick is Professor of Arab and Islamic Studies at Aarhus University, Denmark. His specialization is modern Islam, Sufism, and Islam in the West, and he is best known for his *Against the Modern World: Traditionalism and the Secret Intellectual History of the Twentieth Century* (2004) and *Western Sufism: From the Abbasids to the New Age* (2016).

Meir Hatina is Professor in the Department of Islamic and Middle Eastern Studies and Jack and Alice Ormut Chair in Arabic Studies at the Hebrew University of Jerusalem. He is well known for his *Guardians of Faith in Modern Times: 'Ulama' in the Middle East* (2008), *Ulama, Politics, and the Public Sphere: An Egyptian Perspective* (2010), and *Identity Politics in the Middle East: Liberal Thought and Islamic Challenge in Egypt* (2006).

Nadine Miller is a professional translator living in Cyprus. She translates into English and German from Turkish (modern and Ottoman), French, and Arabic, mostly for publishers in Germany and the UK. Her most recent works include studies in Sufism, Artificial Intelligence, and a historical treatise on Ottoman archery.

Patrick Ringgenberg is a researcher affiliated to the Institut religion, culture et modernité at the University of Lausanne and is best known for his *L'univers symbolique des arts islamiques* (2009) and *La peinture persane, ou, La vision paradisiaque* (2006).

Paul-André Claudel is a maître de conférences at the University of Nantes and is best known for his *Alexandrie: histoire d'un mythe* (2011). He is currently attached to the CNRS in Alexandria.

Per Faxneld is Senior Lecturer in Study of Religions at Södertörn University, Sweden. His specialization is Western esotericism, new religions, and "alternative spirituality," and he is best known for his *The Devil's Party: Satanism in Modernity* (2012) and *Satanic Feminism: Lucifer as the Liberator of Woman in Nineteenth-Century Culture* (2014).

Simon Sorgenfrei is Associate Professor and Lecturer in the Study of Religions at Södertörn University, with an orientation toward Islamic studies. He works on Islam in the past and present, Sufism, and Persian Sufi poetry, and is best known for his *American Dervish: Making Mevlevism in the United States of America* (2013). In 2018, he published *Det monoteistiska landskapet: Ivan Aguéli och Emanuel Swedenborg* (The Monotheistic Landscape: Ivan Aguéli and Emanuel Swedenborg).

Thierry Zarcone is Director of Research at the CNRS in Paris. He works on Islam and systems of thought in the Turco-Persian area, especially on the history of Sufism and shamanism in the Ottoman Empire, Turkey, Central Asia, and East Turkestan (Xinjiang), and on the history of Islam in contemporary Turkey and Xinjiang. He is best known for his prize-winning *Mystiques, philosophes et francs-maçons en Islam* (1993), and also for his English book, *Shamanism and Islam: Sufism, Healing Rituals and Spirits in the Muslim World* (2011).

Viveca Wessel is a former teacher at the Museum of Modern Art in Stockholm and also the former director of a Swedish art school. She published *Ivan Aguéli: porträtt av en rymd* (Ivan Aguéli: Portrait of a Space) in 1988, and is also known for editing and contributing to *Sverige och den islamiska världen: ett svenskt kulturarv* (Sweden and the Islamic World: A Swedish Cultural Heritage, 2002) and for her work in Hans Henrik Brummer's *Ivan Aguéli* (2006).

Index

www.ingramcontent.com/pod-product-compliance
Lightning Source LLC
Chambersburg PA
CBHW060147280326
41932CB00012B/1670